Early Islamic Institutions

Contemporary Arab Scholarship in the Social Sciences

Series ISBN 978 84885 207 5

The Contemporary Arab Scholarship in the Social Sciences (produced by I.B.Tauris in cooperation with the Centre for Arab Unity Studies) aims to introduce an English language audience to the most cutting-edge writings from the Arab world in the fields of politics, sociology, philosophy and history. Hitherto, the majority of social studies on the Arab world have been written by, and from the perspective of, non-Arabs. This series aims to remedy the situation by presenting authentic, indigenous points of view from key influential thinkers and intellectuals. The writers assembled in the series – all highly distinguished experts in their areas of study – tackle the most critical issues facing the Arab world today: Islam, modernity, development, the legacy of imperialism and colonialism, civil society, democracy and human rights. English-language readers are here given an unprecedented window on the vitality and distinctness of contemporary Arab intellectual debate in high-quality, eminently readable translations of the original works.

Democracy, Human Rights Law in Islamic Thought
Mohammed Abed al-Jabri
978 1 84511 749 8

Britain and Arab Unity:
A Documentary History from the Treaty of Versailles to the End of World War II
Younan Labib Rizk
978 1 84885 059 0

The State in Contemporary Islamic Thought:
A Historical Survey of the Major Muslim Political Thinkers of the Modern Era
Abdelilah Belkeziz
978 1 84885 062 0

Early Islamic Institutions:
Administration and Taxation from the Caliphate to the Umayyads and 'Abbāsids
Abd al-Aziz Duri
978 1 84885 060 6

The Formation of Arab Reason:
Text, Tradition and the Construction of Modernity in the Arab World
Mohammed Abed al-Jabri
978 1 84885 061 3

Islamic Land Tax – Al-Kharāj*:*
From the Islamic Conquests to the 'Abbāsid Period
Ghaida Khazna Katbi
978 1 84885 063 7

Contemporary Arab Scholarship in the Social Sciences, Vol 4

Early Islamic Institutions

Administration and Taxation from the Caliphate to the Umayyads and 'Abbāsids

By Abd al-Aziz Duri

Translated for the Centre for Arab Unity Studies
by Razia Ali

Edited with additional annotation by the Centre for Arab Unity Studies

I.B.Tauris Publishers
In Association With
The Centre for Arab Unity Studies

مركز دراسات الوحدة العربية
CENTRE FOR ARAB UNITY STUDIES

The opinions and ideas expressed in this book are those of the author and do not necessarily reflect those of either the publisher or the Centre for Arab Unity Studies.

Published in 2011 by I.B.Tauris & Co. Ltd
6 Salem Road, London W2 4BU
175 Fifth Avenue, New York NY 10010
www.ibtauris.com
Published in association with the Centre for Arab Unity Studies

Distributed in the United States and Canada Exclusively by
Palgrave Macmillan

Centre for Arab Unity Studies
'Beit Al-Nahda' Bldg. – Basra Street – Hamra
PO Box: 113-6001 Hamra
Beirut 2034 2407 – LEBANON
www.caus.org.lb

Contemporary Arab Scholarship in the Social Sciences, Vol. 4

ISBN: 978 1 84885 060 6

A full CIP record for this book is available from the British Library
A full CIP record is available from the Library of Congress

Library of Congress Catalog Card Number: available

Designed and Typeset by 4word Ltd, Bristol, UK
Printed and bound in Great Britain by TJ International Ltd, Padstow, Cornwall

Contents

Preface

The typology of a nation (*ummah*) manifests in the institutions according to which it proceeds, and its vitality and capacity to endure and grow are revealed in the development of its organisations across its history. The various systems and institutions clarify for us the solutions the nation has implemented in order to regulate its affairs and to respond to its exigencies and needs, just as it reveals to us the essence of the particular nation and its genius.

The study of Islamic systems is crucial to understanding the background elements and salient trends which have influenced Islamic society. Thus, research into the various types of these systems – governmental or popular, economic, social, political or cultural – divulges for us the secret of many social and intellectual movements and developments. Are we able to comprehend the origin of Islamic sects and factions without being aware of the problem of the caliphate, or what differences of view derive from it? Or are we able to perceive the civil wars in Islam, the chaos which ensued over the covenant of succession (*'ahd*) or the multitudinous divisions if we are not cognisant of the development of the institution of the caliphate? Or is it possible for us to ascertain the *raison d'être* behind the positions of the *mawālī* (the non-Arab client converts to Islam) in many of the social movements which were afforded a religious patina if we do not comprehend the fiscal policy and systems of taxation according to which the Muslims were operating? Is it possible for us to understand the flourishing of culture if we fail to study the educational institutions and know about the development of schools (*madāris*) and universities in Islam? Would we perceive the influence of the masses on the history of the Muslims if we were not to study the trade and craft guilds, as well as [social] movements such as the ʿAyyārūn, the Shaṭṭār and Fityān? Are not political events, crises and famines manifestations of the influence of political and fiscal systems?

From another perspective, we cannot understand these systems if we consider them to be fixed and stagnant. Just as they had a far-reaching influence on the course of history, likewise we witness their transformation and development across different eras and stages. It is not possible for us to comprehend them unless we attempt to trace their development through the different ages. This is an essential point which has sometimes been neglected by many researchers who therefore remain unaware of the inner vitality of Islamic history. If we analyse the Islamic systems, we see that they did not all arise after the emergence of Islam and did not mature in a short time. Rather, the origins of some of them go back to systems which had been prevalent in the Near East before Islam. Pre-Islamic systems, especially the traditions of chiefdom (*mashyakhah*) and some social traditions, in their original form or in ones reformed and refined, were among the sources of the early Islamic systems. When the Arab conquests expanded east- and westwards, the Arabs utilised extant Sassanian and Byzantine systems, particularly in matters of administration and finance. Similarly, they benefited from the cultural heritage in general. Islamic principles and Arab genius came together to refine these sources and imprint them with an Islamic character. The Muslims created the beginnings of new systems according to their needs, such as the institution of the caliphate (*khilāfah*) and the judiciary (*qaḍāʾ*). With the passing of time and with the influence of new requirements, as well as cultural and intellectual developments, this core grew, expanded and spread, assuming new and distinct forms. Similarly, new institutions appeared with the unprecedented influence of new circumstances, such as institutions for finance and monetary exchange.

In researching these systems, it is insufficient for us to devote attention only to official institutions, such as the system of government, or the financial and administrative systems. To fully comprehend the situation, we must also be concerned with the popular institutions, such as the trade guilds (*ḥiraf*), the craft guilds (*aṣnāf*), charitable endowment (*waqf*) and schools, as well as Sufi lodges (*takāyā*) and orders (*zawāyā*), because they illustrate the vitality of the *ummah*, its natural activity and autonomous growth. This is in addition to the important role which these organisations served in periods of political weakness and some major social movements, such as the Qaramaṭiyah, the Ismāʿīlis and the Futuwwah movements, as well as in economic and social life for the greater part of Islamic history.

Who can study the dispute between the [caliphs] al-Amīn and his brother al-Ma'mūn, or the war between al-Musta'īn and al-Mu'tazz or the Buwayhid era, without referring to the 'Ayyārūn and the Shaṭṭār?[1] Is it possible to understand the rule of al-Naṣr li-Dīn Allāh or the birth of the Ottoman state without studying the Fityān and Ākhīyah movement?[2] Can the researcher understand the progress and rise of industry if he neglects the study of the craft guilds, their qualifications (*sharā'iṭ*) and organisational structures?[3] Can we comprehend cultural development if we overlook the influence of the religious schools, mosques and Sufi lodges?[4] Woe be to us if we were to draw upon what is superficial and abandon what is genuinely beneficial to people!

In another regard, we must distinguish between political systems and theories, or the theories produced by *fuqahā'* (jurisprudents) and Muslim thinkers, in order to define the existing systems, or to reform or accord them legitimacy when they lacked a precedent or basis in the original Islamic principles. Without doubt, failure to distinguish between political systems and theories has been a source of confusion in some of the books on Islamic systems, as our sources for researching the political and fiscal *theories* are the works by the *fuqahā'* and intellectuals for example, the books on statecraft (*al-aḥkām al-sulṭānīyah*) by al-Māwardī, Abū Ya'lā al-Farrā' al-Ḥanbalī and Ibn Jamā'ah, and those on Islamic land tax (*kharāj*) by Abū Yūsuf, Yaḥyā bin Ādam al-Qurashī and Qudāmah bin Ja'far.

As for our sources for the study into Islamic *systems* (as opposed to *theories*), these are numerous and diverse. In addition to the books on statecraft and land tax, they include books of historical anecdotes (*qiṣaṣ*); books for viziers (*wuzarā'*); books for the edification of secretaries (*kuttāb*); general histories; dictionaries; biographies (*siyar*); geographies; as well as some technical works and other [non-literary] sources. However, in these books we find only disjointed fragments of information and observations in which there is much confusion and contradiction. This results from the different periods of the authors, the discrepancies between practice and theory, and the varying purposes for which information was recorded, as well as the instability of the systems themselves, which were not fixed in a uniform or single form and where some expanded while others disappeared, in conjunction with the appearance of new systems with the passing of time. Therefore, the researcher must scrutinise these books with careful precision and take note of the period in which they were written in order to put the information in its proper place.

Inevitably – and obviously – the results of the research are dependent on the extant sources and information available to the researcher. These conclusions will always be subject to revision and modification whenever texts appear with new information, and therefore the researcher cannot affirm or assert decisively the absolute veracity and precision of his contentions – except on the basis of what the available evidence supports.

All that which I have presented here constitutes an initial attempt for which I have followed the methodology of historical analysis. Even if its use is only to stimulate the reader's desire for more information on this subject or to clarify certain points for him, then that is the best for which I can hope. I have dealt with some of the Islamic systems in this volume in the hope that it will be followed by further such studies in the future.

Notes

1. See 'Abd al-'Azīz al-Dūrī, *Dirāsāt fī al-'Uṣūr al-'Abbāsīyah al-Muta'akhirah*. (Baghdad: Sharikat al-Rābiṭah li-l-Ṭab' wa al-Nashr, 1946), pp. 5, 63, 184–185, 280, 282–286; *al-A'māl al-Kāmilah li-l-Duktūr 'Abd al-'Azīz al-Dūrī*, 4, (Repr. Beirut: Centre for Arab Unity Studies, 2007).

2. Abū Ṭālib 'Alī bin Anjab Ibn al-Sā'ī, *al-Jāmi' al-Mukhtaṣar fī 'Unwān al-Tawārīkh wa-'Uyūn al-Siyar*, ed. Muṣṭafā Jawād, Fr. Anastase-Marie al-Karmali [Carmelite] (Baghdad: al-Maṭba'ah al-Suryānīyah al-Kāthūlīkīyah, 1934), pp. 221, 359–361; Paul Wittek, *The Rise of the Ottoman Empire: Studies in the History of Turkey, 13th–15th Centuries* (London: Royal Asiatic Society, 1938); Royal Asiatic Society monographs, vol. xxiii; Köprülü, M. F., *Les Origines de l'Empire Ottoman* (Paris: E. de Boccard, 1935); F. Taeschner, 'al-Nāṣir li-Dīn Allāh', M. Th. Houtsma *et al*, eds., *The Encyclopædia of Islam: A Dictionary of the Geography, Ethnography and Biography of the Muhammadan Peoples*, 4 vols. and Suppl. (Leiden: E. J. Brill and London: Luzac, 1913–1938), vol. 3, pt. 2, pp. 860–862.

3. See Muallim Cevdet, *al-Ākhīyah wa a-Fityān* (Istanbul: [n.p.], 1916); Bernard Lewis, 'The Islamic Guilds', *Economic History Review*, vol. 8, no. 1 (1937–1938), pp. 20–37.

4. Johannes Pedersen, 'Masdjid', *Encyclopaedia of Islam*, vol. 3, pt. 1 (1913–1938), pp. 314–389.

CHAPTER 1

Origins of the Political Systems – *al-nuẓum al-siyāsīyah*

Origins of Islamic political systems

Islamic systems (*nuẓum*)[1] did not begin with the emergence of Islam and did not mature in a short time. Rather, their origins go back to the Arabic systems which existed before Islam. The Prophet Muḥammad engendered the principles of new systems, replacing or altering some of these pre-Islamic systems, while leaving others unchanged. The Arabs subsequently conquered new lands and made use of the (existing) pre-Islamic Arab, Sassanian and Byzantine systems found there. With time, and the (growing) influence of needs, experiences and development over the first three centuries of Islam, this core grew, expanded and branched out, forming systems with specific forms, designated as Islamic systems.

Therefore, it is appropriate to discuss some of the Arab, Sassanian and Byzantine traditions which had some influence, directly or indirectly, on the Islamic systems during their growth and evolution, in order to understand the existing conditions prior to the emergence of the caliphate system.

Introduction

Before analysing the system of the caliphate, we will begin by presenting some Arab political traditions which were among the foundations of this system. We will then deal with some of the Sassanian and Byzantine traditions, which might have had an influence later on, and we shall later discuss the Prophet's political reforms in order to understand the circumstances which preceded the inception of the caliphal system.

Arab traditions

In the pre-Islamic era (*jāhilīyah*), the Arab social system persisted on the basis of the tribe and its divisions. There was great variation in customs (*ʿurf*) and traditions among the Arabs, but it may be said that the tribe constituted the basis of the social and political system in the Arabian Peninsula.[2] Each tribe had a consultative council (*majlis al-shūrā*), composed of its most powerful members and the chiefs of the tribal families. This council used to elect the sheikh of the tribe who was usually known for his tribal solidarity (*ʿaṣabīyah*) and great influence. When selecting a sheikh, old age must be regarded as the word 'sheikh' denotes an elderly man or chief. The sheikh had to distinguish himself through certain characteristics, including: generosity (since it was expected that he would assist the poor and be hospitable to strangers); bravery (and many of the sheikhs were the cavaliers of their tribes); willingness to help and serve; wisdom; experience and forbearance (meaning he would not be angered by any means but, rather, that he would bear much injury and animosity with magnanimity and forgiveness).[3] The following narration best exemplifies how a sheikh ought to be:

> Muʿāwiyah asked ʿArābah ibn Aws ibn Qayẓī al-Anṣārī, 'How did you become the *sayyid* (master) of your people?' He replied, 'I am not their *sayyid* I am one of them.' Muʿāwiyah continued to press him until he said, 'I gave in times of misfortune, was forbearing with the foolish amongst them, and enheartened the forbearing among them. Then, whoever does with them as I do is like me, and whoever falls short of this, I am better than he and as for whoever goes beyond this, he is better than I.'[4]

The principle of inheritance of authority in a sheikhdom (*mashyakhah*) did not arise because the circumstances of life in the tribe required the most intelligent and powerful individuals to assume its leadership. Salam bin Nawfal said: 'As for us, none is master over us except he who spends his wealth upon us, gives us his daughters in marriage and engages himself for the sake of our needs.'[5] Thus, authority used to be transferred sometimes from a sheikh to the son of his brother, or from one sub-tribe/clan (*fakhdh*) to another. Leadership of sheikhs in the same family for three generations in succession was rare. This view is represented in the poem by ʿĀmir ibn al-Ṭufayl:

> Even though I am the son of the cavalier (*fāris*) ʿĀmir, the chief of the tribe, the pure Arab of pure morals,
> ʿĀmir did not make me *sayyid* (chief) on account of inheritance, God

> forbid that I be exalted because of my mother or father!
> But I protect their protected lands and guard it from harm, launching my arrows at those who launch arrows at them from their cohort of horsemen.

The sheikh did, however, have the right to name his successor, especially during circumstances of hardship, but the tribe had to approve of and confirm his leadership. Some families, from whom several sheikhs were produced, became recognised as having a kind of preponderance. The authority of the sheikh extended to the political and social spheres yet it was rare that such would extend to religious authority. In any case, his authority was not absolute and he was obliged to seek the counsel of the *majlis* (council) of the tribe, and without its consent, he was unable to declare war, permit emigration or agree a peace treaty. He had to obtain the blessings of the individuals of the tribe, as remaining in his capacity was contingent on their good opinion of him.[6]

We will examine the political traditions of Mecca since they strongly influenced the political development of the Muslims. Although these traditions were based on tribal fundaments, they did develop in conformity with the needs of a commercial city and important religious centre. The inhabitants of Mecca were known as the *jamā'ah* (the group or community), a word retained by the Prophet to distinguish his followers from others. Authority in Mecca was in the hands of the *mala'*, a council composed of the chiefs of the families and people of influence and financial power, as they were 'given power' (*ulī al-quwwah*) and the '*ahl al-ḥall wa al-'aqd*' ('those who loosen and bind'; i.e. the people of authority who could make and break treaties, etc.), who used to be involved in everything. The *mala'* of Mecca consisted only of elders and typically only those who had reached the age of forty entered it, except for the sons of Quṣayy [the founder of the Qurayshī tribal confederation] for whom this precondition did not apply. Quṣayy had established a special place for the gathering of the *mala'* called the '*dār al-nadwah*', several metres north of the *ka'bah*. The *mala'* would hold their meetings there whenever the need arose, where consultations, deliberations, proclamations of wars and adoption of defensive measures took place, and where important marriages, trade agreements and alliances were concluded. The *mala'* lacked any executive power through which to impose their opinions, but enjoyed great moral power which rendered people content with their decisions. It seems that the impetus for this was, as someone said: 'If you differ, your affairs will become scattered and disparate and others will come to have designs upon you.' The men of the *mala'* became well-known for the soundness and the perspicacity of their opinions, as the poet 'Ubayd bin al-Abraṣ expressed it:

> How many a master there is among them, who bestows upon them chivalrous values, says and does,
> the speaker of words the like of which causes the barren land to blossom.

The word of the head of the *mala'*, or the most prominent person in it, was respected, and Quṣayy is described for us as the master to be obeyed whose words were executed. After his death, he was succeeded by an oligarchy because he divided his different duties among his sons. This may have been the source of the famous 'Council of Ten' that existed before the emergence of Islam since it appears that the general duties of peacemaking, supplying water [to the pilgrims], collecting blood money (*diyah*), and so forth, were distributed among some of the prominent members of the tribe of Quraysh;[7] however, none of them had (any) absolute hegemonic power. Al-Fāsī states: 'None of these was actually sovereign over the rest of Quraysh, but rather, this was with the tribe's consent and deference to him.'

It appears that Abū Sufyān was the most prominent person in the *mala'* of Mecca at the time when the call to Islam (*al-da'wah*) began. Despite that, he said: 'I do not contradict Quraysh, I am one of them, and I do whatever they do.'

The *dār al-nadwah* in Mecca was the general meeting place of Quraysh, and there were also special meeting places for other tribes to assess their particular affairs. The Medinan tribes had similar meeting places, one of which was called the *saqīfah* (the bower, or roofed area). There were designated people in Mecca, termed the *munādī* – the crier or the *mu'adhin* – caller to prayer, who were appointed the task of calling people to the meetings. Subsequently, at the time of the Prophet, they formed a group of callers, the most famous of whom was Bilāl, whom the Prophet charged especially with summoning people to prayer.[8] These are the most salient Arab political traditions of which the Muslims made use at the dawn of Islam. Perhaps they were also influenced, in one way or another, by Sassanian and Byzantine traditions, so let us briefly discuss these.

Sassanian traditions

The Sassanian state had two primary characteristics: the first was the existence of an official religion linked to politics and working with such; and the second was a strong, centralised administrative system. Supreme executive authority was in the hands of the ruler. His rule was absolute and not subject to rejection or criticism under any circumstances.[9] The Zoroastrian religion attributed an aspect of holiness to him, and the principle of the divinity of rulers was deeply rooted in Persia. The authority of the ruler and his subjects' view of him are elucidated in the utterances of the high priest of the Magians: 'If God wishes good for His *ummah*, He chooses the best of them [for its service].'[10] Thus, the subjects obey and God passes judgment. The ruler surrounded himself with displays of pomp and grandeur and lived apart from his subjects.

Only the members of the ruling family were fit for the throne because God had favoured them over the peoples of the world. When the Persians wanted to choose a king after Yazdegerd I and remove his son Bahram V (Gur), he protested this saying: 'This constitutes corruption in the loins of the kingdom that they should appoint a man to rule who is not of its people.'[11]

Supreme judicial authority was in the ruler's hands; and he was the ultimate and final recourse and referential authority for those wronged, just as he was responsible for maintaining justice, being familiar with the affairs of his subjects, and appearing before the people on special occasions to hear their complaints. The early Sassanians were accustomed to allowing the general public to (freely) express their complaints twice a year at *Nawrūz* (the new year) and at the *mahrajān* (the festival), where no one was to be prevented from voicing his complaints before the ruler, who used to attend these occasions alongside the highest religious priest.[12]

However, the ruler had the right to decree life and death for his subjects since they were tantamount to his slaves, and the executioner was beside him at all times to implement his orders immediately. The ruler was assisted by a vizier who was the first person consulted in all matters of the state, though under the supervision of the ruler.[13] It was believed that a prudent ruler would never appoint a powerful vizier, but only one from among his servile underlings.[14]

Byzantine traditions

The head of the Byzantine state was the emperor, the supreme leader and the greatest legislator. The position of emperor accorded its possessor absolute authority and infallible power. Through contact with the Sassanian East, the emperor became an autocrat or a despot, and from the time of the seventh century onwards he became even more excessive in terms of pomp and ostentation and the like of the Sassanian *shāhanshāh* (king of kings). In imitation of the rulers of the East, the emperor was placed above the level of humanity and his subjects were, therefore, like his slaves. Christianity contributed its sanctification, and the emperor became the shadow of God and his deputy on earth. He also became the equal of saints in status, and God inspired him in all which was requisite to the circumstances of his rule, and supported and directed him to the right path. The Emperor Justinian stated: 'We do not put our trust in our arms, nor soldiers, nor intelligence, but in our destiny and the Holy Trinity.' The emperor's wars with enemies were a kind of holy war, since he was the shadow of God (on earth). He was the supreme leader of the religion and its guardian, hence, he was king and bishop at the same time with an absolute, infallible power on the religious and temporal spheres. As Justinian pondered: 'What could be greater or more sacred than the imperial majesty?'

Among the manifestations of the emperor's autocracy was the fact that he surrounded himself with grandeur and abided by elaborately-organised ceremonies, separating him from the people and conferring sanctity on him. The magnificent ceremonies were among the Byzantine diplomatic means used to instil terror in the people and enemies alike. One of the emperors explained: 'By abiding by such extravagent ceremonies imperial power appears more grandiose and magnificent and such commands the amazement of both foreigners and subjects alike.'[15] The emperor was above the law, possessing absolute power over the people, administration, judiciary, politics and religion. Leo VI wrote: 'Everything is subjected solely to the providential care and governance of the Emperor.'[16] He supervised customs and public morals, and had the right to enact and annul laws. The most significant characteristic of his authority was its religious aspect, as he used to rule the Church as he ruled the State; where he appointed priests and convened church assemblies and was the highest arbiter in religious disputes. As defender of the Church, he was the enemy of heresies and the propagator of the religion. In the sixth century, the patriarch Menas declared: 'Nothing can be done in the holy Church in contravention of the orders of the emperor.'

Despite this, the authority of the emperor had some limits. The most important of these was that upon his accession, he had to swear loyalty to the Church and the decisions of its previous councils, in addition to swearing to follow the true religion. He was also limited variously by: the power of the army which curbed his power sometimes and was characterised by repeated revolts; the power of the feudal aristocracy with whom he was compelled to agree; and the power of the people that was expressed in demonstrations and riots. What weakened the authority of the emperor was the absence of any law of inheritance until the ninth century, and in spite of successive wars, Byzantium was in contact with the Islamic East, which might have led to the mutual exchange of influence and factors of such between them.[17]

The era of the Prophet (610AD–11AH/632AD) and the role of the Message

The Messenger of Islam emerged in a Mecca where there was a ruling authority. He adopted a religious, exhortative stance and assumed the role of a social reformer. He became the representative of the opposition to the prevailing status quo, but did not undertake to establish any political systems due to the absence of favourable conditions for such.

His emigration (*hijrah*) to Medina [in 1AH/622AD] was a pivotal segue in the political and religious history of Islam, as it paved the way for the unveiling of his political brilliance and organisational ability. The absence of a ruling authority in Medina, the instability of the situation and the intensity of tribal solidarity represent the causal factors behind the political and social chaos and confusion. However, one must not suppose that his political efficacy expresses a change in his theory[18] since he was always striving to form a new *ummah*, a community of which he was leader and guide. Thus, religion and politics were, and remained, undifferentiated in the call to Islam.[19]

The Messenger's primary aim in Medina was to protect the Muslims, especially as they were few in number, and to maintain security and peace in his new home. Therefore, he initiated a series of reforms in light of the circumstances and need which constituted an important factor for the reinforcement and propagation of Islam. Prior to anything else, the Prophet thought of building a mosque to be the gathering point of Muslims, and a place where they could meet and attend to their worship. Hence, the mosque became the centre of government and a place for consultation where Muslims discussed general matters, and from which delegations and raids would depart; or, more generally, the mosque became the 'heart' of the new community's activity.

When the Messenger sensed the low numbers of Muslims and the poverty of the *muhājirūn* (emigrants from Mecca) who had abandoned their possessions for the sake of their religion, he put into effect the system of *mu'ākhāt* (brotherhood) in which the *muhājirūn* were distributed among the *anṣār* (lit. 'helpers' from Medina), since he made each emigrant live with a member of the *anṣār* as his brother, sharing even in matters of inheritance, thereby solving the problem of assisting the *muhājirūn* and strengthening the cooperation between Muslims.[20] The Arabs had been familiar with the system of *mu'ākhāt* in the pre-Islamic period. However, the Messenger applied it in a broader form and attributed a religious basis to it. He continued to implement it until the battle of Badr, whereafter it was annulled after the position of the Muslims had been consolidated and their financial crisis had ended. This example elucidates how some of the social institutions in Islam evolved as a result of particular circumstances, and then disappeared with the change of these.[21]

After the battle of Badr the position of the Muslims (was) strengthened in Medina, and they came to have a powerful voice as a result of their unity and coterminous schism among other Jewish and pagan groups. The Messenger had perceived the necessity of a new system approriate to the circumstances and which would support him in his struggle against the tribe of Quraysh. Therefore, he aimed to form a balanced group consisting of the various elements of Medina, and since he had realised that blood ties were the cause of the instability in Medina before his emigration, he replaced these with religious ties and established his *ummah* on a religious basis. He drew up a prescript between the *muhājirūn*, the *anṣār*[22] and the Jews in which he clarified the foundations of the new state (*dawlah*) in Medina, and from this document we are able to discern the changes which were introduced to the *ancien* status quo.

Before we discuss the contents of the document, we must indicate that there is some disagreement over the historicity or date of its composition. Wellhausen,[23] like Muslim historians, sees that it was written before the campaign of Badr, whereas Muḥammad Ḥamīdullāh believes that the document was composed in two parts. The first part[24] concerns the *muhājirūn* and *anṣār* and probably dates back to a few months after the *hijrah*. The second part[25] relates to the alliance between the Muslims and the Jews and was written after the campaign of Badr because that can be inferred from the text, according to Ḥamīdullāh.[26] My opinion is that the document in both of its two parts was composed after the battle of Badr because the system of *mu'ākhāt* was not annulled before that, and the Muslims did not come to have a say in Medina except after their position had been improved following on their victory at Badr. Only after that was the Prophet able to make himself the supreme referential authority in Medina, as can be ascertained from the document.[27] Al-Bukhārī points to two events concerning Muslims' protection of Qurayshīs before Badr, whereas the document proscribes the protection of a Qurayshī or his property (para. 20b), and the meaning of that is that this was after Badr.[28] On the other hand, I support Ḥamīdullāh's view that the document was composed in two parts, each independent of the other, as its content indicates.[29] This is especially so as the first part of the document contains a paragraph (16) which is similar to the Jews' proposal that they conclude an alliance with the Muslims, whereas some paragraphs of the second part consider them to be allied to the Muslims (paras. 24, 25, 38 and 45) and placed under the authority of the Prophet (para. 42).

Let us begin now with the analysis of this important document. Ḥamīdullāh terms the first part of the document (paras. 1–23) 'the first constitution (*dustūr*) of the Islamic state'.[30] He begins with the establishment of a community of Muslims, *muhājirūn* and *anṣār* (and all of those inhabitants of Medina who allied with the Muslims and fought alongside them): 'This is a document (*kitāb*) from Muḥammad, the Prophet, to the believers and Muslims from Quraysh and Yathrib [Medina] and those who follow, join and struggle (in *jihād*) with them' (para. 1). This community is distinguished from all others: 'They are one community (*ummah*) to the exclusion of [other] people' (para. 2). Each of the elements of this community had the same rights, especially in times of war (paras. 15, 18 and 19). The peace concerned all, so none was able to maintain the peace alone and without the knowledge of others: 'The peace of the believers is one. No believer shall make peace when fighting for the sake of Allah without other believers unless it is equal and just for all' (para. 17). Each Muslim had the right to protect and defend those he wanted and to deny protection to any of them, even the lowliest, because of any crisis affecting the whole community: 'The protection (*dhimmah*) of Allah is one. The lowliest of them may compel them [the believers]' (para. 15). However, the traders of Quraysh and those who helped them were not protected, and neither was it permitted for any polytheist (*mushrik*) to protect the life or possessions of a Qurayshī (para. 20b).

The community was a collection of alliances as the tribes (*'ashā'ir*, sg. *'ashīrah*) and clans (*afkhādh*, sg. *fakhdh*) had been left intact as they were and had become members in the community, where the *muhājirūn* were considered as constituting a single tribe.[31] The individual participated in the community indirectly through the clan or the (tribal) federation (*qabīlah*, pl. *qabā'il*).[32] The relationship of the clan to the community is clear in that it made payments which were not private, such as the blood money (*diyah*) and redemption money (*fidā'*) for the family, just as before, since there was no central treasury at that time:

> The Banū 'Awf, Banū al-Ḥārith from the Khazraj, the Banū Sā'idah, Banū Jusham, Banū al-Najjār, Banū 'Amr bin 'Awf, Banū al-Nabīt and the Banū

> al-ʾAws shall be responsible for their ward and they shall, according to their former approved practice, and every group shall secure the release of their prisoners by paying the ransom. Moreover, dealing among the believers shall be in accordance with the recognized principles of law and justice.[33]

However, it was necessary for the Muslims to assist their needy brethren with money for the blood money and the ransom: 'Believers shall not leave anyone destitute among them by not paying his redemption money (*fidāʾ*) or blood money (*al-ʿaql*) in kindness.'[34] Similarly, loyalty remained connected to the clans (*fakhdh*) or tribe, and no believer was allowed to ally against him the *mawlā* (charge affiliated to a tribe) of another Muslim.[35]

The clans ceded to the community their right to resolve disputes when it was in the interest of the *ummah* to prevent internal discord, turbulence and disputes. All disputes were dealt with by the Prophet: 'Whenever you differ over a matter, it shall be referred to Allah and to Muḥammad.'[36] If anyone were to break the peace, commit aggression or foment corruption, the entire community would participate, even the relatives of the aggressor, in apprehending the perpetrator and bringing him to justice:

> The God-fearing believers shall be against any who has transgressed among them, engaged in secret machinations or who has sought to spread injustice, or sin, or enmity, or corruption among the believers; the hand of every believer shall be against him even if he be a son of one of them.[37]

This is in addition to making the settlement of a type of punishment by agreement with the kin of the aggressor who had the choice of retaliation or accepting blood money.[38] These measures were an important step towards ending disputes and substituting revenge with punishment because the duty of punishing culprits was incumbent on the community after having previously been undertaken by the family or the clan.[39] Thus, the first objective of the *ummah* (community) was to impose a general peace for all in Medina, which is the peace of the *ummah*.[40] The *ummah* had another important goal which was to be united in defending against outside enemies: 'The believers shall be the protectors of one another against all other people (of the world).' Furthermore: 'A believer shall not kill another believer for an unbeliever (*kāfir*) nor help an unbeliever against a believer.'[41] The duty of retaliation against the enemies of the Muslims did not fall on a brother for a brother, but on one believer for another believer: 'The believers must avenge the blood of one another shed for the sake of Allah.'[42] In this way, the raids were divested of the aspect of bloody revolts, as they had been previously, and became military tasks which concerned all the community, just as peace came to concern all.

The second part of the document (paras. 24–47) concerns the alliance between the Jews and the Muslims, and the clarification of the relationship between them. Both parties had the freedom to worship[43] and the alliance between them was a military one for the purpose of defending Medina, if it were attacked: 'Between them there shall be aid against those who attack Yathrib.'[44] In this case, each group engaged in protecting its own part of Medina.[45] However, making peace demanded a joint decision and everything which the central authority decided bound together the different parties to the alliance: 'There shall be between them [the Muslims and the Jews] mutual aid against those who make war on the people of this document and there shall be between them mutual consultation and advice and honourable dealing without animosity.'[46]

In defensive wars, each party had to bear its own expenses separately.[47] In offensive wars, it was not expected that any group would support another.[48] The right of protection (*jiwār*) and ransom remained as before, however: 'There shall be no refuge for Quraysh or those who assist them.'[49] The application of justice was a public duty and no one was permitted to stand in its way, not even if his relatives were in the wrong: 'There shall be no holding back of retaliation for injury. Whoever commits murder, he and his household shall be responsible for it. Otherwise, it will be unjust and Allah is with those who are most devout in this.' The Messenger was the arbiter in disputes: 'And verily if any dispute arises among the parties to this document from which corruption may be feared, it shall be referred to Allah and to Muḥammad, the Messenger of Allah.'[50] It appears from the particular reference to the rights of each Jewish tribe bound by the document and their duties that the Jews participated in small, separate groups and not as one group. This perhaps explains the presence of this paragraph: 'No one shall bear the consequences of a wrong deed by his ally, and aid shall be given to the wronged;'[51] and likewise the paragraph: 'Whoever commits murder shall be responsible for it himself.' This is also supported by the events pertaining to the expulsion of the Jewish tribes from Medina, one after the other.

The Muslims were representing the vital progressive element in the *ummah*, which expanded with the spread of Islam and with the increase of its power until it became a single Islamic community with one law and one leader. The idea of the 'ruling authority' (*al-sulṭah al-ḥākimah*) outside the limits of the tribe was alien to the tribal environment. Therefore, the Messenger introduced it in the name of Allah and the public institutions and army were attributed to Allah. From this concept, it was understood that there was no human authority but rather a divine authority above humankind which alone had the right of rule, and the Messenger was the representative of Allah and the executor of His will. He was the guide to the truth and the legitimate ruler on the earth. The basis of this rule was justice (*al-ʿadl*) and individuals were equal in their relationship to the ruler. However, He was the source of authority, not the people.[52] Consequently, religion and politics were unified, permitting little distinction between them. The religious authority of the Messenger depended on divine inspiration (*waḥy*) and there was no scope for human endeavour in it. As for temporal powers, the Messenger had advisers from among his Companions (*ṣaḥābah*), and he used to take some customs as well as circumstances into consideration. Therefore, the Islamic measures in the worldly sphere are not described as promulgating a particular constitution from the beginning since they were a collection of practical solutions for specific problems that were propounded in particular and flexible conditions apt to suit the circumstances.

This observation brings us back to the determination of when this document went out of effect. The last Jewish tribe was expelled after the battle of al-Khandaq in 5AH. With that, there was no longer any meaning to the alliance with the Jews. Similarly, the Treaty of al-Ḥudaybīyah in 6AH opened the way for the Messenger to ally with whomever he wanted among the tribes, which undoubtedly led to a great alteration in the significance of the document. Perhaps the document went out of effect after the conquest of Mecca, as the position of the Muslims had changed completely and they had come to represent the most powerful force in the Peninsula. The Messenger had striven to unify the Peninsula under his rule, and the Muslims entered a new stage which demanded a new constitution for a united Arab Peninsula. However, time was not sufficient for the *daʿwah* (call to Islam) to consolidate the entire Peninsula; and, the beginnings of civil strife (*fitnah*) appeared in the final days of the Messenger. The *ṣaḥābah* (Companions of the Prophet) were obliged to complete what he had begun: to unify the population of the Peninsula and lay down a system for the rule of the Islamic *ummah*. The problem of rule after the Messenger's death was the most volatile issue the Muslims had to confront. We shall see in the following sections how the Muslims faced this problem.

The system of the caliphate and its development

The caliphate (*khilāfah*) is a political institution which developed naturally in the circumstances persisting when it came into existence. In order to understand it, we must study both its growth and development across the different periods of Islamic history. The caliphate had a theoretical dimension which was represented in the theories of the *fuqahā'* (jurists) that were posited after the establishment of the Islamic state and after the development of the system of the caliphate. These theories were sometimes influenced by reality, as well as what was near to reality at other times, and these may possibly be considered to be a constitution for the caliphal order. Therefore, we must distinguish between the two aspects[53] and study each of them specifically as well as present reality over and above the theories because it preceded them, and because we only understand the theories after clarifying reality.

The Rāshidūn era (11–40AH/632–661AD)

At the death of the Prophet, the Muslims perceived the need for a leader[54] who would maintain and direct the new community, or as Abū Bakr stated in a speech to the Muslims: 'You must have a man who takes charge of your affair(s) (*amrakum*), leads your prayers and fights your enemies.'[55] However, the Muslims were not a single bloc as they included the groups of the *muhājirūn* and the *anṣār*, each of which was subdivided into factions. The Islamic community passed through periods of hardship which had the most far-reaching of effects on the development of the caliphate.

It appears that tribal traditions had an influence on the election of the first caliph. After each group had nominated its leader, the *anṣār* met at the *saqīfah* (the roofed bower) of the Banū Sā'idah to swear the *bay'ah* (oath of allegiance) to Sa'd bin 'Ubādah, the chief of the Khazraj. They invoked their excellence (*faḍl*) in Islam, and the claim that they were 'the people of glory, numbers and power' and that Medina was their city. However, they were hesitant and unsure of themselves because, as one of them said, the *muhājirūn* were the first Companions of the Messenger of Allah, and they were his kinsmen and close friends.[56] Their position was weakened due to the envy of the 'Aws tribe of the Khazraj, to the extent that some of the 'Aws said at the meeting: 'By Allah, if you put the Khazraj in charge over you once, they will still have that merit over you and they will never afford you a share. So rise and give the oath of allegiance to Abū Bakr.'[57]

The Banū Hāshim among the *muhājirūn* nominated 'Alī bin Abī Ṭālib and contended that the leadership remained in the Prophet's family after his death. Their viewpoint is clear from the narration of Ibn Qutaybah that al-'Abbās said to 'Alī upon the death of the Messenger: 'Stretch out your hand so that I may give you the *bay'ah* and so the people of your household will also give you the *bay'ah*. If the matter is thus, then nothing can be said about it.' 'Alī asked him: 'Is anyone claiming this matter other than us?'[58] 'Alī spoke out against the *bay'ah* to Abū Bakr:

> O you masses of *muhājirūn*, do not remove the authority of Muḥammad among the Arabs from his house and the inner sanctum of his household to your abodes. Do not push his family out from his position among people and his right. By Allah...we have the most right to it because we are the people of his house (*ahl al-bayt*).[59]

He also objected, saying: 'You took this matter from the *anṣār* and you argued against them on the basis of your kinship (*qarābah*) to the Prophet. Would you take it from us, who are his (immediate) family?!'[60] Some of the Umayyads were on the side of the Hāshimites, as were al-Zubayr and Ṭalḥah.[61]

A group of the *muhājirūn* nominated Abū Bakr before the meeting at the *saqīfah*. Ibn Hishām reported the position of the *muhājirūn* after the death of the Prophet: "Alī bin Abī Ṭālib, Zubayr bin al-'Awāmm and Ṭalḥah bin 'Ubayd-Allāh withdrew to the house of Fāṭimah and the remaining *muhājirūn* sided with Abū Bakr.'[62] This latter group was the fastest to get to work, as no sooner had Abū Bakr and 'Umar bin al-Khaṭṭāb heard about the meeting of the *anṣār* at the *saqīfah* than they hurried to them with some of the *muhājirūn*.[63] Abū Bakr argued with the *anṣār* that the *muhājirūn* were the first people to believe and accept the Messenger, and that 'they are his closest affiliates and trustees (*awliyā'*) and kinsfolk.'[64] He indicated the position of Quraysh among tribes, saying: 'We are the most established in the lineage of the Arab tribes. There is not an Arab tribe in existence except that there are descendants from Quraysh in it.'[65] 'Umar asserted that Quraysh had been honoured through the Prophet [having been raised up in their midst], asserting:

> By Allah, the Arabs will not be content to be ruled by you when their Prophet is not from among you. However, the Arabs do not object to their affairs being taken charge of by one from those among whom prophethood sprang and who is the entrusted trustee of their affair(s) (*walī amrihim*)... Who will contest us in the authority of Muḥammad and his rule when we are his close affiliates and trustees and his kinsfolk?[66]

When some of the *anṣār* suggested that there should be a leader from among them and another leader from among the Quraysh, the *muhājirūn* rejected their suggestion. Abū Bakr nominated 'Umar and Abū 'Ubaydah, but they refused to accept this and nominated him instead, pledging the *bay'ah* to him: 'because "he was the second of the two when they were in the cave" [*sūrat al-tawbah*, Q 9:40] and the deputy of the Messenger of Allah in leading the prayer, and prayer is the best part of the religion of the Muslims.' Those *muhājirūn* who were present gave their *bay'ah*, as did the *anṣār*, except for Sa'd bin 'Ubādah.[67] It appears that there was an understanding among the *muhājirūn* in Abū Bakr's group before the day of the meeting at the *saqīfah*, otherwise there would have been no significance to Abū Bakr's going to the *anṣār* and no explanation for the *anṣār*'s considering him a representative of the *muhājirūn*. This is supported by 'Umar's subsequent account of the events of the *saqīfah* when he says:

> There was one who informed us that when the Prophet died, 'Alī, al-Zubayr and those who sided with him remained away from us at the house of Fāṭimah and all the *anṣār* kept away from us while the *muhājirūn* assembled with Abū Bakr. So, I said to Abū Bakr, 'Let us go to our brothers from the *anṣār*', so we set off to confide in them.[68]

The following day, the day after the events of the *saqīfah*, the people gave their *bay'ah* to Abū Bakr at the mosque, except some of the Banū Hāshim who delayed doing so until a later time.[69] The sources emphasise, specifically, Abū Bakr's accompanying of the Messenger in his emigration to Medina and the Messenger's delegating him to lead the prayer during his final illness, and render these two matters the main impetus behind the election of Abū Bakr.[70] Abū Bakr's seniority also had an important influence on his election. When 'Alī objected to the *bay'ah* to him, Abū 'Ubaydah responded: 'O nephew, you are young in years. These are the elder sheikhs of your people; you do not have the like of their experience and knowledge in affairs.'[71] The significance of Abū Bakr's election connoted the victory of the system of free election in choosing the caliph over the system of inheritance, even if only in its general form. The system of election became one of the important precepts in the theories of the caliphate among the Sunnis. According to Arnold: 'The election of Abū Bakr... was in conformity with ancient Arab tribal customs, since when the chief of a tribe died, his office passed to the member who enjoyed the greatest influence, the one who was respected on account of his age, his influence, and his good service.'[72] The naming of Abū Bakr as '*khalīfat rasūl allāh*' (the successor [i.e. caliph] of the Messenger of Allah)[73] signified that he was proceeding according to the *sunnah* of the Prophet in his rule.

It is noteworthy that Medina was unique in the election of the caliph. The election in Medina came to have an influence on the development of the theories of the caliphate with regards to the number of electors and their place. The *bay'ah* of the *saqīfah* was termed the 'private (*khāṣah*) *bay'ah*' and the *bay'ah* in the mosque the 'public (*'āmah*) *bay'ah*'.[74] The existence of two oaths of allegiance subsequently came to be part of the traditions of the caliphate thereafter.

Abū Bakr gave an address in the mosque explaining his policy and position:

> O people, I have been given charge of you, but I am not the best of you. If I do well, then aid me, but if I err, then correct me. Truth is a trust and untruth is betrayal. The weak among you is strong unto me until I deliver him his right, Allah willing. The strong among you is weak unto me until I take the right from him, Allah willing. No one among you should leave *jihād* (struggle) in the path of Allah. It is not abandoned by a people without Allah inflicting them with disgrace, nor does abomination spread amongst a people without Allah spreading trials among them. Obey me in that in which I obey Allah and His Messenger. If I disobey Allah and His Messenger then you are not to obey me. [Then he convened the prayer saying:] Stand up for your prayers. May Allah have mercy on you![75]

Thus, he clarified that he was responsible for the Muslims and that the basis of his rule was justice. Everyone was equal (before the law) in justice, *jihād* was the pillar of state, and the constitution (*dustūr*) of the Muslims was the word of Allah and the *sunnah* of the Messenger. This sermon is considered one of the political foundations of Islam. Abū Bakr affirmed his position in another speech, saying:

> O people, I am like you, but I do not know if perhaps you will charge me to do what only the Messenger of Allah was able to bear. Allah chose Muḥammad over mankind over all the worlds and vouchsafed him from transgression. But I am a follower and not one to be followed. So, follow me if I do right but if I deviate then rectify me.[76]

He thereby affirmed his proceeding according to the *sunnah* of the Messenger, as well as his welcoming of consultation and criticism for the best of the *ummah*.

Abū Bakr had worked as a merchant and he continued as such for six months after his *bay'ah*; then he said: 'No, by Allah, trade is not meet with handling the affairs of the Muslims. There is nothing more beneficial for them than single-minded devotion to their affairs and looking after such.' After that the Muslims paid him an annual stipend.[77] This directive undoubtedly grew out of the circumstances of the caliph and became one of the traditions of the caliphate. At the end of his life, Abū Bakr perceived the necessity of securing a covenant of succession (*'ahd*) for a successor after him in order to avoid *fitnah* (strife).[78] It appears that he tried to determine the reaction to the like of this idea among the *ṣaḥābah*. When he was certain of that,[79] he consulted some of them about appointing 'Umar as successor. Some of them supported him and others opposed him.[80] Then Abū Bakr designated the caliphate for 'Umar: 'The Muslims confirmed his leadership (*imāmah*) during the period of Abū Bakr's tenure.'[81] Abū Bakr's opinion of his successor was that 'I have put in charge over them the best and strongest of them who is most vigilant over what will guide them rightly'.[82]

Arnold[83] and Levi della Vida[84] considered 'Umar's succession to be in accordance with Arab traditions because both the influence of 'Umar and his strong position in the caliphate of Abū Bakr caliphate[85] rendered him the incontrovertible successor to the first caliph, and that the agreement of the Companions and their pledge of the *bay'ah* to him confirmed his authority. 'Umar was thinking about the problem of rule; yet, he was unresolved. Al-Wāqidī reports that: ''Umar said, "I do not know what I shall do with the *ummah* of Muḥammad"; and, this was before he was stabbed.'[86] It seems that some of his companions were asking him to designate a successor, but he refused. It is narrated by al-Wāqidī that ''Umar bin al-Khaṭṭāb was asked while he was in good health to appoint a successor, but he refused'.[87] When he was stabbed, the *muhājirūn* implored him to appoint a successor. However, he appeared hesitant saying: 'If I appoint a successor it will become a *sunnah* [i.e. a normative practice to appoint a successor] and if I do *not* appoint a successor it will become *sunnah* [to not to appoint a successor]. The Messenger of Allah died without appointing a successor. Abū Bakr died and he did appoint a successor.'[88] When he saw the urgency of the situation and his death was immanent, he advocated making the caliphate a *shūrā* (consultation) between six of the leaders of the *ṣaḥābah*, as is apparent from his remark:

> People are advising me to appoint a successor. Allah will surely not neglect His religion or His caliphate. If death overtakes me, then the caliphate will be a consultation (*shūrā*) between those six with whom the Messenger of Allah was pleased when he died.[89]

The rest of the men of Medina were oblidged to pledge the *bay'ah* for the person elected. 'Umar arrived at this directive due to the influence of the circumstances of the Muslims. He considered that these six were leaders (*zu'amā'*) of the Muslims and had said to them: 'I find you to be the chiefs and leaders of the people and this matter (*amr*) [i.e. the caliphate] is only to be among you.' The six men were 'Alī bin Abī Ṭālib (chief of the Banū Hāshim), Sa'd bin Abī Waqqāṣ and 'Abd al-Raḥmān bin 'Awf (leaders of the Banū Zahrah), 'Uthmān bin 'Affān (sheikh of the Banū Umayyah), Ṭalḥah (master of the Banū Tamīm) and al-Zubayr bin al-'Awwām.[90] These men had excellence and precedence in entering Islam, as is clear from 'Umar's words: 'I do not find anyone more deserving of this matter than these in this group with whom Allah's Messenger had been pleased when he died.'[91] On the other hand, 'Umar was not entirely confident in any one of the six so as to be able to recommend him, as is apparent from his observations about them. He was apprehensive about 'Alī's stern vehemence (*shiddah*), as well as his 'sense of levity' (*fukāhah*),[92] 'Uthmān's partisanship and love of his family; al-Zubayr bin al-'Awwām's being 'a believer in approval [of others], a disbeliever in anger [of others] and miserly'; the weakness of 'Abd al-Raḥmān; the arrogance and vanity of Ṭalḥah; and that Sa'd bin Abī Waqqāṣ was a man of war who would not be fit for politics.[93] He knew the ambitions of each of the six and their lack of agreement on any one of them. He had warned them of competition and conflict, saying: 'I fear that you will differ over what is amongst you so that the people will then differ.' He organised the procedure of *shūrā*, specifying a period of three days and put watchers over them, ordering them to kill anyone who did not comply. He did all that to preclude any strife and schism. The details of what took place in the council of the *shūrā* are ambiguous; it appears that mutual approval between them over one person was difficult and that the deliberations were protracted. The candidates designated 'Abd al-Raḥmān bin 'Awf to choose a caliph from among them, and he chose 'Uthmān bin 'Affān.[94]

Thus, it is clear that 'Umar resorted to the *shūrā* after a precise analysis of the circumstances, and perhaps for this he relied on the pre-Islamic Meccan concept of the *mala'* (i.e. recourse to notables).[95] It is appropriate for us to demonstrate that the caliph knew that 'Alī and 'Uthmān were the two main contenders among the candidates.[96] Therefore, he spoke to them individually and expounded on the merits of each of them. The mention of these aspects is important to us in understanding what used to qualify someone for the position of the caliph at that time. 'Umar said to his two Companions: 'O 'Alī, perhaps these people will acknowledge for you your kinship to the Prophet and your relationship to him by marriage, as well as the perspicacity and knowledge which Allah has given you. If you are put in charge of this matter, then be mindful and fearful of Allah in regard to it.' Then he called 'Uthmān and said: 'O 'Uthmān, perhaps these people will acknowledge you on the basis of your relationship to the Messenger of Allah by marriage, your age and your honor. If you are put in charge of this matter, then be mindful and fearful of Allah, and do not burden the necks of the people with the sons of Abū Mu'ayṭ [i.e. his clan].'[97] Several factors led to the choice of 'Uthmān, including the fact that 'Abd al-Raḥmān bin 'Awf made following the policy of Abū Bakr and 'Umar a condition for nomination. On the day of the election, he had requested that both 'Alī and 'Uthmān swear by Allah in front of the Muslims that they would act according to 'the Book of Allah, the *sunnah* of His Messenger and the precedent (*sīrah*) of the two caliphs who came after him'. 'Alī said '*Ijtihād* – independent judgment – is incumbent on me.'[98] In another narration he said: 'No, by Allah, but according to my own effort and capacity (*ṭāqatī*).'[99] And, in a third narration, he is reported to have said: 'I hope to do that and to act according to the utmost of my knowledge and capacity.'[100] At the same time, 'Uthmān swore 'not to contradict or fall short of the precedent (*sīrah*) of the Messenger of Allah or Abū Bakr and 'Umar in aught'.[101] These two responses had an important effect, and the sources which we have come down to us confirm this matter decisively.

The Umayyads (Banū Umayyah) also had an important influence on the election of 'Uthmān. Some of their influence went back to the era of the first two caliphs, when they came to have a strong voice in Medina.[102] It appears that they engaged in a widespread propaganda campaign for 'Uthmān. Al-Ṭabarī narrates that 'Abd al-Raḥmān bin 'Awf consulted the notables among people and the commanders of the armies, and 'he did not pass by any man without admonishing him and commending 'Uthmān to him'.[103] Then he walked about in disguise: 'He did not leave anyone of the *muhājirūn*, *anṣār* or others among the weak among people and their rabble without inquiring of them and seeking their opinion. He did so until he no longer encountered anyone whom he asked and consulted who did not reply, "'Uthmān".'[104] Perhaps the kinship between 'Abd al-Raḥmān and 'Uthmān also had its influence on that matter. 'Alī had evinced fear of this when the *shūrā* was arranged, as he said that Sa'd 'will not disagree with his cousin, 'Abd al-Raḥmān, and 'Abd al-Raḥmān is related by marriage to 'Uthmān and these three will not disagree about it [i.e. the *shūrā*]; and, 'Abd al-Raḥmān will entrust it to 'Uthmān, or 'Uthmān will entrust it to 'Abd al-Raḥmān.'[105] When 'Abd al-Raḥmān chose 'Uthmān, 'Alī spoke frankly to him: 'You have sided with him...This is not the first day that you have gone against us.'[106] 'Alī alluded to the fear of the Quraysh that the Banū Hāshim would enter into the caliphate, fearing that it would not be taken from them. He said: 'The people look to Quraysh and Quraysh look to their house. They [the Quraysh] say that, "If the Banū Hāshim are put in charge over you, it [i.e. the caliphate] will never leave them. As long as it is with those other than Quraysh, it will alternate among you."'[107]

Wellhausen believes that 'Uthmān was elected because he was the weakest of the six. The men of the *shūrā* had desired a weak man and not a strong one like 'Umar.[108] This opinion resembles what used to transpire in the election of popes, during one of the periods of the papacy. Wellhausen was perhaps influenced by this, but – in any case – his assertion about 'Uthmān is incorrect as he was not the weakest of the six. He was the strongest of them in terms of tribal solidarity. Furthermore, 'Umar had considered him to be one of the two foremost contenders among candidates. 'Uthmān was pledged the *bay'ah* and the first *fitnah* [i.e. the first instance of strife among the Muslims] took place. The garrison cities (*amṣār*) revolted against him, and he was killed. The revolt against him combined the grievance of the tribes over the authority of the Quraysh and the discontent of the senior *ṣaḥābah* due to the Banū Umayyah's monopolisation of authority, in addition to the hatred of central rule by certain tribes, as well as the existence of economic disparity and regional conflict. 'Alī was elected after him because he was the most outstanding of the *ṣaḥābah*, and also because of his precedence, kinship, knowledge and excellence. The senior *muhājirūn* supporters stood by his side, whereas Banū Umayyah had incurred the wrath of people. We must recall that the men of the garrison cities sent in delegations to Medina, especially the Iraqis among them, and also supported and advocated him.[109]

Now after this brief, general survey of how each caliph was chosen, we shall discuss the general characteristics of the caliphate in the era of the Rāshidūn (Rightly Guided) Caliphs. The caliphate of the Rāshidūn has a republican tinge insofar as it relied on elections. However, there was no single or systematised method of election. It was sometimes a direct election and sometimes a nomination, having been preceded by the knowledge of the opinion of the electors, followed by their acceptance of the *bay'ah*. At yet another time, it was an election undertaken by the leaders [i.e. as in the case of 'Alī]. In all cases, it was limited mainly to Medina. What can be noticed in the caliphate of the Rāshidūn is the infusion of Arab traditions with an Islamic spirit or, to be more precise, the influence of Arab traditions on the spirit of Islam. So, the concept of election was taken from Arab traditions. However, the concept of the caliph as being dependent on the consent of the people to him in general – and not to his family or his tribe – was taken from Islam. Moreover, the concept of the source of authority as being divine and the necessity of making known the opinion of the *ummah* – which (according to a Prophetic *ḥadīth*) would not agree in consensus upon error – with regard to the candidate was an Islamic concept. The technique followed in election, whether by the selection of the community or by an appointment which was preceded by knowledge of the opinion held, or by *shūrā* (consultation), was drawn from Arab traditions. This is also verified in the reports about the form of the *bay'ah*. We may say that the multiplicity of ways of election in the era of the Rāshidūn points to the Arabs' lack of political experience and the attempt to apply Arab methods, which were germane to a tribe or a city, to new imperial circumstances. Moreover, the qualities of the candidate, such as his experience, age and influence, combined Arab traditions and Islamic principles which affirm a strong connection to the Messenger, precedence in Islam and service to it. Qurayshī lineage was a necessary quality. There is no doubt that there was a tribal spirit in the emphasis on a specific tribe, but the Quraysh were honoured by Islam on the basis of the Messenger coming from among them.

As for the authority of the caliph, it was limited by public opinion. In this respect, it continued the Arab tradition and was constrained by an Islamic constitution – namely the Qur'ān and the *sunnah* of the Messenger. Abū Bakr had said: 'Obey me in so far as I obey Allah and His Messenger. If I disobey Allah and His Messenger then do not obey me.'[110] However, the extent of this authority was broader than the authority of the sheikh over the tribe. The caliph was the chief executive authority and he also held judicial authority, which he would exercise directly or by means of his appointed judges (*quḍāt*) (from the time of 'Umar's caliphate), whereas judicial authority was not in the hands of the sheikh. The caliph oversaw religious affairs, but he did not have spiritual authority and this is an Islamic distinction.[111] Abū Bakr adopted the title '*khalīfat rasūl allāh*', 'the successor of the Messenger of Allah', and this is an indication of the orientation of Islam. The caliph had inherited all the powers of the Prophet, except prophecy. 'Umar initially adopted the title '*khalīfat rasūl allāh*', and this points to following the same orientation. However, the title was shortened to avoid being long-winded and he was then simply called caliph, '*khalīfah*' (successor). Thus, this title appeared as a result of the circumstances. Subsequently, 'Umar was termed 'Commander of the Faithful' (*amīr al-mu'minīn*). This was a temporal title affirming the authority of the caliph, and his being the supreme leader and head of the executive authority.[112]

Finally, we perceive in the development of the caliphate in the era of the Rāshidūn a trend which indicates the ascendancy of Arab traditions and their steadily increasing influence.

The Umayyad era (41–132AH/661–750AD)

'Alī did not appoint anyone as successor. After he was fatally wounded: 'The people came in asking him, "O Commander of the Faithful, do you think that if we lose you, and we may not lose you, we should pledge the *bay'ah* to al-Ḥasan?" He replied, "I neither command you to do so, nor do I forbid you. You best understand your affairs."' Al-Ḥasan was given the *bay'ah* because he fulfilled the requisite conditions of the caliphate, and the Kufans' concurred on pledging him the *bay'ah*.[113] Mu'āwiyah had assumed the caliphate due to the circumstances favouring him during the struggle with 'Alī. In any case, his shrewdness and his sword had their influence in his coming to power. In Mu'āwiyah's triumph over the concept of election to determine the caliphate, or ignoring the principle of precedence and service in Islam, as well as affirming the importance of power and influence and attaining to rule, constitutes a revolt against the Islamic principle which holds that the source of rule is Allah. In Mu'āwiyah's victory was also the triumph of Arab traditions over Islamic principles. Whatever the debate of historians over the relative value of trends and individuals on the development of history, we feel that Mu'āwiyah had a decisive influence on the development of the caliphate. That was due to his introduction of an innovation in rule and the caliphate, namely the principle of *inheritance*. We do not know how Mu'āwiyah arrived at the adoption of this principle, but historians are inclined to think that al-Mughīrah bin Shu'bah advised him in that.[114] Whatever his motives were for wanting to keep power among his descendants, whether it was his observation of the problems which transpired upon the death of each caliph,[115] or his knowledge of the power of tribal solidarity for the Banū Umayyah and their desire to retain power among themselves, he innovated the system of inheritance in 676AH in his attempt to obtain the *bay'ah* for his son Yazīd.

This action of his provoked the displeasure of the Arabs in general, and some of the Umayyads in particular,[116] because it conflicted with the tribal traditions which – even though they acknowledged the right to maintain authority in a tribe or clan – did not recognise direct inheritance from father to son. And this was also for the reason that it negated the principles of Islam which did not consider authority to be a human possession; and therefore the caliph could not bequeath it to whomever he willed.[117] Some historians may perceive the concept of inheritance in the Kufans' *bay'ah* to al-Ḥasan. The 'Alīd faction clung to this principle, but this concept had not been advocated by any caliph before Mu'āwiyah. We notice in Mu'āwiyah's persuasion of the garrison cities to give the *bay'ah* to his son Yazīd that the idea of election was still acknowledged in theory. All its value had been lost in practice because it was supported by force, even if he hesitated to use it openly.[118] Thus, Mu'āwiyah's caliphate headed in a new direction in the constitutional history of Islam since the caliph became a king, in fact, from the standpoint of the power of his family and his personal status, even if the term king (*malik*) was not his official title.[119]

When Mu'āwiyah died, the *bay'ah* to Yazīd was renewed as a confirmation of the covenant of succession, and this became a custom which subsequent caliphs followed. However, the system of dynastic inheritance was not settled in the Umayyad age. This era was one of perpetual conflict between three principles:

1. the Islamic principle which affirmed the selection of the most righteous and best of Muslims;
2. the tribal principle which acknowledged the ascendancy of the tribe or the clan, and accepted the selection of the wisest, eldest and most inclined to service of its individuals;
3. the principle of direct inheritance from father to son.

It is sufficient to mention here some examples to clarify the clash between these principles, while leaving the other details to those who are researching political history.

Mu'āwiyah II (Mu'āwiyah bin Yazīd) came to power on the basis of the principle of inheritance from his father.[120] Nevertheless, his position was representative of the struggle between the Islamic principle and the principle of inheritance. This caliph had been a Qadarite[121] who was faithful to the Islamic principle, and who did not accept inheritance to the extent that he accepted the *bay'ah* but detested it.[122] He criticised his grandfather and his father in a speech, saying: 'My grandfather Mu'āwiyah wrested power from those who were more entitled to it and more deserving of it. Then my father took over power but he was not suitable for it.'[123] He had refused to designate his brother Khālid. The Umayyads asked him to do this when he was on the verge of death, but he said: 'No, by Allah, I will not do so. I found no happiness in its sweetness, so how should I find despair in its bitterness? [i.e. even when circumstances were favourable, he was not in agreement to ceding the caliphate to his brother].'[124] Al-Ṭabarī presumed that the reason for his refusal was that he had not found anyone qualified for the succession,[125] and it appears that he held to the principle of election and left matters to the Muslims so they could choose a satisfactory man for themselves.[126] Thus, Mu'āwiyah II left the field wide open for the collision between the three principles which found those who would epitomise them: Ibn Zubayr represented the Islamic principle; Marwān bin al-Ḥakam – the tribal principle; and Khālid bin Yazīd – the principle of inheritance. Let us discuss the circumstances for the choice of Marwān so that we can understand this situation.

The campaign for Ibn Zubayr was strong in the Ḥijāz and Iraq, and reached Syria itself to the extent that he was supported by the leader of the Qays tribe at that time, al-Ḍaḥḥāk bin Qays al-Fihrī. Al-Balādhurī suggests the reason for that: 'When Mu'āwiyah II died, the majority of the people inclined towards Ibn Zubayr. They said, "He is a man of full maturity and has assisted the Commander of the Faithful 'Uthmān. He is a son of the disciples of the Messenger of Allah and a son of Abū Bakr,...and he has virtue in his soul."'[127] At a gathering in al-Jābiyah there was an indication of the Umayyads' desire to maintain the caliphate among themselves. However, they were not unified. Khālid bin Yazīd represented the Sufyānid house and was the leader of those calling for the principle of inheritance. He was supported by his uncles of the Kalbī tribe under the leadership of their chief Ḥassān bin Baḥdal.[128] There was also 'Amr bin Sa'īd, Marwān's rival for prestige and influence, even if he was young. The al-Jābiyah gathering ended with the victory of the tribal principle without neglecting the principle of inheritance since the *bay'ah* was given to Marwān, then Khālid bin Yazīd, then 'Amr bin Sa'īd al-Ashdaq, just as the sources all elucidate.[129]

It can be noticed that age, wisdom and experience were emphasised in the nomination of Marwān. When Ḥassān bin Baḥdal, the victor of the Sufyānid house, said that Khālid bin Yazīd was 'of the essence of a king (*ma'dan al-malik*), the seat of politics and leadership', it was replied to him that Khālid was 'a young man'.[130] He fell silent and did not add anything to what he had said. The people of al-Urdunn (Jordan) said to Ḥassān al-Kalbī:

> We will give you the *bay'ah*, on the condition of fighting those who opposed you and obeyed Ibn al-Zubayr, and that these two youths [Khālid bin Yazīd and his brother 'Abdullah] are kept away. They are young, and we abhor that the people should bring forth a sheikh while we should bring them a youth.[131]

The supporters of al-Ḍaḥḥāk objected to the *bay'ah* being given to Khālid as he was 'the age of a boy'. Al-Ḥuṣayn bin Numayr said on the same subject: 'By Allah, no. The people will not bring a sheikh to us while we come to them with a boy.'[132] 'Abdullah bin Ziyād objected to Khālid, saying: 'Would you give the *bay'ah* to a young lad who has no worldy experience?'[133] Ḥassān bin Baḥdal acknowledged this weakness of Khālid and said: 'Nephew, the people have rejected you because of your youth.'[134] Marwān bin al-Ḥakam was the experienced and seasoned sheikh. Ibn 'Aḍāh al-Ishwī said of the nomination of Marwān: 'O people, this is our companion for whom the matter is well suited. He is the son of the paternal uncle of 'Uthmān, the Commander of the Faithful, the sheikh of Quraysh and the best of them.'[135] 'Ubayd Allāh bin Ziyād said: 'I see that you are giving the *bay'ah* to Marwān. He has age, perspicacity and virtue.'[136] Al-Ḥuṣayn bin Numayr emphasised his age and experience, saying: 'Marwān is the sheikh of Quraysh, he directs us and governs us. He does not need us to direct and govern him.'[137] The Umayyads took into account experience and age in choosing Marwān. This is described by al-Balādhurī:

> The people of Syria met to consider those to whom to give power. They said, 'There is no good in your appointing a youth, but this is Marwān, sheikh of Quraysh and master of the Banū Umayyah. He is sensible, wily and experienced in war.' Then they said, 'Bring Marwān' and they gave the *bay'ah* to him.[138]

Other sources depict the Umayyads assessing the services of Marwān to the Banū Umayyah and his struggle in the service of their victory.[139] Thus, Marwān was elected on a tribal basis due to his age, experience and lineage. The acknowledgement of Khālid bin Yazīd was because he was satisfactory to Ḥassān bin Baḥdal and those who asserted that Khālid was of the 'essence of a king.'[140] It appears that Marwān promised to cede to Khālid. Nevertheless, he reverted to the system of inheritance in 65AH and gave the *bay'ah* to his two sons 'Abd al-Malik and 'Abd al-'Azīz.[141] This was the first time that it was pledged to two men, and perhaps the disturbances Mu'āwiyah II's position created and the many who coveted the caliphate pushed Marwān to this. Thus, began a normative practice which increased the problems of the Banū Umayyah.

We will not go into the details of the remaining history of the Umayyads since it is sufficient for us to elucidate that the revolts of the Khārijites, 'Ālids and the 'Abbāsids were in the name of the Islamic principle. It is also enough for us to clarify that the failures of 'Abd al-Malik in removing his brother 'Abd al-'Azīz from power and of al-Walīd in trying to remove his brother Sulaymān were a blow to the principle of inheritance,[142] and the ceding of Sulaymān to 'Umar bin 'Abdul 'Azīz, Yazīd II's designation of his brother Hishām, then Hishām's to al-Walīd II (the son of his brother

Yazīd), were a triumph for the tribal principle.[143] With the coming to power of Yazīd III and the killing of al-Walīd II was a threat to the ascendancy of the tribal principle due to the Yamānī tribe's hostility to al-Walīd II and their revolt against him, and also because al-Walīd had challenged tribal sentiment by designating his two young sons. The morals of al-Walīd II were a secondary issue, on the evidence that Hishām tried to remove him on the pretext of his reprehensible conduct. However, he failed in his attempt. Then the coming of the last Umayyad caliph Marwān II was a triumph of the tribal principle over the principle of inheritance because Marwān, even though he was from the descendants of Marwān I, was not from the main Marwānid branch. However, the influence of the Qays and their support of him, as well as his power and wisdom, raised him to the caliphate. Therefore, it can be reasoned that the tribal principle was the more influential among the Umayyads, whereas the Islamic principle was the impetus driving the movements which rose up against them.

The restriction of the caliphate to the Umayyad house was the aim of all the Umayyads. Al-Balādhurī reports: 'When the *bay'ah* was given to Marwān, the Banū Umayyah turned to him and said, "All praise belongs to Allah who did not take it from us."'[144] The initial trend had been towards making the caliphate Sufyānid. When that shifted to the Marwānid branch, they began to say: 'No one should be appointed successor to it except Marwān.'[145] The introduction of inheritance into the caliphate and its clash with the other principles precipitated the emergence of two orientations: firstly, the view of the caliphate towards its powers; and, secondly, the view of the *fuqahā'* towards caliphate. The first caliphs were kings and sheikhs of the tribes at the same time, so their authority did not persist on a religious basis but rather on the power of the tribes. Therefore, the Umayyad caliph came to monitor and regard vigilantly the sentiments of the chiefs of the tribes and behave as though he were one of them, even if he were more senior to them. The Umayyads had begun to take interest in giving consideration to tribal traditions and customs (*'urf*) in their policy more than their interest in Islamic principles. Their rule became Arab because the Arab aristocracy had not been applying the principles of the religion of brotherhood and equality. Rather, they used to look back to Arab traditions and boast of the pre-eminence of the Arabs.[146] However, the frequent reliance of the caliph on inheritance rendered the form of rule gradually oriented more and more towards despotism.[147]

On the other hand, the *fuqahā'* considered the caliphate of the Umayyads to be a worldly possession because it was incompatible with the divine law (*al-shar'*). The *fuqahā'* in Medina were against the Umayyads. This divergence between the caliphs and the *fuqahā'* influenced the theory of the caliphate, since it had been formulated against the will of the *fuqahā'* who were far from rule and continued to be far-removed from the knowledge of the political practice of it. So they did not pay heed to reality but neglected it, intentionally or inadvertently.[148] Thus, religion had its influence in the Umayyad age, with the caliph adhering to certain religious protocols. He led the people in prayers, delivered the sermon (*khuṭbah*) to them on Fridays and sent his armies to distant regions to bring them under the banner of Islam. Moreover, religion had an influence on some of the Umayyad caliphs. For example, it has come down to us that Mu'āwiyah II was deeply devout; 'Umar bin 'Abdul 'Azīz was influenced by religion in his policies; and Yazīd III came to rule in the name of Islamic principles.[149] Finally, we can assert that the caliphate system in the Umayyad era was a period of transition from the stage of election to that of absolute inheritance, which obtained in the 'Abbāsid era.

The first 'Abbāsid era (132AH/750AD) until the death of al-Mutawakkil (247AH/861AD)

The coming to power of the 'Abbāsids had an impact on the development of the system of caliphate. The principle upon which they constructed their right to rule, the development of the system of administration in their time, and the involvement of non-Arab elements in their rule, were all factors which influenced the growth and development of the caliphal order in this period, even though no significant change in the status of the caliph transpired during it.

The 'Abbāsids affirmed the system of inheritance and dealt tribal traditions a severe blow when they established their right to the caliphate on the basis of their kinship to the Prophet. This is manifest in their statements and propaganda. Abū al-'Abbās stated in his opening address: 'Allah has distinguished us by kinship to the Messenger of Allah...He made us descendants of his tree...and He sent down a Book wherein He said, "Say [Muḥammad]: I ask of you no reward for this save for affection for kin (*al-qurbah*)."'[150] The suggestion was that the intent here was that Allah had imposed on the Muslims' inheritance by the relatives of the Prophet. This verse was the slogan for the legitimate right to rule of the 'Abbāsids.[151] It was only natural that they considered the rule of the Umayyads an epoch of injustice and usurpation, and that they saw in their arrival the return of the right to its people. Furthermore, Abū al-'Abbās pointed to the justice of the Rāshidūn caliphs and then said: 'The Banū Ḥarb and the Banū Marwān sprang up and usurped it [the caliphate]. They monopolised it, doing injustice to its people. Then, in the end, Allah returned the right to its people.'[152]

They disseminated these views widely in their propaganda, stressing to the people that Allah had ordained the transfer of rule to the people of merit among the lineage of prophets as a reward unto them. He had imposed obedience to the people of the Prophet's house (*ahl al-bayt*) on the Muslims in the verses of operative injunctions (*muḥkam*) of His book (i.e. the Qur'ān), without the Prophet asking for that. The *Risālat al-Khamīs* by Aḥmad bin Yūsuf (the scribe of al-Ma'mūn), one of the treatises which used to be written upon the *bay'ah* of each caliph to be read to the 'Abbāsid Shī'ites in Khurasān, declares that:

> The choice of those of excellence from his relations and kin for the inheritance of his caliphate derives from the great closeness which the Prophets of Allah desired to attain unto Him...He favoured His Prophet by commanding him with his request for his community to render affection to his kinsfolk...Their virtue from Allah (the Most Mighty and Magnificent) was great, without the Messenger asking Allah to impose this conferral upon His creation or imposing upon them to abide by it. He said: "I ask of you no reward for this save for affection for kin (*al-qurbah*)." This was what necessitated for them thereby the right of inheritance in the clear verse of His revelation: "Those of kin [lit. those of the same womb *arḥām*] are closer to one another in the Book of Allah."[153]

The 'Abbāsids claimed that Allah had purified them and removed any impurity (*rijs*) from them so that they would be the best rulers.[154] Moreover, they claimed that they came to revive the Prophetic *sunnah* and to follow the Book of Allah in rule, namely that the basis of their rule was religious and persisting on the divine *sharī'ah*, not on Arab traditions or customs (*'urf*). Dāwūd bin 'Alī said in a speech to the people upon the *bay'ah* of Abū al-'Abbās: 'You have the protection (*dhimmah*) of Allah, the protection of His Messenger and the protection of al-'Abbās...so we shall rule you in accordance with what Allah has sent down and deal with you according to the Book of Allah and conduct ourselves in accordance with the *sunnah* of His messenger.'[155]

The 'Abbāsids began surrounding themselves with *fuqahā'* and drawing close to them in order to demonstrate their adherence to the religion. Al-Manṣūr advised al-Mahdī, saying: 'Let the people of religion be your strength.'[156] They came to show their zeal for the religion by fighting against apostacy and heresy. They began emphasising religious aspects in their ceremonies. The *burdah* (mantle) of the Prophet became the first symbol of the caliphate. The caliph would wear it on public occasions, such as the prayers for the two *'eid* festival days, Friday prayers and when he announced *jihād* (as al-Mu'tamid did when he fought against Layth al-Ṣaffār [leader of the Ṣaffārid state, who ruled between 879 and 902AD] and as al-Muqtadir did when he fought Mu'nis).[157] The religious influence appears prominently in the title '*imām*', which al-Ma'mūn was the first to adopt officially and which had been commonplace before him.[158]

After the Umayyads had depended for their authority on the good pleasure of the tribal chiefs, authority with the 'Abbāsids became sacrosanct and derivative from Allah. Al-Manṣūr said in an address in Mecca: 'Oh people, I am the sultan of Allah on His earth. I rule you by His success [conferred upon me] and direction,...So follow me, and implore Him to favour me with right guidance and proper conduct and to inspire me with mercy and beneficence towards you.'[159] Thus, the people did not have a hand in the caliphate. They only had to pledge the *bay'ah*, to be loyal and obey. As it stated in the *Risālat al-Khamīs*:

> If the people of the east and west, those deficient and perfect, were to choose for themselves, then there is no hope that their opinions will be in agreement until the end of time because of their divisions and differences...It is Allah's kindness and mercy that He lifts dispute and absolves the believers of the burden of choosing to raise up the *ahl al-bayt* [i.e. caliphs] and to connect their lineage to the Messenger of Allah and to impose affection for them on His creation.[160]

The result of what we have mentioned is that the sacrosanct character of the caliph increased, to the extent that he came to be called '*khalīfat allāh*' – the viceregent of Allah. 'Abdullah bin 'Amr bin 'Utbah conveyed his condolences to al-Mahdī, saying: 'There is no greater calamity than an *imām*'s loss of his father, nor a more splendid consequence than the caliphate of Allah for those near unto (*awliyā'*) Allah.'[161] The *Risālat al-Khamīs* also indicates: 'It is the duty of those whom Allah has appointed as deputies on His earth and made a trust unto His creation...' and so on.[162] It appears that this view of the caliph was acceptable to the people and in common parlance, so that even when Bashār bin Burd lampooned al-Mahdī he referred to him as '*khalīfat allāh*'. One of those in revolt against al-Mutawakkil described him as 'the rope (*ḥabl*) stretching between Allah and His creation'.[163]

The 'Abbāsids began to circulate and disseminate among the people the concept that they were above the level of mankind. 'Abd al-Ṣamad bin 'Alī said upon his oath to al-Amīn in 175AH (when he was five years old): 'O people, do not be indignant of his young age, for it is the blessed tree, whose root is firmly fixed and whose branches reach unto the heavens (Ibrāhīm, Q 14:24).'[164] They were not content with doing this only, but also informed the people from the outset that the caliphate would remain in their hands for eternity. The evidence of this is what al-Ṭabarī relates to the effect that the *imām* Ibrāhīm dispatched a flag to Abū Muslim which he called 'the shadow'. The explanation for this (as al-Ṭabarī says) was that the earth would never be devoid of shadow, and likewise it would not be devoid of a 'Abbāsid caliph until the end of time.[165] Dāwūd bin 'Alī said in a sermon: 'Know that this matter [the caliphate] is unto us and not other than us until we surrender it to 'Īsā bin Maryam [i.e. Jesus].'[166]

The result of their sharing rule of Persia was that they were influenced, to no small extent, by Persian systems of rule, although to less of a degree than is imagined by the sources affected by the populist/chauvinist non-Arab movements of the *shu'ūbīyah*. The 'Abbāsids adopted many of the elaborate ceremonies of the Persian kings and were influenced by their despotic outlook. Anyone perusing the *Kitāb al-Tāj* (*The Book of the Crown*) attributed to al-Jāḥiẓ can perceive this clearly. E. H. Palmer contends: 'When the 'Abbāsids owed their rise entirely to Persian influence, it was only natural that Persian despotic views should prevail over them.'[167] Arnold comments on the 'Abbāsid caliphate:

> This autocratic character of the Muslim caliphate was probably a legacy of the Persian monarchy...for pre-Islamic Arab society had never known any such form of political institution, nor was it in harmony with the Qur'ānic doctrine of the equality of all believers or with that attitude of independence which characterized the relations between the first Caliphs and the Arabs who had so recently come out of the desert.[168]

He explains that the pomp seen in the palace ceremonies helped to augment the caliph's authority and foster others' awe of him.[169] However, we must not exaggerate the effect of Persian influence on the despotic system, which the 'Abbāsids followed because the core of that system was inherent in their claim to the holiness of their authority. This is clear from the address by al-Manṣūr and in the natural development of the caliphate. Pomp, the isolation from subjects and tyranny exhibited their prototypical beginnings in the Umayyad state. Likewise, intermixing with the Persians and being influenced by their opinions had an effect on the strengthening and ingraining of this trend. Among the influences of the Persians on the first 'Abbāsid period was that the 'Abbāsids adopted the ministerial system (*wizārah*) from them. With that, the caliphs availed themselves of aids, or what resembled pseudo-partners to them in authority sometimes. However, the caliph remained the real master and absolute ruler, overseeing the viziers and punishing them when they exceeded their bounds of their power, or when their influence became a danger to him (which occurred with the Barmakids and the Banū Sahl).

The caliphate in this period relied on the period of the previous caliph. However, the problems of inheritance resulted from the 'Abbāsid's perpetuation of an error, which the Umayyads had committed before them and this was of engaging more than one man in a pact (of succession). We see in Abū al-'Abbās' pledge to cede to his brother al-Manṣūr, and after him to 'Īsā bin Mūsā, a direct continuation of what took place sometimes with the Umayyads, the conclusion of a pact with two of the most prominent members of the royal family. This had been a political exigency dictated by the grave situation of the caliphate. However, al-Manṣūr refrained from the plan of direct inheritance when he renounced 'Īsā bin Mūsā and designated al-Mahdī. Al-Mahdī confirmed this when he overthrew 'Īsā and pledged the *bay'ah* to al-Hādī. One of the effects of ignoring public opinion was the abrogation of tribal traditions in regard to the matter of age (al-Amīn was designated when he was five years old) in confirmation of the bequeathing of rule from father to son. This principle was abandoned abruptly due to the impact of the system of multiple bequests of the pact of succession. Therefore, the first 'Abbāsid era was the age of struggle between the principle of pledging the succession to more than one son and the desire of each caliph that his son should succeed him.

The period of Turkish influence (247–334AH/861–945AD)

The advance of the Turks and the increase of their influence had negative and distressing effects on the caliphal system and the status of the caliphs. This is not odd as the Turks had no prior civilised traditions and al-Jāḥiẓ referred to them as '*badū al-'ajam*', non-Arab Bedouin. They had no awareness of matters of policy and administration, nor an understanding of its theoretical bases, as had been the case with the Persians.[170] Despite the fact that the period of the domination of the Seljuk Turks was brief, spanning the years between the killing of al-Mutawakkil (247AH) and the coming of al-Mu'tamid (256AH), their influence was potent and its effect remained obvious until the Buwayhid (also Buyid) invasion (334AH). Therefore, it has become incumbent upon us to consider the period between 247 and 334AH as one of the periods of the caliphate, while acknowledging certain exceptions. The prestige of the caliphate returned at the time of al-Muʿtamid and al-Muktafī (279–295AH) when the influence of the Seljuk Turks waned manifestly.

On the other hand, we can consider the period of Buwayhid rule to be the end of the period (324–334AH) of the *imārat al-umarāʾ* (the emirate of the emirs) in many aspects. However, the fact that the Buwayhids were Zaydīs and foreign conquerors clearly distinguishes their role from the constitutional aspect of the role of the *amīr al-umarāʾ* (chief emir of emirs). We would not be in error if we were to say that that period of the *imārat al-umarāʾ* resembles the period of Nine Years (247–256AH) in many ways, with one important difference; namely, that it is distinguished from the latter by the unity of the ranks of the Turks and the distinction of having one person from among them as their leader. This allows us to consider the period between 334 and 347AH as a single, discrete period (despite our feelings about the difficulty of delimiting this), and to term it the period of Turkish influence and attribute to it some general characteristics. This period is distinguished by the influence of the Turks and their interference in the selection of the caliphs, which ranged from exercising some influence to full appointment.

Al-Wāthiq had opened the door to chaos in the caliphal system because he refused to cede the pact of succession to anyone,[171] thereby leaving the matter to the court entourage (*ḥāshiyah*) and the army to nominate whomever they wanted. A council met, formed of the chief judge, the vizier (*wazīr*), two of the chief scribes (*kuttāb*) and two of the Turkish commanders, who were Itākh and Waṣīf. They chose al-Mutawakkil (the brother of al-Wāthiq) and rejected the son of al-Wāthiq due to his young age.[172] The Seljuk Turks had an important influence on the choice of al-Mutawakkil. Waṣīf was the first to object to giving the *bayʿah* oath to the son of al-Wāthiq, and it seems that they were the ones who suggested al-Mutawakkil to the council and were the reason for this.[173] Subsequently, al-Mutawakkil was killed after a long struggle between him and the Turks over power.[174] The results of this were extremely detrimental to the caliphate as it opened the way for a series of appointments to the caliphate, and for hostilities against the caliphs including killing, imprisonment and overthrow without justification. This precedent proved the *coup de grâce* for the traditional respect, and with this the Turks became the masters of the situation.[175]

This was followed by a period of nine years (247–256AH) during which the Turks were alone in appointing whomever they wished, or ousting him according to their whims and desires. They did not take into account the merits of their candidates. Rather, their concern was to maintain their interests and to distance the sons of al-Mutawakkil, out of fear of their reprisal.[176] The caliphate was weakened by the establishment of independent emirates in the east (such as the Ṣaffārid and Sāmānid dynasties), as well the Zanj revolt, which shook the foundations of the state, in addition to the Qarmatian propaganda and the independence of Ibn Ṭūlūn. There then followed a nine-year period of recovery in which the prestige of the caliphate was restored due to the efforts of al-Muwaffaq (al-Manṣūr II)[177] and his son, al-Muʿtaḍid. The influence of the Turks waned temporarily but returned again during the caliphate of al-Muqtadir (295–321AH), due to the conflict between the functionaries of the administration and their covetous self-interests, the weakness of the caliph and the interference of the female members of the family. This period ended with a war between the caliph and the Seljuk Turks, which culminated in his being killed[178] and the caliphate being shaken once more. The importance of the event can be sufficiently ascertained in that ʿAbd al-Raḥmān al-Nāṣir named himself caliph when he heard of this farce. With this, the Turks regained control of power. After the deliberations between Mu'nis and his group, Mu'nis appointed al-Qāhir (the brother of al-Muqtadir) as caliph.[179] When al-Qāhir attempted to vanquish the Turks, they attacked him in his palace, deposed him and empowered Abū al-ʿAbbās bin al-Muqtadir as caliph (al-Rāḍī) in 322AH.

However, the bankruptcy of the treasury and the corruption of the administration, together with the secession of the Ḥamdānids in Mosul, the Buwayhids in Persia, al-Jibāl (Kurdistan) and Rayy and the Barīdis in Khūzestān, as well as Ibn Rā'iq's monopolisation of revenue in Basra, and Wāsiṭ and the leadership of the army there, all led to the institution of the *imārat al-umarā'*.[180] The caliphate was compelled to accept Ibn Rā'iq's proposal that he pay all the costs of the administration and put aside sufficient allowances for the caliph on condition that he head the army in Baghdad. That took place on 19 Dhū al-Hijjah 324AH/9 November 936AD. The caliph appointed Ibn Rā'iq

> supreme commander and leader of the army, made him the *amīr al-umarā'* (emir over all emirs); and he reassigned the management of the kingdom to him. Ibn Rā'iq ordered that his name be read in the [Friday] sermon from all the *manābir* (pulpits) in the principalities, and that he be referred to by the *kunyah* (honorific title) of *amīr al-umarā'*. From that day forward, the matter of [the office] the *wizārah* was void. Ibn Rā'iq and his scribe (*kātib*) came to oversee every affair and, likewise, all those who took over the emirate after Ibn Rā'iq.[181]

Wealth came to be in the hands of the *amīr al-umarā'* (Ibn Rā'iq) and the caliph had no share except that which the emir gave to him. This was a blow to the masters of the pen (i.e. the scribes) and a reason for the transfer of rule to the men of the army.[182]

Al-Rāḍī has left us a striking description of the state of the caliphate shortly before the establishment of *imārat al-umarā'* and after it:

> People may say, 'Is this caliph content with a Turkish slave managing his affairs, even controlling his wealth, and administering [the dominion] by himself?' They do not know that this matter was corrupted before me and that people entered me into it against my wishes. Then, would blackmail me, keeping in confinement under guards who acted presumptuously towards me, making me sit with them several times in the day and coming to me in the night. Each of them wanted me to favour him over his companions and to have his own treasury. I used to fear for my life, so I did not attempt to avoid them until Allah spared me finally of their affair. Then Ibn Rā'iq took charge of it and acted even more presumptuously in his extortion and exploitation of the treasury. He was unmatched in his drinking and pleasures.[183]

Thus, the caliph became like a phantom beside the *amīr al-umarā'*, simply the companion of the actual ruler. There was no strangeness then in the fact that al-Rāḍī was 'the last to speak on the day of the Friday prayer'.[184]

When al-Rāḍī died, Bajkam, the then *amīr al-umarā'*, was in Wāsiṭ so he sent his *kātib* (scribe) to oversee the choice of a new caliph. He held a council headed by the vizier, which was attended by each vizier and his *kātib*, as well as the 'Ālid and 'Abbāsid tribal nobles (*ashrāf*), the judges and the local notables (*wujūh*), so that the election would be complete in form. Each pair of them cast two votes together, but they knew Bajkam's candidate was al-Muttaqī so they elected him.[185] When al-Muttaqī differed with Tūzūn (the new emir), he escaped to the Ḥamdānids. When they lost in the war with Tūzūn, al-Muttaqī was forced to negotiate with him. Tūzūn received an oath from him and his *kātib*, in the presence of the judges and nobles (*ashrāf*), to respect his authority. However, al-Muttaqī deceived him, so Tūzūn blinded him and deposed him. Then al-Mustakfī rose to the position of caliph after Ḥasan al-Shīrāzīyah conspired with Tūzūn through al-Qahramānīyah. Al-Mustakfī remained until the coming of the Buwayhids.[186]

We will here make note of the particular circumstances of the period in which Turkish influence weakened somewhat. During the reign of al-Mu'tamid (r. 256–279AH), the position of the caliph was unique in the history of the caliphate for the reason that he was a figurehead and actual

Then al-ʿAbbās said: 'This is the [correct] opinion.'[191]

Four months after al-Muqtadir's accession to the caliphate, a group under the leadership of the al-Jarrāḥ family revolted against him, demanding that the caliphate be given to Ibn al-Muʿtazz. The basis of their contention was that al-Muqtadir was too young of age and not mature enough to rule: 'It ended in failure. One of the judges was killed because he was asked, "Would you give the *bayʿah* to al-Muqtadir?" and he replied, "He is young and it is not permissible to give the *bayʿah* to him."'[192] The increase in Turkish influence resulted in the weakening of the caliphate's authority. Al-Mutawakkil and al-Muqtadir constituted a deadly blow to the authority and prestige of the caliphate, and in a period of nine years the caliphate was merely a plaything in the hands of the Turks and those contending for power. With the revival of caliphal authority through the efforts of al-Muwaffaq and al-Muʿtaḍid, their influence decreased even if the prominent viziers still sought their friendship.[193]

Their influence was restored to the Turks during the caliphate of al-Muqtadir and reached its peak upon his death. They reverted to their machinations and ambitions, and established the position of *amīr al-umarāʾ*. Their leaders began competing for control of Baghdad. The *amīr al-umarāʾ* was not content to simply take actual power into his hands and render the caliph an official who received a particular salary; instead, he began to share with the caliph in the symbols of his caliphate, with his name being mentioned in the Friday sermon and minted on coins along with the name of the caliph.[194]

Despite the fact that the selection of the caliph was dependent on personal ambitions, and sometimes demanded the failure of the genuinely well-qualified candidate with the right merits, there were some qualities which were taken into consideration in his selection. It was taken into account as to whether he was free from any deficiency in hearing, sight or speech and free from any physical disability, as well as whether he was from the tribe of Quraysh. The Qurayshī precondition was out of concern to abide by some of the prophetic *ḥadīth*. The ʿAbbāsids had strengthened their position through the existence of *aḥādīth* that were to their benefit, attributed to the Prophet. With this, they were able to avail themselves of an attribute of sanctity in the view of the Sunnis (*ahl al-sunnah*), and this explains the Turks' lack of boldness at any time in considering any change. Moreover, it was impossible to remove the caliph from his post unless he himself renounced it. For example, al-Ṭabarī narrates that Muḥammad bin al-Wāthiq 'would not accept the pledge of the *bayʿah* from anyone until al-Muʿtazz had been brought before him and abdicated himself'.[195]

There were two main reasons which necessitated removal: immorality and physical deficiency. These were the best weapons in the hands of opposition groups as they could be used to contrive arguments against the caliph whenever they desired. The Turks had accused the caliph al-Muhtadī [of impropriety] in his confrontation with them when he refused to abdicate himself, as they alleged that

> he had written in his own hand to Mūsā bin Bughā, Bāyakbāk and a group of commanders that he would not harm, seize or kill them, nor attempt to do that. If he were to do that to them – to any or all of them – they would stand against him as they would be free from their oath of the *bay'ah* to him.[196]

The Turks found blinding (by gouging out the eyes) the simplest way to do away with the caliph since the caliph's right to the caliphate would drop naturally as a result of that [given considerations about the impermissibility of physical defects]. An example of this is what happened to al-Qāhir:

> When they decided to depose him, they sent the judge (*qādī*) 'Umar bin Muḥammad with three witnesses, accompanied by Ṭarīf Subkarī to witness the deposition of al-Qāhir. The judge was disturbed when al-Qāhir affirmed his right to remain as caliph so he said to Ṭarīf: 'Why is it that we were summoned to a man who had not been overcome or had his signet seal taken away in the presence of the *kuttāb* (scribes) and the army? This should have been done beforehand, and then we should have been summoned before him.' When this judge related what had happened to 'Alī bin 'Īsā, 'Alī responded, 'Abdicate and do not think about it. His behaviour is infamous and his actions are flagrant. What he deserves is obvious.' I said, 'Dynasties are not founded by us. That is done by those who wield swords. We are only fit to witness and attest.'[197]

Al-Qāhir was blinded the day after that. When Tūzūn wanted to remove al-Muttaqī, he gouged out his eyes as well. Metz believes that the Muslims adopted this custom of blinding from the Byzantines.[198]

Despite this deplorable situation, the caliph enjoyed the respect and loyalty of the Muslims. Therefore, it was difficult to stand against him openly because this meant provoking the wrath of the masses against anyone who might attempt it. Thus, it was necessary to promulgate a legal reconciliation between a man's enjoying real power and the appearance of him being subordinate to the caliph. The caliph, even if he was theoretically responsible for administration, was not in a position which would facilitate his conducting it. Therefore, orders used to be issued in his name while his hands were tied. The books of *fiqh* (jurisprudence) are contrary to this matter and suggest an alternative picture of the caliph.[199] This also explains to us why the emirs in the independent states were always insisting on ceremonial pacts to inherit the throne and overt displays, attempting thereby to accord their power a patina of legitimacy before the *fuqahā'* and the public. If we exclude the period of revival, we can say that the significance of the pact/covenant (*'ahd*) did not persist. The nomination of the caliphate was carried out by influential figures among the Turks or the viziers. After that, the people used to give the *bay'ah* to the caliph in public. It appears that the system of the private *bay'ah* and the public *bay'ah* in their most extreme manifestations began during this period. To summarise, the errors of al-Wāthiq and al-Muktafī paved the way for the Turks and the men of the entourage to take charge of selecting the caliphs, and to eliminate the authority and prestige of the caliphate, leaving it only with its name and moral influence. The interference of the military led to the shake-up of the administrative institutions and the waning of their importance, just as it led to the corruption of the administration. Subsequently, the diminishing of the lands of the caliphate was an important factor in weakening the import of the caliphate.

The Buwayhid era (334–447AH/945–1055AD)

It can be said that the period of the *amīr al-umarā'* and what it constituted of divesting the caliphate of all authority made Baghdad the object of ambitions. This led naturally to the Buwayhid (also Buyid) attack, which appeared to the people to be a substitution of one *amīr al-umarā'* for another. However, it had far-reaching effects on the caliphate system and the administrative institutions attached to it, and in all aspects of public life.[200] The change was merely the substitution of one emir for another. Indeed, the Buwayhid age was a culmination of the age of the *amīr al-umarā'* in its orientations since the Buwayhids adopted this title and took the place of the previous emirs. The caliph remained a phantom, and the forces of the military took command of the institutions of state.[201] However, some of the new circumstances effected a transition in the station of the caliph from bad to worse. The Buwayhids had arrived at the head of a foreign army and established a hereditary emirate. They were Zaydī Shī'ites[202] and did not recognise the right of the 'Abbāsids to rule the Islamic world.[203] The Buwayhids only allowed the 'Abbāsid caliphs to remain out of political considerations.[204]

Mu'izz al-Dawlah had wanted to transfer the caliphate to the Zaydī Abū al-Ḥasan Muḥammad bin Yaḥyā, but his retinue warned him about the discontent of the people and their opposition because: 'The common people in the garrison cities are accustomed to the 'Abbāsid claim. They consider their dynasty to be an article of faith and obey them in accordance with Allah and His Messenger. They regard them as having been given the right to rule (*ūlī al-amr*).'[205] The retinue propounded to him the advantage of the caliph being a 'Abbāsid: 'Today you are with a caliph whom you and your companions do not believe to be of the people of the caliph. If you were to order them to kill him, then they would kill him, deeming it Islamically-lawful to shed his blood.' They also showed him the danger to his position in the event of his appointing an 'Ālid caliph, saying: 'If you enthrone one of the 'Ālids as caliph, you will have someone whom you and your companions believe is entitled to the caliphate, but if he were to order them to kill you, then they would obey him;' and power would come into the hands of the caliph, whereas Abū al-Ḥasan would become merely a follower: 'If you give him the *bay'ah*...the Daylamites shall obey him and reject you; and whatever he commands to be done with you, they will do.'[206] Therefore, the emir abandoned his decision and preferred to rule despotically in the shadow of a pseudo-caliph [which would allow him a free hand], instead of being subservient to a legitimate caliph whose *imamate* would be held legitimate by the masses.[207]

With the coming of the Buwayhids, the position of the caliph worsened further, and he lost the remaining respect and influence which he had in the running of the state: 'Among the greatest reasons for this was that the Daylamites were Shī'ite and extreme in their Shī'ism. They believed that the 'Abbāsids had usurped the caliphate and taken it from those who had the right to it. So for them there was no religious motive impelling them to obey.'[208] The Buwayhid's lack of respect for the 'Abbāsid caliphs soon manifested and twelve days after they entered Baghdad (Thursday 21 Jumādā al-Ākhirah 334AH/29 January 946AD), Mu'izz al-Dawlah deposed al-Mustakfī because he accused him of conspiring with his commanders against him and of trying to obtain aid from the Ḥamdānids, just as he was also not pleased with the arrest of the leader of the Shī'ah.[209] The caliph's removal was carried out in a disgraceful way. Two Daylamites approached the caliph when he was in his *majlis* (council) and in the presence of Mu'izz al-Dawlah:

> They seized him and threw him to the ground, then tied his turban-cloth round his neck and dragged him away. At that moment, Mu'izz al-Dawlah got up and the people became confused. The two Daylamites took al-Mustakfī bi-Lāh to the palace of Mu'izz al-Dawlah. He was arrested there and the palace of the sultan was plundered so that nothing remained in it.

Mu'izz al-Dawlah fetched Abū al-Qāsim al-Faḍl bin al-Muqtadir and offered him the caliphate, giving him the title al-Muṭī' li-Lāh (lit. the one who obeys Allah).[210] When the al-Ḥamdānid Nāṣir al-Dawlah attacked Baghdad in 335AH 'he was rising up in defence of the caliph', so Mu'izz al-Dawlah imprisoned the caliph. When Nāṣir al-Dawlah's campaign failed: 'Mu'izz al-Dawlah again installed al-Muṭī' li-Lāh as caliph assuring him that he had not intended him ill will or animosity towards him. After that, he [again] stopped his appointment of him and returned him to his palace.'[211] On 19 Ramaḍān 381AH/911AD, Bahā' al-Dawlah was covetous of the wealth of al-Ṭā'i' and took his possessions.[212] He carried this out in a dreadful fashion. He visited the caliph, and while he was sitting [in his palace] Bahā' al-Dawlah approached him with his companions: 'Then, they pulled al-Ṭā'i' down from his throne by the straps of his sword. More Daylamites came and he was wrapped up in a cloak and carried him off to some small boats (*zabāzib*), then they imprisoned him in a storeroom in the *dār al-mamlakah* [the Buwayhid residence in Baghdad].' Then he was deposed.[213] The caliph used to be visited but did not visit anyone. However, 'Aḍud al-Dawlah did not abide by this. Upon his arrival from Hamdān in Baghdad in 370AH, he went down to the bridge of al-Nahrawān and asked al-Ṭā'i' to meet him. So al-Ṭā'i' went out and met him.[214]

With the coming of the Buwayhids, a hereditary dynasty was established in the heart of the caliphate. After the caliph had had, in the previous period, a vizier and the emir had had a *kātib*, the situation was now reversed.[215] The Buwayhids even came to be involved in appointing the *kātib* of the caliph.[216] They monopolised wealth while they allocated a salary to the caliph. Mu'izz al-Dawlah paid al-Mustakfī 5,000 *dirhams* per day,[217] then this was reduced with the appointment of al-Muṭī' to 2,000 *dirhams* per day.[218] After the Buwayhids conquered Basra in 336AH, Mu'izz al-Dawlah cut off the salary of the caliph and gave him private estates (*ḍay'ah* pl. *ḍiyā'*), which could bring in 200,000 dinars per year.[219] However, the Buwayhids used to tax the revenue of these estates to the extent that their revenue was decreased to 50,000 dinars per year.[220] Miskawayh states:

> The funds which were designated for the caliph had been dispersed (in the year 364AH) and encroached on by the dependants of Mu'izz al-Dawlah and subsequently Bakhtiyār: some of them had seized them or requested some of these [estates] as an *iqṭā'* (land grant) from the caliph, and others had farmed some of them unfairly and it was not easy to remove them from control of them. 'Aḍud al-Dawlah reclaimed all this as his right.[221]

Sometimes the emir would force the caliph to give him some money, as Bakhtiyār did in 361AH when he demanded 400,000 *dinars* on the pretext of [conducting] a *jihād*. He forced the caliph to sell his jewels and accoutrements to meet the demand.[222] The wealth of the caliph was sometimes subject to confiscation, as Muʿizz al-Dawlah did with the wealth of al-Mustakfī and Bahāʾ al-Dawlah did to al-Ṭāʾiʿ.

The end of the caliph's authority is clear from a letter of Muṭīʿ in 361AH/971AD to Bakhtiyār when he asked him for money for *jihād*, claiming that *jihād* was incumbent upon the ruler. Al-Muṭīʿ wrote:

> Forays (*al-ghazw*) would be incumbent on me if the world were in my hands and if I had control over the management of monies and men. Now, I have none of it except meager a subsistence which is inadequate for me. These are in your hands and those of the governors in the provinces. Neither forays nor the *ḥajj* (pilgrimage), nor anything expected of the *imām* is incumbent on me. All you can have from me is this name which you mention in the Friday sermons from the pulpits of your *minbārs*, thereby reassuring your subjects. If you would like me to withdraw, I will withdraw from even this as well and leave the entire matter up to you.[223]

Upon his appointment to the caliphate in 381AH, al-Qādir wrote a letter to Bahāʾ al-Dawlah in which he said: 'You have become the sword of the Commander of the Faithful unto his enemies, favoured above others with the beauty of his countenance, the sole and absolute protector of his territory, the care of his subjects and the mediator between him and that which is entrusted to him by Allah.'[224] The Buwayhids were not content to take power in practice, but also took it in theory in that they made the caliphs delegate it to them officially and publicly. In 369AH, at a solemn ceremony, al-Ṭāʾiʿ delegated power to ʿAḍud al-Dawlah, saying:

> I have decided to delegate to you that which Allah, may He be exalted, has charged me with of affairs of my subjects in the east and west of the earth and their management in all aspects, except for my private affairs and means of subsistence. Take charge of this seeking guidance from Allah.

He ended by saying: 'I command you to do what Allah commands you, and I forbid you to do what He forbids you. I absolve myself before Allah for anything other than that.'[225] In 381AH, the nobles (*ashrāf*), judges and witnesses came to al-Qādir and they heard his oath of loyalty to Bahāʾ al-Dawlah: 'He pronounced the handing over of all beyond his gate to which claim had been laid.'[226]

The Buwayhids were not satisfied with taking power. Rather, they endeavoured to share with the caliphate in its last privileges and symbols. The *khuṭbah* (Friday sermon) in Baghdad was the symbol of the caliph's political sovereignty. It was not more than a quarter of a century before the Buwayhids exploited this distinction. Their names came to be mentioned along with the name of the caliph in the Friday sermon. 'Aḍud al-Dawlah began this practice in 369AH, then it subsequently became a custom for those emirs who came after him.[227] The significance of the *khuṭbah* to the emir was the acknowledgement by the caliph of his sovereignty in Baghdad.[228] More unusual than this was that 'Aḍud al-Dawlah had a disagreement with al-Ṭā'i' and removed his name from the *khuṭbah* for a period of about two months (20 Jumadā al-Ūlā–10 Rajab 364AH).[229]

Coinage became the second primary symbol of the caliph's sovereignty in the hands of the Buwayhids. They removed the title 'Commander of the Faithful' and were content to mention the name of the caliph on the coins. However, the Buwayhid emir was not content to imprint only his name but added also his title and *kunyah* (*agnomen*). Sometimes the name of the head of the Buwayhid family and his titles were added, and occasionally even the titles of the heir apparent, and all this was on the coins in Baghdad.[230] The Buwayhid's supervision of the minting led to their sometimes engraving titles on the coins which the caliph had not conferred upon them. For example, the title '*shāh-han-shāh*' is found next to the name of 'Aḍud al-Dawlah on a coin struck with the date 370AH, even though this title was not one granted before the reign of Jalāl al-Dawlah. Numismatic study of the coins of the Buwayhid era elucidates the vacillation of power between the emir and the caliph. Thus, when the *imārat al-umarā'* was the stronger, the caliph's name would appear on the reverse, whereas it would be struck on the obverse when the *imārat al-umarā'* was weak.[231] Among the other symbols of the caliphate was the beating of drums at the caliph's gates at the times of the five ritual prayers. Mu'izz al-Dawlah attempted to share in this priviledge and failed. However, 'Aḍud al-Dawlah forced al-Ṭā'i' (in 368AH) to grant him the right to have drums beaten at his gate in Baghdad three times a day (at midday, sunset and evening).[232] The custom continued thus and for each ruler of the state until Ṣulṭān al-Dawlah, Abū Kālījār and Jalāl al-Dawlah superceded it, and the drums were beaten for them five times a day, despite the protests of the caliph.[233]

In this way the Buwayhids wrested authority from the caliphs and shared with them, for the first time in the history of the 'Abbāsids, all the emblems and distinctions of privilege of the caliphate. 'Aḍud al-Dawlah conceived of a plan as he desired to transfer the caliphate to the Buwayhid house. Miskawayh says:

> (In the year 369AH) ʿAḍud al-Dawlah contrived to effect a connection between himself and al-Ṭāʾiʿ li-Lāh by [marrying off] his eldest daughter. He did that and the marriage contract was concluded in the presence of al-Ṭāʾiʿ li-Lāh, with the witnessing of the bridal dower of one-hundred thousand *dinars* by the notables (*aʿyān*) of the state and judges. The emir hoped that he [the son al-Ṭāʾiʿ li-Lāh] might be blessed with a son by her who would then inherit the throne. The caliphate would come to the house of the Buwayhids and power and the caliphate would both be gathered together within the Buwayhid dynasty.[234]

ʿAḍud al-Dawlah also exceeded familiar custom in ceremonies. In 367AH he rode to the palace of the caliph where he was conferred, crowned, given a necklace and belt, and:

> The caliph presented two banners to him by hand, one of them was the emblem of the emirs in silver and the other was the emblem of the heirs to the throne (*wulāt al-ʿuhūd*) in gold. This second banner had not been awarded to anyone else before him who had been in his position. A covenant was written for him and read in his presence. This had never been the custom. Pacts used to only be given to the heirs in the presence of the caliphs. If a man among them received the pact, he would say to him, "This is my covenant to you, so carry it out."[235]

Was ʿAḍud al-Dawlah dreaming of being appointed successor? There is no further need to demonstrate that all the caliphs of the fourth century were chosen by the Buwayhids, who appointed and removed them according to their interests.

All that remained for the caliph was his religious influence, and therefore he began to cling to this and assert it. Al-Bīrūnī wrote during the caliphate of al-Qāʾim:

> The state and the dominion have been transferred...from the family of al-ʿAbbās to the family of Buwayh [Buwayhids]. What remains in the hands of the ʿAbbāsids is only religious and creedal, but nothing of the sovereign or temporal. It resembles that possessed by the Resh Galutha among the Jews, religious leadership without dominion or state.[236]

In 363AH, al-Muṭīʿ was explicit in his covenant (conceding succession) to al-Ṭāʾiʿ about the reality of his position; he said in his letter of abdication:

> I testify to the contents of this that the Commander of the Faithful, *al-Faḍl al-Muṭīʿ li-Lāh*, when he considered his religion and his subjects, endeavoured

> perpetually to provide for them in the obligatory religious matters, but his clearness of speech was cut off [i.e. he was unable to speak having suffered a stroke] in some of what Allah has commanded, so he decided to abdicate...[237]

It is no coincidence that the historical accounts make known the religiosity of al-Qādir and his great piety, alms-giving and contact with the ascetics.[238] Al-Qādir had intervened in doctrinal matters and had written a treatise on the foundations of the school of the *ahl al-ḥadīth* (lit. the 'people of the *ḥadīth*', those who based praxis on collecting narrative traditions on the Prophet). He used to teach a circle of the *ahl al-ḥadīth* every Friday in the al-Mahdī mosque.[239] He authored another document which he read to the nobles (*ashrāf*), judges, witnesses (i.e. those formally entrusted to witness official matters) and *fuqahā'*: 'It contains admonition, the merit of the Sunni *madhab* (doctrinal school) and a discrediting of the Mu'tazilah.'[240] In this, is there not evidence of the caliph's focusing his efforts on the religion, as well as his feelings that he constituted its final pillar of support in the face of the political strength of the Buwayhids? For this reason, the functionaries among the adherents of the religious schemes always followed the caliph. The appointment of judges was one of the privileges of the caliph even when he was in the weakest of states, and the judge was not permitted to make a ruling, if he were not designated by him. In 350AH/961AD, one of them attempted to vouchsafe the post of chief judge (*qāḍī al-quḍāt*) for 200,000 *dirhams* a year. The caliph refused to appoint him or even to meet him, even on reception days. When he withdrew after two years, his successor refused all his rulings (*aḥkāmahu*) because he had purchased his post from the Buwayhid emir.[241] When Bahā' al-Dawlah attempted to entrust the post of chief judge to a Shī'ite, he did not succeed because the caliph refused to appoint him.[242]

The *imāms* of the mosques were responsible directly to the caliph and they usually carried out his orders. The *imāms* used to be vigilant that no heresy occurred. In 420AH/1029AD, the Shī'ites of al-Karkh introduced an innovation in the *khuṭbah* (the Friday sermon). The caliph appointed a special *khaṭīb* (preacher) in al-Karkh, but he cursed the caliph at the time of prayer. The leaders of the Shī'ites apologised to the caliph and sought forgiveness from him so that the *khuṭbah* again would be read in his name as usual, and he allowed that.[243] This clarifies why the *fuqahā'*, judges and preachers used to constitute a single group supporting the caliph. The caliphs utilized them in periods of weakness of the Buwayhids as a means to threaten the emirs and constrain their actions. When al-Qā'im became angered at Jalāl al-Dawlah because he had not disciplined a servant of his who had usurped a plantation of the caliph: 'In the year 426AH, he ordered the judges to desist from making rulings, and the *fuqahā'* to desist from *fatwās* (giving legal opinions) and *khuṭabā'* (preachers) from having anything to do with [buying or dealing with] lands or to conclude contracts.'[244] Jalāl al-Dawlah was forced to appease him.[245] Thus, despite the weakness of the caliph, his religious influence had an effect on the masses because he remained, in relation to the Sunnis, the source of authority and a symbol of the Islamic *sharī'ah*. The *fuqahā'* continued to affirm that he was the supreme leader for the Muslims, just as is clear from the book *al-Aḥkām al-Sulṭānīyah* (*The Principles of Rule*) by al-Māwardī, who confirmed the political and religious sovereignty of the caliph. By means of this influence, the caliphs regained some of their authority in the first half of the fifth century AH. Al-Fakrī bin al-Ṭaqṭaqī refers to this revival when he mentions al-Qādir who died in 422AH: 'In his time, the prestige of the 'Abbāsid state returned and its splendour was augmented. It regained power in its affairs.'[246] He says of his successor al-Qā'im: 'The prestige of state increased with him; and, its power grew.'[247]

Similarly, the religious influence of the caliph clearly indicates that the Buwayhids, despite their ambitions, were compelled to maintain the legitimacy of the caliph. It was necessary to issue a pact for the investiture of the emir upon the replacement of the caliph or the emir; and this was in order to satisfy public opinion. A meeting was held, to which was summoned the senior officials, the men of the entourage, commanders, *fuqahā'* and judges. The emir would come forward, in humility and deference, in front of the caliph and kiss his hand, putting the deeds of the covenant on his head [in a symbolic gesture] out of respect for him. Then the contents of the covenant were read out in a loud voice and both the emir and the caliph swore two oaths, the first for honesty and obedience, and the second for loyalty and devotion.[248] In order to confirm their status, the victors over the different sides had to acknowledge – in theory – the sovereignty of the caliph and obtain the covenant for investiture from him.[249] This covenant was important as the decisive factor in the case of any struggle between two emirs, for example.[250] However, it can be observed that the pacts in the Buwayhid period used to depend to a great extent on the desire of the emir and were not issued without his agreement. The truth is that the most ambitious came forward with a request for the covenant from the emir, not from the caliph who had to issue it at that time.[251]

The caliph had another distinguished privilege, namely that of granting titles and honours. He was able by this means to please or flatter the emir. At a time when the emirs were obsessed with requesting magnificent titles from the caliph, there was a wariness about giving such to them, and the caliph used to try to invent a suitable title for each situation. In 367AH, he granted 'Aḍud al-Dawlah a new title which was '*Tāj al-Millah*' (Crown of Denomination).[252] In 381AH, al-Qādir granted Bahā' al-Dawlah the honorific '*Ghiyāth al-Ummah*' (Succour of the Nation).[253] In 429AH, the titles '*shāhanshāh al-A'ẓam, Malik al-Mulūk*' (Greatest Shah of Shahs, King of Kings) were added to the titles of Jalāl al-Dawlah. The *khuṭbah* was read in his name according to this title, however the public was enraged and they castigated the preachers. The *fuqahā'* sought a *fatwā* ruling on the permissibility of this title and two among them decreed its permissibility, but the famous al-Māwardī rejected it.[254] Even so, the emir continued to use it and, in 430AH, he was granted the title '*al-Malik al-'Azīz*' (the Beloved King).[255] The caliphs used to occassionally refuse to grant some titles. When the emir Abū Kālījār requested the title '*al-Sulṭān al-A'ẓam, Malik al-Umam*' (the Greatest Sultan, King of the Nations), his request was refused. The Buwayhids were not satisfied with the titles of the caliphs. Rather, they used to sometimes accord themselves titles which the caliph had refused to grant, such as the title of '*shāhanshāh*' which was used by 'Aḍud al-Dawlah.[256]

This religious influence of the caliph and its importance in assuaging public opinion led the Buwayhids to show great respect for the caliphs and to exaggerate in displays of the pomp of the caliphate on public occasions, and that was to please the masses. At the investiture ceremony of 'Aḍud al-Dawlah in 369AH,

> al-Ṭā'i' sat on a high couch and around him were a hundred men with swords and finery. In one hand [he held] the *muṣḥaf* (the written redaction of the Qur'ān) of 'Uthmān, and on his shoulders was the Prophet's mantle (*burdah*) and in his [other] hand was the Prophet's staff, and before him was the sword of the Prophet. A curtain was put up which had been sent by 'Aḍud al-Dawlah. He asked that there be a curtain for al-Ṭā'i' so that the gaze of none from the army arrayed in front of him would fall on him. The Turks and the Daylamites entered there and none of them had any armour. The nobles and the men of rank stood on either side. Then 'Aḍud al-Dawlah was summoned, and he entered. The curtain was raised and 'Aḍud al-Dawlah kissed the ground. The commander, Ziyād, was alarmed by this and asked in Persian: 'What is this, O king? Is this Allah, the Almighty and Magnificent?' He turned to 'Abd al-'Azīz bin Yūsuf and he said to him, 'Help him to understand. Tell him: "This is God's *khalīfah* on earth".' Then he ['Aḍud al-Dawlah] continued moving forward, and he kissed the ground seven times. Al-Ṭā'i' turned to the *khāliṣ*

> *al-khādim* [his chamberlain] and said, 'Let him come closer.' 'Aḍud al-Dawlah arose, approached and kissed the ground twice. He said to him, 'Come closer to me. Come closer.' So he came nearer and kissed his foot and al-Ṭā'i' took his right hand and ordered him to sit on a chair after he had repeatedly commanded him: 'Sit'. He ['Aḍud al-Dawlah] asked his pardon [in refusing to sit out of deference], but al-Ṭā'i' replied to him, 'I swear, you will sit.' So he kissed the chair and sat...[257]

It would be difficult to conceive of a more peculiar political farce.

For political reasons, the Buwayhids used to issue important orders in the name of the caliph and with his signature.[258] Likewise, the caliph would be asked to sign important communications to the provincial governors,[259] even the contracts which were made with the tax farmers.[260] Whatever the case, the emir used to do as he wished and he would send the documents to the caliph for him to sign.[261]

Theories of the caliphate

The Sunni theory of the caliphate

The Sunni *fuqahā'* had sought recourse to the Qur'ān and *aḥādīth* in order to posit the foundations of their theories of the caliphate. They searched for any reference to the institution of the caliphate in the Qur'ān but to no avail. The term *khalīfah* appears in the plural form – *khulafā'* – in indication of certain groups (*sūrat al-a'rāf*, Q 7:69 and 7:74; *sūrat al-naml*, Q 27:62); however, such have no relation to these political institutions. It is also used in the singular form in two places, one referring to Adam: 'When your Lord said to the angels, "I will make a *khalīfah* on the earth";'[262] and another in verse addressing the Prophet David: 'O Dāwūd (David)! We have made you a *khalīfah* on the earth.'[263] Hence, the word *khalīfah* was explained exegetically as connoting a representative (*mumathil*) or deputy (*nā'ib*); and that both were prophets to guide and warn people according to the strictures of Allah. These two verses were often cited and interpreted for the purpose of corroborating the system of the caliphate. Yet, the most important source for corroborating and explaining the system of the caliphate was the corpus of the *ḥadīth*. Therefore, the initial theory of the *fuqahā'* on the duties and rights of the caliph comprised a collection of moral maxims. This is shown clearly in the introduction to Abū Yūsuf's *Kitāb al-Kharāj* (*The Book of Land Tax*), which was addressed to the 'Abbāsid caliph Hārūn al-Rashīd; Abū Yūsuf may be considered to have been among the vanguard of those who wrote about political theories in Islam.

Abū Yūsuf affirms the necessity of absolute obedience to the ruler (*imām*) and adduces accounts from the *ḥadīth* to support this contention: 'Whoever obeys me obeys Allah and whoever obeys the *imām* obeys me;' and: 'Even if a cleft-nose Abyssinian slave is made ruler over you, listen to him and obey.' Abū Yūsuf regards obedience as compulsory even if a ruler is immoral/unjust because such is the will of Allah and His wish: 'When Allah wishes well for a people, He appoints the forbearing over them and puts their wealth in the hands of the generous. When He wants to try a people, He appoints the foolish over them and puts their wealth in the hands of the misers.' Thus, whenever Allah desired to punish mankind, He would put evil men in charge over them and no one could oppose this because to do so was in contravention of the will of Allah. Ḥasan al-Baṣrī reported on the authority of the Prophet:

> Do not curse your rulers, for if they do good, they will receive reward and you should be grateful. If they do evil, they will bear the burden of this, and you should be patient. They are a punishment from Allah upon those whom He wills. Do not take the punishment of Allah with resentment and anger, but accept it in quiet tranquillity and humble supplication.

Thus, obedience was a perpetual obligation; that was because the ruler represented Allah by the will of Allah. Abū Yūsuf says: 'Allah... has put you in charge of the affairs of this *ummah*.' The caliph was charged with preserving the religion and the *sharī'ah*: 'Allah...has made those who have been put in authority [the rulers] representatives on His earth and made a light for them which illuminates for the subjects those affairs among themselves which have been made obscure to them and those rights which appear doubtful to them.' Abū Yūsuf then explains the duties of the caliph and continues saying: 'The essence of this light is in those who have been given authority; enforcing the the *ḥudūd* (the limits and penalties of Islamic law); restoring the rights to those entitled to them...and reviving the normative practices (*sunan*) established by the righteous people.' Then he provides evidence to clarify the first duty of the caliph:

> 'Umar made an address...he said, 'The greatest commitment the shepherd makes for the sake of his flock is that they fulfil the duties of their religion imposed on them by Allah...and it is incumbent upon us to command you to do what Allah has commanded you to do in the way of obedience to Him and to forbid you to do what Allah has forbidden you to do of disobedience to

> Him and to establish the religion among people both near and far. We do not pay heed to anything except who is on the side of truth'.

However, there were no direct or tangible restrictions on the caliph since he was not questioned, except before Allah. Consequently, Abū Yūsuf draws attention to this: 'Beware that you do not lose track of your flock, for its Owner may exact its full due from you.' He warns him of the Day of Reckoning: 'The Messenger of Allah said, "The most beloved and closest of the people sitting near me on the Day of Judgement will be the just *imām*. The most despicable person unto me on the Day of Judgement and subject to the most severe punishment will be the unjust *imām*."' Continuing, he clarifies for him that 'the injustice of the shepherd is tantamount to the ruination of the flock'. Although the caliph was not responsible to the people, Abū Yūsuf encourages the caliph to listen to their views magnanimously. He narrates that when a person repeatedly told 'Umar insistently, 'Fear Allah', another person scolded him to be silent. 'Umar said to him: 'Leave him. There is no good in them [the people] if they do not say this to us; and there is no good in us if we do not accept this [i.e. what they say].' Finally, Abū Yūsuf mentions the right of the caliph over his subjects according to 'Umar bin al-Khaṭṭāb: 'O people, we have a right over you for you to admonish us of the unseen (*al-naṣīḥah bi-l-ghayb*) [i.e. to be pious and god-fearing] and to assist us in doing good.' From this it is clear that the corpus of the *ḥadīth* constituted the primary source for the Sunnis (*ahl al-sunnah*) to formulate a theory of the caliphate; however, it was a first step which took the form of advice and maxims of guidance only.

The formulation of the theory and its practical elaboration was a gradual matter, which had a strong relationship to doctrinal and legal arguments during the first three centuries. On the other hand, the problematic of the caliphate played the major role in the political and legal disputes between the Islamic factions. The Sunnis had been accused by their enemies of error sometimes when pledging the *bay'ah* to some of the caliphs. Their *fuqahā'* were compelled to find arguments to defend or justify the historical events since they could not acknowledge any principle from which it might be inferred that the [Sunni] group (*jamā'ah*) had committed an error, or that their religious and legal works were not legitimate. Therefore, the Sunni (political) theory of the caliphate was not, at its maturity, anything except that which was merely drawn from the Qur'ān and the *ḥadīth* (in contrast to the Khārijites and the Shī'ites). It relied only on the explanation of these sources in view of later political developments and the strict adherence to the principle of the infallibility of *ijmā'* or consensus (deriving from the prophetic *ḥadīth*: 'My *ummah* will never agree on error'). Thus, almost every generation left its mark on political theory as new precedents were formed and political theory came to conform to these accordingly.

This reliance on historical facts manifests in another aspect of the Sunni theory, which is the fact that it did not formulate principles for situations which had not arisen in practice, except in the form of ambiguous generalisations or logical deductions. This is shown clearly by al-Māwardī. However, in the main he only gives veiled reference to the disputes which had led to the appearance of some of the principles and tenders what he believes is a final positive form. With this, he gives the impression that he is referring to something which had existed from the beginning, and was – therefore – extant in his time and must always remain so. Although we sense that al-Māwardī made use of earlier sources for his theory (which he asserts is a summary of the views of the *fuqahā'*), complete studies on the caliphate dating from before the fifth century AH are not available to us. There is the *Uṣūl al-Dīn* (*Foundations of the Religion*) of al-Baghdādī (d. 439AH/1027AD), which includes a synopsis of the principle of the *imamate* (in the 13th chapter) and discussions around each point, sometimes in a more complete way than al-Māwardī's work, even though al-Baghdādī was a contemporary of his.

Al-Māwardī's theory has some particular characteristics. The authoring of his work had an important political significance, as he wrote in the introduction to his book:

> Since the principles of rule have primacy for those in authority, and since their coalescence with all [other] principles inhibits their being scrutinised by those people preoccupied with policy and planning, I have devoted a book to them, in doing so I have complied with the order of one whom I am obliged to obey, so that he may know the doctrinal positions of the *fuqahā'* on his rights in regard to them [those principles] so that he may exact them in full, and his duties among them so that he may fulfil them in view of justice in his execution and judgement(s) and in accordance with equity in his receiving and giving.

This introduction refers to the caliph, especially given that al-Māwardī was honoured with the title of *aqḍā al-quḍāt* (the most decisive of the judges) and was the caliph's representative in his negotiations with the Buwayhids, so the issue, then, was also one for the caliph. Moreover, it should be remembered that the power of the Buwayhids had weakened since the beginning of the fifth century because of internal struggle and military revolts. Maḥmūd al-Ghaznawī's loyalty to the 'Abbāsids made both the caliph al-Qādir (d. 422AH/1031AD) and his son al-Qā'im (d. 467AH/1031AD) the two hopes for the return of power to the 'Abbāsids. The first step to restoring that power was a legal demonstration of their neglected rights, which had almost been forgotten. This situation justifies his attitude to anyone who might find it unusual that he should have composed a book on the theory of the caliphate, which renders everything in the state dependent on the caliph during the worst periods of the caliphate. Whereas some writers have contended that al-Māwardī sought to describe the supreme ideal of the state – a perfect utopian state the bases of which were Islamic – al-Māwardī was not a philosopher in fact. For him, purely theoretical thinking played a minor role. Rather, he was a *faqīh* (jurist) who built on the opinions of his predecessors and expanded upon them to a certain extent. He utilised his intellect to apply those opinions to the situation at his time. His primary distinguishing characteristic then is that he avoids mere abstract theorisation but applies the theories of the *fuqahā'* to contemporary realities. Similarly, he was not simply collecting or explicating the opinions of his predecessors, but he was also demonstrating his independence in judgement (*ra'y*) and he sometimes arrived at opinions, which were in opposition to those of his predecessors or entirely new.

We will restrict ourselves to examining the main points in al-Māwardī's theory in juxtaposition with the older legal discussions on the one hand and the contemporary political situation on the other hand, in order to assess it properly.

1 The *imamate* (leadership) is necessary by divine law, not reason (*lā 'aqlan*): 'and its investiture in those who undertake it in the *ummah* (community) is obligatory by consensus – *ijmā'*.' This is also the view in al-Baghdādī,[264] who explains that it was the opinion of al-Ash'arī in opposition to the Mu'tazilitah.

2 The *imamate* is by election (*intikhāb*) and undertaken by those who combine the suitable qualifications, the *ahl al-ikhtiyār* (electors). This is contrary to the Shī'ite principle of *wiṣāyah* (delegation) or *ta'yīn* (appointment). However, al-Māwardī expunges what al-Baghdādī says; that is, if the choice is made by an immoral/corrupt person, then the *imamate* is not sound (*ghayr ṣaḥīḥah*) – even if such a person comprises the necessary pre-requisites of the *ahl al-ikhtiyār*. This omission of al-Māwardī's was due to the Buwayhids' interference in the appointment of the caliphs.

3 Among the qualifications taken into account in regard to the candidates is the seventh, which specifies is Qurayshī lineage.[265] By mentioning the opinions of the Sunnis (*ahl al-sunnah*) and their arguments in support of this point, perhaps al-Māwardī was demonstrating that in his time there were those who considered it to be permissible to elect a non-Qurayshī. Perhaps, it may have been a veiled attack against the claims of the Fāṭimids, whose lineage to the Quraysh was disavowed by the supporters of the 'Abbāsids.

4 The election of the *imām* is sound even by one person (among the *ahl al-ḥall wa al-'aqd*); and this is the principle of al-Ash'arī.[266] Perhaps this is a step to justify the nomination which he discusses in another section.

5 There is a discussion about the preference of one of two candidates who are equally suitable. The preference is posited, so it seems, on legal inference in *fiqh*, and this is not found in al-Baghdādī.

6 The *imamate* of a preferable candidate is permissible even with the existence of a more preferable candidate. It is not possible to remove the *imām* (after his selection) in order to install someone more preferable than he in his place. This justifies many of the cases in which unsuitable caliphs were found and perhaps was also possibly a response to the Shī'ites.

7 The election is obligatory even if there is one voter. It seems also that this stipulation was directed against the Shī'ites.

8 It is not permitted to have two *imāms* at the same time. With this, al-Māwardī rejects al-Ash'arī's opinion which did not favour the existence of two *imāms,* but which did permit it in distant lands which were far apart.[267] Al-Māwardī's emphasis on the rejection of two *imāms* may echo the refusal of the 'Abbāsids and their supporters to acknowledge their Fāṭimid enemies and the Umayyads of al-Andalus (i.e. Muslim Spain).

9 The pact (*al-'ahd*) does not become legally-binding except after the nominee's acceptance of it. Then it is not possible for the current *imām* to revoke it nor for the nominee to resign except in special cases. It appears that this fell under the category of legal inference from the principles of the *sharī'ah* because there were no historical precedents for it. The inference itself was applicable to the covenant pledged to someone who was not present and to the delimiting of the authority of the nominee.

10 The *imām* could limit and constrain the choice of voters after his death to certain people and also appoint a council of election according to the precedent of the *shūrā* of 'Umar bin al-Khaṭṭāb.

11 The *imām* may pledge the covenant to two or more people and to specify the succession of one after the other. A weak justification for this is the example of the Messenger's decision regarding the leadership of the campaign of Mu'tah and in discussions of *fiqh*, which were weaker still in their probative value.

12 The first heir to the succession – after becoming *imām* – may displace the other heirs. Al-Māwardī clarifies that this is the opinion of al-Shāfi'ī and is agreed upon by the majority of the *fuqahā'* in contrast to the previous view which does not permit such. Here historical precedents are arrayed against al-Māwardī. He admits the actions of al-Manṣūr in delaying 'Īsā bin Mūsā, but he ignores the refusal of 'Umar II to remove Yazīd II and al-Amīn's attempt to depose al-Ma'mūn. Here al-Māwardī follows the legal *fiqh* opinions and ignores precedent. This is strange and with this he sought perhaps to diminish the disadvantages of the system of succession.

13 It is not necessary for all the individuals in the *ummah* to know the caliph personally or by name. This is directed against the Zaydī principle, which is germane on this matter in particular.

14 The naming of the caliph as '*khalīfat allāh*' (deputy of Allah) is unlawful: 'The commission of an abomination (*fujūr*) is attributed to anyone saying this.'

15 There is detail for ten articles on the duties of the *imām*: the religious, legal and military duties agree with those mentioned by al-Baghdādī, but here with greater legal detail in terms of *fiqh*. On the administrative side can be noticed – in particular – the emphasis on the personal duty of the *imām* and his responsibility for overseeing general matters, even when their undertaking is delegated to others. We see that the later writers sometimes consider the *imām* to have had two main duties. However, the stress which al-Māwardī places on the administrative duties of the caliph was directed especially against any view which regarded the caliphate as strictly a religious and judicial institution, or primarily so, as the institution was almost on the verge of becoming (in fact). This is the central point of al-Māwardī's theory and the basis of all his work because most of the remaining chapters constitute only details of the caliph's administrative duties. Of course, this was a point of contention between the caliph and the Buwayhid emirs, since they, even if they had not clearly formulated their opinion, had freely neglected the caliphate in matters of administration in a way which renders it understood that these matters were outside of their sphere.

16 Al-Māwardī enters into a lengthy legal discussion about the circumstances which render forfeiture of the *imamate* obligatory. These are:

a Committing an offence against justice.[268] This is either as a result of following a base desire or a 'dubious belief or interpretation which would impinge upon the caliphate of truth'. Al-Māwardī recognises that 'many of the scholars of Basrah' denied that error in interpretation (*al-ta'wīl*) should precipitate forfeiture of the *imamate*. Perhaps he is inclined towards the initial view which held that error necessitates forfeiture of the *imamate*, and this is a view in which there is greater logic than the second, and perhaps it was influenced by the fear that a Shīʿite caliphate might rule in Baghdad, and this was not inconceivable at the time of his writing.

b Deficiency in mind and faith in a way which affects the ruler's ability to undertake his duties and position.

c Deficiency in conduct. This has a strong connection to the problem of the caliphate in his time. Quite possibly his words were put with the utmost care, especially if we imagine that they had a political significance.

i The first case for deficiency in conduct was when the *imām* was under confinement: 'it is when he is arrested and restrained by those of his entourage who appropriate the running of affairs without doing so openly.' These are words which describe precisely the situation of the ʿAbbāsids, as it had been for a century. Was it possible for anyone in this situation to be termed an *imām*? It is difficult to reconcile this with the *imamate* of al-Muṭīʿ li-Lāh and his successors. He responds succinctly by affirming this, then skilfully segues into the discussion of the relationship between the caliph and the usurper – namely the Buwayhid emir. If the actions of the usurper 'conform with the legal rulings of the religion and the dictates of justice', he permits the situation to be accepted so that 'what leads to the corruption (*fasād*) of the *ummah*' will not occur. And if not, it is obligatory for the caliph to 'seek assistance from those who would stay the hand of the usurper and put an end to his mastery'. Furthermore, this was no doubt a threat to the Buwayhids if they persisted in their misbehaviour.

ii Coercion or 'imprisonment'. In this case, 'it is the duty of the entire *ummah* to hasten to his rescue because of what the

> *imamate* makes obligatory of rendering him aid'. If such is not the case, then the situation differs. The captors may be unbelievers (*kuffār*). The details which al-Māwardī mentions in this case are theoretical. In the case that such are among 'Muslim transgressing oppressors (*bughāt*)', his situation is that of a caliph under confinement (i); however, a deputy must be appointed for him and this is also theoretical. If the 'oppressors have appointed an *imām* for themselves', or in clearer terms, if they are among the supporters of the Fāṭimids, then his rights are dropped naturally. However, al-Māwardī does not say that the *imām* of the oppressors takes his place. Rather, it is incumbent on 'the *ahl al-ikhtiyār* (qualified electors) in the *dār al-ʿadl* (house of justice) to pledge the *imamate* to someone with whom they are satisfied for it'. In reality, this discussion signifies that the takeover of Baghdad by the Fāṭimids did not lead automatically to the end of the 'Abbāsid caliphate, but it was left to the *ahl al-ikhtiyār* to pledge the *bayʿah* to the Fāṭimids or to set up an 'Abbāsid *imām* in another place.

We must note after this that al-Māwardī differs from many of the Sunni *fuqahā'* because he does not explicitly deny the right of the *ummah* to disobey a corrupt *imām* (*imām fāsiq*). On the other hand, he does clarify that obedience to one who has been given command (*ūlī al-amr*) is obligatory (in such a case), and confirms this with a *ḥadīth* on the authority of Abū Hurayrah; nonetheless, the weakness of his argument and his citation of a *ḥadīth* from Abū Hurayrah, while leaving aside another stronger one related by Abū al-Ḥasan al-Baṣrī (Abū Yūsuf), is striking, and especially so if it is compared with the statement of al-Ashʿarī. Similarly, he confirms openly that the injustice of the ruler (*jarḥ fī ʿadālat al-imām*) removes him from his post. His position is, therefore, something of an intermediate one between the Khārijites who necessitated revolt against the unjust ruler (*imām jā'ir*) and the traditional Sunni principle, which imposed obedience.

There is another point related to this. Although he discusses removal from the *imamate*, he does not posit a method whereby to dispute and challenge the *imām* (this agrees with the traditions of Sunni theories for which there were no precedents or general opinion to rely upon here). Indeed, many of the caliphs were deposed, but he knows that this was by force. As for the cases in which there was a *fatwā*, he intimates that the *fatwā* was but *force* thinly veiled. So while it was possible to depose the caliph legally, there was no legal mechanism for doing that. Thus, we see that the theory of the caliphate among the Sunnis was a refinement of political developments. The theory followed precedents and this theory was but a justification of the previous events that had been agreed upon by *ijmā'* (consensus).

Here, let us move on to another point in al-Māwardī's theory, namely to what he terms 'the emirate of usurpation' (*imārat al-istīlā'*). This refers to a strange case since here the emir imposes his authority by force instead of being accepted because he removes or changes the caliph. The situation becomes more delicate when the usurper cannot be considered to be in revolt, even from the legal standpoint of *fiqh*. For example, Maḥmūd al-Ghaznawī (prominent ruler of the Ghazanvid dynasty, d. 1030AD) did not at any time adopt a measure which could be considered as being against the caliph or his heir. It must be noted that this situation was not new because it was about two centuries before that al-Rashīd had acknowledged the hereditary emirate of the Aghlabids in North Africa. Thus, precedents were extant and available, and the flexibility of Sunni *fiqh* and its adaptability to the circumstances saved the principle of the unity of the caliphate through a kind of agreement that the caliph would acknowledge the separation of the emir in policy and administration, and – in exchange for acknowledging this – the emir would submit to the caliph and his right to oversee religious matters. This case is referred to often, although it is theoretical. However, it was not this way in the beginning, even if the relationship became more and more symbolic with the passing of time.

Even in this case, practical *ijmā'* provides the solution and the problem became one of the legal forms for supporting it. Al-Māwardī's predecessors had avoided this task; they covered their eyes before this clear deviation from the law. Al-Māwardī did not do so as he was not content to simply find a legal justification for what happened. Rather, he was more concerned with positing the rules for the contemporary situation and established what might be applied in the near future. When the matter is one of the impossibility of restoring the caliphate to its previous prestige, al-Māwardī's concern turns towards the systemisation of the relationship in the present, and the future between the caliph and the six independent emirs, such as Maḥmūd al-Ghaznawī. At that time it was necessary that his theory should not contradict the principles of *fiqh* and what was incumbent upon the caliph, as he mentions. So, for example, he accords authority to the rulers of distant territories without this encroaching upon the rights of the caliph who is the actual ruler of the central territories. It is noticeable that al-Māwardī implicitly denies such a system of this type in the centre. With this definition, which limits the ceding of authority strictly to distant territories, he allows no sphere for contradiction with his previous statements (relating to confinement).

Al-Māwardī clarifies that ceding (of authority) was permissible only under certain circumstances, including that there be agreement between the two sides with the stipulation that this be a genuine agreement and not one of external appearances. Therefore, the emir had to manifest respect for the caliph in a way which would nullify any appearance of separation on his part. Then he had to rule in accordance with the *sharīʿah* and maintain the religion in speech and action. The caliph for his part verified all the appointments and religious decisions of the emir (which up until that time were unlawful), and he afforded to these a legal patina. Thus, the two sides were party to a symbiotic alliance of 'mutual understanding and assistance'. If these conditions are not extant, al-Māwardī suggests that the caliph pledge a pact/covenant (*ʿahd*) to the emir to obviate the danger of his resorting to revolt 'calling for his obedience and averting his harrassment and disobedience'. In this case, it was necessary to appoint the caliph a representative to represent him in the execution of rulings.

However, what were the legal bases upon which al-Māwardī relied to posit the legal permissibility of these major licenses? The sole source is *necessity* (*ḍarūrah*): 'Necessity waives the conditions which lack possibility of fulfilment' and al-Māwardī acknowledges this. Thus, necessity permits abandoning the conditions of implementation. He adds to this a political principle, which is that fear of harming common interests/public good (*al-maṣāliḥ al-ʿāmmah*) calls for 'leniency in conditions'.[269]

Khārijite views on the caliphate[270]

Political conflicts between Muslims catalysed the emergence of sects. However, political issues in a society founded on religion inevitably take on a religious form. Hence, religion gradually entered into the arena of political conflict and conferred upon it a religious cast. It is religious interest itself which gives political conflict its distinctive cast.[271] The essential basis of the conflict was the problem of rule after the death of the Prophet. Al-Shahrastānī states: 'The greatest dispute among the *ummah* is the dispute over the *imamate*.'[272] About this dispute were formed the most significant sects: the Khārijites, the Shīʿites and the Murjiʾites.

Upon the death of the Prophet, there was a group who were dissatisfied with the accession of the first three caliphs. The group protested the neglect of the principle of *qarābah* (kinship) which incontrovertibly dictated the swearing of the *bay'ah* to 'Alī bin Abī Ṭālib, the son of the Prophet's paternal uncle and the husband of his daughter Fāṭimah. This constituted the core of the 'Ālid faction and, when 'Alī became caliph, it realised its desire.

When the struggle occurred between 'Alī and Mu'āwiyah, 'Alī's concession to submit the matter of contention to arbitration (in order to bring an end to the battle of Ṣiffīn which pitted one Muslim army against another) was the impetus behind the formation of the first Islamic sect, the Khārijites (*khawārij*, sg. *khārij* – from the Arabic root *kh-r-j* meaning 'to go out [against]' or 'to revolt against').[273] The first Khārijites are considered by al-Ṭabarī to have come from the *qurrā'* (Qur'ān reciters) and Ibn al-Athīr concurs with this. Wellhausen may be relying on al-Ṭabarī when he attributes the movement to the *qurrā'*, who condemned 'Alī for accepting the arbitration because the caliph had been chosen by the *ummah*. By disregarding this, he had betrayed the trust, so they condemned him.[274] Levi della Vida sees that those who seceded and revolted against 'Alī when he conceded to arbitration were a group of fighters, most of whom came from the tribe of Tamīm. They objected to the arbitration of men, marshalling in support the Qur'ānic verse: 'There is no judgement/arbitration except unto Allah (*lā ḥukm illā li-lāh*)' (*sūrat al-an'ām*, Q 6:57); and they withdrew to Ḥarūra'. Their number increased gradually with others who seceded, especially with the result of the arbitration which did not please the *qurrā'* and some of them went secretly from Kūfah to the camp of 'Abdullah bin Wahab al-Rāsibī (the first caliph of the Khārijites).

According to Levi della Vida, the term *khārijite* may be derived from this group's departure from Kūfah, not from their departure from the *ummah*. Apparently, his opinion differs from that of Wellhausen (which Caetani and Lammens followed), who disassociates the arbitration from the Khārijite movement and even situates the battle of al-Nahrawān [in which 'Alī bin Abī Ṭālib fought the Khārijites] *before* the arbitration. Levi della Vida ascribes the original Khārijites to the Bedouin, who were subsequently joined by the *qurrā'* due to their dissatisfaction with the result of the arbitration.[275] This concurs with Bruno's opinion that the genuine Khārijites were Bedouin and not *qurrā'*, as evidenced by their names, and that the *qurrā'* desired the arbitration. However, the text of the agreement revealed to them their error, so they hastened to reject it. They hoped that 'Alī would reject it as they did, just as some of the Shī'ites had done, and left with those who seceded because 'Alī had consented to cast doubt on his own caliphate which was from Allah. However, the backbone of the

Khārijites, who had stood against 'Alī and continued to do so, were the men of the tribes. They had formulated their objection to the arbitration with their entreaty: 'Why did you submit to the arbitration of men when "there is no judgement/arbitration except unto Allah (*lā ḥukm illā li-lāh*)"?'[276] Bruno explains this movement, clarifying that the majority of the Khārijites were from the tribes of the Jazīrah who had settled in Basra and Kūfah after the conquest. It is worthy of note that they never accepted the holiness of the Quraysh or its right to the caliphate. The murder of 'Uthmān inspired them with the idea that it was possible to remove the caliph when he acted against the good of the *ummah*.[277] These Bedouin were not accustomed to, nor did they want to be, arbitrated by a judge who was not related to them. They deplored that they should be controlled forcefully by a caliph from his faraway palace. They had joined 'Alī, but in the arbitration he had conceded the influence afforded him by kinship to the Prophet. So these Bedouin felt free to follow their inclinations and choose a leader from among themselves.

To summarise, we can say that the Khārijites were of three groups. The first group were the majority and the most important division. They were a group of Bedouin fighters, and most of them were from the tribe of *banī* Tamīm. They represented the tendency to not submit to centralisation and they despised authority. Hence, they exploited 'Alī's action in accepting the arbitration as 'he had relinquished his position as *amīr al-mu'minīn* (Commander of the Faithful)', and so they revolted against him. The second group were some of the Shī'ites who had departed because [in their view] 'Alī had consented to cast doubt on his caliphate which was from Allah. The third group were a faction of the *qurrā'* who had seceded because of the arbitration, which did not settle the dispute but only exacerbated it.

The majority of the Khārijites had been Bedouin among whom there was a strong tendency towards equality. The logical result of this principle was that they did not specify one tribe or clan for the caliphate. Rather, any Arab from among them could be nominated.[278] Therefore, the welfare (*maṣlaḥah*) of the Muslims dictated that the best person be chosen for election by the entire *ummah*. Al-Shahrastānī says that [a Khārijite sect known as] the Muḥakkimah (i.e. those who rejected the arbitration and repeated the Khārijite slogan) 'saw the legal permissibility of the *imamate* to be given to other than [the tribe of] Quraysh'. It appears that after a large number of *mawālī* (non-Arab converts) had joined them over time, they extended this right to non-Arabs, finally even permitting the election of an Abyssinian slave. Al-Shahrastānī cites them as saying: 'It is permitted for the *imām* to be a slave, a free man, a Nabatean or a Qurayshī.'[279] Ibn al-Jawzī says: 'One of the views of the Khārijites is that the *imamate* should only specify an individual in whom is combined knowledge and asceticism (*al-zuhd*), for if these are found in combination he is an *imām*, even if he is Nabatean.'[280] Thus, they stood against the Shī'ite view of the *wiṣāyah* (designation), as well as the Sunni theory of the legality of election, which is closer to the doctrine of *ta'yīn* (appointment). This theory was the reason for their revolt against the Umayyad and 'Abbāsid caliphs on the basis of their conviction that these caliphs were unjust and did not fulfil the requisite preconditions for the caliphate. Some of the Khārijites demonstrated freedom of opinion and a particular appreciation for women in a way which reflected the Bedouin viewpoint of them. The Shabībah, the followers of Shabīb bin Yazīd al-Shaybānī, saw the legal permissibility of the *imamate* of a woman. Al-Shahrastānī commented: 'They maintained the legal permissibility of the *imamate* of a woman if she undertook their affairs and fought against their opponents. They claimed that Ghazālah Umm Shabīb (i.e. the mother of Shabīb) was the *imām* after the murder of Shabīb until she was killed.'[281] This viewpoint was not explicitly acknowledged by any other Islamic group.

However, the Bedouin Khārijites' tendency to dislike central authority manifested itself in the claim of some of them that the *imamate* was not necessary. Ibn Abī al-Ḥadīd says: 'In the beginning of their affair, the Khārijites were of the opinion that there was no need for an *imām*. Then, they desisted from this contention when they put 'Abdullah bin Wahab al-Rāsibī over them (as emir).' What supports this is when 'Alī heard their cry of '*lā ḥukm illā li-lāh*'; he said: 'It is a just [and true] word whereby injustice is desired. They say, "there is no leadership (*lā imārah*)", yet leadership is unavoidable, be it righteous or immoral.'[282] This tendency continued in some of their sects. Al-Shahrastānī says about the Muḥakkimah (i.e. the Khārijites): 'They considered it legally permissible for there to be no *imām* in the world at all.' He says about another sect, the Najadāt (followers of Najdat bin 'Āmir al-Ḥanafī): 'They all concurred that there was never a need for people to have an *imām*, but that it was obligatory for them to be just and equitable with one another. If they decide such cannot happen unless an *imām* induces them to do it, then it is permitted for them to appoint one.'[283]

The Khārijites demanded that the ruler submit completely to Allah and follow precisely the injunctions of the *sharī'ah*. Whenever he transgressed, the community was able to depose him. They also agreed over the obligation of revolting against an unjust ruler (*imām jā'ir*).[284] Al-Mastawrid bin 'Ullafah – the 'Commander of the Faithful' (i.e. who had been pledged the *bay'ah*) – wrote to an Umayyad governor:

> We have taken revenge against our people for their injustice in the legal injunctions, neglect of the *ḥudūd* punishments and monopolising of the spoils (*fay'*). I call you to the Book of Allah, the Almighty and Magnificent, the *sunnah* of His Prophet and the trusteeship (*wilāyah*) of Abū Bakr and 'Umar, and to absolution from 'Uthmān and 'Alī for their innovation in the religion and their forsaking of the judgement of the Book (i.e. the Qur'ān).[285]

Al-Baghdādī mentions that the Khārijites were divided into twenty subsects which were grouped together on the basis of their presumption of 'a duty to revolt against the unjust ruler'.[286] Al-Shahrastānī says: 'They consider revolt against the *imām*, if he contradicts the *sunnah*, to be a mandatory obligation.'[287] With this, they opposed the Murji'ite principle of neutrality [of the *ummah*] and likewise the Shī'ite principle of dissimulation (*taqīyah*). They were explicit in their words and actions, as is apparent from their history. It can be noticed that they began as a political sect, the basis of which was the subject of the caliphate. Then they gradually promulgated legal researches in *fiqh* for themselves from the middle of the Umayyad reign onwards, attempting above all to judge against those who opposed them in principle and creedal doctrine. Nonetheless, simplicity remained paramount in their legal theory. Moreover, they lacked military or political unity and did not formulate a set of unified principles.[288]

The Twelver Shī'ite theory of the caliphate

For the Shī'ites, *imāmism* (*imāmīyah*) is defined as:

> the knowledge of those who profess the necessity of the *imamate* and its existence throughout all time, attest to the explicit designation (*al-naṣṣ al-jalī*), the infallibility (*'iṣmah*) and perfection of every *imām*, then to restrict the *imamate* [after 'Alī bin Abī Ṭālib and al-Ḥasan] to the offspring of al-Ḥusayn bin 'Alī and to transfer it to al-Riḍā 'Alī bin Mūsā.[289]

This means that the *imamate* is limited to the Twelver or Ja'farī Shī'ah. In order to understand the Shī'ite theory of the caliphate, two points must be noted. Firstly, the *imamate* is an essential part of the religion for the Shī'ah and accordingly the trusteeship (*muwālah*) to the *imām* is a part of belief: 'The slave [i.e. a person] is not a believer until he acknowledges Allah, His Messenger, all the *imāms* and the *imām* of his time, having recourse to him submitting himself unto him'.[290] Knowledge (*ma'rifah*) of Allah and worship of Him are only realised with the acknowledgement of the *imām* and to follow him. Abū Ja'far stated: 'Knowledge (*ma'rifah*) of Allah...is the belief in Allah and His Prophet, and the trusteeship of 'Alī and to follow the example of the *imāms* of guidance (i.e. the twelve *imāms*).'[291] He added: 'Only those who recognise Allah and His *imām* from us, the *ahl al-bayt* (family of the Prophet), know Allah and worship him.'[292] Secondly, there are no practical historical precedents among the Shī'ah (excepting the caliphate of 'Alī bin Abī Ṭālib) to which they may find recourse in order to establish their theory, just as is the case with the Sunnis. Therefore, their theory of the *imamate* relied on the Qur'ān and the *sunnah*, as well as the sayings of the *imāms*, and thus it became an idealised theory.

It shall be sufficient for us to examine the Shī'ite theory of the caliphate here as represented in the *Uṣūl al-Kāfī* by Muḥammad bin Ya'qūb al-Kulaynī (d. 328–9AH/939AD):[293]

1 The *imām* is the *khalīfah* (deputy/successor) of the Messenger and the *khalīfah* (deputy) of Allah on earth. Al-Riḍā says: 'The *imāms* are the *khulafā'* (deputies) of Allah on His earth;'[294] and 'The *imām* is the trustee (*amīn*) of Allah for His creation, His authoritative contention (*ḥujjah*) over His slaves and His *khalīfah* (deputy) in His lands.'[295] He also says: 'The *imamate* is the caliphate (*khilāfah*) of Allah and the caliphate of the Messenger.'[296]

2 The *imamate* is binding by (textual) designation (*al-naṣṣ*). The Messenger appointed 'Alī bin Abī Ṭālib as his *khalīfah* (successor) during his lifetime, and he designated him for after his death: 'Whoever expunges that, he has expunged a duty from the religion.'[297] Al-Riḍā says: 'The *imamate* is too exalted in measure, importance, magnificent status and profundity for people to attain to it by their reason, or to attain to it with their views, or to establish an *imām* by their choice.' Then he mentions that Allah specified Abraham for the *imamate* after prophethood (*nubuwwah*) and friendship (*khullah*),[298] and his descendants subsequently inherited it until Allah distinguished the Prophet by it. Al-Riḍā says: 'He conferred it upon 'Alī by the command of Allah according to what Allah had ordained. It then came into his pure offspring to whom Allah granted knowledge and faith. It will remain exclusively among the descendants of 'Alī until the Day of Judgement.'[299]

3 Similarly, the passing of the trusteeship (*wilāyat al-'ahd*) from one *imām* to another is 'a covenant (*al-'ahd*) from Allah to be entrusted to one *imām* after the other'.[300] Abū 'Abdullah inquires: 'Do you see that

one of us can entrust [the *imamate*] to whomever he wants? No, by Allah, but it is a covenant (*al-'ahd*) from Allah and His Messenger to one man, then another man, until the matter arrives at its (true) possessor.'[301]

4 The *imāms* exclusively possess special eminent virtues, the most important of which are:
   - **Infallibility (*'iṣmah*).** The *imāms* are infallible like the Prophets.[302] Al-Riḍā says that the *imām* is 'infallible, granted support and success and guided [in a way that does not permit him to err]. He has been rendered safe from fault, error and stumbling. Allah has favoured him with this so that he will be the contention [of Allah] over His slaves.' He is free from any fault/defect, and distinguished by Allah in virtue and perfection. Al-Riḍā says: 'The Imam is pure of sins, free from any faults and distinguished by knowledge...The Imam is unique in his age, no one can come close to him [in his rank], none is equal to him in knowledge. He is distinguished by all virtue without having to ask for or acquire it. Rather, he was distinguished by the most Perfect Bestower (Allah).'[303]
   - **Knowledge (*'ilm*).** The *imām* 'cannot be equalled by any scholar' since 'Allah did not teach His Messenger any knowledge without commanding him to teach it to 'Alī, the Commander of the Faithful, and he shared in his knowledge'. Abū Ja'far said: 'We are the repositories of the knowledge of Allah, and we are the transmitters and exegetes/translators (*tarājimah*) of Allah's revelation.'[304] Abū 'Abdullah said: 'The Commander of the Faithful ('Alī) was the gateway to Allah who cannot be approached except through him and His path wherein those who follow any others will be destroyed.'[305] Al-Kulaynī composed a chapter in which he explained that 'no one collected all of the Qur'ān except the *imāms* and they possess all its knowledge'. Abū Ja'far said: 'No one can claim to possess all of the Qur'ān – its manifest and hidden meanings – except the *awṣiyā'* (the designees, i.e. the *imāms*).'[306] Abū 'Abdullah says: 'By Allah, I swear that I know the Book of Allah from its beginning to its end as if it is in the palm of my hand. It contains the knowledge of the heavens and the earth, of what has been and what will be. Allah said that: "In it is the explanation of every thing" (*al-Naḥl*, Q 16:89).'[307]

Al-Kulaynī composed a chapter entitled 'The Imams Inherited the Knowledge of the Prophet and all the Prophets and *awṣiyā'* before them'[308] and another entitled 'The Imams Possess all the Books which were Revealed by Allah and They Know them in all their Various Tongues'.[309] This knowledge is inherited successively by the *imāms* and there is a chapter on this: 'The Imams are the Inheritors of Knowledge which they Inherit from One Another.'[310] Abū Ja'far says: 'The knowledge which came down from Adam was not rescinded. The knowledge is inherited successively. 'Alī was the most knowledgeable of this community and the most knowledgeable among us never dies without being succeeded by someone from his family who has knowledge the like of his or that which Allah wills.'[311] Thus, the *imāms* knew all the (divine) sciences and al-Kulaynī includes a chapter entitled 'The Imams Know the Knowledge of What has been and What will be and Nothing is Unknown to Them'.[312] Abū 'Abdullah explains: 'I know this from the Book of Allah, wherein He says "In it is the explanation of everything".'[313]

5 The *imāms* are the guides for mankind and the cornerstone of the *sharī'ah*. Al-Riḍā says: 'The Imam is Allah's trustee (*amīn*) over His creation, His contention (*ḥujjah*) over His slaves and His *khalīfah* (deputy) in His lands.'[314] That is because for the *imāms* 'Allah has favored them and gives unto them from the wellsprings of His knowledge and His wisdom that which He does not grant to others. Hence, their knowledge transcends the knowledge of the people of the age.'[315] He says: 'The imamate constitutes the reins of the religion, the system of the Muslims, the salvation of the world and the pride of the Muslims. Abū Ja'far explained the Qur'ānic verse 'We bestowed on the people [i.e., family] of Abraham the Book and wisdom and gave to them a mighty dominion' (*al-nisā'*, Q 4:54):[316] 'The mighty dominion is that He made the *imāms* among them. Whoever obeys them obeys Allah. Whoever disobeys them disobeys Allah, for He is the Mightiest King.'[317] Abū Ja'far said about the verse: 'You are a warner only, and for every people there is a guide' (*sūrat al-ra'd*, Q 13:7).[318] 'The Messenger of Allah said, "I am the warner (*al-mundhir*) and 'Alī is the guide (*al-hādī*). By Allah, it never departed from us and will not cease to be with us until the final hour (Day of Judgement)".'[319] For this reason, the world cannot be devoid of a *ḥujjah* and the presence of the *imām* is an incontrovertible necessity: 'As long as the earth persists, the *ḥujjah* (i.e. the *imām*) will be upon it, who knows the lawful and the forbidden, and who calls people to the path of Allah, and if the *imām* were to be removed from the earth for an hour, people would be swept to and fro just like a wave does with people at sea.'[320] Abū 'Abdullah

says of the *imāms*: 'Allah has made them the cornerstones of the earth, so that it does not fall on its people and [they are] His decisive contention (*ḥujjah*) over those on the earth and those below the ground.'[321]

6 The *imām* has important and wide-ranging duties:

- The *imām* applies the commands and prohibitions of Allah, enforces the *ḥudūd* punishments, and he preserves and propagates the faith. Al-Riḍā says: 'The Imam declares lawful what Allah has made so and declares unlawful what Allah has made so. He implements the *ḥudūd* (penalties) of Allah and defends the religion of Allah. He calls to the path of His Lord with wisdom, in good counsel and decisive authority.'
- The *imām* engages in *jihād*, protects the borders and distant provinces and supervises financial spheres: 'alms-giving (*zakāt*)... war (*jihād*) and the provision of *fay'* (conquered lands) and charity (*ṣadaqāt*), as well as the protection of the borders and distant provinces...are achieved through the *imām*.'[322]
- The *imām* rules with justice among the people and apportions amongst them equally. Abū Ja'far mentions that the subjects' right over the *imām* is that he 'apportions [e.g. spoils of war and distributable wealth] amongst them equally and is just with his subjects'.[323]
- Al-Kulaynī reports some of the *aḥādīth* by which the duties of the *imām* are performed: 'Whenever a believer or Muslim dies and leaves a debt which is not due to corrupt or extravagant behaviour, then it is incumbent on the *imām* to settle that debt. If he does not settle it, then he incurs the sin for that. There is a *ḥadīth* which admonishes the *imām* to honour the elderly; to have mercy and compassion for the weak and to respect the scholars; not to beat his subjects so as to humiliate them, and not to impoverish them and thus make them unbelievers, and not to ignore them so that the strong among them encroach on the weak, and not to amass them [i.e. all the males of a single family] to dispatch them [on campaigns] and thereby cut off the lineage of the Islamic *ummah* [i.e. in a situation where they might all be killed in battle].'[324]

7 Al-Kulaynī also mentions *aḥādīth* to affirm the necessary qualities of the *imām*: 'The *imāmah* is only meet for a man with three qualities: god-fearing pious reserve (*wara'*) which prevents him from disobeying Allah, forbearance (*ḥilm*) whereby he controls his anger and good rule over his followers so that he is like a merciful father towards them.'[325]

Then he draws on a *ḥadīth* from ʿAlī's biography as an example for the *imāms* with regard to their food and clothing. He reports that ʿAlī said: 'Allah has made me an *imām* unto His creation. He made it incumbent upon me to be the like of the weakest of people in my person, my food, my drink and my attire so that the poor will be guided by my poverty and the rich will not be excessive in their wealth.'[326] Abū ʿAbdullah said: 'The best raiment for every time is the raiment of its people, so that when any of the *ahl al-bayt* arises he goes out in the raiment of ʿAlī and behaves according to the example of ʿAlī.'[327]

8 Al-Kulaynī also discusses the duties of the subjects. He makes compliance with the opinions and commands of the *imāms* an essential religious obligation (*farḍ*). Abū Jaʿfar said: 'It is the right of the *imām* over the people that they listen to and obey him.'[328] Abū ʿAbdullah said: 'We are a people to whom obedience has been made obligatory by Allah;' and, 'The *awṣiyā'* (i.e. the designated *imāms*) merit and enjoy the same obedience as the messengers.' He said: 'We are those to whom obedience has been made obligatory by Allah. The people can only recognise us and the people will not be excused for their ignorance of us. Whoever recognises us is a believer and whoever denies us is an unbeliever (*kāfir*)'. Al-Riḍā says: 'The people are slaves unto us in obedience to us, our charges [for whom we are responsible] – *mawālī* – in the religion.'[329] This is a natural result because the *imām* was above the level of the ordinary human being and the possessor of knowledge and guidance.

9 Lastly, al-Kulaynī cites some *aḥādīth* to confirm the right of the family of ʿAlī to the imamate. For example, he mentions Abū Jaʿfar's commentary on the verse 'Say [Muḥammad], "I ask of you no reward for this save for affection towards the kin" (*al-qurbah*)'. According to Abū Jaʿfar, the *qurbah* were the *imāms*.[330] He also indicates al-Riḍā's exegesis wherein those referred to as 'truthful (*al-ṣādiqīn*)' in the verse 'O you who believe, fear all Allah and be with the truthful'[331] as being the *imāms*, and those who are strictly observant and scrupulous in their obedience.[332]

Al-Kulaynī also mentions a *ḥadīth* which stresses the guidance of the community by the *imāms* and their attachment to them, in addition to warning those who dissent: 'Woe to those who oppose them from my community. O Allah, I ask that you not grant my intercession [on the Day of Judgement] to them.'[333] In this way, al-Kulaynī presents to us the Shīʿite theory of the caliphate through the *aḥādīth* of the Prophet which he reports and the verses which he explains exegetically, as well as the sayings of some of the *imāms*.

Notes

1. The Arabic root (*n-ẓ-m*) connotes organising or arranging things in proper order (including poetry), and throughout this text *niẓām* and its plural, *nuẓum*, refer to *systems* – or institutions – (including regulations and standards) and systemisations in the various spheres, from administration to taxation and revenue to recruitment, and records and pensions for the army with the institution of the *diwāns*. Such are also referred to as *tanẓīmāt* – coming from the same Arabic root – in the form of the word which, in a much later period, would refer to the late Ottoman reforms begun in 1839 in order to reorganise the government, its administrative systems and apparatuses. [Editor's note]

2. See W. Robertson Smith, *Kinship and Marriage in Early Arabia* (Cambridge: Cambridge University Press, 1885), p. 2.

3. See Reinhart Dozy, *Histoire des Musulmans d'Espagne jusqu'à la Conquête de l'Andalousie par les Almoravides* (711–1110), new edn, revised by E. Lévi-Provençal, 3 vols. (Leiden: E. J. Brill, 1932), vol. 1, p. 4; B. Faris, *L'Honneur chez les Arabes avant l'Islam* (Paris: Adrien Maisonneuve, 1932), pp. 54–56.

4. Abū al-'Abbās Muḥammad bin Yazīd al-Mubarrad, *al-Kāmil* (*The Kāmil of al-Mubarrad*), edited for the German Oriental Society from the manuscripts of Leiden, St. Petersburg, Cambridge and Berlin by William Wright, 2 vols. (Leipzig: F.A. Brockhaus/Kreysing, 1874–1893), pp. 166–167.

5. Ibid., p. 166.

6. See Jurjī Zaydān, *Tārīkh al-Tamaddun al-Islāmī*, 5 vols. (Cairo: Dār al-Hilāl, 1918–1922), vol. 4, pp. 9–29; Dozy, ibid., p. 4; H. Lammens, *L'Islam: Croyances et Institutions*, trans. by E. Denison Ross as *Islam: Beliefs and Institutions* (London: Methuen and Co. Ltd, 1929), ch. 1; Guidi, Ignazio, *L'Arabie Antéislamique*: *Quatre Conférences Données à l'Université Égyptienne du Caire en 1909* (Paris: Librairie Paul Geuthner, 1921), pp. 30–32; Philip K. Hitti, *History of the Arabs*, 2nd rev. ed. (London: Macmillan and Co. Ltd, 1940), ch. 3.

7. For this, see Abū 'Umar Aḥmad bin Muḥammad Ibn 'Abd Rabbih, *al-'Iqd al-Farīd* (*The Unique Necklace*), edited with explanations on its obscure utterances by one of the most distinguished personages of the age, 4 vols. (Cairo: Maḥmūd Shākir, 1913), pp. 203–204.

8. Jabbūr 'Abd al-Nūr, *Naẓrāt fī Falsafat al-'Arab* (Beirut: Dār al-Makshūf, 1945), p. 20 ff. For the systemisations in Mecca, see Muḥammad Ḥamīdullāh, 'The City State of Mecca', *Islamic Culture*, vol. 12 (1938), p. 265 ff; Henri Lammens, '*La Mecque à la Veille de l'Hégire*', Mélanges de l'Université Saint-Joseph, vol. 9 (Beirut: Imprimerie Catholique, 1924), pp. 158–178.

9. See Arthur Christensen, *L'Iran sous les Sassanides* (Copenhagen: Levin and Munksgaard, 1936), p. 92 ff.

10. Ibid., p. 297.

11. Abū 'Uthmān 'Amr bin Baḥr al-Jāḥiẓ, *al-Tāj fī Akhlāq al-Mulūk* (Cairo: Aḥmad Zakī Pāshā, 1914), p. 165.

12. Christensen, ibid., pp. 295–296.

13. Ibid., pp. 108–109.

14. Abū ʿAbdullah Muḥammad bin ʿAbdūs al-Jahshiyārī, *al-Wuzarāʾ wa al-Kuttāb*, edited and indexed by Muṣṭafā al-Saqqā, Ibrāhīm al-Ibyārī and ʿAbd al-Ḥafīẓ Shalabī (Cairo: Maṭbaʿat Muṣṭafā al-Bābī al-Ḥalabī, 1938), p. 10.

15. The Cambridge Medieval History, vol. 4, *The Eastern Roman Empire* (717–1453), ed. H. M. Gwatkin and J. P. Whitney (Cambridge: Cambridge University Press: 1923).

16. Ibid.

17. See Charles Diehl, *Byzance: Grandeur et Decadence* (Paris, E. Flammarion, 1919) p. 25 ff; Norman H. Baynes, *The Byzantine Empire* (New York, London: H. Holt and Company, 1939; Home University Library of Modern Knowledge, no. 114), pp. 59–75; H. M. Gwatkin and J. P. Whitney (eds.) *The Cambridge Medieval History*, vol. II, *The Rise of the Saracens and the Foundation of the Western Empire* (Cambridge: Cambridge University Press, 1913).

18. See Muḥammad Ḥamīdullāh, *Documents sur la Diplomatie Musulmane à l'Epoque du Prophète et des Khalifes Orthodoxes*, préface de Monsieur M. Gaudefroy-Demombynes (Paris: G.-P. Maisonneuve, 1935), p. 19.

19. Julius Wellhausen, *Das Arabische Reich und Sein Sturz*, trans. Margaret Graham Weir as *The Arab Kingdom and its Fall* (Calcutta: University of Calcutta, 1927), p. 4 ff; Tor Andrae, *Mohammed: sein Leben und sein Glaube*, trans. Theophil Menzel as *Mohammed: The Man and His Faith* (London: George Allen & Unwin, 1936), p. 186.

20. See Abū Muḥammad ʿAbd al-Malik Ibn Hishām, *al-Sīrah al-Nabawīyah*, edited and indexed by Muṣṭafā al-Saqqā, Ibrāhim al-Ibyārī and ʿAbd al-Hafīẓ Shalabī, 4 vols. (Cairo: Muṣṭafā al-Bābī al-Ḥalabī, 1936), vol. 2, p. 152; Ḥamīdullāh, ibid., p. 19; Andrae, ibid., p. 191.

21. ʿAbd al-Rāzzāq Aḥmad Sanhoury, *Le Califat: son Evolution vers une Société des Nations Orientale*, préface d'Edouard Lambert; Travaux du Séminaire Oriental d'Études juridiques et Sociale, tome 4 (Paris: Librairie Orientaliste Paul Geuthner, 1926), p. 264.

22. See the critical edition of the document in Muḥammad Ḥamīdullāh [al-Ḥyderābādī], ed., *Majmūʿat al-Wathāʾiq al-Siyāsīyah fī al-ʿAhd al-Nabawī wa al-Khilāfah al-Rāshidah* (Cairo: Lajnat al-Taʾlīf wa al-Tarjamah wa al-Nashr, 1941), pp. 1–7.

23. Abū ʿAbdullah Muḥammad bin Manīʿ Ibn Saʿd, *al-Ṭabaqāt al-Kubrā*, Eduard Sachau *et al* (eds.) 8 vols. in 3 parts (Leiden: E. J. Brill, 1904–1918), vol. 2, pt. 1, ed. Josef Horovitz, p. 19; Ḥamīdullāh, *Documents sur la Diplomatie Musulmane à l'Epoque du Prophète et des Khalifes Orthodoxes*, p. 20; Wellhausen, *The Arab Kingdom and its Fall*, p. 12.

24. See al-Ḥyderābādī, ibid., pp. 1–4, paras. 1–23. I have followed al-Ḥyderābādī in dividing the document into [numbered] paragraphs for ease of reference.

25. Ibid., paras. 24–27.

26. Ḥamīdullāh, ibid., p. 20. Here we notice that Andrae Tor's book about the Prophet suffices to say that the document was composed in 2AH. See Tor, *Muḥammed: The Man and His Faith*, p. 190.

27. See al-Ḥyderābādī, ibid., paras. 23 and 42.

28. See al-Ḥyderābādī, ibid., margin no. 4; Ḥamīdullāh, ibid., p. 20.

29. See al-Ḥyderābādī, ibid., document 1 (*al-Wathīqah al-ʾŪlā*), paras. 1, 16, 19, 23, 24, 37, 38b, 42 and 45.

30. Ḥamīdullāh, ibid., p. 20.

31. al-Ḥyderābādī, ibid., para. 3.

32. See Wellhausen, *The Arab Kingdom and its Fall*, p. 13.

33. al-Ḥyderābādī, ibid., pp. 2–3, paras. 4–11.

34. Ibid., p. 2, para. 12.
35. Ibid., p. 4, para. 2b.
36. Ibid., p. 4, para. 23.
37. Ibid., p. 3, para. 13.
38. Ibid., p. 4, para. 21.
39. See Wellhausen, ibid., pp. 13–14.
40. al-Ḥyderābādī, ibid., pp. 2–3, paras. 4–11.
41. Ibid., p. 3, paras. 14 and 15.
42. Ibid., para. 9.
43. Ibid., paras. 5–35.
44. Ibid., para. 44.
45. Ibid., para. 45b.
46. Ibid., para. 37.
47. Ibid., paras. 24, 28 and 37.
48. Ibid., para. 45.
49. Ibid., para. 43.
50. Ibid., p. 6, para. 42.
51. Ibid., para. 37b.
52. See ʻAbd al-Rāzzāq Aḥmad Sanhoury, *Le Califat: son Evolution vers une Société des Nations Orientale*, pp. 268–272.
53. See ibid.; Thomas W. Arnold, *The Caliphate* (Oxford: Clarendon Press, 1924).
54. See Abū al-Ḥasan ʻAlī bin Muḥammad al-Māwardī, *al-Aḥkām al-Sulṭānīyah wa al-Wilāyāt al-Dīnīyah* (Cairo: [Maṭbaʻat al-Saʻādah], 1909), p. 2; Sanhoury, ibid., p. 280.
55. Abū Muḥammad ʻAbdullah bin Muslim Ibn Qutaybah, *al-Imāmah wa al-Siyāsah* (Cairo: Maṭbaʻat al-Nīl, 1904), vol. 1, p. 32.
56. Abū Jaʻfar Muḥammad bin Jarīr al-Ṭabarī, *Tārīkh al-Rusul wa al-Mulūk*, 12 vols. (Cairo: al-Maṭbaʻah al-Ḥusaynīyah, 1336/1917), vol. 3, p. 218.
57. Ibid., vol. 3, pp. 221–222.
58. Ibn Qutaybah, ibid., vol. 1, p. 6.
59. Ibid., vol. 1, p. 19.
60. See ibid., vol. 1, p. 19 and Aḥmad bin Abī Yaʻqūb al-Yaʻqūbī, *Tārīkh al-Yaʻqūbī*, 3 vols. (al-Najaf: al-Maktabah al-Murtaḍawīyah, 1358/1939), vol. 2, p. 103.
61. al-Yaʻqūbī, ibid., vol. 2, pp. 103–105.
62. Ibn Hishām, *al-Sīrah al-Nabawīyah*, vol. 4, pp. 306–307; al-Ṭabarī, ibid., vol. 3, p. 205.
63. al-Yaʻqūbī, vol. 2, p. 102.
64. al-Ṭabarī, ibid., vol. 3, p. 220.
65. Ibn Qutaybah, *al-Imāmah wa al-Siyāsah*, vol. 1, p. 9.
66. al-Ṭabarī, ibid., vol. 3, p. 220.
67. Ibid., vol. 3, p. 221; Ibn Saʻd, *al-Ṭabaqāt al-Kubrā*, vol. 3, ed. Eduard Sachau (Leiden: E. J. Brill, 1904–1918), pt. 2, pp. 126 and 129.
68. al-Ṭabarī, ibid., vol. 3, p. 205.
69. Ibid., vol. 3, p. 210; al-Yaʻqūbī, vol. 3, p. 103.
70. See Ibn Saʻd, *al-Ṭabaqāt al-Kubrā*, vol. 2, pt. 2, ed. Friedrich Schwally (Leiden: E. J. Brill, 1904–1918), p. 126.
71. Ibn Qutaybah, ibid., vol. 1, p. 19.
72. Arnold, *The Caliphate*, p. 20.
73. Ibn Saʻd, *al-Ṭabaqāt al-Kubrā*, vol. 2, pt. 2, p. 203; Idem, ibid., vol. 3, pt. 1, p. 130.

74. al-Ṭabarī, ibid., vol. 3, p. 210.

75. Ibid., vol. 3, p. 210; Ibn Hishām, *al-Sīrah al-Nabawīyah*, vol. 4, p. 311. See the other narration about his address in Ibn Sa'd, ibid., vol. 2, pt. 2, p. 129; Idem, ibid., vol. 3, pt. 1, p. 129.

76. al-Ṭabarī, ibid., vol. 3, p. 224.

77. Ibn Sa'd, ibid., vol. 2, pt. 2, p. 132. His salary was 2,500, 3,000 or 6,000 *dirhams* per annum, according to various narrations.

78. Ibid., vol. 2, pt. 2, p. 142.

79. Ibn Qutaybah, ibid., vol. 1, pp. 32–33; al-Ṭabarī, ibid., vol. 3, pp. 428–429.

80. Abū al-'Abbās Aḥmad bin Yaḥyā al-Balādhurī, *Ansāb al-Ashrāf*, 5 vols. (Jerusalem: Maṭba'at al-Jāmi'ah al-'Ibrīyyah, 1936–1940), vol. 5, pp. 156 and 364. Ibn Sa'd reports that he sought the opinion of 'Abd al-Raḥmān bin 'Awf, who said: 'By Allah, he is better than you think of him.' And he consulted 'Uthmān who told him: 'What he ['Umar] does in private is better than what he does openly [i.e. he does more good deeds than we are aware] and there is no one like him among us,' as well as seeking the opinion of 'Sa'd bin Zayd, Usayd bin al-Ḥuḍayr and others from the *muhājirūn* and *anṣār*. However, some of the (Companions) *ṣaḥābah* objected, including Ṭalḥah bin 'Ubayd Allāh and 'Alī, but the opposition was moderate. See Ibn Sa'd, ibid., vol. 2, pt. 2, pp. 141–142 and 196.

81. al-Māwardī, *al-Aḥkām al-Sulṭānīyah*, p. 7.

82. Ibn Sa'd, ibid., vol. 2, pt. 2, p. 142.

83. Arnold, *The Caliphate*, pp. 20–21.

84. See article ''Umar' in *Dā'irat al-Ma'ārif al-Islāmīyah*, eds. Ibrāhīm Zakī Khurshīd, Ahmad al-Shintināwī, 14 vols. (Cairo: Dār al-Shāb, 1908–1938).

85. See al-Ya'qūbī, *Tārīkh al-Ya'qūbī*, vol. 2, p. 116.

86. al-Balādhurī, *Anṣāb al-Ashrāf*, vol. 4, pt. 1, p. 501.

87. Ibid., vol. 4, pt. 1, p. 503.

88. Ibn Sa'd, ibid., vol. 1, pt. 2, pp. 248 and 256; al-Ṭabarī, ibid., vol. 5, p. 228; (Pseudo) Ibn Qutaybah, ibid., p. 38.

89. al-Balādhurī, ibid., vol. 5, p. 500; al-Ṭabarī, ibid., vol. 4, p. 228; Ibn Sa'd, ibid., vol. 2, pt. 2, p. 243.

90. (Pseudo) Ibn Qutaybah, ibid., vol. 1, p. 19.

91. Ibn Sa'd, ibid., vol. 3, pt. 1, p. 245; al-Balādhurī, ibid., vol. 5, p. 503.

92. This is something of an obscure account in attributing this quality to 'Alī bin Abī Ṭālib, as the quality is not uniformly attributed to him. [Editor's note]

93. See (Pseudo) Ibn Qutaybah, ibid., vol. 1, p. 41; al-Māwardī, ibid., pp. 9–10; al-Ṭabarī, ibid., vol. 5, p. 34; al-Balādhurī, ibid., vol. 4.

94. See the details in al-Māwardī, ibid., pp. 9–10; Ps.-Ibn Qutaybah, ibid., vol. 1, p. 42; al-Balādhurī, ibid., vol. 4, pt. 1, pp. 504–508; al-Ṭabarī, ibid., vol. 4, pp. 231–232; al-Ya'qūbī, ibid., vol. 2, p. 138; Ibn Sa'd, ibid., vol. 3, pt. 1, p. 245.

95. See Ḥamīdullāh, 'The City State of Mecca', p. 262 ff.

96. See al-Balādhurī, ibid., vol. 4, pt. 1, p. 501; Ibn Sa'd, ibid., vol. 5, pt. 1, p. 247.

97. al-Balādhurī, ibid., vol. 4, pt. 1, p. 501 ff; Ibn Sa'd, ibid., vol. 5, pt. 1, p. 247 ff.

98. al-Balādhurī, ibid., vol. 4, pt. 1, p. 508.

99. al-Ṭabarī, ibid., vol. 4, p. 238.

100. See ibid; (Pseudo) Ibn Qutaybah, ibid., vol. 5, pp. 45–46.

101. al-Balādhurī, ibid., vol. 4, pt. 1, p. 508.

102. See article ''Uthmān' in *Dā'irat al-Ma'ārif al-Islāmīyah*.

103. al-Ṭabarī, ibid., vol. 4, p. 231.

104. (Pseudo) Ibn Qutaybah, ibid., vol. 1, p. 42.

105. al-Ṭabarī, ibid., vol. 4, p. 230; al-Balādhurī, vol. 1, pt. 1, p. 505.

106. al-Ṭabarī, ibid., vol. 4, p. 233.

107. Ibid.

108. Wellhausen, *The Arab Kingdom and its Fall.*

109. Levi della Vida considers that the election of ʿAlī was attributable mainly to the support of the *anṣār* for him.

110. al-Ṭabarī, ibid., vol. 3, p. 210.

111. See Sanhoury, *Le Califat: son Évolution vers une Société des Nations Orientale*, pp. 287–288 and 290–291.

112. Ibn Saʿd, *al-Ṭabaqāt al-Kubrā*, vol. 2, pt. 2, p. 202; Arnold, *The Caliphate*, pp. 39–40.

113. Abū al-Ḥasan ʿAlī bin al-Ḥusayn al-Masʿūdī, *Murūj al-Dhahab wa Maʿādin al-Jawhar*, edited with commentary by Muḥammad Muḥyī al-Dīn ʿAbd al-Ḥamīd, 4 vols. (Cairo: Dār al-Rajā', 1938), vol. 2, p. 42.

114. al-Ṭabarī, *Tārīkh al-Rusul wa al-Mulūk*, vol. 5, p. 302; ʿIzz al-Dīn Abū al-Ḥasan ʿAlī bin Muḥammad Ibn al-Athīr, *Tārīkh al-Kāmil*, 12 vols. (Cairo: Maṭbaʿat Muṣṭafā al-Bābī al-Ḥalabī, 1303/1885), vol. 3, p. 252; See Wellhausen, *The Arab Kingdom and its Fall*, p. 141 ff. This alludes to the fact that the principle was taken from the Sassanians, whereas Marwān bin al-Ḥakam's comment indicates a Byzantine source. See (Pseudo) Ibn Qutaybah, *al-Imāmah wa al-Siyāsah*, vol. 1, pp. 262 and 237.

115. It is narrated that al-Mughīrah bin Shuʿbah said to Muʿāwiyah: 'I have seen what there was of bloodshed and conflict after ʿUthmān.' See Ibn al-Athīr, ibid., vol. 3, p. 252; (Pseudo) Ibn Qutaybah, ibid., vol. 1, p. 263.

116. Marwān bin al-Ḥakam objected to the *bayʿah* to Yazīd and said: 'You have brought hereditary succession like Heraclius which you pledge to your sons.' See Ibn Qutaybah, ibid., vol. 1, p. 277.

117. See Wellhausen, *The Arab Kingdom and its Fall*, p. 110.

118. For Muʿāwiyah's efforts towards this, see ibid., p. 140; al-Ṭabarī, *Tārīkh al-Rusul wa al-Mulūk*, vol. 5, pp. 302–304; Ibn al-Athīr, *Tārīkh al-Kāmil*, vol. 3, p. 252 ff; Ibn Qutaybah, ibid., vol. 1, p. 263 ff; al-Yaʿqūbī, *Tārīkh al-Yaʿqūbī*, vol. 2, p. 302; al-Masʿūdī, *Murūj al-Dhahab wa Maʿādin al-Jawhar*, vol. 2, pp. 328–329; Arnold, *The Caliphate.*

119. Georgio Levi della Vida, 'Umayyads', *Encyclopedia of Islam*, vol. 4, pt. 2, pp. 998–1012.

120. al-Balādhurī, *Anṣāb al-Ashrāf*, vol. 4, pt. 1, p. 356; al-Ṭabarī, ibid., vol. 5, p. 503.

121. al-Muṭahhar bin Ṭāhir al-Maqdisī, *al-Bid' wa al-Tārīkh (al-mansūb) li-Abī Zayd Aḥmad bin Sahl al-Balkhī* (*Le Livre de la Création et de l'Histoire de Motahhar ben Tahir el-Maqdisi, attribué à Abou-Zéïd Ahmed ben Sahl el-Balkhi*), 6 vols., ed. and trans. into French by Clément Huart (Paris, Ernest Leroux, 1899–1919), vol. 6, p. 46.

122. al-Balādhurī, ibid., vol. 4, pt. 1, p. 358.

123. Bar Hebraeus (Ibn al-ʿIbrī Abū al-Faraj Yūḥannā Gregorius), *Tārīkh Mukhtaṣar al-Duwal*, ed. Fr. Antoine Ṣālḥānī (Beirut: al-Maṭbaʿah al-Kāthūlīkiyah, 1890), p. 190; al-Maqdisī, ibid., vol. 6, p. 46.

124. al-Balādhurī, ibid., vol. 4, pt. 1, p. 359.

125. See ibid., vol. 4, pt. 1, p. 356; (Pseudo) Ibn Qutaybah, vol. 2, p. 18; al-Ṭabarī, *Tārīkh al-Rusul wa al-Mulūk*, p. 383.

126. al-Ṭabarī, ibid., vol. 7, pp. 530–531.

127. al-Balādhurī, ibid., vol. 4, pt. 1, p. 359.

128. Ibid., vol. 4, pt. 2, pp. 11 and 19; al-Ṭabarī, ibid., vol. 5, p. 533.

129. See al-Ṭabarī, ibid., vol. 5, p. 537; al-Mas'ūdī, *Murūj al-Dhahab wa Ma'ādin al-Jawhar*, vol. 2, p. 106; al-Ya'qūbī, *Tārīkh al-Ya'qūbī*, vol. 3, p. 3; al-Maqdisī, *al-Bid' wa al-Tārīkh*, vol. 6, p. 18. It refers to the *bay'ah* of 'Āmr bin Sa'īd. See al-Balādhurī, ibid., vol. 4, pt. 2, p. 21.

130. al-Balādhurī, ibid., vol. 4, pt. 2, p. 12.

131. Ibid., vol. 4, pt. 2, p. 20. The same text is found in al-Ṭabarī, ibid., vol. 5, p. 532.

132. Ibid., vol. 4, pt. 2, p. 20 ff; al-Ṭabarī, ibid., vol. 5, p. 536 ff.

133. al-Balādhurī, ibid., vol. 4, pt. 2, p. 34.

134. al-Ṭabarī, ibid., vol. 5, p. 537.

135. al-Balādhurī, ibid., vol. 4, pt. 2, p. 12.

136. See ibid., vol. 4, pt. 2, pp. 34–45; al-Ṭabarī, ibid., vol. 5, pp. 34–35.

137. al-Balādhurī, ibid., vol. 4, pt. 2, p. 20.

138. See ibid., vol. 4, pt. 2, p. 26; al-Ṭabarī, ibid., vol. 5, p. 536.

139. al-Mas'ūdī, *Murūj al-Dhahab wa Ma'ādin al-Jawhar*, vol. 2, p. 106; al-Ṭabarī, ibid., vol. 5, pp. 13, 21 and 536–537; Ps-Ibn Qutaybah, vol. 2, p. 42; al-Balādhurī, ibid., vol. 4, pt. 2, pp. 34–35.

140. See al-Balādhurī, ibid., vol. 4, pt. 2, p. 21.

141. For details, see ibid., vol. 4, pt. 4, pt. 2, pp. 44–45; Ibn al-Athīr, *Tārīkh al-Kāmil*, vol. 4, p. 93; al-Ya'qūbī, *Tārīkh al-Ya'qūbī*, vol. 3, p. 4; al-Ṭabarī, ibid., vol. 5, p. 640.

142. Philip Hitti says: 'but the antiquated Arabian tribal principle of seniority in succession stood in constant conflict with the natural ambition of the ruling patriarch to pass sovereignty on to his son.' See Philip K. Hitti, *History of the Arabs*, p. 281.

143. Maslamah bin 'Abd al-Malik asked his brother Yazīd II: 'Who do you prefer, your brother or the son of your brother?' He replied: 'My brother.' Then he said: 'Your brother has more right to the succession!' Yazīd then replied: 'If it was not for my son.' See Ibn al-Athīr, ibid., vol. 5, p. 46.

144. al-Balādhurī, *Anṣāb al-Ashrāf*, vol. 4, pt. 2, p. 13.

145. See Ibn Qutaybah, *al-Imāmah wa al-Siyāsah*, vol. 1, pp. 178–180.

146. Arnold, *The Caliphate*, p. 24.

147. Sanhoury, *Le Califat: son Evolution vers une Société des Nations Orientale*, pp. 297–298.

148. Arnold, ibid., p. 24; Levi della Vida, 'Umayyads', pp. 297–298.

149. See al-Ṭabarī, *Tārīkh al-Rusul wa al-Mulūk*, vol. 7, p. 268; Wellhausen, *The Arab Kingdom and its Fall*, p. 362 ff.

150. *sūrat al-shūrā*, Q 42:23.

151. See al-Ṭabarī, ibid., vol. 7, p. 425; 'Abd al-Raḥmān Sunbuṭ al-Irbilī, *Khulāṣat al-Dhahab al-Masbūk, Mukhtaṣar min Siyar al-Mulūk* (Beirut: Maṭba'at al-Qiddīs Georgios li al-Rūm al-Orthodox, 1885), p. 39. Abū Muslim printed this verse on his coins in Khurasān. See Henri Lavoix, *Catalogue des Monnaies Musulmanes de la Bibliothèque Nationale*, 3 vols. (Paris: Imprimerie Nationale, 1887–1896), p. xvii. See also how the Qaramaṭiyah/Qaramites were indignant about this claim in 'Abd al-Qāhir al-Baghdādī, *al-Farq bayna al-Firāq*, edited with commentary by Muḥammad Muḥyī al-Dīn 'Abd al-Ḥamīd (Cairo: Maktabat al-Ma'ārif, 1910), pp. 281–282.

152. 'Abd al-Raḥmān Sunbuṭ al-Irbilī, *Khulāṣat al-Dhahab al-Masbūk, Mukhtaṣar min Siyar al-Mulūk* (Beirut: Maṭba'at al-Qiddīs Georgios, 1885), p. 40; al-Ṭabarī, ibid., vol. 7, p. 436.

153. *sūrat al-aḥzāb*, Q 33:6.

154. Aḥmad Zakī Ṣafwat, ed., *Jamharat Rasā'il al-'Arāb fī 'Uṣūr al-'Arabīyah al-Zāhirah*, 4 vols. (Cairo: Maṭba'at Muṣṭafā al-Bābī al-Ḥalabī, 1937–1938), vol. 3, p. 383.

155. al-Irbilī, ibid., p. 126; al-Ṭabarī, ibid., vol. 7, p. 427.

156. al-Ya'qūbī, *Tārīkh al-Ya'qūbī*, vol. 3, pp. 126–127.

157. See Muḥammad bin 'Alī Ibn al-Ṭaqṭaqī, *al-Fakhrī fī al-Ādāb al-Sulṭānīyah wa al-Duwal al-Islāmīyah* (Cairo: Sharikat Tab' al-Kutub al-'Arabīyah, 1317/1899), p. 101; 'Abd al-'Azīz al-Dūrī, *al-'Aṣr al-'Abbāsī al-Awwal: Dirāsah fī al-Tārīkh al-Siyāsī wa al-Idārī wa al-Mālī* (Baghdad: Maṭba'at al-Tafīḍ al-Ahlīyah, 1945; Manshūrāt Dār al-Mu'allimīn al-'Āliyah), p. 42; also published by the Centre for Arab Unity Studies – Beirut, 2006; *al-A'māl al-Kāmilah li-l-Duktūr 'Abd al-'Azīz al-Dūrī* (3); Arnold, *The Caliphate*, p. 562; Wellhausen, *The Arab Kingdom and its Fall*, pp. 17–18 and 89–91.

158. See al-Mas'ūdī, *Murūj al-Dhahab wa Ma'ādin al-Jawhar*, vol. 3, p. 239.

159. Ibn 'Abd Rabbīh, *al-'Iqd al-Farīd*, vol. 3, p. 370.

160. Aḥmad Zakī Ṣafwat, ed., *Jamharat Rasā'il al-'Arab fī 'Uṣūr al-'Arabīyah al-Zāhirah*, vol. 3, p. 384.

161. al-Mas'ūdī, vol. 3, p. 239.

162. Ṣafwat, ibid., vol. 3, p. 406.

163. al-Ṭabarī, *Tārīkh al-Rusul wa al-Mulūk*, vol. 10, p. 170.

164. al-Ya'qūbī, *Tārīkh al-Ya'qūbī*, vol. 3.

165. al-Ṭabarī, ibid., vol. 7, p. 356.

166. al-Irbilī, *Khulāṣat al-Dhahab al-Masbūk, Mukhtaṣar min Siyar al-Mulūk*, vol. 40; Arnold, *The Caliphate*, p. 81.

167. On Islamic systems, see Ḥasan Ibrāhīm Ḥasan and 'Alī Ibrāhīm Ḥasan, *al-Nuẓum al-Islāmīyah* (Cairo: Maktabat al-Nahḍah al-Miṣrīyah, 1939), p. 64.

168. Edward G. Browne, *A Literary History of Persia*, 4 vols. (Cambridge: Cambridge University Press, repr. 1928–1929), p. 255.

169. Arnold, ibid., pp. 29 and 48.

170. See the 'Risālah fī Manāqib al-Turk' in al-Jāḥiẓ, Abū 'Uthmān 'Amr bin Baḥr in *Rasā'il al-Jāḥiẓ: al-Rasā'il al-Siyāsīyah* (n.p: n.pb., n.d.), p. 43; Edward G. Browne, *A Literary History of Persia*, 4 vols. (Cambridge: Cambridge University Press, repr. 1928–1929), vol. 1, pp. 204–205; Amīr Ḥasan Ṣiddīqī, 'Caliphate and Kingship in Medieval Persia', *Islamic Culture*, vol. 9 (1935), pp. 560–579, p. 561.

171. Al-Ya'qūbī says: 'He [al-Wāthiq] was told about the *bay'ah* to his son. He said, "Allah will not deem it incumbent on me to assume it, dead or alive."' See al-Ya'qūbī, *Tārīkh al-Ya'qūbī*, vol. 3, p. 208.

172. The son of al-Wāthiq was said to be 'a beardless youth'. Waṣīf said: 'He is not allowed to lead the prayer.' See al-Ṭabarī, *Tārīkh al-Rusul wa al-Mulūk*, vol. 10, p. 154.

173. Ibid., vol. 10, p. 154; al-Ya'qūbī, ibid., vol. 3, p. 218. Al-Ya'qūbī says: 'The first to pledge the oath to him were Sīmā the Turk and Waṣīf the Turk.' See Harold Bowen, *The Life and Times of "Alī Ibn 'Īsā', 'the Good Vizier'* (Cambridge: Cambridge University Press, 1928), p. 3.

174. See 'Abd al-'Azīz al-Dūrī, *Dirāsāt fī al-'Uṣūr al-'Abbāsīyah al-Muta'akhirah*. (Baghdad: Sharikat al-Rābiṭah li-l-Tab' wa al-Nashr, 1946), pp. 45–48 and 56–58; repr. *al-A'māl al-Kāmilah li-l-Duktūr 'Abd al-'Azīz al-Dūrī* (4) (Beirut: Centre for Arab Unity Studies, 2007).

175. See Ṣiddīqī, 'Caliphate and Kingship in Medieval Persia', p. 564.

176. See al-Dūrī, ibid., pp. 59–73; al-Ṭabarī, ibid., vol. 10, pp. 75–76 and 256; al-Ya'qūbī, ibid., vol. 3, p. 228; Ibn al-Ṭaqṭaqī, *al-Fakhrī fī al-Ādāb al-Sulṭānīyah wa al-Duwal al-Islāmīyah*, p. 220; Bowen, '*The Life and Times of 'Alī Ibn 'Īsā*', p. 4; Abbott-Chicago, Nabia, 'Arabic Papyri from the Reign of Ga'far al-Mutawakkil 'ala-llāh (AH 232–47/AD 847–61)', *Zeitschrift der Deutschen Morgenländischen Gesellschaft* (ZDMG), vol. 92, nos. 1–3 (1938), pp. 88–135, p. 89 ff.

177. See Abū al-Faraj ʿAbd al-Raḥmān bin ʿAlī Ibn al-Jawzī, *al-Muntaẓam fī Tārīkh al-Mulūk wa al-Umam*, 10 vols. (Hyderabad-Deccan: Dā'irat al-Maʿārif al-ʿUthmānīyah, 1357–1358/1938–1939), vol. 5, p. 122.

178. See al-Dūrī, ibid., pp. 193–218.

179. Bowen, ibid., pp. 321–322.

180. Ibid., pp. 336–351; Ibn Miskawayh, Abū ʿAlī Aḥmad bin Muḥammad, *Tajārib al-Umam*, with selections from various histories relating to the matters mentioned therein, ed. H. F. Amedroz, 7 vols. (Cairo: [n.pb.], 1920–1921), vol. 1, pp. 350–352.

181. Bowen, ibid., p. 351 ff; Ibn Miskawayh, ibid., vol. 5, p. 352 ff.

182. See Ibn al-Ṭaqṭaqī, *al-Fakhrī fī al-Ādāb al-Sulṭānīyah wa al-Duwal al-Islāmīyah*, pp. 254–255.

183. Abū al-Fidā' Ismāʿīl bin ʿUmar Ibn Kathīr, *al-Bidāyah wa al-Nihāyah fī al-Tārīkh*, 14 vols. (Cairo: Maṭbaʿat al-Saʿādah, 1929–1939), vol. 11, p. 184.

184. Ibid., vol. 11, p. 197.

185. Ibn Miskawayh, *Tajārib al-Umam*, vol. 2, pp. 2–3; Bowen, *The Life and Times of "Al Ibn ʿĪsā'*, p. 364.

186. Ibn Miskawayh, ibid., vol. 2, pp. 72–75.

187. See Ibn al-Ṭaqṭaqī, *al-Fakhrī fī al-Ādāb al-Sulṭānīyah wa al-Duwal al-Islāmīyah*; Ibn al-Jawzī, *al-Muntaẓam fī Tārīkh al-Mulūk wa al-Umam*, vol. 5, p. 122.

188. Ibn al-Jawzī, ibid., vol. 5, p. 123; Bowen, *The Life and Times of "Alī Ibn ʿĪsā'*, p. 25; E. Lévi-Provençal, 'Muʿtaḍid', *Encyclopedia of Islam*, vol. 3, pt. 2, pp. 777–778.

189. Ibn al-Jawzī, ibid., vol. 5, p. 68; Ibn Miskawayh, vol. 1, p. 3; Bowen, ibid., p. 86.

190. See Bowen, ibid., pp. 62–65.

191. Abū al-Ḥusayn Hilāl bin al-Muḥsin al-Ṣābī, *Tuḥfat al-Umarā' fī Tārīkh al-Wuzarā' = The Historical Remains of* Hilāl al-Ṣābī: *first part of his Kitāb al-Wuzarā' and fragment of his History, 389–393 AH*, edited with notes and glossary by H. F. Amedroz (Beirut: Catholic Press [Maṭbaʿat al-Ābā' al-Kathūlīkiyīn], 1904), pp. 115–116; Ibn Miskawayh, ibid., vol. 1, pp. 2–3.

192. See al-Qurṭubī, ʿArīb bin Saʿd al-Kātib, *Ṣilat Ta'rīkh al-Ṭabarī*, ed. M. J. de Goeje (Leiden: Brill, 1897), p. 28; Ibn al-Jawzī, *al-Muntaẓam fī Tārīkh al-Mulūk wa al-Umam*, vol. 7, p. 69; Bowen, ibid., p. 62.

193. See Ṣiddīqī, 'Caliphate and Kingship in Medieval Persia', p. 565.

194. See ibid., pp. 566–567; Stanley Lane-Poole, *The Mohammedan Dynasties: Chronological and Genealogical Tables with Historical Introductions* (London: A. Constable and Company, 1894), p. 190; Idem, *Catalogue of Oriental coins in the British Museum*, 10 vols. (London: Trustees of the British Museum, 1875–1890), p. 256.

195. al-Ṭabarī, *Tārīkh al-Rusul wa al-Mulūk*, vol. 10, p. 391.

196. Ibid., vol. 10, p. 462.

197. Ibn Miskawayh, *Tajārib al-Umam*, vol. 1, p. 29.

198. See Adam Metz, *Die Renaissance des Islams*, trans. Muḥammad ʿAbd al-Hādī Abū Raydah as *al-Ḥaḍārah al-Islāmīyah fī al-Qarn al-Rābiʿ al-Hijrī*, 2 vols. (Cairo: Lajnat al-Ta'līf wa al-Tarjamah wa al-Nashr, 1940–1941), vol. 1, p. 17; Ṣiddīqī, 'Caliphate and Kingship in Medieval Persia', p. 570.

199. See al-Māwardī, *al-Aḥkām al-Sulṭānīyah*; Ṣiddīqī, ibid., p. 566.

200. For the influence of the Buwayhids on the financial and social situation, see ʿAbd al-ʿAzīz al-Dūrī, *Dirāsāt fī al-ʿUṣūr al-ʿAbbāsīyah al-Muta'akhirah*, pp. 262–270 and 278–290.

201. See Ibn Miskawayh, *Tajārib al-Umam*, vol. 1, p. 355.

202. Ibn Ḥassūl reports that most of the Daylamites were Shī'ite as they had converted at the hands of the Nāṣirīyah (who were Zaydīs). See Abū 'Alā' Muḥammad bin 'Alī Ibn Ḥassūl, *Tafḍīl al-Atrāk 'alā Sā'ir al-Ajnād*, ed. 'Abbās al-'Azzāwī, Istanbul: [n.pb.], 1940, p. 32.

203. Ibn al-Athīr, *Tārikh al-Kāmil*, vol. 7, p. 149.

204. See art. *'al-Buwayhīyīn'*, Dā'irat-al-Ma'ārif al Islāmīyah.

205. Ibn al-Athīr, ibid., vol. 7, p. 249; Abū al-Rayḥān Muḥammad bin Aḥmad al-Bīrūnī, *al-Jamāhir fī Ma'rifat al-Jawāhir*, ed. F. Krenkow (Hyderabad-Deccan: Jam'īyat Dā'irat al-Ma'ārif al-'Uthmānīyah, 1355/1936), pp. 23–53.

206. See footnotes in Ibn Miskawayh, *Tajārib al-Umam*, vol. 2, p. 87.

207. That is, it was preferable to not appoint an 'Ālawid caliph for the reason that such would enjoy the popular support of the people – in his being perceived to be the rightful or legitimate claimant to the caliphate – where they would follow his commands.

208. Ibn al-Athīr, ibid., vol. 7, p. 149.

209. Ibn Miskawayh, ibid., vol. 2, p. 86; Vladimir Minorsky, *La domination des Dailamites* (Paris: 1932; Publications de la Societé des études Iraniennes 3), pp. 12–23.

210. Ibn Miskawayh, ibid., vol. 3, pp. 86–87; Ibn al-Jawzī, *al-Muntaẓam fī Tārīkh al-Mulūk wa al-Umam*, vol. 6, pp. 342–344.

211. Ibn al-Jawzī, ibid., vol. 6, p. 350.

212. Ibn Miskawayh, ibid., vol. 3, p. 301.

213. Ibn al-Jawzī, vol. 7, p. 156.

214. Ibid., vol. 7, p. 102.

215. Ibn al-Athīr, *Tārikh al-Kāmil*, vol. 7, p. 147.

216. See Metz, Adam, *al-Ḥaḍārah*, vol. 1, p. 22.

217. Ibn al-Athīr, ibid., vol. 4, p. 148.

218. Ibn Miskawayh, *Tajārib al-Umam*, vol. 2, p. 87.

219. Ibid., vol. 2, p. 108; Ibn al-Jawzī, ibid., vol. 6, p. 357.

220. Ibn al-Jawzī, ibid., vol. 6, p. 357.

221. Ibn Miskawayh, ibid., vol. 2, p. 334.

222. Ibid., vol. 2, p. 308.

223. Ibid., vol. 2, p. 307.

224. Ibid., vol. 2, p. 308.

225. See the footnote in ibid., vol. 2, p. 318.

226. Ibn al-Jawzī, ibid., vol. 7, pp. 150–169.

227. Ibid., vol. 7, p. 100; Ibn Miskawayh, ibid., vol. 2, p. 396; Quṭb al-Dīn al-Ḥanafī [al-Nahrawālī], *al-I'lām bi-A'lām Bayt Allāh al-Ḥarām* (n.p.: n.pb., n.d.), p. 78.

228. Ibn al-Jawzī, ibid., vol. 7, p. 160.

229. Ibid., vol. 7, p. 115; Ibn Miskawayh, ibid., vol. 2, p. 396.

230. Ṣiddīqī, 'Caliphate and Kingship in Medieval Persia', pp. 11–12.

231. Ibn al-Jawzī, ibid., vol. 7, p. 76.

232. Ibn Miskawayh, *Tajārib al-Umam*, vol. 2, p. 85; ibid., p. 112.

233. Ṣiddīqī, ibid., p. 113.

234. Ibn Miskawayh, ibid., vol. 2, p. 396; Ibn al-Jawzī, *al-Muntaẓam fī Tārīkh al-Mulūk wa al-Umam*, ibid., vol. 7, p. 94.

235. Ibn al-Jawzī, ibid., vol. 7, p. 87.

236. Al-Bīrūnī, Abū al-Rayḥān Muḥammad bin Aḥmad, *al-Āthār al-Bāqiyah 'an al-Qurūn al-Khāliyah = Chronologie orientalischer Völker*, ed. Eduard Sachau (Leipzig: [n.pb.], 1878), p. 132.

237. Ibn al-Jawzī, ibid., vol. 7, p. 66.

238. Ibid., vol. 7, pp. 160–161; Taqī al-Dīn Aḥmad bin al-Ḥusayn Abū Shujā' al-Iṣfahānī, *Matn al-Ghāyah 'alā Madhhab al-Imām al-Shāfi'ī* [*Mukhtaṣar Abū Shujā'*] (n.p.: n.pb., n.d.), p. 308; Ibn al-Ṭaqṭaqī, *al-Fakhrī fi al-Ādāb al-Sulṭānīyah wa al-Duwal al-Islāmīyah*, p. 391.

239. Ibn al-Jawzī, ibid., vol. 7, p. 161; Idem, ibid., vol. 8, p. 109; Adam Metz, *al-Ḥaḍārah*, vol. 1, p. 23.

240. Ibn al-Jawzī, ibid., vol. 8, p. 42.

241. Ibn Miskawayh, *Tajārib al-Umam*, vol. 2, pp. 189 and 196.

242. Ibn al-Athīr, *Tārikh al-Kāmil*, vol. 9, p. 129.

243. Ibid., vol. 9, p. 279; Ṣiddīqī, 'Caliphate and Kingship in Medieval Persia', pp. 128–129.

244. Ibn al-Jawzī, *al-Muntaẓam fī Tārīkh al-Mulūk wa al-Umam*, vol. 8, p. 82.

245. Ibn al-Athīr, ibid., vol. 9, pp. 128–129.

246. 'Izz al-Dīn Abū al-Ḥasan 'Alī bin Muḥammad Ibn al-Athīr, *al-Kāmil fī al-Tārīkh* (*Ibn-El-Athiri Chronicon Quod Perfectissimum*), ed. Carolus Johannes Tornberg, 12 vols (Leiden: Brill, 1851–1871), pp. 391–392.

247. Ibid., p. 392.

248. Ibn Miskawayh, *Tajārib al-Umam*, vol. 3, p. 84.

249. See Ibn al-Jawzī, *al-Muntaẓam fī Tārīkh al-Mulūk wa al-Umam*, vol. 8, p. 35.

250. See Ibn Miskawayh, ibid., vol. 2, p. 339.

251. Ibid., vol. 2, p. 156.

252. Ibn al-Jawzī, ibid., vol. 7, p. 78.

253. Ibid., vol. 8, pp. 97–98.

254. Ibid., vol. 8, p. 9.

255. Ibid., vol. 8, p. 65.

256. Ṣiddīqī, 'Caliphate and Kingship in Medieval Persia', p. 120.

257. See the margin in Ibn Miskawayh, *Tajārib al-Umam*, vol. 2, pp. 417–418; al-Ḥanafī [al-Nahrawālī], *al-I'lām bi A'lām Bayt Allāh al-Ḥarām*, p. 79; Ibn al-Jawzī, ibid., vol. 7, pp. 98–100.

258. Ibn Miskawayh, ibid., vol. 2, p. 344.

259. Ibid., vol. 2, p. 123.

260. Ibid., vol. 2, p. 179.

261. Ṣiddīqī, 'Caliphate and Kingship in Medieval Persia', p. 125.

262. *sūrat al-baqarah*, Q 2:30.

263. *sūrat ṣād*, Q 38:26.

264. 'Abd al-Qāhir al-Baghdādī, *Uṣūl al-Dīn* (Istanbul: Maṭba'at al-Dawlah, 1928), p. 272.

265. See the discussion in ibid., pp. 275–277.

266. Ibid., pp. 28–29.

267. al-Ash'arī does not see the permissibility of this except where there is an intervening sea between the two lands which prevents the assistance of each of the two peoples from reaching the other, and he allows each of the two peoples to conclude a covenant for an *imamate* for one of the people on their respective sides. See ibid., p. 274.

268. al-Baghdādī explains that if the *imam* deviates from the *sharī'ah*: 'The *ummah* (community) shall reproach him (voluntarily) to desist from his error and return to the right course, or to remove and replace him with someone else.' See ibid., p. 278.

269. See al-Māwardī, *al-Aḥkām al-Sulṭānīyah*, p. 2 ff; Haroon Khan Sherwani, *Studies in Muslim Political Thought and Administration* (Lahore: Sh. Muḥammad Ashraf, 1945), p. 94 ff. I have benefited particularly from these two studies: H. A. R. Gibb, 'al-Māwardī's theory of the Khilāfah', *Islamic Culture*, 11 (1937), pp. 291–302;

Aḥmad Mian Akhtar, *Studies: Islamic and Oriental*, with a foreword by Muḥammad Shafi (Lahore: Sh. Muḥammad Ashraf, 1945), p. 159 ff.

270. For the development of the Khawārij and their principles, see al-Ṭabarī, *Tārīkh al-Rusul wa al-Mulūk*, vol. 5, pp. 64–66 and 72–93; al-Mubarrad, *al-Kāmil*, p. 528 and 550; al-Minqarī Naṣr bin Muzāḥim, Abū al-Faḍl, *Waq'at Ṣiffīn* (n.p.: n.pb., n.d.), pp. 560–563 and 589; Abū Ḥāmid 'Abd al-Ḥamīd bin Hibat Allāh Ibn Abī al-Ḥadīd, *Sharḥ Nahj al-Balāghah*, 4 vols. (Cairo: Dār al-Kutub al-'Arabīyah al-Kubrā, n.d.), pp. 186, 202 and 314–315; al-Balādhurī, *Anṣāb al-Ashrāf*.

271. Goldziher, Ignác [Ignaz], Vorlesungen über den Islam, trans. Felix Arin as *Le Dogme et la Loi de l'Islam: histoire du développement dogmatique et juridique de la religion musulmane* (Paris: Librairie Orientaliste Paul Geuthner, 1926), pp. 158–159.

272. Abū al-Fatḥ Muḥammad bin 'Abd al-Karīm al-Shahrastānī, *al-Milal wa al-Niḥal*, [repr. of William Cureton's ed., 1846], ed. Goberton, 2 vols. (Leipzig: Otto Harrassowitz, 1923), p. 9.

273. Goldziher, ibid., p. 160.

274. Reynold A. Nicholson, *A Literary History of the Arabs*, 2nd edn. (Cambridge: Cambridge University Press, 1930), p. 210.

275. See Wellhausen, *The Arab Kingdom and its Fall*, p. 85 ff; G. Levi Della Vida, 'Kharijite', *Encyclopædia of Islam*, vol. 2, pt. 2, pp. 904–908.

276. See Bruno, in Salahuddin Khuda Bukhsh, *Contributions to the History of Islamic Civilization*, 2 vols. (Calcutta: University of Calcutta, 1924), vol. 2, pp. 160–166; al-Shahrastānī, *al-Milal wa al-Niḥal*, p. 66.

277. Khuda Bukhsh, ibid., pp. 159–169.

278. See ibid., p. 159.

279. al-Shahrastānī, ibid., p. 66.

280. See Abū al-Faraj 'Abd al-Raḥmān bin 'Alī Ibn al-Jawzī, *Talbīs Iblīs*, ed. Muḥammad Munīr al-Dimashqī (Cairo: Maktabat al-Nahḍah, 1928), p. 96; Goldziher, *Le Dogme et la Loi de l'Islam*, p. 160.

281. al-Shahrastānī, ibid., pp. 89–90.

282. Ibid., p. 67; Ibn Abī al-Ḥadīd, *Sharḥ Nahj al-Balāghah*, vol. 1, p. 215.

283. al-Shahrastānī, ibid., p. 70.

284. See al-Ṭabarī, *Tārīkh al-Rusul wa al-Mulūk*, vol. 5, p. 191.

285. See ibid., vol. 5, p. 191.

286. al-Baghdādī, *al-Farq bayna al-Firāq*, p. 55.

287. al-Shahrastānī, *al-Milal wa al-Niḥal*, p. 66; Goldziher, *Le Dogme et la Loi de l'Islam*, p. 163.

288. In addition to the sources and references mentioned previously, see Suhayr al-Qalmāwī, *Adab al-Khawārij fī al-'Aṣr al-Umawī* (Cairo: Lajnat al-Ta'līf wa al-Tarjamah wa al-Nashr, 1945); Jabbūr 'Abd al-Nūr, *Naẓrāt fī Falsafat al-'Arab* (Beirut: Dār al-Makshūf, 1945), pp. 132–168; Aḥmad Amīn, *Fajr al-Islām* (Cairo: Maktabat al-Nahḍah al-Miṣrīyah, 1945), pp. 314–326; Idem, *Ḍuḥā al-Islām* (Cairo: [n.pb.], 1936), vol. 3, p. 331 ff.

289. Muḥammad bin al-Nu'mān al-Shaykh al-Mufīd, *Awā'il al-Maqālāt fī al-Madhāhib wa al-Mukhtārāt*, ed. Mahdī Muḥaqqiq. (Tehran: Institute of Islamic Studies, McGill University, Teheran Branch, 1323/1944), pp. 38–39.

290. Abū Ja'far Muḥammad bin Ya'qūb al-Kulaynī, *Uṣūl al-Kāfī* [includes the gloss (*sharḥ*) of al-Mullā Muḥammad Ṣāliḥ al-Māzandarānī in the notes] (Tehran; Tab' Ḥajar, [n.d.]), p. 63.

291. Ibid., p. 83.

292. Ibid., p. 64.

293. Al-Kulaynī was one of the greatest Imamī (Twelver) Shī'ite scholars of *ḥadīth*.
294. Ibid., p. 69.
295. Ibid., p. 72.
296. Ibid., p. 161.
297. al-Shaykh al-Mufīd, ibid., pp. 41–42.
298. This is in reference to the Qur'ānic verse which specifies that Allah took Ibrāhīm (Abraham) as a 'boon friend' – *khalīl* (*sūrat al-nisā'*, Q 4:125), and who is, therefore, referred to as *khalīl allāh* or *al-khalīl*. [Editor's note]
299. al-Kulaynī, ibid., p. 72.
300. Ibid., p. 101.
301. Ibid.
302. See al-Shaykh al-Mufīd, ibid., p. 33.
303. al-Kulaynī, ibid., p. 71.
304. Ibid., p. 68.
305. Ibid., p. 70.
306. Ibid., p. 81.
307. Ibid., p. 82.
308. Ibid., p. 89.
309. Ibid., p. 11.
310. Ibid., p. 89.
311. Ibid., p. 89.
312. Ibid., p. 91.
313. Ibid., p. 95.
314. Ibid., p. 72.
315. Ibid., p. 73.
316. *sūrat al-nisā'*, Q 4:45.
317. al-Kulaynī, ibid., p. 74.
318. *sūrat al-ra'd*, Q 13:7.
319. al-Kulaynī, ibid., p. 68.
320. Ibid., p. 62.
321. Ibid., p. 70.
322. Ibid., pp. 71–72.
323. Ibid., p. 161.
324. Ibid., p. 166.
325. Ibid., p. 161.
326. Ibid., p. 163.
327. Ibid.
328. Ibid., p. 611.
329. Ibid., p. 66.
330. Ibid., p. 166.
331. *sūrat al-tawbah*, Q 9:119.
332. al-Kulaynī, ibid., p. 75.
333. Ibid.

CHAPTER 2

Fiscal Systems – *al-nuẓum al-mālīyah*

The measures of the Prophet

In 9AH, the Qur'ānic verse of the *jizyah* (the tax on non-Muslims) was revealed:

> Fight [against] those who do not believe in Allah or in the Last Day, and who do not forbid what Allah and His Messenger have forbidden, and who do not follow the religion of truth [*dīn al-ḥaqq* – i.e. Islam] among those who have been given the Book (*min al-ladhīna ūtū al-kitāb*), [fight] until they pay/give the *jizyah* willingly while they are humbled.[1]

However, there appeared no mention in the Qur'ān of anything on the *kharāj* in the connotation of an Islamic land tax: 'Or do you [Muḥammad] ask them for any payment? But the bounty/recompense (*kharāj*) of your Lord is best and He is the Best of providers.'[2] Therefore, the Prophet followed a policy which comprised a collection of practical measures characterised by their flexibility and regard for the objective conditions of the situation. He took into consideration the way in which the conquered lands had surrendered to the Muslims, whether this had been by force (*'anwah*) or by a peace agreement (*ṣulḥ*), and whether their inhabitants were Arabs or non-Arabs. Furthermore, he took notice of their living conditions and whether they owned land or not. In the light of this, he promulgated his measures and some of these became precedents for what took place after him.

The measures of the Prophet can be categorised as follows:

1 Lands conquered by force (*ʿanwatan*)

a Non-Arab lands

These were lands whose inhabitants were non-Arabs, namely Khaybar and Wādī al-Qurah. The Prophet began with Khaybar, and instituted a temporary solution and then a semi-permanent one which he applied to Wādī al-Qurah:

i Khaybar was conquered by force after fighting; and the Prophet divided it into five and apportioned four-fifths of it among the Muslims.[3] That was because he considered it as *ghanīmah* (pl. *ghanāʾim*), or *booty*, in accordance with the Qurʾānic verse: 'Know that whatever you take as booty, a fifth of it belongs to Allah and to the Messenger (*wa aʿlamū annamā ghanimtum min shayʾin faʾinna li-Lāhi khumusahu wa li-l-rasūl*), and to close relatives, orphans, the poor and needy and the *ibn al-sabīl*[4]...'[5]

Let us consider the issue of *al-khums* (lit. a fifth [part]) and the Messenger's share so as to clarify whether it is distinct from the share of Allah or not, before we go into the details of the verse. Abū ʿUbayd discusses this and reports several narrations:

- The share of the Prophet was a fifth of the fifth (*khums al-khums*, reported in two narrations with the connotation that there was no separate share for Allah).
- The fifth was divided into four parts. A quarter for Allah, the Messenger and the close relatives; that is, those related through kinship (*qurābah*) to the Prophet. He did not take anything from this share himself. The second quarter was for the orphans, the third for the poor and needy, and the fourth for the traveller, the *ibn al-sabīl* – the needy person who was a guest of the Muslims.
- The Messenger set aside the fifth, and then he reached his hand into it and whatever he grasped [not necessarily in a literal sense] he put towards the *kaʿbah*. This was the share for the House (*bayt*) of Allah and he divided the remainder into five parts.
- The fifth of Allah and the fifth of the Messenger were the same. The Messenger used to carry some of it (on his person) and give it away, or spend it and do with it as he wanted.

- Abū 'Ubayd explains that Allah attributed the fifth to Himself, then he mentioned its [designated] people after him. Likewise, for the close relatives he referred it to Himself then restricted mention to its/his people.[6] Subsequently the decision became that of the *imām*, to spend it for everything Allah wished [i.e. to distribute it among the five groups].[7]

It appears from this that the fifth (a special tithe called *al-khums*) of the five categories mentioned was a substitute for the share of Allah; and that the Prophet apportioned it according to whatever necessitated it and disposed of the remainder as dictated by the common interest/good (*al-maṣlaḥah*). So the *khums* of Khaybar was for Allah. The Prophet gave part of it to his wives and relatives. As the need among the Banū 'Abd al-Muṭṭalib was greater, he gave them more. He gave to the orphans, poor Muslims (men and women), the men who had mediated the peace settlement between the Prophet and the inhabitants of Fadak, as well as a man from the inhabitants of al-Ḥudaybīyah (Jābir bin 'Abdallah bin Ḥarām al-Anṣārī) who had been absent from [the battle of] Khaybar. What the Prophet distributed was agricultural produce, consisting of 'wheat, barley, dates, fruit kernels, and so forth', which he apportioned according to their need.[8] The four remaining fifths were divided among the Muslims who conquered Khaybar. Each cavalier received a share and his horse two shares, and each foot-soldier received one share, meaning that he apportioned for each rider three shares and each foot-soldier a single share.[9]

However, necessity led the Prophet to alter this arrangement. He gave the land to its owners for the sharecropping (*muqāsamah*) of one-half. Ibn Hishām reports: 'When the inhabitants of Khaybar yielded to that, they asked the Messenger of Allah to share half of the property with them. They said, "We know more about it [i.e. the land] than you and we are best able to exploit it."'[10] Abū 'Ubayd states: 'When the property came into the hands of the Messenger of Allah, he did not have sufficient labourers to work the land. So the Messenger handed it over to the Jews for them to work in exchange for half of what was produced from it.'[11] Therefore, because of the influence of the lack of labour and the [horticultural] expertise of the inhabitants of Khaybar, the Prophet made a peace treaty (*ṣulḥ*) in their favour with them for half of the crop, saying: 'It is up to us: if we want to evict you then we will evict you.'[12]

ii The Prophet conquered Wādī al-Qurah by force: 'The Muslims obtained from it an abundance of goods and accoutrements. The Messenger of Allah divided this into fifths. He left the date palms and the land in the hands of the Jews and he dealt with them as he had done with the people of Khaybar.'[13]

b Arab lands

The Prophet pursued a special policy with the lands of the Arabs which was that he did not impose the *kharāj* tax on them, but rather the *'ushr* (lit., a tenth or tithe of one-tenth). In doing that, he had a social and political aim. The *kharāj* carried with it the connotation of submission and humiliation, and he desired political unity for the Arabs. Abū 'Ubayd confirms: 'The reports (*akhbār*) about the Messenger of Allah are sound and to the effect that he conquered Mecca and was gracious towards its inhabitants. He returned it [i.e. the lands of Mecca] to them, and did not distribute it nor make it common property (*fay'*).'[14] Abū Yūsuf says: 'The Messenger had left what he did not divide of the villages and conquered Mecca by force and other dwelling places of the Arabs. He did not divide anything other than Khaybar. Similarly, when he conquered other dwelling places of the polytheist Arabs (*mushrikī al-'arab*), he left them as they were.'[15] Elsewhere he says: 'We have heard that the Messenger of Allah conquered Arab land and imposed the *'ushr* on it, but he did not set a *kharāj* on any of it. He applied this procedure to all of the Arab land.'[16]

2 Lands conquered by peace agreement (*ṣulḥ*)

a Here, it is problematic to posit any general rule except with regard to the *kharāj* tax. In Yemen, the Prophet 'settled them [the inhabitants] on their lands'[17] and imposed on them the payment of *'ushr* (one-tenth) of the produce irrigated naturally, and half of the *'ushr* (i.e. half of one-tenth) on what was irrigated by instrument (i.e. through human intervention/irrigation); [that is, and for example:] one-tenth on what was irrigated by spring water, one-tenth on what was watered by rainwater and half of one-tenth on what was irrigated through use of camels.[18] In Bahrain, he left the land to them on condition that 'they spare us the work and divide the yield with us'.

b Only the *jizyah* was imposed on the northern cities. This was one of two types:

i A collective *jizyah* (*jizyah mushtarakah*). For example, the inhabitants of Taymā' 'made peace terms for the *jizyah*, and they remained in their towns and on their land'.[19] Similarly, as for Tabūk: 'the Messenger stayed in Tabūk for some days and made peace with its people for the *jizyah*.'[20] Likewise, the Prophet made peace with the inhabitants of Adhruḥ for one hundred *dinars* (annually) every month of Rajab. The principle may also have been applied to the inhabitants of al-Jarbā'.[21]

ii A *jizyah* of one *dinar* 'on the heads' of individuals [i.e. per person], together with the stipulation of hospitality (*ḍiyāfah*) for those Muslims passing through the region. For example, the Prophet had settled the people of Tabālah and Jerash, according to the terms of their surrender, and fixed one *dinar* on each adult male (*ḥālim*) of the non-Muslims (*ahl al-kitāb*, 'people of the Book') among them (and he also stipulated that they provide hospitality to the Muslims).[22] In Aylah, he set one *dinar* per year on each adult landowner, which yielded a total of 300 *dinars*. Additionally, he stipulated a hospitable reception (*qiran*) from them for those Muslims passing their way.[23]

iii The people of Maqnā made peace with a written document which stated: 'There shall be no injustice or enmity against you. The Messenger of Allah shall protect you from that which he protects himself. Your seige ladders, your arms and armour (war materials) will belong to the Messenger of Allah, except that which is exempted by the Messenger or the emmisary of Allah's Messenger. Besides that, one-quarter of what your palm trees produce, one-quarter of whatever your fishermen catch, and one-quarter of what is woven by your women is incumbent on you. You shall have what is left after that. The Messenger of Allah has relieved you of any *jizyah* and forced labour (*sukhrah*).'[24]

iv In Yemen there was a *jizyah* of one *dinar* for each person or the equal value of that in quantities of a local garment (*ma'āfir*).[25]

v The *jizyah* imposed on Najrān was 'one thousand *ḥallah* (pl. *ḥilal*, coppers) in Ṣafar, one thousand *ḥallah* in Rajab, each *ḥallah* shall be equivalent to the value of one *wiqīyah* (ounce) of silver [where one *wiqīyah* = forty *dirhams*]; to pay according to the surplus if the value of the *ḥallah* is more than the *wiqīyah*; and to pay the deficit if it is less than the *wiqīyah*; he [Muḥammad] will accept from them whatever they give in the way of weapons, camels, horses or whatever they offer which is of the same value as a substitute for the *ḥilal*.' The Prophet asked them 'to give hospitality to the emmisaries of Allah's Messenger for a month or what is less, and that they would not be obligated to do so for more than a month'. He also asked them for the following assistance in the event of any trouble: to loan the Muslims thirty coats of mail and thirty camels, on condition that the Muslims replace whatever is destroyed or lost from what is borrowed.[26]

vi The Prophet imposed the *jizyah* on those protected non-Muslims (*ahl al-dhimmah*) in Mecca and Medina after his return from the raid of Tabūk. He imposed 'one *dinar* or its equivalent on the men, but the women or the youths were not [included] in that'.[27] At first, the Prophet imposed the *jizyah* on the Jewish and Christian 'people of the Book' only, then he subsequently added the Magians (*al-majūs*) to this. Abū Yūsuf reports: 'The Messenger of Allah had accepted the *jizyah* for the Magian inhabitants of Bahrain and he allowed them to remain devotees of Magianism.'[28] Similarly, he imposed the *jizyah* of 'one *dinar* or the equivalent value of local *maʿāfirī* garments on all those who had attained to maturity among the Magians of Yemen, whether male or female'. There is no other reference to imposing the *jizyah* on women in any narration other than this.[29]

vii The Prophet took Fadak 'without the charge of horse or camel'[30] (i.e. without mobilisation for fighting), and 'it belonged exclusively to the Messenger of Allah',[31] and nothing of it belonged to the Muslims.

viii The Prophet stipulated on the general ownership of water, pasture and fire [i.e. tinder]. He said: 'The people are sharing partners (*shurakā'*) in water, pasture and fire.'[32] The pasture which had not been sown or planted by anyone was necessary for cattle and sheep. Water was likewise a general necessity. The meaning of 'fire' here was probably *firewood*, which was used as fuel.[33]

From the facts mentioned above, it is possible to derive some paradigms:

- The Prophet divided up Khaybar and Wādī al-Qurah, which had been conquered by force, among the Muslims, or he abided by the principle of distributing these lands as booty.

- He considered the lands of the Arabs to be *'ushr* land [land paying a 'one-tenth' tithe].
- He set the individual *jizyah* at one *dinar*, and imposed it on the people of the Book (Jews and Christians) and subsequently added the Magians. He exempted women and children from it.
- He introduced the principle of hospitality (*ḍiyāfah*) for the Muslims due to the necessity which became military (i.e. as in quartering).
- He was content to impose the *jizyah* on lands conquered by a *ṣulḥ* agreement and to fix its amount.
- He made water, pasture and fire (i.e. tinder) public property.

These measures of systemisation (*tanẓīmāt*) were important precedents for the Rāshidūn caliphs: at times, they took them literally and at others they were guided by the approaches towards which they were directed. The task of those caliphs was extremely arduous because their conquests encompassed ancient lands which had their own deep-rooted indigenous fiscal systems and traditions.

The fiscal systemisations – *tanẓīmāt* – of 'Umar bin al-Khaṭṭāb

Introduction

In the early period of Islam, the greatest preoccupation for the Muslims after the issue of the caliphate was the issue of taxation and dealing with the conquered peoples. 'Umar bin al-Khaṭṭāb, the second caliph, undertook a vital role in treating this problem. During his rule (13–23AH/634–644AD), the first conquests took place and the foundations of the administrative systems were laid down. Wellhausen considers 'Umar bin al-Khaṭṭāb to be 'the founder of the second theocracy, or the theocracy without a prophet'.[34] In this light, the study of his systemisations – *tanẓīmāt* – is very important, as it reveals the foundations of the Islamic state and the source from which the majority of the *fuqahā'* (jurists) drew in promulgating their legislation regarding financial matters. However, the *fuqahā'* attributed to 'Umar measures which took about a century to be put into effect. This was so that they could impart them with an aspect of religious legitimacy after these measures had been the product of particular practical circumstances. In his systemisation of taxation in the conquered lands, 'Umar had recourse to the *spirit* of Islam and the systemisations of the Prophet and Abū Bakr on the one hand, and to the circumstances prevailing in the conquered lands on the other. Moreover, he formulated his own opinion through *ijtihād* (independent judgment) and seeking council of the Companions (*ṣaḥābah*), and from this resulted the first framework for Islamic fiscal systemisations.

We will refer to the local circumstances in due course, but it is sufficient for us to discuss here the systemisations carried out by the first caliph since we have already examined those of the Prophet. During the caliphate of Abū Bakr (11–13AH/632–634AD), [his commander] Khālid bin al-Walīd conquered Busra and agreed with its inhabitants 'that they shall pay one *dinar* and a *jarīb* of wheat[35] for every adult male'.[36] In this agreement we can see the beginning of the *kharāj* tax. Khālid made peace terms with the people of Ḥīrah for a specific *jizyah*. The men had to pay fourteen *dirhams* per year of a weight of five *dawānīq* [ancient coins, each valued at approximately one-sixth of dirham] (or ten *dirhams* of a weight of seven *dawānīq*),[37] and he excluded the chronically ill of which there were 1,000 men.[38] Jarīr bin 'Abdullah al-Bajlī (one of Khālid's commanders) made peace with the inhabitants of Bāniqyā, near to Kūfah, for 1,000 *dirhams* and [1,000] *ṭaylasān* [(from a Farsi term) black-coloured cloaks, worn over the shoulder] every year,[39] and Ḥīrah and Bāniqyā became *ṣulḥ* lands. Thus, in the caliphate of Abū Bakr precedents were established relating to *ṣulḥ* land (land whose ownership remained in the hands of its owners – through a peace treaty – and which was not considered the property of the Muslims), as well as collecting tax on the produce [of the land], in addition to the precedent of the tax in cash as in Busra. These were the Islamic precedents with which the second caliph was confronted when he initiated his grand plan to systemise taxation in the conquered lands.

Before exploring the details of the systemisation of taxation during the caliphate of 'Umar bin al-Khaṭṭāb, we will mention its approaches in order to understand their essence:

a 'Umar was content to apply the Qur'ānic verse on booty (*sūrat al-anfāl*, Q 8:41) to movable spoils, but he did not distribute the conquered lands among the fighters as the Prophet had done at Khaybar. Consequently, he met with great opposition from the ranks of the conquering soldiers. When the *sawād* (fertile alluvial lands, in the vicinity of the Tigris and Euphrates) was conquered, the fighters said to the caliph: 'Divide it among us, for we conquered it by force with our swords.' He refused, saying: 'But what would be apportioned for those Muslims who come after you?'[40] Abū Yūsuf relates that the

Companions of the Prophet and a group of the Muslims wanted 'Umar bin al-Khaṭṭāb to divide Syria, just as the Messenger of Allah had divided Khaybar. However, 'Umar replied, "Then I would leave nothing to those Muslims who come after you."'[41] When Egypt was conquered, the fighters urged 'Amr bin al-'Āṣ (the governor of Egypt) to divide it, but he refused to do it without asking 'Umar for advice. 'Umar wrote to him: 'Leave it so that future generations (lit. the foetuses of the pregnant women – *ḥabal al-ḥabalah*) may profit by it.'[42] 'Umar had decided upon this arrangement after consulting the senior Companions who differed in their opinions: 'As for 'Abd al-Raḥmān bin 'Awf, his opinion was that their just deserts should be divided among them.'[43] Al-Zubayr bin al-'Awām agreed with him;[44] however, the opinion of 'Uthmān, 'Alī, Ṭalḥah and Ibn 'Umar was that of 'Umar.[45] Al-Ya'qūbī states that 'Alī opposed the division of the land and remarked to 'Umar: 'If you divide it today there will be nothing for those who will come after us. However, if we leave it in their hands [the inhabitants on the land] they will work it, and it will be for us and for those after us.'[46] Yaḥyā bin Ādam adds that 'Alī said to 'Umar: 'Let them [the inhabitants] be a resource for the Muslims.'[47] Moreover, Mu'ādh bin Jabal pointed out that Syria had not been divided.[48] 'Umar had various motives for making the land a religious endowment (*waqf*), including those relating to the interest of the state and those especially relevant to the Arabs as a conquering nation.

Abū Yūsuf narrates that he ['Umar] said: 'By Allah, no land will be divided up after me, so that it will become a burden for the Muslims later. If I divide the land of Iraq among its influential and powerful (*'ulūj*), the lands of Syria and Egypt according to the same, then who will defend its borders? And who among the people of Syria and Iraq will be left for the offspring and the widows in this land and others?' He explained that the fighters needed a stipend (*'aṭā'*): 'From where will it be given if I distribute the land and its inhabitants?'[49] Yaḥyā bin Ādam reports that 'Umar said: 'Were it not that the last of the people would be left with nothing for them, I would have divided into shares any village which Allah has granted conquest of, just as Khaybar was divided into shares.'[50] 'Alī also affirmed this viewpoint. Mu'ādh bin Jabal told the caliph: 'If you divide it [i.e. the land], the great returns will come into the hands of the people. Then they will die and that will go to a single man and woman [i.e. a few]. Then people will come after them, people who do not have any means in Islam, and they will not find anything. So consider a solution which will suffice for the first of them and the last of them.'[51] Thus, the caliph wanted the conquered land to be a stable financial resource for the Muslims and for the state during his reign and after it, so he did not distribute it. Furthermore, it appears that he feared dispute among the Muslims over the land. He said, 'I fear that if I divide it [the *sawād*], you will come into conflict with one another over its waters.'[52] Ibn al-Athīr says: 'He [ʿUmar] also feared strife (*fitnah*) among the Muslims.'[53] Likewise, ʿUmar noticed the Arabs' lack of familiarity with agriculture and the necessity for them to remain as a fighting military *ummah* [engaged in *jihād*], and the danger of their being dispersed across the lands, given their small number in comparison to the conquered peoples. ʿUmar had also relied on some of the Qur'ānic verses which pertained to the *fay'* (common property). One verse reads: 'What Allah has given [as spoils (*afā'a allāh*)] to His Messenger from the people of the inhabitants of the villages, it is for Allah and his Messenger, and for close relatives, for orphans, for the poor and for the *ibn al-sabīl* [traveller/stranded wayfarer/individual engaged in *jihād*]...'[54] Another reads: 'And [it is] for the poor and the emigrants who were driven out from their homes and their belongings...Those who were in the city and had entered the faith before them show love for those who migrated to them for refuge...' [i.e. the *muhājirūn* and the *anṣār*] and also mentioned are 'those who came [into the faith] after them'.[55]

b ʿUmar took advantage of the Sassanian and Byzantine systems of taxation, and he retained them with some necessary modifications. It is therefore instructive to briefly examine those systems:

i Until the sixth century AD, the Sassanians used to levy the land tax through the method of sharecropping (*muqāsamah*) [or proportional taxation], which involved taking a specified proportion of the yield. This proportion ranged between one-tenth and one-half depending on the method of irrigation, the distance of the land from the market places and the quality of the crop.[56] Then Qubādh, son of Firuz (d. 531AD), attempted to reform the tax system. He ordered a survey of the lands and a count of the date palms and (fruit) trees, as well as a head count of the people. However, he died and his son Khusrau Anushirvan (r. 531; d. 578AD) completed the census. The latter appointed a special committee to set the taxes, and they decided unanimously to levy the land tax – *al-kharāj* – on 'whatever sustains people and animals'; namely, wheat, barley, rice, grapes, clover and olives. They then imposed: 'one *dirham* on every *jarīb* of land sown with wheat and barley'[57]; 'eight *dirhams*; on every *jarīb* of land with grapes'; 'seven *dirhams* on every *jarīb* of land with clover (*riṭāb*)'; 'one *dirham* on every four Persian date palms' and 'the same amount on every six poor-quality date palms (*daqal*)'; and 'the same amount on every six olive trees'. They levied the tax 'only on date palms in (walled) gardens or growing together, not isolated trees [i.e. in the orchards, not the trees dispersed around]. They left [untaxed] everything other than these seven crops.'[58] Anushirvan ordered that the *kharāj* should be reduced on those crops which had been afflicted by some disaster by an amount commensurate with the damage.[59] Thus, Anushirvan annulled the sharecropping system and replaced it with the land tax – *kharāj* – based on the land survey. Then Anushirvan systemised the poll tax *al-jizyah*, putting it into four grades of twelve, eight, six, and four *dirhams* 'according to the [relative] wealth or poverty of the person'. He did not take the tax from those who were below the age of twenty or those above fifty and exempted the poor and the chronically ill.[60] Also, he did not impose it on all the social classes, but waived it for 'the notables, people of good families (*ahl al-buyūtāt*), great men, warriors, *herbadhs* (fire-priests), scribes (*kuttāb*) and those in the service of the king'.[61] This has prompted the belief that he imposed the tax on the common people in Iran and on the conquered peoples. It appears he ordered the *jizyah* to be collected in three instalments of one-third, every four months.[62]

Al-Ṭabarī and Ibn Miskawayh mention that 'Umar emulated the reforms of Khusrau Anushirvan, and that 'in Iraq in particular, he did not contradict the tax amounts put in place (*waḍāyi'*) by Khusrau for the *jirbān* [plural of *jarīb*] of land, the date palms, olive trees and people'. They mention some of 'Umar's changes which were that the caliph 'levied each *jarīb* of uncultivated land according to what it could bear similar to the amonut which he imposed on cultivated land. For every *jarīb* of land sown with wheat or barley, he increased one *qafīz* to two[63] and provided for the army from it', and 'just as the Sassanians had only imposed the *kharāj* on date palms in gardens or clumped together, not isolated trees and left [untaxed] everything other than that, so the people were secured and made prosperous in their means of subsistence'. 'Umar likewise 'excluded what Khusrau had excluded in people's means of subsistence'.[64] Yaḥyā bin Ādam mentions that the peasants (*fallāḥīn*) of the *sawād* who were Nabateans used to pay the *kharāj* to the people of Persia; when the Muslims appeared they imposed the *kharāj* on them.[65]

The *dihqāns* (Arabicised Farsi term: *dahāqīn* – village chiefs) during the Sassanian age used to carry out local administration; their essential task was to collect the taxes from the villages. After the Islamic conquest, they continued to collect and send the taxes to the provincial governors (*wulāt*, sg. *wālī*), just as they had done before.[66] 'Umar retained the local bureaus – *dīwāns* – in Iraq and Iran.[67] Al-Jahshiyārī mentions: 'The kings of Persia had two *dīwāns*: one of them was the *dīwān* (bureau) of land tax – *dīwān al-kharāj* – and the other the *dīwān* of expenditure – *dīwān al-nafaqāt*. Everything which was yielded went to the *dīwān* of the *kharāj* and everything which was expended on the army or otherwise was in the *dīwān al-nafaqāt*.'[68]

ii The land tax for the Byzantines was the most important of their financial resources. In 275AD, Diocletian introduced the system of sharecropping, but he did not delimit the percentage of the tax, but rather left that up to the circumstances. After the government had made an assessment of the necessary expenditure for the new year, it would issue orders for the amount which the people would have to pay. The cultivated lands were usually divided into taxation units. The basis of the unit was that each – known as a *jugum* – was enough to provide for the sustenance of one person – *caput*. Therefore, the taxation unit had two aspects: on the material side it represented an area of cultivated land and on the human side it was represented by the individual who cultivated the land. It is inferred from this that the land tax – *jugato* – and the poll tax – *capitatio* – were two parts of a single tax.

The method of levying was to apportion [the payment of] what the state required across the provinces, then divide the share of the provinces across the regions and then divide their share across the cities. The municipal councils decided what the neighbouring villages would pay. Finally, the village council – *majlis* – decided which taxation unit – *jugum* – would be levied for the specified village. In assessing the tax, the council took into account the fertility of the soil, the method of irrigation and the type of crops. The village was responsible jointly for paying the amount imposed on it. This meant that the responsibility for the insolvency of one of its individuals, or his flight from the village, fell on those remaining there.[69]

'Umar used these measures and left them unchanged in the main. Al-Suyūṭī reports: "'Umar bin al-Khaṭṭāb wrote to 'Amr bin al-'Āṣ ordering him to ask the *maqūqas* (Coptic chief) of Egypt: "From whence does its prosperity and its ruin come?" So 'Amr asked him.'[70] Ibn 'Abd al-Ḥakam says: 'When 'Amr bin al-'Āṣ had taken command for him ['Umar], he left its Copts to continue with the taxation of the Byzantines.'[71] Similarly, the village chiefs continued to collect the tax as before.[72] The changes which 'Umar implemented will be seen later in the detailed research into his systems.

c The change in local systems and their confusion, as well as the Arabs' inexperience in the financial sphere and the absence of Islamic legislation at that time (other than the division of booty), resulted in the systems of taxation during 'Umar's caliphate being unstable yet flexible at the same time, and we have much evidence to this effect. 'Umar gave the Bajīlah tribe one-quarter of the *sawād* because he had promised to give them 'one-quarter of what they conquered of the *sawād*' when he sent them to Iraq.[73] That quarter remained in their possession for about two years, then the caliph said to their chief, Jarīr bin 'Abdullah al-Bajlī: '"If I were not responsible for the division, then I would be for what you obtained, but I see that the people have multiplied so return this to them." So he did and they [the tribe] did and 'Umar recompensed them with eighty *dinars*.' It was said that: 'A woman from the Bajīlah said, "I am not a Muslim, so would you bear me on a female riding camel with a red riding-cloth on it and would you fill my hand with gold [in order that I should convert]?"' So 'Umar did that.[74] Al-Ya'qūbī mentions: 'Eighty million *dirhams* were yielded from the *kharāj* of the *sawād* in the first year and one hundred and twenty million *dirhams* in the coming [the second year].'[75]

The lack of any specific rules for the *jizyah* and the *kharāj* is clear from the fact that the caliph left their assessment in the *sawād*, for example, to 'Uthmān bin Ḥunayf and Ḥudhayfah bin al-Yamān. When they had completed their work, 'Umar said to them: 'Perhaps you two have burdened the land with [an amount] that it cannot bear!' 'Uthmān was in charge of the bank of the Euphrates, and Ḥudhayfah was in charge of the land beyond the Tigris from Jawkhī and what was watered by the Tigris in the east. 'Uthmān said: 'I have levied the land [an amount] within its capacity. If I had wished, I could have doubled it.' Ḥudhayfah said: 'I have imposed on it [an amount] which it can bear and in which there is a large surplus.'[76] In the peace agreements made with the inhabitants of Māh [i.e. the district of] Bahrādhān, Māh Dīnār [another term for Nahāwand], Isfahan, al-Rayy, Qūms, Jurjān (province in North Persia) and Azerbaijan, the *jizyah* was imposed according to capacity (*ṭāqah*).[77]

The rates of the taxes continued to remain unstable in Egypt. Al-Maqrīzī narrates that the chief of the Akhnā said to 'Amr bin al-'Āṣ: 'We have been informed that there is no *jizyah* on any one of us, so that we should pay it.' 'Amr told him: 'Rather, you are a resource [lit. storehouse] for us. If our demands are high for us, then we make it high for you and if they are light for us, then we make it light for you.'[78] The lack of specification of taxes in Egypt is clear from the fact that 'Amr bin al-'Āṣ raised 12 million *dinars* from it, then 'Abdullah bin Sa'd raised 14 million *dinars* during the caliphate of 'Uthmān. 'Uthmān said to 'Amr: 'The milk of the milk-camel has flowed abundantly in Egypt after you.' 'Amr responded: 'Because you have emaciated her offspring [i.e. he levied them heavily to the extent that he caused hardship for the local population].'[79]

Ibn 'Abd al-Ḥakam says that the levying of the *kharāj* in the Egyptian villages was 'by *ta'dīl* (reassessment survey). If the village was prosperous and its people became numerous, it was increased for them. If the people became few and it [the village] was ruined, it was decreased for them.'[80] 'Umar urged that the protected non-Muslims – *ahl al-dhimmah* – 'should not be charged beyond their capacity'.[81] Al-Awza'ī says: ''Umar wrote of the protected non-Muslims that those who do not have the capacity to pay the *jizyah* should have it waived for them and those who are [disabled and] unable to pay it [all] should be helped with it because we do not need them for a year or two.'[82] Therefore, we can describe the caliphate of 'Umar as being a very important experimental period. This is why the systems – *anẓimah* – were flexible and subject to modification, and this is the best evidence of the genius of this caliph.

d The result of conforming to local fiscal systems was that the *jizyah* and the *kharāj* continued to connote their ancient meanings. The *jizyah* was originally a tax which the slave paid to his master and the *kharāj* was a tax which the farmer paid the landowner. Then the two taxes became symbolic of the submission of one people to another by the right of conquest. It was natural that the inhabitants of the *sawād* continue to pay the (*kharāj*) taxes to the landowners (who were theoretically Muslims) and the *jizyah* on their heads to their new masters. Al-Ṭabarī narrates: 'They took from them [the people of the *sawād*] the *kharāj* of Khusrau and the *kharāj* of Khusrau was imposed on the *heads* of men according to the share [of the crop] and the wealth in their hands.'[83] The *faqīh (jurist)* Sharīk stated: 'The people of the *sawād* are slaves;' and: 'The *jizyah* which is taken from them is but the *kharāj*, like the *kharāj* which was taken from the slave and that is not abrogated by their conversion to Islam.'[84]

Therefore, both the *jizyah* and the *kharāj* were symbolic of the subjugation of non-Muslims to Muslims. As regards the view which holds that Islam exempted some from the *jizyah* but not from the *kharāj*, and that there was no humiliation (*ṣaghār*) in the *kharāj*, this appeared at a later time. The *faqīh* Yaḥyā bin Ādam acknowledges that there was humiliation (*ṣaghār*) in the *kharāj* and that it was a symbol of slavery when he says: 'It is reported that 'Umar prohibited anyone from purchasing anything of *kharāj* land or its slaves. He said: "It is not moot for the Muslim to permit humiliation (*ṣaghār*) to rest upon his neck."'[85] Abū 'Ubayd reports from Qabīṣah bin Dhu'ayb that 'Umar said: 'Whoever buys land with its *jizyah* has brought upon themselves what the *ahl al-dhimmah* have brought upon themselves of humiliation (*al-dhull*) and submission (*ṣaghār*).'[86] Therefore, the Muslim was not to pay the tax on the land. Rather, he was to pay the *'ushr* from its crops and this was for Allah and not for humans.[87] The lack of distinction between the two words *jizyah* and *kharāj* is evidence of the agreement between their two denoted meanings. Many references were transmitted in regard to the '*jizyah* on the land' and the '*kharāj* on the heads', or to the two words connoting a single meaning.[88]

Farmers in Iran, before the Muslim conquest, only paid the tax on the land to its owners. Therefore, in the agreements concluded with some of the Iranian regions after the conquest, we find reference to a single tax instead of the two as in Iraq. However, this was to the benefit of the nobility that they imposed this tax per person not on the land because the nobles had extensive land holdings.[89] In brief, the Muslim was exempted from the *jizyah* and the *kharāj* during the caliphate of 'Umar. If he owned land, he only paid the *'ushr* from it.[90] Similarly, the *kharāj* lands which the Arabs bought from the protected non-Muslims – *ahl al-dhimmah* – used to pay the *'ushr*.[91] If the protected non-Muslim converted to Islam, he paid the *'ushr* from his land. Al-Balādhurī says: 'There were lands by the Euphrates whose inhabitants had adopted Islam when the Muslims entered them, so they were made *'ushr* lands when they had been *kharāj* lands.'[92]

ʿUmar's system resulted in the (Arab) Muslims becoming a military *ummah* (community) whose task was war, whereas the non-Muslims had to work and offer money and crops. The caliph expressed this best himself when he said in an address to the Arabs: 'You are appointed as successors (*mustakhlafūn*) on the earth and conquerors of its people...There are only two communities who have come to be a community contrary to your religion: a community subjugated to Islam which pays the *jizyah* to you and you take the best part of their means of subsistence, their toil and the sweat of their brows. The burden is incumbent on them and you have the benefit...and [another] community whose hearts Allah has filled with fear...'[93] Von Kremer describes the situation: 'The people of the conquered states used to plow and sow and the Muslims used to harvest, and there was no work for them other than war and making raids.'[94] This viewpoint, although it seemingly resembles that of the Byzantines and the Sassanians, differs from it in one essential point, which is that neither race nor military supremacy were considered a basis for distinguishing between those who ruled and those who were ruled. However, religion was regarded as a criterion, and the conquered peoples could enjoy the distinctions of the conquerors when they embraced their religion.

As a consequence of ʿUmar's policy, the *kharāj* and the *jizyah* became '*fay*' (common property) of the Muslims, the fighters and their offspring, and those who come after them'. ʿUmar had made the distinction between *kharāj* land and other lands. He did not prevent the Arabs from buying land which was not *kharāj* land in the conquered territories since he made land grants (*qaṭīʿah/qaṭāʾiʿ* or *iqṭāʿ/iqṭāʿāt*) from the *ṣawāfī* (state lands) to others, such as Ṭalḥah, Jarīr bin ʿAbdullah, al-Rufayl bin ʿAmr, Abū Mayfarzadān and Abū Mūsā al-Ashʿarī.[95] Yaḥyā bin Ādam says that the caliph wrote to Saʿd: 'to grant land to Saʿīd bin Zayd. So he granted him land for the Banū Rufayl.' ʿUmar also ordered his governor for Basra to give a man land 'which was not *jizyah* land'.[96] Likewise, he allowed the Muslims to purchase the land of Ḥīrah because it was *ṣulḥ* land. Yaḥyā bin Ādam states: "ʿUmar bin al-Khaṭṭāb returned their lands to them (i.e. the people of Ḥīrah) and left it for them, making peace with them for the *kharāj*. He did not see any harm in its purchase.'[97] He gave the governor ʿIyāḍ bin Ghanm some of the land of al-Raqqah which had been surrendered by its owners to the Muslims 'for the *ʿushr*',[98] and the caliph also granted a man in Egypt 1,000 *feddans* of land.[99]

As well as this, ʿUmar permitted the revival of *mawāt* land (lit. 'dead land' or wasteland). He said: 'Whoever revives *mawāt* land that is not in the possession of a Muslim or under contract, it belongs to him.' Yaḥyā bin Ādam relates: 'he [ʿUmar] wrote...to the people: "Whoever revives *mawāt* [land], he has the most right to it."'[100] Thus, there is no truth to Van Vloten's assertion that the Arabs 'were forbidden to own land during the caliphate of ʿUmar';[101] or to Von Barsham's contention that ʿUmar promulgated a land restriction and distinction between the Arabs and others, which did not permit them to own land outside of the Arabian Peninsula.[102]

On the other hand, ʿUmar did not encourage the Arabs and perhaps *did* prohibit them from buying *kharāj* land because it was a financial resource for all the Muslims.[103] Yaḥyā bin Ādam reports: "ʿUmar prohibited the buying of the land of the *ahl al-dhimmah* and their slaves;' and: "ʿUmar bin al-Khaṭṭāb said, "Do not purchase any of the immovable property (*ʿaqār*) of the *ahl al-dhimmah* or their lands."'[104] Moreover, he did not encourage the army to become occupied in agriculture. His herald announced in the midst of the soldiers in Egypt: 'Your stipend still stands and provision for your dependants is flowing, so do not sow.'[105] Despite this, Al-Balādhurī and Abū ʿUbayd mention that he allowed someone (*shakhṣ*) to cultivate in Basra.[106]

The classification of lands during the caliphate of ʿUmar

Conquered lands were classified into three categories: *ṣawāfī* lands; *ṣulḥ* lands; and lands of the protected non-Muslims – *ahl al-dhimmah*:

1 *Ṣawāfī* land. This was special land set aside for the caliph; or in other words, it was the property of the state. It was called the *ṣawāfī* of the *imām* (*ṣawāfī al-imām*);[107] and he enumerated ten types of *ṣawāfī* land in this category:[108] i) the lands of Khusrau; ii) lands of other members of the Persian royal family; iii) postal waystations and postal roads; iv) fire temples (lit. 'fire houses' – *buyūt al-nīrān*);[109] v) marshlands (*ājām*); vi) lands of those killed in the war; vii) wetlands (*maghāyiḍ al-māʾ*) or swamps (*mustanqaʿāt*), such as the Baṭīḥah in southern Iraq; viii) the lands of those inhabitants who fled during the period of war; ix) all land that Khusrau had designated state land – *ṣawāfī*; and x) walls (*arjāʾ*). The last category is mentioned by

Ibn al-Athīr and may be a corruption of the Arabic word *arḥā'*, meaning *mills*.[110] Al-Balādhurī mentions that the revenue of the *ṣawāfī* reached 7 million *dirhams* annually.[111] Yaḥyā bin Ādam concurs with him in one of his narrations,[112] whereas in another he narrates from 'a learned Kūfan man' that it had reached 4 million *dirhams*.[113]

The *ṣawāfī* in Syria were specified by Ibn 'Asākir: 'When Allah defeated Rome (i.e. the Byzantines), the petrarchs fled from those plantations which had been in their possession. As for the land of the Rome (i.e. Byzantium) and those among them who were killed in the battles were linked...these fields and villages became state land – *ṣawāfī* – for the Muslims.'[114] Some of the *ṣawāfī* were divided up and granted as land grants to the senior Companions[115] and, at that time, only *'ushr* was paid on them.[116] The remainder was dispersed through temporary sharecropping contracts (*muzāra'ah*) and Ibn 'Asākir said that the caliph 'accepts it [i.e. the sharecropping system] just as the man accepts his farm'.[117] Al-Iṣṭakhrī speaks about 'sharecropping (*muqāsamāt*) in villages which became the property of the treasury – *bayt al-māl* – and so the people farmed on them',[118] and these villages were among the *ṣawāfī*.

2 *Ṣulḥ* land. These were lands whose owners had made peace terms with the Muslims to pay them a single tax while they retained ownership of their lands.[119] The percentage of lands in this category is minute. The *ṣulḥ* lands in the *sawād* were the lands of Ḥīrah, Bāniqyā (one of the districts of Kūfah), and Alīs or al-Layth (in the region of Iraq in the district of al-Bādiyah near al-Anbār).[120] The tax was communal and imposed on the inhabitants of the region, then distributed among them on the individuals or per head. In Ḥīrah, Khālid bin al-Walīd imposed a tax on the inhabitants of 80,000 *dirhams* (weight of fifty *dawānīq* [where a *dāniq* is variably a unit of weight as well as square measure, but is also a coin valued at one-sixth of a *dirham*]) annually, and each indivdual's share was fourteen *dirhams*.[121]

3 Lands of the protected non-Muslims (*ahl al-dhimmah*). This was the *kharāj* land, and included in it were the remaining lands and public lands.

We will be content here to mention 'Umar's systemisation of these lands in Iraq, Greater Syria and Egypt.

Systemisations – *al-tanẓimāt* – in Iraq (the *sawād*)

'Umar bin al-Khaṭṭāb appointed two with experience from the Companions – 'Uthmān bin Ḥunayf and Ḥudhayfah bin al-Yamān, to survey the lands of the *sawād*, and conduct a census of its inhabitants in order to assess the *kharāj* and the *jizyah*. He sent 'Uthmān to the lands located west of the Tigris and Ḥudhayfah to the lands beyond that,[122] 'and he ordered them both not to burden anyone beyond his capacity'.[123] The two began to survey the land, turning to help from the inhabitants. Abū Yūsuf describes their degree of success in this saying: "'Uthmān was knowledgable in the *kharāj* so he surveyed it [his region] like a Persian silk brocade (*dībāj*) [i.e. in a very precise fashion]. As for Ḥudhayfah, the people of Jawkhī (a region east of the Tigris) were cunning and they played with him in his survey.'[124] After finishing the work of surveying, they levied the *kharāj* 'on the lands which were cultivable (i.e. with cultivation on them)'.[125] They disregarded the lands which were not cultivable, and these were 'mountainous regions, foothills, hills, elevations, thickets and marsh lands (*ājām*), salt lands (*sibākh*), highways, stables, river waterways, locations of cities and villages, and other lands in which there is no arable land'.[126] The *kharāj* was imposed on everyone who owned land: whether male, female, young boy, self-emancipated slave/freedman who had purchased his freedom (*mukātab*) or slave, and none was excluded.[127] The amount paid varied in accordance with the various crops. However, the sources prevent us from reaching any definitive conclusions in this area. Imposed was 'one *qafīz* of wheat (*ḥinṭah*) or one *qafīz* of barley and one *dirham* on every *jarīb* of cultivated or uncultivated land which was reached by water'.[128] Al-Ya'qubī specifies that amount for the region of 'Uthmān bin Ḥunayf, and terms it the land of Kūfah. It appears that the caliph wrote afterwards to Abū Mūsā al-Ash'arī to impose the same tax on the inhabitants of Basra as *kharāj*.[129]

As for the remaining lands, four *dirhams* were imposed on every *jarīb* of wheat and two *dirhams* on every *jarīb* of barley.[130] The difference between the two taxes is only outward, as the price of a *qafīz* of wheat at that time was equivalent to three *dirhams*,[131] and the price of a *qafīz* of barley equalled one *dirham*. Perhaps this point explains to us the conflicting narrations about the *kharāj* on wheat and barley. Hence, we find Al-Balādhurī saying in one of his narrations that Ḥudhayfah and 'Uthmān 'imposed on each *jarīb* one *qafīz* and one *dirham*',[132] but he says elsewhere (and Ibn Ḥawqal agrees with him) that the tax was four *dirhams* on every *jarīb* of wheat and two *dirhams* on every *jarīb* of barley.[133] However, we are unsure if these taxes were imposed on both cultivated or uncultivated lands alike; and, perhaps, there was some differentiation between the two. Al-Balādhurī states in one of his narrations that 'one *dirham* was imposed on every *jarīb* which had the capacity to be cultivated'.[134] However, this distinction is not understood from other sources.

The *kharāj* on other crops was as follows: ten *dirhams* was levied on every *jarīb* of grape vines. The majority of sources agree that a single tax was imposed on date palms[135] at a rate of eight *dirhams*.[136] One *dirham* was levied on Persian date palms and one *dirham* on two low-quality *daql* date palms.[137] Abū Yūsuf clarifies that nothing was imposed on those crops which were cultivated under date palms,[138] just as al-Balādhurī mentions that nothing was levied on crops cultivated under the grape vines.[139] Six *dirhams* were imposed on every *jarīb* of sugar cane (as mentioned by Abū Yūsuf and al-Balādhurī); five *dirhams* on every *jarīb* of sesame;[140] five *dirhams* on every *jarīb* of cotton;[141] and – according to most of the narrations – five *dirhams* on every *jarīb* of trefoil (*ruṭab*)[142] and three *dirhams* on every *jarīb* of green vegetables 'from the summer crop'.[143] In addition, Abū 'Ubayd mentions that twelve *dirhams* were imposed on every *jarīb* of olives.[144]

'Umar bin al-Khaṭṭāb imposed personal taxes on the protected non-Muslims (the *ahl al-dhimmah*) and put them into classes, taking from each class according to its ability to pay. It seems that he arrived at this systemisation gradually. Perhaps he had initially treated the people equally, as is understood from the narration of Abū 'Ubayd: 'He levied on their heads...fourteen *dirhams* every year.'[145] He may have proceeded gradually after that in dividing the people into two classes, as is undertood from al-Sha'bī's statement: 'He imposed one *dirham* on the men in one month, and two *dirhams* in another month.'[146] What is important is that the people were divided finally into three classes: the wealthy paid forty-eight *dirhams*; the middle class paid twenty-four *dirhams*; and the poor paid twelve *dirhams*.[147] The caliph said: 'One *dirham* a month does not render a man destitute.'[148] The basis for the difference between the people was as Al-Balādhurī narrates: 'forty-eight *dirhams* on each man of the *dihqāns* who ride coarse-bred work horses and wear gold; twenty-four *dirhams* per *annum* on the head of each of those merchants among them of average means; and, twelve *dirhams* on every tiller of the land (*akarah*) and [whomever else among] the rest of them.'[149] The necks of the protected non-Muslims (*ahl al-dhimmah*) were sealed with lead, which was to distinguish them and be a personal instrument of certificate.[150] Al-Balādhurī says: "Uthmān bin Ḥunayf sealed the necks[151] of five-hundred-thousand unbelievers (*ʿilj*);'[152] while Ibn Ḥawqal estimates the number of those sealed to be 500,000.[153] He excluded women and 'boys (*ṣibyān*)',[154] and likewise 'those with chronic illness'.[155]

In addition to this, the protected non-Muslims were expected to provide hospitality (*ḍiyāfah*) to 'those Muslims who passed their way'.[156] The period of hospitality was three days according to one narration,[157] but the more likely is a second narration which relates that the caliph 'made the [condition of] hospitality on the inhabitants of the *sawād* one day and one night, and that he [i.e. the Muslim] should not exceed this of what these had of food or fodder'.'[158] Ḥārithah bin Muḍarrab reads to us ʿUmar's document: 'We have made the hospitality on the people of the *sawād* one day and one night. If he [the guest or messenger] is kept detained because of rain or sickness, he shall spend from his own wealth.'[159] This is supported by al-Aḥnaf bin Qays, who also adds: 'If a man of the Muslims is killed on their land then the blood money (*diyah*) is incumbent on them.'[160]

Systemisation in the Jazīrah *(the northern part of Iraq)*

The *jizyah* was imposed on al-Raqqah in cash and in kind. Al-Balādhurī mentions that the governor ʿIyāḍ bin Ghanm 'imposed one *dinar* on every man among them for every year', and likewise 'a number of *qafīz* of wheat and some oil, vinegar and honey'. He exempted 'women and boys (i.e., children)',[161] and imposed the same taxes on Qarqīsiyā. He concluded the major *ṣulḥ* agreement with al-Ruhā (also Edessa). In accordance with this, ʿIyāḍ stipulated in the treaty which he drew up for them that each man of this city 'shall pay one *dinar* and two *mudd* of wheat for every man...and you must guide the lost and repair the bridges'.[162] The *ṣulḥ* agreement of al-Ruhā became a model for the agreements with all the districts of the Jazīrah. Al-Balādhurī says: 'The people of the Jazīrah entered into that which had been entered by the people of al-Ruhā.'[163] Therefore, it appears that the Muslims initially imposed a cash *jizyah*, together with some foodstuffs for sustenance, and the caliph had fixed the tax, as al-Balādhurī mentions, by imposing 'two *mudd* of wheat, two *qisṭ* [a measure of weight and volume considered to be one-half of a *ṣāʿ*, or between 1.4 and 1.7 litres or between 1 and 1.6 kilogrammes] of oil and two *qisṭ* of vinegar on every person along with his *jizyah*'.[164] We can attribute the narration which appears in Abū Yūsuf to this period since he says that ʿIyāḍ levied 'one *dinar*, two *mudd* of wheat, two *qisṭ* of oil and two *qisṭ* of vinegar on every head and made them one class (*ṭabaqah wāḥidah*)'.[165] This is a narration which reminds us of the first stage of the sytemisation of the *jizyah* in the *sawād*.

However, it appears that the caliph resystematised the *jizyah* on more stable bases. The difficulty of supplying the conquering army had ceased after they established a firm foothold in the (lands of) conquest. Similarly, the provision of foodstuffs had an inevitable influence on food prices and led to their increase. There is evidence that the caliph observed the overburdening of the people in levying wheat, vinegar and oil, and this was among that which impelled him to re-examine the issue. Al-Balādhurī narrates from Maymūn bin Mahrān: 'He ['Umar] took the oil, vinegar and crops for the ease of the Muslims in the Jazīrah for a while, then he relieved them of some of it and thereby it was reduced to forty-eight *dirhams* out of 'Umar's concern for the people.'[166] This means that the caliph rendered the *jizyah* payable in cash only and that he applied in the Jazīrah what had been previously applied in the *sawād*. Since some of the regions of the Jazīrah used to deal in the Persian *dirham* and some others in the Byzantine *dinar*, as a result of some of them surrendering to the Persian and others to the Byzantines, we find mention of the *jizyah* in the *dinar* sometimes and in the *dirham* at other times (the exchange rate at that time was equivalent to 1:12). Hence, al-Balādhurī states that the *jizyah* for each person in Ra's al-'Ayn was four *dinars* annually.[167] This gradualism in the systemisation, together with the existence of two types of currency, may have led to some confusion on the part of certain researchers on the subject, or so it seems.[168]

Systemisations – tanẓīmāt – *in Greater Syria* (bilād al-shām)

The narrations on this subject are confused due to the lack of precision in the historicism of the *fuqahā'*, and due also to the lack of distinction between Syria and Damascus, as well as the actual nature or variability of some of the measures. In the city of Damascus, one *dinar* and a *jarīb* of wheat (fixed weight) was levied on each *jarīb* of land, and levied on each person, as well as was 'vinegar and oil for the sustenance of the Muslims'.[169] Al-Ṭabarī explains that a part of the region of Damascus had made terms (in a *ṣulḥ*) for 'one *dinar* and crops for every *jarīb* whether it was easy for them or not', whereas what was levied on the other part was according to the circumstances and to capacity.[170] In the city of Homs, the taxes which were imposed were the same as those in the city of Damascus,[171] just as the region of Homs was similar to the region of Damascus. So a sector of it paid fixed taxes and a sector paid according to ability.[172] The region of al-Urdunn (Jordan) and the region of Qinnasrīn[173] paid the same as the region of Damascus. The inhabitants of Busra agreed to peace terms to 'pay one *dinar* and one *jarīb* of wheat for each male adult'. Adhruʿāt,[174] Antioch,[175] Manbaj (also Manbej)[176] and Iliyā'[177] followed suit. The inhabitants of al-Lādhqiyīah (i.e. Latakia) 'were bound to a [fixed rate of] *kharāj* which they would pay, whether they were few or many'.[178] Abū ʿUbaydah was content to take the *jizyah* from the Samaritan Jews in Palestine and Jordan (al-Urdunn); and exempted them from the *kharāj* because they were the guides and informants of the Muslims.[179]

From what we have mentioned above, we may notice that the prevailing method in Syria was to impose the *dinar* on each person and a *jarīb* of wheat on each *jarīb* of land. Similarly, we perceive the influence of the lack of accurate distinction between the *jizyah* and the *kharāj*, just as was the case during the era of the Byzantines when the two were considered as two parts of one tax. The protected non-Muslims – *ahl al-dhimmah* – pledged to the Muslims to guide the lost, build arched bridges [over rivers] along roads from their own wealth and to provide hospitality to 'each Muslim wayfarer according to the average of what we find [i.e. according to what one typically consumes] to provide such [board] for three days'.[180] The people of Syria complained to the caliph on the occasion of one of his visits to them: 'Our guests impose on us a burden more than we can bear. They cost us chickens and sheep.' He said: 'Only feed them that which you are eating.'[181] The Muslims exempted women and children from the *jizyah*.[182] The caliph took the lands of the fleeing Byzantine petrarchs and the lands of the war dead and made them *ṣawāfī*. Some of these lands were in Damascus, Abū Qubays, al-Balqā' and near Homs.[183]

Systemisation in Egypt

The narrations conflict over the systemisation of taxes in Egypt due to the confusion of the narrators over the reports of the conquest of Egypt. They confuse the city of Miṣr near the fortress of Bāb al-Yūn and the country of Egypt (Arabic, *Miṣr*), as well as confusing the first *ṣulḥ* agreement of Alexandria and the military retaking of it after its revolt. We should not forget that the first writing we have about the conquest of Egypt [of Arab sources] was written two centuries after that event.[184]

There were two *ṣulḥ* agreements between the Muslims and the Egyptians. One of them was temporary, and this was the *ṣulḥ* for the surrender of the fortress of Bāb al-Yūn and the city of Miṣr on 9 April 641AD.[185] In accordance with this, a small and temporary *jizyah* was imposed, which was to pay each soldier from the Arab armies one *dinar* and one *kiswah* (a woollen *jubbah*, burnus hooded cloak, turban and kaftan).[186] The second and more important agreement was the *ṣulḥ* of Alexandria which applied to Egypt. Here we will mention the narrations about it.

Ḥannā al-Nīqūsī (the Nicosian) mentions that the *jizyah* was assessed in *dinars* for every man, and the very old and young were exempted from it. This is in addition to some possessions on the land and landed properties.[187] Abū Ṣāliḥ al-Armanī (the Armenian) shows that 'Amr bin al-'Āṣ imposed an annual *jizyah* which equalled twenty-six and two-thirds *dirhams*, and that he used to impose two *dinars* and three *arādib* (*ardabb*) of wheat on the affluent. The revenue from that *jizyah* reached 12 million *dinars*, excluding what was imposed on the Jews of Egypt.[188] Al-Maqrīzī[189] and al-Suyūṭī[190] mention that the *jizyah* was two *dinars* for every man and did not increase. Al-Balādhurī narrates on the authority of 'Abdullah bin 'Amr bin al-'Āṣ that 'Amr bin al-'Āṣ 'levied two *dinars* for the *jizyah* on every adult male'.[191]

If we note that Ḥannā al-Nīqūsī and Abū Ṣāliḥ al-Armanī mean the *jizyah* and the *kharāj*, and we leave aside the tax on the land, it is clear to us from all the sources that 'Umar set the amount of the *jizyah* at two *dinars* for every man annually, and exempted the poor,[192] women, juvenile boys and the elderly from it.[193] Al-Maqrīzī says that the caliph commanded that 'they should not impose the *jizyah* except on those who had grown beards [i.e. had attained to the age of maturity] and that they should not impose it on women and children'.[194] The amount of the *kharāj* was not specified. Al-Maqrīzī mentions that 'Amr bin al-'Āṣ imposed – in addition to the *jizyah* – 'the provisioning of (*arzāq*) the Muslims',[195] and Ibn 'Abd al-Ḥakam clarifies that every farmer was 'obligated to the extent of the land and crops'; that is, according to his capacity.[196] Al-Maqrīzī and al-Suyūṭī explain the situation, saying: 'Their levying [of the *kharāj*] was by *ta'dīl* (cadastral) survey. If the village prospered and its inhabitants became many, it was increased for them. If its inhabitants became few and it [i.e. the village] went to ruin, it was decreased for them.' This was precisely the same method as the Byzantines: '['Amr bin al-'Āṣ] specified for the Copts [of Egypt] the levy of Rome [i.e. Byzantium].'[197] Thus, the Muslims used to assess the levy every year, taking into consideration the need of the state and the condition of the land, then distributing that among the villages.

Ibn 'Abd al-Ḥakam has described the method of levying. He tells us that 'The *gharāfasū* and *māzūt*[198] of every village' used to collect annually and set up a committee for assessment, which decided what each village would pay from the total levy, taking into account 'the village's ability to bear [this] and the capacity of its farms'. Then the nobles (*ashrāf*) of the village met to distribute what their village had been allotted to its individuals, each according to his capacity, after they specified a part of the revenue of the village for common/public interests (such as the expenditure on churches and baths), and for the hospitality of Muslims passing through and the governor or his men (if they happened through the area). He says:

> Then each village returned with their share and they collected their share and the *kharāj* for every village and the cultivated land in it. They began by taking *feddans* from the land for their churches, baths and properties from among the total land. Then the requisite quantities for the hospitality for the Muslims and the board and lodgings for the ruler were taken from it. When they finished, they considered what craftsmen and labourers there were in the village and divided it among them according to their ability. If there were a group of emigres (*jāliyah*) in it, they divided it among them according to their ability. Subsequently they considered what remained of the *kharāj* and divided it among them according to the quantity of the land. They apportioned this among those from among them who wanted to cultivate according to their capacity. If one of them was unable and complained of weakness in cultivating his land, they distributed what he was unable to cultivate to those who were able. If there were from among them someone who wanted more, he was given what the weak people were unable to cultivate. If any of the tax remained, they divided that over their number and their share was in *qirāṭs* of the *dinar,* twenty-four *qirāṭs* (pl. *qarārīṭ*; sg. *qirāṭ*: a measure of area as well as weight for silver and gold – in modern parlance; *karat*). They divided that over the land (1 *feddan* = 24 *qirāṭs* using accurate division).[199]

There are references to the rate of the *kharāj* which the individual paid. However, it should not be inferred from these that the *kharāj* tax was fixed. It indicates what the levy was on each individual in some years after following the method which I have previously explained; therefore, it differs widely in amount. Al-Balādhurī says that ʻAmr bin al-ʻĀṣ ʻimposed on every owner of land in addition to two *dinars,* three *arādibb* (sg. *ardabb*; also *ardeb*) of wheat, two *qisṭ* of honey, two *qisṭ* of vinegar as provision for the Muslims, which was deposited in the supply depot (*dār al-rizq*)'. It seems that this was in the year following the conquest.[200] Ibn ʻAbd al-Ḥakam mentions that ʻhalf an *ardabb* of wheat and two *waybah* [i.e. 1/3 of an *ardabb*] of barley' were imposed on every *feddan.*[201] It appears that the burden of taxes was lightened in Egypt after the Arab conquest,[202] such that the caliph considered what ʻAmr collected to be meagre in comparison with what the Byzantines collected. Correspondence passed between him and his governor, and the caliph wrote in his letter: ʻI do not accept from you

['Amr] less than that which has been taken (from Egypt) of the *kharāj*.'[203] He censured him for the delay in sending the *kharāj*. 'Amr replied that the increase was harmful and that the postponing of the *kharāj* was in response to the wish of the farmers to delay the collection until the crops had ripened: 'So, I sought council of the Muslims who held that kindness towards them [i.e., the Copts] was preferable to being excessive with them and to proceed in such a way when we cannot do without them [and their cultivation of the land].'[204] The caliph was convinced by his governor of the soundness of his view, and he commended his policy. We do not know the revenue of Egypt exactly. Most of the historians have mentioned that the *kharāj* (revenue) of Egypt reached 12 million *dinars* during the governorship of 'Amr.[205] However, this was the revenue of the *jizyah* alone, as Ibn Ḥawqal says,[206] and al-Maqrīzī supports him, asserting: 'This is what 'Amr collected and it was only on the heads, apart from the *kharāj*.'[207]

Taxes on trade (*ḍarā'ib al-tijārah*)

The imposition of these taxes was a result of the necessities of the economic conditions. Yaḥyā bin Ādam narrates that Abū Mūsā al-Ash'arī (the governor of Iraq) informed the caliph that when the Muslim merchants entered the territory of non-believers (*dār al-ḥarb*, lit. 'the house of war') the *'ushr* was taken from them,[208] so the caliph ordered his governor to take the same as that from their merchants. Thus, the caliph followed traditions of precedent in commercial taxes. This is supported by a narration in Abū 'Ubayd's book to the effect that Mālik bin Anas asked Ibn Shihāb al-Zuhrī: 'Why did 'Umar take the *'ushr* from the *ahl al-dhimmah*?' (perhaps meaning here the *ahl al-ḥarb*; i.e. the people of the *dār al-ḥarb*). He replied: 'It was taken from them in the *jāhilīyah* (i.e. the so-called pre-Islamic 'era of ignorance'), so he left this in place...'[209] Then the caliph took 'one-half of the *'ushr* from the merchants of the *ahl al-dhimmah* and one-quarter of the *'ushr* from the merchants of the Muslims [who undertook their trade in the lands of the *dār al-ḥarb*]' for their trade.[210]

The Christians of the Banū Taghlib were treated specially, Ziyād bin Ḥudayr says: "Umar ordered me to take the *'ushr* from the Banū Taghlib.'[211] A special rule was followed in the treatment of the merchants from *dār al-ḥarb*, who remained in Muslim lands. Yaḥyā bin Ādam reports that Ziyād bin Ḥudayr said: 'He wrote to 'Umar about people from the *ahl al-ḥarb* who entered the "land of peace" (i.e. *dār al-salām*, lit. 'the house of peace' in contradistinction to *dār al-ḥarb*) and then remained. He said, "So

ʿUmar wrote to me: If they stay six months, take the *ʿushr* from them; and, if they stay a year, take half of the *ʿushr* from them."'[212] Perhaps the caliph intended thereby to invite these people to the faith of Islam, or to strengthen trade and commercial activity. It appears that the caliph did not impose a minimum limit on commercial wealth upon which the tax could be taken,[213] and the tax was taken once a year.[214]

The tax system in the Umayyad era

Introduction

ʿUmar bin al-Khaṭṭāb had imposed a fiscal system based on circumstance and need, in which he had taken into consideration the welfare of the conquered peoples to some extent and recommended kind treatment of them; and, hence, he was characterised as just.[215] Because of this system, the *jizyah* and the *kharāj* became the backbone of the central treasury. Therefore, its perpetuation without any change presumes that the protected non-Muslims of the *ahl al-dhimmah* remained as they were, paying the *jizyah* and the *kharāj*, and the Arabs remained a community engaged in war. However, circumstances did not endure, and the situation changed with the conversion to Islam by a portion of the *ahl al-dhimmah*. This meant that they were exempt from the *jizyah* and the *kharāj*. Also, with the Arabs' purchase of *kharāj* lands, they came to pay the *ʿushr* on them in lieu of the *kharāj*. There was an increase in the Umayyad age in the state's need for monies to control the internal situation, and for spending on the royal court's needs within a developing and cultured society in Damascus, as well as for the extensive administrative machine and its burgeoning costs. Thus, the new circumstance demanded a change in ʿUmar's system in accordance with the new situation. This is what the Umayyads attempted to do in the form of temporary measures, or in the form of a fundamental re-examination, as ʿUmar bin ʿAbd al-ʿAzīz did and those who followed his example, such as Naṣr bin Sayyār.[216]

There was a new factor in policies, which was the Umayyad's attention to custom (*ʿurf*) in their policies, whether such was Arab or local, since they encouraged Arab traditions and revived local customs in many cases. One of the most important manifestations of inherited local custom was that which considered conquered lands and its people to be the property of the conquerors who could deal with them according to need.[217] This viewpoint was extant in the age of the Rāshidūn caiphs. ʿUmar had written to Abū ʿUbaydah about the *ahl al-dhimmah*: 'Those are [from whose toil] the

Muslims will eat as long as they are alive. When we die and they die, our children will eat [from the labours of] their children forever.'[218] 'Uthmān's governor, Sa'īd bin al-'Āṣ, said: 'The *sawād* is the garden (*bustān*) of [the tribe of] Quraysh. We take what we want, and we leave what we want.'[219] 'Amr bin al-'Āṣ considered Egypt to be a storehouse/treasury (*khizānah*) for the Muslims.

This viewpoint was not limited to the Umayyads. Rather, it was the view of the Arab tribes as well. Al-Ṭabarī tells us about the protest of the Kūfans against al-Mukhtār, saying:

> You have betaken our *mawālī* [i.e. our non-Arab client charges who entered into Islam] and they are a *fay'* granted to us by Allah and all these lands. We manumitted them hoping for reward, recompense and gratitude for that. However, you were not satisfied with this, even to the extent that you made them our partners to our *fay'*.[220]

Ibn 'Abd al-Ḥakam relates: 'Abū Salamah bin 'Abd al-Raḥmān left heading to Alexandria by boat. He needed a man to row it, so he compelled a man from the Copts [to do this]. He talked about this saying, "They [the Copts] are in the status of slaves (*fī manzilat al-'abīd*) if we need them."'[221] This view also gained currency among some of the *fuqahā'*. Al-Ṭabarī mentions a jurist named Sharīk, who used to say: 'The people of the *sawād* are slaves (*ariqqā'*);' and 'the *jizyah* which is taken from them is but the *kharāj*, just like the *kharāj* which is taken from the [ordinary] person (lit. *al-'abd*),[222] and this is not waived for them upon their [conversion to] Islam'.[223] Perhaps the Umayyads went further than the Rāshidūn in this view due to their support for Arab policy, their following of the principle of decentralisation in administration and their expansion of the authority of the governors, in addition to their increasing needs.

On the other hand, we must note that the bias of historians against the Umayyads and their disregard for much of the Umayyads' reform, restoration and building during their era made them focus their attention on the atypical cases. This affords the researcher a particular impression of this period, and this is what can be observed from some of the extraordinary expressions. For example, Mu'āwiyah due to financial need attempted to increase the levy by a *qirāṭ* on every Copt, but his governor refused to do that, out of respect for familiar custom. It is narrated: 'Mu'āwiyah bin Abī Sufyān wrote to Wardān: "Increase [the levy by] one *qirāṭ* on every man among them." Wardān wrote to Mu'āwiyah: "How can you impose an increase on them when in their pact/covenant (*'ahd*) stipulates that there shall be no increase upon them?"'[224] Al-Maqrīzī informs us that Hishām bin

'Abd al-Malik 'wrote to Egypt to act in accordance with the pact/covenant (*'ahd*) with the Christians in regard to their profits – *'awāyid* – and what they possess'.[225] It can be understood from this that for the *'awāyid* – customary profits – there was protection of the taxpayer against any excess or unjust oppression. There is no need for us to emphasise the importance of the reforms which 'Umar bin 'Abd al-'Azīz introduced in various parts of the dominion, the influence of which persisted posthumously after him, despite the attempt by some of his successors to ignore these. We perceive their influence strongly in the reforms of Naṣr bin Sayyār in Khurāsān, and they had become the basis for the systemisation of the *jizyah* and the *kharāj*. This reformist trend is clear in the address of Yazīd III when he attained to rule: 'I do not burden those who pay your *jizyah* with that which will compel them to abandon their lands and cut off their descendants.'[226]

Similarly, the paucity of information about the Umayyad age and the decentralised administrative system constrains and confuses the researcher wanting to distinguish the influence of the caliphs from that of their governors in these inconsistencies. The broad authority of the governors used to encourage them to act recklessly and to needlessly squander the wealth of the state and its subjects.[227] This is why often the efforts of some of the caliphs for reform were brought to no avail by the greedy aspirations of governors for wealth and their various machinations.[228] 'Umar bin 'Abd al-'Azīz was explicit that the injustice in Iraq was a result of 'a wicked custom practised against them [the Iraqis] by agents of evil'.[229] Al-Ya'qūbī informs us that al-Jarrāḥ, the governor of Khurāsān for 'Umar bin 'Abd al-'Azīz, persisted in his ways until he was removed by the caliph.[230] Moreover, he mentions that Ḥanẓalah bin Ṣafwān, the governor of Egypt for Hishām 'Abd al-Malik, increased the *kharāj* and became stricter in his levying, against the recommendations of the caliph.[231] Furthermore, the role of the *dihqāns* in hindering every reform in Khurāsān is shown clearly by al-Ṭabarī.[232]

There is another issue which bears indicating, and this is the fact that the historians and the *fuqahā'* regarded the system of 'Umar bin al-Khaṭṭāb as a measure for gauging their own judgements about the Umayyads. However, it was the system as they understood it in its idealised form, as had been drawn from the imagination of later generations and which differed from the system which we have described. They neglected its development and forgot an important point to which we have referred; namely, that the Umayyads restored many of the local administrative traditions which 'Umar bin al-Khaṭṭāb had ignored or neglected and of which our information is still meagre. The historians had considered these traditions, such as the gifts of *Nawrūz* and *Mihrajān*, to be unbearable misdeeds. Furthermore, the contraventions which the historians recorded against the Umayyads in taxation were only a record of what they considered to have been contraventions of the system of ʿUmar bin al-Khaṭṭāb. (There is no need here to discuss Van Vloten because he did not understand the foundations of the Umayyad measures, just as he went to extremes in his opinions in a way unsupported by academic research.)

All that I would confirm is that the Umayyad system was a continuation of the system of the Rāshidūn caliphs on the one hand, and a necessary result of it under the circumstances in the midst of which it found itself. Thus, it is a perpetuation of the system of the Rāshidūn caliphs, and it served as the precursor to the system of the ʿAbbāsids, so there was no leap nor break [between them]. The system of ʿUmar and the local differences were responsible for the variations in the policy of the Umayyads in different provinces. Therefore, the situation in each region must be studied separately in order to understand the Umayyad fiscal system. We will restrict ourselves to the most important regions, namely: Iraq, Greater Syria, Egypt and Khurāsān.

Taxes in Iraq and Greater Syria (bilād al-shām)

In Iraq, the collection of the *kharāj* continued to be undertaken by the *dihqāns* due to their financial expertise and ability. Ziyād bin Abīhi used to say: 'There should be a book on the *kharāj* from the chiefs of the Persians (or non-Arabs) who are knowledgable in matters of the *kharāj*.'[233] It appears that the lack of maturity of the concept of state among the Arab tribes and the difficulty in accounting for its individuals in financial matters were among the sum of motives for this. This is clear from ʿUbayd Allah bin Ziyād's complaint:

> If I employ the Arab, he will cut off [not collect] the *kharāj*. Then if I fine his clan or demand it [the *kharāj*], I will enrage them. If I leave him, I leave the wealth of Allah when I know its place. I found the *dihqāns* more knowledgeable about levying, superior in trustworthiness and more adept in exacting it than you, although I have made you trustees over them so that they will not oppress anyone.[234]

The *dihqāns* in Iraq rushed to embrace Islam and ally themselves with the Arabs. Hence, they maintained their local influence and gathered riches for themselves through tax collection. The burden of the taxes fell on the common people, and therefore this class was the most hostile of the people towards the Arabs.[235]

It appears that the Umayyads did not increase the rate of the *jizyah* and the *kharāj* in Iraq, except in rare cases. We do not have any clear reference to this except Abū Yūsuf's mention that the *jizyah* which the inhabitants of the Jazīrah (northern Iraq) paid was considered to be too meagre by 'Abd al-Malik. He wrote to his governor al-Ḍaḥḥāk bin 'Abd al-Raḥmān about the matter. Then the governor conducted a head count, and considered all the people to be labourers and commensurate with the annual earnings of the labourer; he then deducted his expenses for his food staples, fat/oil (*idām*) and clothing, and deducted the festival days for the year. He found that after this four *dinars* ought to be obtained in a year from each person. Therefore, he imposed this sum on them all and rendered them a single class.[236] This meant that he made the wealthy, the middle class and poor (lit., 'weak' – *ḍu'afā'*) equal in the *jizyah*, and that he only left for the common class [of the masses] (*ṭabaqah al-'āmah*) enough for their necessary requirements. This information, despite its importance, appears only in one book of *fiqh*, and the soundness of its narrators is not certain. However, it is supported additionally by local Syriac narration.

The Umayyads reimposed some of the Sassanian taxes which had been annulled or ignored by 'Umar bin al-Khaṭṭāb. These were 'the gifts of *Nawrūz* and *Mihrajān*' – taxes which the [local] people had become accustomed to offering in the name of gifts for the Sassanian kings during the two festival days of *Nawrūz* and *Mihrajān*. This was from the time of the caliphate of Mu'āwiyah, as he 'demanded the people of the *sawād* give him gifts on the occasions of *Nawrūz* and *Mihrajān*. So they did that and its worth reached ten thousand *dinars*.'[237] We do not have anything in addition to this except for what al-Ṭabarī mentions about 'Umar bin 'Abd al-'Azīz's measures. He advised his governor for Kūfah:

> Do not tax barren land (*kharāb*) as you do cultivated land (*'āmir*) nor tax cultivated land as you do barren land. Examine the barren land then take from it only what it can bear and reclaim it so it can be cultivated. Only take the specified amount of *kharāj* from cultivated land in kindness for the ease and comfort of the people of the land, and only take the *kharāj* in the weight of seven [*mithqāl*] not including in it the *āyyīn* (charges), nor the wages of the minters (*ujūr al-ḍarrābīn*) [or, the wages of the money changers (*ujūr al-ṣarrāfīn*)],[238] nor the gifts of *Nawrūz* and *Mihrajān*, nor the price of the papers (*thaman al-ṣuḥuf*), the wages of the messengers (*ujūr al-fuyūj*), the rents of the houses (*ujūr al-buyūt*), nor the *dirhams* for marriage (*nikāḥ*); and, there is no *kharāj* for those people of the land who become Muslim.[239]

This text implies the existence of aberrations at the start of the caliphate of ʿUmar bin ʿAbd al-ʿAzīz. We do not know, with the exception of the gifts of *Nawrūz* and *Mihrajān*, who was responsible for them and when they appeared.

What we deduce from this text is the following:

- First, a single tax was imposed on cultivable land, whether it was cultivated or not. We do not know whether or not this was the practice of ʿUmar bin al-Khaṭṭāb because the sources differ. Some of them mention that he distinguished between cultivated and uncultivated land, and some others mention that he treated them identically.
- Second, some customary duties (*āyyīn*) were taken from the farmers in addition to the *kharāj*. The word *āyyīn* refers to traditional duties which were a legacy of the Sassanian era; however, we do not know what they were or their value.
- Third, it is difficult to consider the wages of the minters (*ujūr al-ḍarrābīn*) as a tax. That is because the money mint (*dār al-ḍarb*) was open to the public for them to bring precious metals to be struck into coins at their own expense. They only had to pay the fee for the workers and the price of the firewood, so this was a *fee* not a tax.[240]
- Fourth, the price of the papers (*thaman al-ṣuḥuf*) concerns the parchment which was used for writing in order to settle in the interests of the people, and this was a valuable commodity. It was to the advantage of whoever was given a written record; however, he was obliged to pay its price. This was not a tax and cannot be compared with the tax on seals (*ṭawābiʿ*).
- Fifth, the *dirhams* for *nikāḥ* were explained by Abū ʿUbayd as 'the *dirham* of prostitutes (*baghāyā*) from whom the *kharāj* was taken'.[241]
- Sixth, it seems that they imposed the rents on houses and on some buildings for storing crops.
- Seventh, it appears that the governors exploited the differences in the weights of the *dirham*[242] to increase their levy. Whereas ʿUmar bin al-Khaṭṭāb made the *dirham* – weighing fourteen *qirāṭ* of silver – the basis of the levy, we find some governors demanding a *dirham* whose weight was more than this. That used to lead to a practical substantial increase in the rate of the tax because the governors took the *dirham* in *number*, while its *value* depended on its weight. It is understood from al-Yaʿqūbī that some of the governors used to charge the people for acts of forced labour.[243] Bandalī Jawzī believes that the Umayyads imposed taxes on crafts (*ṣināʿāt*) and trades (*ḥiraf*), and that these taxes were

> not fixed. Rather, they used to depend on the desires of the governors and, therefore, may have constituted a more severe burden than the *jizyah* and the *kharāj*.[244] However, while he does not mention their origin, I do not find any reference to support his view. From the above, it is clear that *'urf*, or custom, prevailed in the Umayyad's fiscal measures, such as the gifts of *Nawrūz* and *Mihrajān* and the *āyyīn*, and some did not fall into the category of taxes, as in the case of the price of papers and the wages of the minters [or money changers].

Some of the tax collectors (sg. *jābī*, pl. *jubāh*) did not refrain from using violent means in their collection which gave rise to grievances,[245] and some of the Umayyads referred to these conditions. 'Umar bin 'Abd al-'Azīz writes in his letter to his governor in Kūfah: 'The people of Kūfah have been befallen by calamity, hardship and injustice in the rulings (*aḥkām*) of Allah and a wicked custom practised against them by the agents of evil.' He attempted to compel the governors to annul the gifts of *Nawrūz* and *Mihrajān*, increases in the weight of the *dirham*, the '*dirhams* for *nikāḥ*' and the wages of the minters [or money changers]. He ordered them to differentiate between cultivated land and barren land, saying: 'Examine the barren land (*kharāb*) then take from it only what it can bear and reclaim it so it can be cultivated. Only take the specified amount of *kharāj* from cultivated land (*'āmir*) in kindness for the ease and comfort of the people of the land.'[246] Among the new cases of Umayyad measures was that Mu'āwiyah 'took the *zakāt* (*alms*) from the stipends (*al-a'ṭiyah*)'.[247] Was he intending to render the *zakāt* a tax on income? Another case was the abuse of the right to hospitality, as when the army of Marwān bin 'Abd al-Ḥakam, who were sent against Ibn Zubayr, 'used to stay with the people and not give anyone the price of anything. When they came to Wādī al-Qurah, they imposed a tax on its people which they paid to them.'[248] However, the most dangerous and far-reaching innovation of the Umayyads in the history of that period was taking the *jizyah* (and the *kharāj*) from new Muslims. They had been compelled to do this due to the incompatibility of the system of 'Umar bin al-Khaṭṭāb with the new conditions, which threatened their treasury with a great financial crisis. There is no doubt that the change in conditions was responsible for this, and that this change resulted from the conversion of the protected non-Muslims – the *ahl al-dhimmah*; the purchase of lands by the Muslims; and the assignment of land grants (*iqṭā'*). Let us discuss these factors in order to understand this financial development.

'Umar bin al-Khaṭṭāb had granted some of the Companions a small amount of the *ṣawāfī* land as a land grant, or *iqṭā'*. The granting of *iqṭā'* increased during the time of ʿUthmān to an extent that generated complaint. Then, the Umayyads increasingly granted lands as *iqṭāʿ* to their close associates and relatives from the beginning of their reign. Al-Yaʿqūbī narrates that Muʿāwiyah 'after he had taken from each region the choice cultivated estates which the kings of Persia used to designate as *ṣawāfī* land [i.e. state land] for themselves, and he made these *ṣawāfī* for himself. Then, he granted them as an *iqṭāʿ* to a group of people from his family.'[249]

Al-Balādhurī indicates this of some swamplands, which Muṣʿab bin al-Zubayr reclaimed for himself and which were then transferred to the caliph ʿAbd al-Malik: "Abd al-Malik granted them as *iqṭāʿ* to people.'[250] Similarly, al-Walīd bin ʿAbd al-Malik granted his brother Maslamah extensive lands in the *sawād*.[251] These lands had not formerly paid the *kharāj* because they became property of the Muslims. Rather, they paid *ʿushr* and, as a result of this, the revenue of the treasury decreased. The situation was made more complicated by the combining of these *iqṭāʿ*, the *iqṭāʿ al-mulk* – lands of property with another type – the *iqṭāʿ al-ījār* (these were lands which were given to the farmers on condition that they pay a rent on them, while they remained property of the state).

After the sedition of Ibn Ashʿath, the owners of the *iqṭāʿ al-ījār* claimed that those lands were their property, and they stopped paying *kharāj*, which impacted on the treasury extremely adversely. Al-Māwardī says:

> among the reasons for the widespread properties among the Muslims is that ʿUthmān himself and his successors granted *iqṭāʿ* of some lands without binding their owners to pay something to the treasury in exchange for the *ījār* or the *ḍamān* (tax farming guarantee)...when the sedition of Ibn Ashʿath took place (82AH), the register (*dīwān*) was burned and the accounts were lost so all the people took what they had been working [of the lands].[252]

The Muslims also began competing in the purchase of land. The Umayyad caliphs, such as ʿAbd al-Malik and al-Walīd, had allowed them to purchase *kharāj* land and pay the *ʿushr* alone on the crop,[253] which reduced the revenue of the treasury. This was in addition to the spread of Islam among the farmers, which was accompanied by their exemption from the *kharāj* and a corresponding decrease in the revenue as a result. Thus, the area of *kharāj* land in the *sawād* diminished, and it was the mainstay of the treasury, as is clear from ʿUmar bin ʿAbd al-ʿAzīz's statement on it: 'I do not know of anything more vital to the fortunes of the Muslims and their material resources than these [*kharāj*] lands which Allah has made *fay*' for them.'[254] Hence, the Umayyads were faced with a crucial financial crisis; that is, a deficit in their finances.

Al-Ḥajjāj bin Yūsuf al-Thaqafī was the first to attempt to deal with this problem seriously, especially as warning had come to him from his officials that 'the *kharāj* has abated [lit., been broken] and the protected non-Muslims – the *ahl al-dhimmah* – have become Muslims and moved to the garrison towns (*amṣār*)'.[255] He imposed his policy aiming at rescuing the treasury, and in this he did not consider the wishes of the Arabs or the *mawālī* (non-Arab converts, attached as 'clients') since he imposed the *kharāj* on the Arabs who had bought *kharāj* lands, as well as both the *jizyah* and the *kharāj* on the non-Arabs who had converted to Islam and remained in their villages. When they emigrated to the cities in order to escape his draconian measures, he ordered their forced return to their villages. He 'wrote to Basra and other cities: "Whoever has family in a village, he shall go back to it."'[256] These measures created an uproar among the Arabs and the *mawālī* who were affected by them. They protested that Islam forbade this, but al-Ḥajjāj paid no heed. He wanted to increase the taxes, but the caliph prevented him. Al-Māwardī mentions that al-Ḥajjāj wrote to 'Abd al-Malik: 'seeking permission to take the surplus from the profit of the *sawād*', but the caliph forbade him from doing that and wrote to him: 'Do not be more covetous and eager for the *dirham* which you have not taken than for the *dirham* which you have, and leave them their meat instead of just the scraps [i.e. leave them with something].'[257]

This situation persisted until 'Umar bin 'Abd al-'Azīz came to power. He demonstrated extreme flexibility and far-sighted vision by imposing a solution which maintained the rights of the treasury and observed Islamic principles. In an official decree, he distinguished – for the first time in history – between the *jizyah* and the *kharāj*. He considered the *jizyah* to be a tax paid by the non-Muslim for whom it was waived upon conversion to Islam. He considered the *kharāj* to be a rent (*ījār*) for the land. He stated that *kharāj* land was originally a common property held jointly among the Muslims, and that it had been left among the conquered peoples to cultivate it in return for a rent which they paid to the Muslim community, and this was the *kharāj*. Therefore, when the Muslim bought *kharāj* land, it was incumbent on him to pay its *kharāj* as rent (*ījār*) on the land since it was an endownment (*waqf*) for the Muslims. Yaḥyā bin Ādam narrates on the authority of al-Ḥasan bin Ṣāliḥ: 'It is disliked [in terms of Islamic law] for a Muslim to purchase *kharāj* land;' and said 'that if he has done that, he must pay from the land what used to be remitted from it [i.e. the *kharāj*]. He mentions [that] from 'Umar bin 'Abd al-'Azīz.'[258] In the case of conversion by a non-Muslim, he was exempted from the *jizyah*, but his land remained *kharāj* land. This is clear from his assertion: 'Whoever among the people of the land becomes a Muslim, he retains of family and wealth what he had upon his conversion. As for his abode and his land, they are among the *fay'* of Allah for the Muslims.' Therefore, the convert could continue to cultivate the land and pay the *kharāj* on it, or leave it to the people of his village to cultivate, while he emigrated to the city.[259] In this way, 'Umar bin 'Abd al-'Azīz was able to render the land a permanent source for the state treasury, and reconcile need and principle. His view of the *ṣawāfī* indicates a concern for the affairs of the treasury. He did not resort to granting them as *iqṭā'*. Rather, he preferred that they be given by a sharecropping contract, '[give it] for one-half. What cannot be cultivated, give it for one-third. If it is left uncultivated, give it [for less] until it reaches one-tenth. If no one will cultivate it, then grant it [for nothing]. If it is [still] not cultivated, spend on it from the treasury of the Muslims.'[260] However, he did not interfere with the *iqṭā'* land grants which were made by his predecessors. Al-Ya'qūbī mentions about him that 'he left in place the *iqṭā'*, which had been granted to his family'.[261]

However, the policy of 'Umar bin 'Abd al-'Azīz came to an end with his death and the Umayyads reverted to the previous conditions. In Iraq, 'Umar bin Hubayrah increased his levy on date palms and fruit trees, and overburdened the smaller peasant farmers and harmed the *kharāj* payers just as he 'restored socage/forced labour (*sukhrah*) as well as the gifts and what was taken at *Nawrūz* and *Mihrajān*'.[262] It seems that the Umayyads in this unstable period overburdened the protected non-Muslims of the *ahl al-dhimmah* and the *mawālī* (i.e. those who had converted) to such an extent that many were forced to abandon their farms to escape from the taxes. This is clear from the letter of Yazīd III which promised reform, where he says: 'Do not charge those who pay your *jizyah* what will force them to flee from their lands and cut off their descendants.'[263] However, there was no opportunity for Yazīd III to execute his pledge. Among the effects of the bad policy of the Umayyad tax collectors in Iraq was the spread – in Iraq – of the system of *iljā'* (lit. entrusting land to persons of influence). Here the cultivator registered his land in the name of someone more powerful (the protector) in order to protect himself from excesses in the levying. At the time of al-Ḥajjāj, a large number of landowners entrusted their lands by *iljā'* to Maslamah bin 'Abd al-Malik.[264] However, the registering of land in the *diwān* in the name of the protector and with the passing of time both led to the transfer of ownership of some of the lands which had been entrusted to the protectors (through *iljā'*).[265]

Now let us mention some of the construction works which the Umayyads undertook in the *sawād*. 'Abdullah bin Darrāj, 'governor for Mu'āwiyah over the *kharāj* of Iraq', had drained and reclaimed some of the swampland for Mu'āwiyah, and their revenue reached 5 million *dirhams*. That was because he cut the reeds and diverted waterflow with dams.[266]

It appears that the floodgates in the diversion channels (*buthūq*) had become numerous along the rivers in southern Iraq, especially after the revolt of Ibn Ash'ath. This can be inferred given that when waters flooded over the lands, al-Ḥajjāj wrote to al-Walīd to inform him of that:

> He estimated the cost to drain the lands of the water to be three million *dirhams*: al-Walīd thought that to be too much. Then his brother Maslamah came forward and promised him that he would spend that amount of money on condition that the lands extracted from the water be given to him. Al-Walīd agreed and Maslamah implemented his plan. Many *ṭasāsīj* [sg. *ṭasūj*, where one *ṭasūj* is equal to four *danānīq*] of lands were obtained for him, and he dug the two canals known as al-Sībayn. The tillers and the farmers became united and those lands were restored.[267]

He thereby salvaged extensive fertile land, just as 'Ḥasan al-Nabaṭī...reclaimed for al-Walīd bin Hishām, and then for 'Abd al-Malik much of the swampland'.[268] The caliph used to do as he wished with these lands.

'Umar bin Hubayrah undertook a survey of the *sawād* during the caliphate of Yazīd II in 105AH. This was the second time in which the *sawād* had been surveyed since the Islamic conquest. There is no doubt that this was a monumental task, with the evidence being that this survey continued to be relied upon during the 'Abbāsid era. As al-Ya'qūbī (who wrote during the second half of the third century AH) says: 'The land survey (*misāḥah*) which was taken as a reference was the survey of Ibn Hubayrah.'[269]

Taxes in Khurasān

In Khurasān, there is reference to a single tax at the beginning, and this was paid in cash since the princes of Khurasān had previously made pacts with the Arab conquerors in which they pledged to pay them a specific annual *jizyah*.[270] This is what we understand from the sources, and perhaps we can add to this the fact that the Arabs in initially perpetuating the framework of the prevailing system implemented a single tax in Iran. This was the tax on the land as Iran had been the seat of the ruling family in the Sassanian age, so the Muslims retained that tax without specifying whether it was a *jizyah* or *kharāj*.

It appears that the local nobility (the *dihqāns*) exploited this ambiguity to their own benefit. They cooperated with the state tax collectors in the collection of the taxes, and thereby the interests of the Arabs and the *dihqāns* were in agreement, at the expense of the people.[271] Their attitude in this is reflected in the words of a Persian to an Arab: 'The noble of each people is a relative of the noble of any people.'[272] The benefit derived for the *dihqāns* was that they dispersed the taxes to be distributed on the heads of the people and not on the area of the land. In doing so, they removed the burden from their own shoulders and put it on the common people because if it were imposed on the land, they would have been the most burdened.[273] This is clear from some of the narrations. Al-Ṭabarī reports from 'Ammār bin Yāsir that he 'made peace with the great of Herat, Barshanj and Badhis. They made terms (in a *ṣulḥ*) with him for their lowlands and mountains and to pay a *jizyah* for that which they agreed with him, and to divide this across the lands justly among them.'[274] Al-Balādhurī narrates: "Abdullah bin Khāzim made peace [at the time of 'Uthmān] with the people of Nisapur for three million *dirhams*, or as some other narrations report, that it was to be according to the land's capacity to support [the levying of] the *kharāj*.'[275]

Al-Ṭabarī mentions 'the *kharāj* of Khurasān on the heads of the men',[276] and al-Ya'qūbī clarifies 'their *kharāj* was on the heads of the men, mandating for each male of maturity a *jizyah*'.[277] These narrations explain the confusion over describing the tax and reveal the ruse used by the *dihqāns* in changing the tax from one on the land to one on the heads of the men. Thus, the *dihqāns* returned to their influence and power at the social and financial level. Barthold comments: 'The *dihqāns* were content in the first Islamic periods in Iran with the cessation of their political jeopardy in exchange for what they received by way of social and economic distinctions and priviledges.'[278] We have indications to support this. Al-Ṭabarī mentions that when Sa'īd Khudaynah (Sa'īd bin 'Abd al-'Azīz) came to Khurasān 'he summoned a group of the *dihqāns*. He sought their council about whom he could send out to the districts. They indicated to him a group of Arabs. However, the Arabs were angered and they called him "Khudhaynah" [lit. little lady; i.e. because of his weakness].'[279] When Muslim bin Sa'īd, the tax collector for Ibn Hubayrah, wanted to take the remaining funds from some of the local nobility: 'he was told, "If you do this to those nobles (*ashrāf*), there will be no power for you in Khurasān because those from whom you want to take this money are of the nobility of this land."'[280]

We also have evidence pointing to the license of some of the governors. For example, it is reported about Aslam bin Zur'ah, the governor of

Mu'āwiyah, that he was unjust and oppressive and 'he doubled the *kharāj* on the people of Merv.'[281] Additionally, it is mentioned that al-Ashras, the governor of Hishām bin 'Abd al-Malik, 'increased the tax amounts of Khurasān and belittled the *dihqāns*',[282] and there are other examples of the misconduct of some of the governors.[283] However, the greed of the *dihqāns* was more dangerous and influential. One of the best examples of this is that Tughshada, the local prince of Bukhāra, who was killed by two *dihqāns* in 121AH after they had complained to Naṣr bin Sayyār that he had oppressed them and seized their property by force. They also complained about Wāṣil bin 'Amr, the tax collector of Bukhārā, due to his complicity with Tughshada in the unjust seizure of peoples' property.[284]

The spread of Islam was incompatible with the cultural and material interests of the *dihqāns* because the Muslims among the non-Arabs were equal in the view of the Umayyads and had a better status than non-Muslims, among whom were the Magian *dihqāns*. This meant the influence of the *dihqāns* and their resources were reduced, and they were a manifest obstacle in the path of reform. The spread of Islam had led to the decrease in the revenue of the treasury. Therefore, some of the Umayyads adopted the precarious measure of imposing the tax on new Muslims. This was in addition to their depriving the fighters among the Khurasān *mawālī* of their stipend. This was an issue fraught with danger if we take into account the multitude Khurasānī fighters in the Arab armies in the east. Such created an outcry among the *mawālī*, as is obvious from the complaint of the *mawā* in the delegation sent by al-Jarrāḥ (governor of Khurasān) to 'Umar bin 'Abd al-'Azīz: 'O Commander of the Faithful, twenty thousand of the *mawālī* are fighting without a stipend or rations, and a similar [number] of them from the *ahl al-dhimmah* have converted and pay the *kharāj*.' 'Umar bin 'Abd al-'Azīz tried to end these abuses. He exempted the *mawālī* from the *jizyah* and implemented a stipend for them like the Arabs in Khurasān. He wrote to al-Jarrāḥ: 'Look to whomever prays towards your *qiblah* [i.e., in the direction of Mecca] and waive from him the *jizyah*.' He affirmed equity in the stipend and called for kindness in levying taxes. When he noticed some hesitation by his governor [to act on this], he removed him.[285] This encouraged the spread of Islam.

It appears that the measures of 'Umar bin 'Abd al-'Azīz failed to treat the fiscal aspect of the issue in Khurasān as he had done in Iraq, focusing only on one tax in Khurasān instead of two as in Iraq. Thus, Yazīd bin 'Abd al-Malik rescinded these measures, and perhaps he increased taxes in order to shore up the fiscal deficit incurred by his mighty ancestors.[286]

A new attempt to deal with the problem of taxation in Khurasān occurred during the caliphate of Hishām. His governor Ashras bin 'Abdullah al-Sulamī (767–769AD) promised to exempt the Muslims in Transoxiana from the *jizyah*, and his appeal succeeded to a large degree. The governor was alarmed due to the decrease of revenue because, as he said, 'the strength of the Muslims is in the *kharāj*'. He censured the *dihqāns* because 'they do not want the spread of a religion in which is the spirit of equality', as Barthold says. Al-Ṭabarī mentions:

> The *dihqāns* of Bukhārā came to him [Ashras] and they said, 'From whom will you take the *kharāj* when all the people you take it from have become Arabs [i.e. Muslims]?' So Ashras wrote to Hānī [his governor]: 'Take the *kharāj* from those you were [taking it from]' and they restored the *jizyah* for those who had become Muslim.[287]

A general revolt took place in Transoxiana, which lasted until the governorship of Naṣr bin Sayyār. Thus, the role of the *dihqāns* in hindering reform is clear.[288]

Eventually, Naṣr bin Sayyār (738–748AD) attempted to implement a fixed and just solution to the problem of taxation in Khurasān. He had acted according to the policies of 'Umar bin 'Abd al-'Azīz in Iraq and decided to exempt the Muslims from the *jizyah*. There was no difficutly in that as he found 30,000 men paying it, but 80,000 men among the polytheists (*mushrikūn*) for whom the *jizyah* had been waived (and perhaps they were among the minions of the *dihqāns*). So he reinstated the *jizyah* on them and exempted the Muslims. Subsequently, he divided the lands of Khurasān into regions and imposed a specified fixed amount on each region which was levied on the land, whatever the religion of its owner.[289] This measure was a severe financial blow to the *dihqāns*, which cost them most of their privileges and sent them rushing to support and enlist in the 'Abbāsid claim [to power]. However, the measures of Naṣr bin Sayyār came too late in relation to the masses.

Taxes in Egypt

The discussion of the problem of taxation in Egypt provokes many questions since we are faced with a lack of information in the history books on the one hand, and with the various results of what we obtain from the papyri on the other hand. Similarly, the study of the papyri yields decisive proof of the Umayyads' preservation of local traditions since they afford much information about these traditions. However, the papyri have not been studied sufficiently until now, and this is what leaves some of the points unclear to the researcher.

Scrutiny of the Umayyad directives in Egypt, such as is in evidence from the history books, indicates that they tried one of two things: to increase the *kharāj* by the rate of one *qirāṭ* (by approximately 4.5 per cent) for every *dinar/feddan*; and to take the *jizyah* from monks (*al-ruhbān*) from time to time. Other than this, we only hear of the harshness in the *kharāj* without being told what this entailed. The attempts to increase the tax began during the caliphate of Mu'āwiyah, who ordered an increase of one *qirāṭ* on every *feddan* for each person from the Copts. However, his governor Wardān refused, as it was in contravention of what was customarily followed.[290]

After this, we do not hear anything of the matter until the caliphate of 'Abd al-Malik. The caliph ordered his brother 'Abd al-'Azīz to take the *jizyah* from the monks (*al-ruhbān*) and he ordered the commander to count them: 'The *jizyah* taken from them was one *dinar* from each monk, and it was the first *jizyah* taken from the monks.'[291] Jurjī Zaydān believes that the reason for this was that people donned the clothing of the monks in order to evade the taxes. The Umayyads observed this and adopted this measure accordingly.[292] Severus (bin Muqaffa') mentions that al-Aṣbagh bin 'Ubayd al-'Azīz bin Marwān undertook the census of the monks and the heads of the monasteries 'so that no one could join the monastery after those whom he had counted'. Severus is unique in saying that 'Abd al-Malik increased the *kharāj* and 'he fixed on all of those paying one *dinar* as *kharāj* [i.e. on the *feddan*] (a new tax of) one *dinar* and two-thirds, such that many churches were ruined for this reason'.[293]

It seems that the continued application of the system of 'Umar bin al-Khaṭṭāb precipitated a financial crisis in Egypt as well because of the conversion of people to Islam and their concomitant release from the *jizyah*. This led the governors during the caliphate of 'Abd al-Malik and his son al-Walīd to become stricter at times in their levying.[294] They began to impose the *jizyah* on the new Muslims, as al-Ḥajjāj had done in Iraq.[295] Apparently, that sometimes rendered them negligent even to the extent that they taxed crops during the time of flooding. In a narration, the governor of Egypt said to Sulaymān:

> O Comander of the faithful, what I have brought you has ruined and exhausted your subjects. If you would consider being kind to them and providing some comfort to them by lightening from their *kharāj* that which will augment the prosperity of their land and the good condition of their living standards, then do so and it will be realized in the coming year.

Sulaymān replied to him: 'May your mother be bereaved of her son. Draw the milk and if it ceases then draw blood and guts (*najā*)!'[296]

The caliph 'Umar bin 'Abd al-'Azīz was not pleased with these measures, and he attempted to apply his fiscal policy of distinguishing between the *jizyah* and the *kharāj* in Egypt. He began and 'waived the *jizyah* from those of the *ahl al-dhimmah* among the inhabitants of Egypt who had become Muslim'.[297] On the other hand, he attempted to consider the *kharāj* of each region fixed in amount and distributed among its inhabitants. Perhaps this was a manifestation of his regarding the *kharāj* as a rent (*ījār*) on the land. Then he wrote to his governor Ḥayyān bin Shurayḥ to 'levy the *jizyah* of the dead Copts on their living'.[298] What was intended by '*jizyah*' here is the *kharāj*. Similarly, the Arabs who bought *kharāj* land began paying the *kharāj*.[299]

Severus clarifies that 'Umar bin 'Abd al-'Azīz exempted church lands from the *kharāj*. He says, 'He ordered that there should be no *kharāj* on the lands of the churches and the bishops.' He adds: 'and he abolished the duties';[300] that is, additional charges. However, Yazīd bin 'Abd al-Malik restored them.[301] It seems that 'Umar's reforms in Egypt were provisional and perhaps he did not realise the importance of the *jizyah* in Egypt in relation to the many protected non-Muslims there. Where the number of payers of the *jizyah* in Iraq at the time of conquest had been about half a million, in Egypt they numbered 6 million. Al-Maqrīzī informs us that the non-Muslims in Egypt rushed to embrace Islam during the caliphate of 'Umar bin 'Abd al-'Azīz, which affected revenue. 'Umar's governor, Ḥayyān bin Shurayḥ, wrote to him: 'Islam has damaged the *jizyah* such that I borrowed twenty-thousand *dinars* with which I covered the stipend for the *diwān* [of the army]. If the Commander of the Faithful will consider ordering the settling of this, it will be done.' 'Umar replied, 'Allah sent Muḥammad as a guide and not as a tax collector.'[302]

Therefore, we find those who succeeded 'Umar bin 'Abd al-'Azīz rescinding his policy in Egypt.[303] In 104AH: 'Usāmah bin Zayd al-Tanūkhī, who was in charge over the *kharāj* [for Yazīd II], was harsh towards the Christians, punishing them and taking their wealth.' He also tried to control the collection of the *jizyah* from the monks:

> He marked the hands of the monks with a ring of metal[304] with the name of the monk, the name of his monastery and the date. For all those whom he found without a mark, he cut off their hands...Then, he raided the monasteries and arrested a number of monks without a mark. He cut off the heads of some, and the remainder of them he flogged until they succumbed from the blows.

He confimed that each Christian should carry an identification paper (*manshūr*), otherwise he would be fined ten *dinars*.[305] The brutality in collecting the taxes and the burdening of the protected non-Muslims of the *ahl al-dhimmah* is clear from this.

This situation, however, did not persist as it was reformed by Hishām: 'he wrote to Egypt to act in accordance with the pacts made previously with the Christians.' In other words, he commanded desisting from any harassment. However, the governors did not follow his order since the commander Ḥanẓalah bin Ṣafwān 'became harsher' towards the Christians, 'and he increased the *kharāj*'. He had the image of a lion tattooed/branded on each Christian, and whomever was found without it had his hand cut off.[306] From this it is understood that the Christians tried in various ways to conceal their identity. In addition, for the first time we hear of an augmentation in the systemisation of the *kharāj* by the caliph in 156AH, and this was at the suggestion of his governor: ''Ubayd Allah bin al-Ḥabḥāb who was in charge of its *kharāj* wrote that the land of Egypt could bear an increase, so he increased one *qirāṭ* on every *dinar* [from the tax on the land];' that is, a 5.4 per cent increase. This led to a revolt among the masses of eastern Ḥawf, and this was the first revolt of the Copts. The rebellion was quashed and the relationship between the Umayyads and the Copts worsened, until they rebelled once again in 121AH and once more in 134AH due to the oppressive taxation.

The Umayyads appear to have imposed taxes on craftsmen to the extent that they could bear; although, it seems that these taxes had existed since the age of the Rāshidūn caliphs.[307] Similarly, the Umayyads imposed excise/sales taxes on trade which were called *mukūs* (sg. *maks*), at a rate of 1–40 for the Muslims and 1–20 for the protected non-Muslims. 'Umar bin 'Abd al-'Azīz wrote to his tax collector about the *mukūs* that:

> he should oversee those Muslims whom he encounters while they are passing through and take one *dinar* for every forty *dinars* which comes out of their wealth and their merchandise. Whoever has wealth assayed below twenty *dinars*, leave it and take nothing from it. If he encounters someone of the *ahl al-dhimmah* passing through, he should take one *dinar* for every twenty *dinars*; and he should continue to assess as such until the value of their merchandise reaches ten *dinars*. If it is lower than that, he should not take anything from it. And in this case, he assays and levies the merchandise another time before the end of the year; and he should write up a document for them about what he has taken from them.[308]

Our information from the papyri which are from the period between 80AH and 100AH includes other details not mentioned elsewhere. They are a collection of contemporaneous administrative prescripts and herein lies their value. In the papyri there is no reference to the Muslims paying taxes. As regards the *jizyah*, there is no mention of any women paying it, nor is there anything to indicate that the monks paid it, or that some of men of the religion among the priests paid it while some others did not.[309]

The system of taxes in the early ʿAbbāsid period

Introduction

When the seat of the caliphate moved to Iraq, the caliphs' interest in it increased, especially its southern part known as the *sawād*.[310] They revived and organised the ancient system of irrigation, and dug waterways (*turaʿ*) and new canals (*qanawāt*), particularly in the region of Baghdad.[311] The new irrigation works included the following canals:

- The Nahr Abī al-Asad in the swamp lands, the opening of which was dug or widened by al-Manṣūr's commander Abū al-Asad.[312]
- The Nahr al-Ṣilah, the digging of which was ordered by al-Mahdī among the works at Wāsiṭ: 'They revived the lands which were along it, and its crops were given as assistances and gifts to the inhabitants of the *ḥaramayn* (i.e. "two holy places", Mecca and Medina) and as charitable gifts [for the poor] there.'[313]
- The Nahr al-Rayyān, which was dug by al-Khayzurān [mother of al-Hādī and Hārūn al-Rashīd].[314]
- The Nahr al-Qāṭūl called 'Abū al-Jund' (lit. 'father of the army'), which was dug by al-Rashīd 'to facilitate what would water the lands to provide provision for his army', and on which he spent 20 million *dirhams*.[315]
- The Nahr al-Maymūn, which 'was dug by an agent of Umm Jaʿfar Zubaydah [mother of al-Amīn]'.[316]

The caliphs were concerned about maintaining the system of irrigation, such that we find Abū Yūsuf detailing the state's duties in this field. He says: 'If the inhabitants of the *sawād* require the digging [or dredging] of their great waterways which branch from the Tigris and the Euphrates, they are dug for them and the cost is paid from the treasury and the *kharāj* payers (*ahl al-kharāj*).'[317] He adds: 'As for the breaches/floodgates in the diversion channels and the dams (*musannayāt*) which are in the Tigris, the Euphrates, and other great rivers, the cost of spending on these is from the treasury (*bayt al-māl*) – nothing of that falls on the *kharāj* payers because the concern for this is incumbent solely on the *imām* as it is a general public matter for all the Muslims.'[318] The caliphs also directed their concern towards maintaining the dams, preventing against their bursting and the risk of flooding. Therefore, it is no wonder that the *sawād* came to be covered by a wide network of canals, supporting and propagating farms and villages.[319] From this, we may deduce the importance of the *kharāj* or land tax, which was the principal resource for the treasury (*bayt al-māl)*.

Let us now consider the various taxes in this period.

The kharāj *(land tax)*

The *kharāj* was taken from the greatest part of the lands of the *sawād*. Therefore, the 'Abbāsids took an interest in its levying and systemisation; they showed their interest in it initially in Khurasān. Khālid bin Barmak 'was...in the camp of [the general] Qaḥṭabah, in charge of the *kharāj* of all the provinces, which Qaḥṭabah had conquered...It was said that there was not one of the people of Khurasān to whom Khālid did not show assistance and kindness because he distributed the *kharāj* and acted well in it towards its payers.'[320] It would appear from this that the 'Abbāsids attempted to systematise the levying of the *kharāj* and to reduce it in Khurasān when they came to power.

In the *sawād*, the *kharāj* was taken in cash according to area (*misāḥah*), whether the land was cultivated or uncultivated on the basis of that which had been imposed by 'Umar bin al-Khaṭṭāb.[321] This continued until al-Mahdī replaced it with the *muqāsamah* (sharecropping) system for the fields, where he took a specified proportion of the crop: 'one-half of what was irrigated by running water (*sayḥ*), one-third on what is by *dāliyah* waterwheel (pl. *dawālī*); one-quarter by *dūlāb* waterwheel (pl. *duwālīb)* or *nā'ūra* (pl. *nawā'īr*)', taking into consideration in this the costs of irrigation at a corresponding rate.[322] However, there were rates other than these in special cases. When the Nahr al-Ṣilah [canal] was dug, al-Mahdī 'brought the sharecroppers (*muzāri'ūn*) and beguiled them into paying a share of two-fifths of the produce for fifty years. Once the fiftieth year had passed, they would not be obliged to continue with the condition imposed on them.'[323]

The *muqāsamah* system did not include date palms, fruit trees or grape vines, on the condition that it remained on the fixed tax rate (*kharāj al-waẓīfah*) and took into account in the assessment of its tax 'the proximity to markets'.[324] However, the *kharāj* tax was not fixed and varied according to the circumstances. When Khālid al-Barmakī was appointed governor of Persia at the time of al-Mahdī: 'he waived from them the *kharāj* on fruit trees, when they had previously been obliged to pay a heavy *kharāj* for this.'[325] Similarly, the proportion of the *muqāsamah* changed since the *'ushr* was added to one-half so that the [resulting] tax became 60 per cent of the crop.[326] It is likely that this occurred in the later days of al-Mahdī due to his multitude expenditures and the bankruptcy of his treasury.[327] It seems this proportion of 60 per cent was exorbitant for the cultivators, and the continuation of the tax on date palms, trees and grape vines on the fixed *kharāj* was beyond their capacity. Abū Yūsuf affirms this, explaining: 'The *kharāj* imposed on their land is onerous for them. We have seen that their land cannot bear it, and we have seen the [collectors] taking it, thereby causing them to flee from the land and abandon it.'[328]

The officials and the tax collectors used to take additional taxes on top of the amount of the *muqāsamah* tax. Abū Yūsuf points out the 'provisions/sustenance of the official (*rizq 'āmil*)', 'the rate of two *mudd* (*ajr mudday*)' or the 'wages of the measurers/weighers (*ujūr al-kayyālīn*)', 'food and lodgings for the ruler (*nuzūlah wa ḥumūlah ṭa'ām li-l-sulṭān*)', 'the price of the papers and the papyri (*thaman ṣuḥuf wa qarāṭīs*)' and their allegation 'that there is a deficit on them, so it is taken from them', and 'what they call a *rawāj* of the *dirhams,* which they pay in the *kharāj*...a man among them brings the *dirhams* to pay them his *kharāj* and a part of the sum is deducted, and this is said to be their *rawāj* and fee [i.e. for the *dirhams*]'.[329] In addition to this, the farmers were sometimes ordered to dig canals at their own expense[330] with the knowledge that 'the canals which are made to flow to their land, farms, orchards and herb gardens and the like, their digging is incumbent upon them exclusively and there is nothing of [the financial burden of] that on the treasury'.[331] At the time of al-Manṣūr, if the crop suffered from being barren or no rain fell on it, then the *kharāj* was not dropped but delayed until the next year. At the time al-Mahdī was deputy for his brother al-Manṣūr in Baghdad, when 'Amārah bin Ḥamzah mediated with his *kātib* (scribe), Abū 'Ubayd Allah, in the matter of a man whose 'estates were parched, barren and ruined...so he asked him to waive his *kharāj*, which was two-hundred thousand *dirhams* [Abū 'Ubayd] told him: "I cannot do this but I will delay his *kharāj* to the coming year."'[332] However, waiving the *kharāj* from close associates became a well-known practice by the governors, until it was pointed out to Abū Yūsuf and he prevented it being done.[333] However, the advice of Abū Yūsuf was implemented. When 'Īsā bin Farkhashah took charge of the *kharāj* of Egypt, he visited Muḥammad bin Yazīd al-Umawī and waived 'for him all his *kharāj* for that year'.[334] The governors used to sometimes give the *kharāj*, or some of it, to their close associates or relatives. Al-Faḍl bin Yaḥyā al-Barmakī, the governor of Khurasān at the time, gave his official over Sijistān the *kharāj* of his estate (*muqāṭa'ah*) for a complete year, the amount of which was 4 million *dirhams*.[335]

When al-Rashīd came to power (r. 170–193AH), he paid close attention to the matter of the *kharāj* and requested that his *faqīh* (jurist) Abū Yūsuf

> compile a comprehensive book for him, which could be used as a reference in his levying of the *kharāj*, *'ushr*, *ṣadaqāt* and *jawālī* (poll tax of non-Muslim exiles) and other than these which required his consideration and action. With this, he wanted only to lift injustice from his subjects and make good their affairs.[336]

Therefore, Abū Yūsuf composed his great book '*al-Kharāj*', in which he explained the correct foundations for the rate of the taxes mentioned and the method of their collection. His proposals regarding the *kharāj* were firstly to levy 'a two-fifths share of the wheat and barley irrigated by running water (*sayḥ*) from all the inhabitants of the *sawād*; one-fifth and a half share of crops irrigated by waterwheel (*dawālī*)...one-quarter share of summer crops', taking into account the problems of irrigation, its costs and the capacity of the *kharāj* payers. Secondly, he proposed that 'the *kharāj* payers share...whatever bears fruit from the date palms, fruit trees and grape vines'; that is, to apply the *muqāsamah* (sharecropping) system to the fruit trees instead of the fixed-rate *kharāj*. He fixed the amount of the tax: 'one-third on date palms, grapes, clover and orchards.'[337] Abū Yūsuf had defended these suggested changes to the system of 'Umar bin al-Khaṭṭāb, saying: "Umar, who is the one who imposed the *kharāj* on them, used to inquire of them: "Are they able to bear that or not?", and he proceeded to not charge them beyond their capcity.'[338] Thirdly, he also proposed the abolition of the additional taxes and assistance from the government for the farmer in the digging of major canals.[339]

Nevertheless, there is nothing to indicate that al-Rashīd applied Abū Yūsuf's advice outside of the *sawād* because of the low level of supervision over the governors – even if al-Rashīd was inclined towards justice – paved the way for them to accumulate wealth and become rich at the expense of the people. This is just as 'Alī bin 'Īsā bin Māhān did; his confiscation of funds reached 8 million *dirhams* after being in charge of Khurasān for ten years.[340] However, when al-Rashīd ascertained the injustice on the part of his governors, he removed them, just as he did with 'Alī bin 'Īsā and the governor of Egypt Mūsā bin 'Īsā al-Hāshimī after 'much complaint about him and caluminy reached him, which threatened to discredit him'.[341] In the *sawād*, al-Rashīd lowered the amount of the *kharāj* in 172AH by nullifying 'the tenth which used to be taken after the half'.[342]

The levying of the *kharāj* continued in the *sawād* at one-half until 204AH when al-Ma'mūn set 'the *muqāsamah* of the people of the *sawād* at two-fifths instead of one-half'.[343] It appears that al-Ma'mūn was intent on reducing the burden of the *kharāj* (even if his motives were political) since he 'reduced the *kharāj* from Khurasān by one-quarter'.[344] Similarly, his governor 'Abdullah bin Ṭāhir, in his attempt to subdue the situation in Syria, 'reduced the *kharāj* from some of it' around the year 210AH.[345] In 214AH, al-Ma'mūn stayed in Damascus in order to survey the lands of Syria and brought land surveyors (*massāḥ*) from Iraq, al-Ahwāz and al-Rayy: 'He made a *ta'dīl* (cadastral survey) of its *kharāj* lands [Damascus and Jordan] and levied each land [the amount] what was commensurate with it.' In 218AH, he advised his governors in Syria of: 'judicious conduct, lightening burdens and restraint from doing harm.'[346]

The abuses connected with the methods of tax collection were numerous, and Abū Yūsuf had frequently called attention to the arbitrary and draconian treatment by the tax collectors. The abuses included guessing by conjecture (*ḥazr*) what was stored on the threshing-floors, then estimating more than their actual contents and then with that 'taking the deficit in the conjectured amount'. Abū Yūsuf drew attention to the fact that 'in this there lies the ruin of the *kharāj* payers and the ruination of the lands. The tax collector sometimes claims the loss of the crop by the *kharāj* payers, and for that reason he takes more than is stipulated.' The tax collector used to sometimes measure the crop after the threshing:

> so he leaves it on the threshing-floor for a month or two, then he apportions it to them [the *kharāj* payers] and he measures it a second time. If it [the second measure] is less than the first measure he says, 'Make up the deficit for me' and takes from them what does not belong to him.[347]

Abū Yūsuf also refers to the misconduct of the aides of the tax collectors who may

> not be pious nor righteous people. He (the tax collector) appoints them and sends them into his districts and through this harasses the people. So, they are not mindful of what they are entrusted to uphold, nor are they just with those with whom they deal. Their way is only to take something, whether from the *kharāj* or from people's possessions, and then they take this...through tyranny, oppression and transgression.[348]

The aides of the tax collector used to sometimes demand special wages, and 'if he [i.e. the cultivator] does not tender it, he beats him, brutalises him, herds away cattle and sheep and whatever he can from the weakest farmers such that he takes this unjustly and aggressively'.[349]

Among the abuses in the levying of the *kharāj* was the collection of the tax before the crops had ripened. Al-Maqrīzī relates a narration from a work which is now lost, entitled 'The Accounts of the Commander of the Faithful, al-Muʿtaḍid bi-Lāh, by Abū al-Ḥusayn 'Abdullah bin Aḥmad bin Abī Ṭāhir'. The narration from a member of the court of al-Mutawakkil reports that this caliph:

> Passed by some crops and he saw they were green. He remarked to the man with whom he was travelling, 'O 'Alī, the crop is still green and has not matured. 'Ubayd Allah bin Yaḥyā has asked me for permission to begin [levying] the *kharāj*. How was it that the Persians used to begin levying the *kharāj* in *Nawrūz* when the crops had not yet matured?' He [The narrator] said: I told him, 'The matter does not proceed as it used in the days of the Persians...because they used to intercalate one month every one-hundred and twenty-one years. It was *Nawrūz* if you went forward one month and it became the fifth of Ḥazīrān/June, if one intercalated that month it became the fifth of Ayyār/May; and if one dropped a month, one would take it back to the fifth of Ḥazīrān, so it did not used to go past this. When Khālid bin 'Abdullah al-Qasrī took charge of Iraq and the time came in which the Persians intercalated, he prevented them from doing so'. He said, 'This is something which Allah has prohibited, and I will not allow it until I seek permission for it from the Commander of the Faithful.' So they spent large sums of money on that but he did not accept it, and he wrote to Hishām bin 'Abd al-Malik to inform him of this...So, he [Hishām bin 'Abd al-Malik] ordered that they be prevented from doing this. When they were precluded from the intercalation (*kabs*), *Nawrūz* advanced rapidly until it came to fall in Naysān/April when all the crop are green.[350]

Al-Bīrūnī adds:

> During the reign of al-Rashīd, they [the *dihqāns*/landowners] convened with Yaḥyā bin Khālid bin Barmak, and they asked him to delay *Nawrūz* by approximately two months. Yaḥyā was resolved on doing so; however, his enemies spoke about him saying, 'He is siding with the Magians', so he reneged on this. The situation continued until the time of al-Mutawakkil when he was informed, 'This has harmed the people. They are incurring loans and borrowing money and fleeing from their homes. Their suffering and

> oppression has increased.' At that moment, al-Mutawakkil ordered him [or one of the Magian priests, according to al-Bīrūnī] 'auger for this...to return *Nawrūz* to the time which it was in during the days of the Persians. 'Ubayd Allah bin Yaḥyā knew about this and sent him (al-Mutawakkil) a letter commending to commence the start of the [levying of the] *kharāj* in it [*Nawrūz*]....' When the court informed the vizier of the matter, he said, 'O Abū Ḥasan, by Allah you have relieved me and the people. You have done much to increase your reward [with Allah] and earned reward and thanks [among people] for the Commander of the Faithful.'

Al-Mutawakkil made a calculation for the extent of the intercalation and postponed the time for levying of the *kharāj* from Naysān to the fifth (al-Maqrīzī) or (according to al-Bīrūnī) the seventeenth of Ḥazīrān, and a document was sent to the districts [telling them] about the matter and this was in Muḥarram 243AH. The poet al-Buḥturī spoke of this in a *qaṣīdah* (poem) in which he praises al-Mutawakkil:

> The day of *Nawrūz* has returned to the time which Ardeshir established,
> You have changed it to its original state when it was going round bewildered,
> You have begun the *kharāj* in it, so for the community there is an acknowledged kindness,
> From them is praise and laudation, and from you is justice for them and reaping of gratitude.

However, al-Mutawakil was killed 'and what he planned was not completed until al-Mu'taḍid came into rule (r. 2792–89AH)'.[351]

It may be noted that in Egypt, the practice intercalation (*kabs*) of the years was followed throughout the first 'Abbāsid era.[352]

The *kharāj* payers used to sometimes be treated harshly. Until the time of al-Mahdī's coming to power, they were

> punished through types of torture by beasts of prey, hornets and wild cats...When he assumed the caliphate, [al-Mahdī] consulted Muḥammad bin Muslim about them. Muḥammad told him: 'O Commander of the Faithful, this is a position which has more to it [than is apparent]. They are debtors (*ghuramā'*) of the Muslims. Therefore, they must be exacted as debtors.' On hearing this, the caliph ordered his vizier '[to write] a letter to all the tax collectors to lift the torture from the *kharāj* payers'.[353]

However, it appears that this did not last long since Abū Yūsuf says (addressing al-Rashīd): 'I have heard that they [the tax collectors] make the *kharāj* payers stand in the sun and flog them severely, they hang upon them [heavy] earthenware jars which they must drag and shackle them in a way which prevents them from praying. This is a great sin unto Allah and abominable in Islam.'[354] Among the unusual anecdotes mentioned by al-Maqrīzī is that a tax collector in charge of the *kharāj* of Egypt in 178AH managed the collection of all the *kharāj* 'without a whip or a cane'.[355] We have accounts of the punishment of *kharāj* payers during the period of al-Rashīd until 184AH, when the caliph ordered the torture of them to be discontinued.[356] However, the effect of this was temporary since the tax collectors returned to their ways and torture continued in the time of al-Ma'mūn. Dionysius of Tell Mahre describes the tax collectors in Iraq around 200AH/815AD as being 'a group from Iraq, Basra and al-'Āqūlā'. They are insolent, without mercy or faith in their hearts, more evil than the viper. They beat the people, imprison them and suspend the corpulent man from one arm until he almost dies.'[357]

The tax farming contract (*ḍamān* or *qibālah*) was another of the abuses in any given region, carried out by individuals who paid a specified amount of money to have a free hand in the tax collection. Al-Faḍl bin Yaḥyā al-Barmakī narrates that his father 'had contracted Fāris from al-Mahdī, and he paid him one million *dirhams*'.[358] Abū Yūsuf warned against doing this and explained its consequences, saying:

> I deem that none of the *sawād*, nor other lands, should be subject to a tax farming contract (*qibālah*). The tax contractor/farmer (*mutaqabbil*), if there is a surplus over and above the *kharāj* in his contract, overburdens the *kharāj* payers and imposes on them what is not obligatory for them, oppressing them and harming them in order to be protected from that which he has entered.[359] In that and what is the like of it, there is the ruination of the land and the ruin of the subjects. The tax contractor does not care about their ruin so long as his own concern is guaranteed in his contract (*qibālah*); and, he might even derive greater benefit after [receiving] a large surplus by [the contract]. However, he can only do this except by means of draconian force against the subjects. He flogs them brutally, he makes them stand in the sun and hangs stones around their necks. This is the excessive punishment which he metes out to the *kharāj* payers.[360]

This tax farming method (*ḍamān*) was followed outside Iraq in particular.

After the disturbances in Egypt of 183AH: 'Layth [governor of Egypt] went to al-Rashīd and asked him to send the armies with him because he was not able to exact the *kharāj* from the people of al-Aḥwāf except with an army. Maḥfūẓ bin Sulaymān proposed that he would guarantee (*yaḍman*) the [payment] *kharāj* of Egypt in full, without [using] a whip or a rod, so al-Rashīd put him in charge of the *kharāj*.'[361] It appears that the *ḍamān* tax farming system was particularly widespread in Egypt. Al-Maqrīzī says:

> The administrator of the *kharāj* of Egypt was sitting in the mosque of 'Amr bin al-'Āṣ in Fuṣṭāṭ [Cairo] at the time when preparations were being made for the tax contract (*qibālah*)[362] of the lands. The people from the villages and the cities gathered. A man then stood and called out the lands [to be auctioned for the tax contract] shouting out 'contracts (*ṣafaqāt*), contracts'. The *kuttāb* (scribes) for the *kharāj* were before the administrator and recording the amounts which had been settled for the districts (*kuwar*) and the contracts (*ṣafaqāt*) for those people who had made [bids for] the contracts. The lands were set aside through *qibālah* by their contractors for four years in case of drought or rent and so forth. When this ended, anyone who had contracted land would undertake working it and annex it to his land; then he and his family and whoever he assigned for that would be in charge of its cultivation, repairing its bridges, and all remaining aspects of its work. He paid the *kharāj* on it in full, but separating it into instalments and he would be credited from the sum of his contract and his tax farming of those lands what he had spent on the building of bridges, damming of waterways and digging canals with a proportional tax specified in the bureau of the *kharāj* and [some] was kept back from the amount of the *kharāj* every year from the provinces of the tax farming and the contractors.[363]

The *ḍamān* tax farming system only spread in Iraq in the late third century AH and the fourth century AH.[364]

There was a second type of *ḍamān* where a wealthy man would guarantee the *kharāj* of the inhabitants of the region, with their consent. Abū Yūsuf approved this on condition that the caliph appointed with the guarantor (*ḍāmin*) a trustee (*amīn*) 'whose faith and loyalty are trusted by the state treasury which pays him out of the treasury [funds]'.[365] This type of *ḍamān* was termed *īghār*.[366]

When Iraq was the seat of the caliphate, the abuses in the tax collection were fewer than in the provinces. We can cite Egypt as an example of this, since al-Maqrīzī reported numerous examples of the brutal injustice of the 'Abbāsid governors there. In 177AH, Isḥāq bin Sulaymān bin 'Alī was put in charge of [leading the] prayer and the *kharāj*: 'He dealt with the matter of the *kharāj* and added to the farmers an increase which ruined them and the people of al-Ḥawf rose against him so he fought them.'[367] In 182AH, the inhabitants of al-Ḥawf revolted 'and they stopped the *kharāj*'.[368] In 190AH, 'the people of al-Ḥawf rebelled and they stopped paying the *kharāj*'.[369] In 198AH, al-'Abbās bin Mūsā bin 'Īsā bin Mūsā bin Muḥammad was put in charge of prayer and the *kharāj* for al-Ma'mūn: 'He brutalized and oppressed the subjects and threatened them all, so they revolted.'[370] In 213AH, the emir Abū Isḥāq al-Mu'taṣim was governor of Egypt and 'he put Ṣāliḥ bin Shirzād in charge of the *kharāj*. He oppressed the people and increased their *kharāj*, to the extent that the people of Lower Egypt (*asfal al-ṣa'īd*) became impoverished.' The revolt continued until it reached its climax in 216AH when 'Īsā bin Manṣūr was placed in charge of the prayer (for Abū Isḥāq): 'The people of Lower Egypt, its Arabs and Copts rebelled in [the month of] Jumādā al-Awwal and the agents were dismissed for their bad conduct, but they refused to obey.' Al-Ma'mūn was forced to come himself (10 Muḥarram 217AH): 'He was enraged with 'Īsā and dismissed him...He attributed the incident to his agents; he fell upon the corrupt among the people; he took the Copts captive, killing their fighters.'[371] His view of the rebels is clear from his statement: 'These are unbelievers (*kuffār*) who have a covenant of protection (*dhimmah*). If they are oppressed they should complain. It is not for them to seek succor with their swords.'[372] Thus, Egypt became a focal point for the revolts due to the evil conduct and oppression of the tax collectors in the collection.

In the province of Fārs (Persia), the *kharāj* was oppressive. Al-Muqaddasī reports: 'I read in a book in the treasury of 'Aḍud al-Dawlah: "The people of Fārs were the most useful and obedient people to the sultan, the most patient of oppression, the most burdened by the *kharāj* and the most humble of souls." In it [it also said]: "The people of Fārs have never known justice."'[373] In presenting the account about Fārs, he says: 'And do not inquire about the burden of the taxes and their abundance.'[374] There was a large number of nobles holding land *iqṭā'* grants among those who owned lands. Al-Muqaddasī says: '[In] most of the estates (*ḍiyā'*) [there] are *iqṭā'*.'[375] Hence, the injustice of the nobility was compounded by the oppression of the tax collectors. The rate of the *kharāj* there depended on the method of irrigation. The *kharāj* of land irrigated by some sort of mechanical implement or device (*ālah*) was equivalent to two-thirds of that which was land irrigated by [freely] running water 'and the unirrigated land (*bakhs*, pl. *bukhūs*) accounted for one-third [of land irrigated by] running water'.[376]

The injustice in the tax collection pushed some of the farmers to protection in the name of one of the senior men [and influential personages] of the state, such as the vizier, and in exchange for that they paid him an amount of money for the year. This was termed *iljā'*[377] and is mentioned in al-Jahshiyārī (through Ardeshir bin Sabur), and in Ibn Abī al-Ḥadīd:

> Whoever among the *kharāj* payers entrusts his land and his estate to the retinue and entourage of the king [does this] for one of two reasons: either protection against the injustice of the tax collectors and oppression by the governors, and in this can be perceived the adverse effect of the tax collectors; or [he does this] to escape paying the due that is incumbent on them and to 'break it' (i.e. to be exempt from payment of the *kharāj*).[378]

Al-Jahshiyārī gives a clear example of *iljā'*:

> A man from the people of al-Aḥwāz came to Abū Ayyūb [al-Mūriyānī] when he was vizier (*wazīr*) [for al-Manṣūr] and said to him: 'The tax collectors have burdened me on my estate in al-Aḥwāz. If the vizier would see fit to loaning me his name, I will put it [the estate] in his name, and I will bring him one-hundred thousand *dirhams* every year!' So he said, 'I have given you my name, so do what seems acceptable to you.'

In the following year: 'The man brought the money and called on Abū Ayyūb.... He informed him that he had made use of his name and that he had brought him the money' and Abū Ayyūb was much delighted.[379]

Al-Iṣṭakhrī mentions:

> In Fārs, the owners of the estates entrusted them to important men from the entourage of the ruler in Iraq and they were run in their names. A quarter [of their land tax] was reduced for them and this was done by means of their owners with the names which they inherited and bought from one another.[380]

There must be reference to a special category of lands which used to pay special taxes, and these were the lands of some of the powerful estate owners and *dihqāns* whose ancestors had made special contracts with the Arabs at the time of the conquest. They paid a specified fixed rate of the *kharāj* in accordance with this that did not change. This was typical particularly in Fārs and Khurasān.[381] There were 'estates of the ruler' (*ḍiya' sulṭānīyah*) or 'estates of the caliphate' (*ḍiya' al-khilāfah*).[382] These estates were extensive and dispersed across the different lands of the caliphate, such as Iraq, Syria, Egypt,[383] Ṭabaristān, al-Yamāmah,[384] Khurasān and Fārs,[385] and a *dīwān al-ḍiyā'* – bureau of the estates was established for them.[386] These estates were given for sharecropping according to the agreement contracted between the cultivator and the *dīwān*. Al-Iṣṭakhrī mentions in his account about Fārs: 'The estates of the ruler were outside of the cadastral survey (*misāḥah*). They were only taken from the ruler by sharecropping or land grant.'[387]

The origins of the estates of the caliphate were the Umayyad lands which had been confiscated by the 'Abbāsids when they came to power,[388] then they were extended gradually in various ways. We will mention one of the most standard ways, as is stated by al-Balādhurī: 'Al-Manṣūr liked to reclaim an estate from the swamp land. He ordered the extraction of the *sabīṭah* [i.e. draining off of water which had submerged it], and it was reclaimed for him.'[389] Elsewhere he says: 'One of the people of knowledge told me about the estates of Basra. He said, "The people of the al-Shu'aybīyah of the Euphrates made them [i.e. the estates] for 'Alī bin al-Rashīd...during the caliphate of al-Rashīd on condition that they would be the sharecroppers for him and he would reduce their *muqāsamah* tax on it for them. Hence, it was made *'ushr* from the *ṣadaqah* (charity), and its people apportioned it however it pleased them."'[390]

The 'Abbāsids took the estates of the al-Sībayn from the children of Maslamah bin 'Abd al-Malik and granted them as *iqṭā'* to Dāwūd 'Alī. Then 'this was subsequently purchased from his heirs and came to be counted among the estates of the ruler'.[391] Another example are estates termed '*īghār Yaqṭīn*' and the story behind them was that 'Yaqṭīn [bin Mūsā], the head of ['Abbāsid] propaganda (*ṣāḥib al-da'wah*), was given estates of several *ṭasāsīj* of *ighār*. This subsequently came to belong to the *sultan* but it retained its name as *īghār Yaqṭīn*.'[392] Some of the estates were sometimes made a family bequest/endowment (*waqf dhurrīyah*): 'Al-Mu'taṣim bequeathed some of the estates of al-Yamāmah to his sons.'[393]

Some of the lands paid *'ushr* only. The lands surrounding Basra were *'ushr* lands because 'the estates of Basra were *mawāt* land revived during Islamic times'.[394] Ibn Khurdādhbah pointed out that the al-Sībayn lands and the *waqf* (endowed) lands in the *sawād* were *'ushr* land.[395] The lands of the *iqṭā'* grants were also *'ushr* lands and paid 'the *'ushr* which "was measured" in kind in the regions assessed by the *muqāsamah*, and cash *'ushr* in the regions assessed by the fixed tax (*kharāj al-waẓīfah*)'.[396] These lands were part of the *ṣawāfī* (lands of the crown).[397]

Abū Yūsuf says: 'The *'ushr* was only taken for what the owner of the *iqṭā'* had to pay for the trouble of digging canals, [constructing] houses/buildings (*buyūt*) and work on the land.'[398] Abū Yūsuf estimates the revenue of these estates in the *sawād* to have been 4 million *dirhams* annually.[399] Qudāmah mentions that 'the *ṣadaqāt* of Basra [the *'ushr* from the products of its land] increased in the year to six million *dirhams*', according to the value for 204AH.[400] There were lands which transferred from *kharāj* [status] to *'ushr*. Al-Balādhurī reports: 'In the Euphrates there are lands whose inhabitants converted to Islam when the Muslims entered. There are other lands which went out from the possession of their owners to Muslims as gifts and other reasons of ownership. They became *'ushr* land after having been *kharāj*.

Al-Ḥajjāj reverted them to their status as *kharāj* lands, then 'Umar bin 'Abd al-'Azīz reverted them to a status of *ṣadaqah*;' and, subsequently, they were restored to *kharāj* status until the rule of al-Mahdī who made them all *ṣadaqah*.[401] Al-Ṭabarī narrates during the events of 241AH that al-Mutawakkil 'made the subdistrict of Shimshāṭ one of *'ushr* and transitioned them [i.e., the people] from [paying] the *kharāj* to the *'ushr* and produced a document specifying this'.[402]

The jizyah *(poll tax)*

The collection of the *jizyah* in the *sawād* proceeded according to the customary practice of 'Umar bin al-Khaṭṭāb and the 'Abbāsids followed this. Dionysius wrote around 200AH: 'According to the law (*qānūn*) of Iraq, the wealthy pay forty-eight *dirhams*, the middle [class] twenty-four *dirhams* and the poor twelve *dirhams*.'[403] The conditions of the *jizyah* stated by the *fuqahā'* were followed (in theory) by the caliphs. In an agreement by the caliph al-Ṭā'i', dated 366AH, it is stated:

> To the tax collectors on the heads (*jamājim*) of the *ahl al-dhimmah*: that they shall take the *jizyah* from them according to their status in wealth and what they possess of works; and according to the categories classified in it, and the fixed limits imposed for it. They shall not take it from the women, nor from those males who have not reached the age of majority, nor from those of a very old age, nor from those with a visible infirmity, nor the poor and destitute or those chaste ascetics who have entered the monastery.[404]

In another agreement it said: 'they shall be forebearing towards them so that they obey, or be firm with them until they comply [lit. change].'[405] These agreements, even if they were late, were applied in accordance with the viewpoint of the caliphs of the first 'Abbāsid age.

However, the collection of the *jizyah* was most often left to the governors or tax collectors, and they behaved in an evil fashion and were brutally unjust. Abū Yūsuf advised al-Rashīd:

> No one among the *ahl al-dhimmah* should be beaten in the taking of their *jizyah*, nor should they be made to stand in the sun or other [such torture], nor should anything reprehensible be inflicted on their bodies. Rather, they should be treated with kindness and imprisoned until they pay what is incumbent on them, and not leave the prison until the *jizyah* is exacted in full from them.[406]

Over and above this punishment, the tax collectors used to sometimes take from the protected non-Muslims 'something from their possessions' without any right and charge them 'beyond their capacity'.[407] Dionysius, who visited Egypt in around 200AH, narrates one example of oppression and excess in the *jizyah* concerning the city of Tinnīs, famous for its textile production. He reports:

> Although the city of Tinnīs is populated with inhabitants and has many churches, I have never seen suffering in any land greater than that of its people. I asked them about the source of this misery and they answered, 'Our city is surrounded by water but we are unable to farm or raise livestock. The water which we drink is brought to us from far away, and we buy jars of it for four *dirhams*. There is no work for us other than weaving flax, so our women spin it and we weave it. We are given half a *dirham* for that a day from the cloth merchants. Even though our wages are not enough to feed our dogs, it is incumbent on each of us to pay a tax of five *dinars* and along with that we are beaten, imprisoned and forced to give our sons and daughters as hostages. They force us to work like slaves for two years for each *dinar*. This is to the extent that if a woman or girl among them bears a child, they take an oath from us not ask for it; and it has occurred sometimes that there are new taxes before the release of these women.[408]

Al-Mutawakkil was harsh towards the protected non-Muslims of the *ahl al-dhimmah*: 'He ordered...the taking of the *'ushr* from the homes of the *ahl al-dhimmah*' in *addition* to the *jizyah* in 235AH.[409] The *jizyah* of a village or region was sometimes guaranteed (through *ḍamān*) by one of its wealthy inhabitants or its chiefs, who paid a specified amount to the treasury and then would be able to collect the *jizyah* after that.[410] Qudāmah mentions that, for instance, the *jizyah* for the protected non-Muslims in Baghdad in 204AH reached an annual revenue of 200,000 *dirhams*.[411]

The assessment taken into account in the collection of the *jizyah* or the *jawālī* was not a single assessment: 'because the *jawālī* (poll tax) in *surra man ra'ā* [i.e., Sāmarrā'], the "city of peace" [i.e. Baghdad] and the capitals of the well-known cities was levied according to the lunar months, and what was on the heads (*jamājim*) of the people of the villages...was levied according to the solar months.' This practice persisted until the time of al-Mutawakkil as 'the year 241AH moved to the year 242AH' when there was levied 'the *jawālī* and the *ṣadaqah* for the year 241AH and 242AH at one time', meaning that the *jawālī* was paid an additional year: 'thus, the books were updated and the governors informed so that their accounts of the *jawālī* would be for the lunar months, and the matter continued like this.'[412]

The ṣadaqah *(charity tax)*

In addition to the *'ushr* on crops, the *ṣadaqah* was levied on livestock in accordance with the principles elucidated by the *fuqahā'*.[413] The levying of the *ṣadaqah* was usually left to the collectors/agents of the *kharāj*,[414] who did not conduct themselves judiciously. Abū Yūsuf says: 'I have heard that the *kharāj* tax collectors send men on their behalf to collect the *ṣadaqah*, and they oppress and tyrannise, taking what is not lawful and unheard of.' Therefore, Abū Yūsuf recommended to the caliph that he should appoint a special official for the *ṣadaqah* 'for all the lands and to instruct him. Then let him send to [these towns] people with whom he is satisfied and inquire about their beliefs, methods, conduct and their trustworthiness to collect the *ṣadaqah* of the lands for him.'[415] Hence, there were sometimes special collectors for the collection of the *ṣadaqah*.[416]

Other taxes

The resources of the treasury included the taking of fifths (*khums*) of metals, such as the gold on the Abyssinian frontier. These used to be exploited, and the *khums* on them was paid to the treasury until the time of al-Mutawakkil. The Bujah (i.e. a people in the region beyond Upper Egypt) expelled the owners of the mines and harassed them: 'The gold, silver and precious minerals which were extracted from the mines and which used to be taken for the ruler by right of the *khums* were cut off because of that.' However, al-Mutawakkil defeated and drove out the Bujah, and the Muslims returned to exploit the mines[417] and these included mother lodes (*rikāz*); buried treasures from pre-Islamic times; the *khums* of valuable commodities washed ashore on the sea and from which ambergris, for example, was extracted; the sale costs of escaped slaves (*ubbāq min al-'abīd*); money and goods taken from thieves whose owners had not come searching for such; and what was taken from the inheritance of those who died without leaving behind an heir.[418] Likewise, the taxes on exports were also taken. The *fuqahā'* stipulated the necessity of armed forces for the *imām* for the [border] regions which led to non-Muslim territories (literally of 'idolatry' – *shirk*) who would inspect the goods of traders and prevent the possibility of sending communications which might harm the welfare of Islam.[419]

There were other new taxes not mentioned by the *fuqahā'*; however, these taxes were not numerous in the first 'Abbāsid age. Rather, they increased after the assassination of al-Mutawakkil because of the influence of increasing affluence, growing expenditure, diminishing tax collection, the waning of the dominion and the weakness of the central authority. These taxes included the tax on markets (*ḍarībat al-aswāq*): 'Al-Manṣūr did not impose a revenue tax on the markets up until the time he died. When al-Mahdī became his successor, Abū 'Ubayd Allah pointed this out to him. He ordered it and imposed the *kharāj* on the shops (*ḥawānīt*), and that was in 167AH (873AD).'[420] The tax on markets was part of the *mustaghallāt* (revenue-generating properties) which were 'the ground for markets (*turbat aswāq*) and other than markets built upon for people, where they paid rents (*ujrah*) for the land and mills to the sultan'.[421] Al-Ya'qūbī says: 'The rent for all the markets in Baghdad together with Raḥā al-Batrīq (the Patrician's Mill) and land annexed to it for each year [and al-Ya'qūbī died in 264AH] was twelve million *dirhams*.'[422] He reports that 'the revenue, *mustaghallāt* and markets of Sāmarrā' reached ten million *dirhams* a year'.[423] This indicates the fact that the *mustaghallāt* had become a considerable resource for the treasury. In Fārs, the mills were a monopoly of the sultan and likewise the rents for the buildings used for making rose water.[424] In the cities of Fārs, the lands of the markets and the streets were the property of the government, which took a rate for them.[425]

The *maks* was a tax taken on ships coming from the sea to Basra when special observation posts were set up for the collection of this tax.[426] The traders coming from China and India paid the tax which amounted to one-tenth – *'ushr*[427] – and this was termed the "*ushr* of ships [lit., *a'shār al-sufun*]'. This tax was dropped at the time of al-Wāthiq. Al-Ṭabarī says that in 232AH 'al-Wāthiq ordered the discontinuation of the *'ushr* of the ships on the sea',[428] and al-Ya'qūbī supports this.[429] This tax was not significant in the first 'Abbāsid age, but its importance increased in the second 'Abbāsid age. According to the revenue list of [the vizier] 'Alī bin 'Īsā, its revenue for 306AH reached 22,375 *dinars* a year. The additional resources included *aḥdāth*, which were indemnities taken by the *gendarme* for crimes.[430] Al-Jahshiyārī says: 'al-Mahdī put 'Amārah bin Ḥamzah in charge of the *kharāj* in Basra. He wrote to him to include the *aḥdāth* in the *kharāj*, so he did that.'[431]

Finally, we must refer to the practice of confiscation (*muṣādarah*) [of the wealth] of the scribes (*kuttāb*) and viziers in the way of obtaining wealth. After the governors and the viziers had had their funds confiscated as punishment for pilfering the funds of the state, the practice of confiscation of funds of these became a standard one and a resource for the treasury after the time of al-Wāthiq. Al-Wāthiq was the first caliph who confiscated the funds of the *kuttāb* in order to obtain wealth. Al-Ṭabarī says of the events of 299AH: 'From that, and what there was of the arrest by al-Wāthiq bi-Lāh of the *kuttāb* and assaying them for money', when he took: 80,000 *dinars* from Isḥāq bin Yaḥyā bin Mu'ādh; 400,000 *dinars* from Sulaymān bin Wahāb (the *kātib* of the Turkish commander Ītākh); 14,000 *dinars* from al-Ḥasan bin Wahāb; 100,000 *dinars* from Aḥmad bin al-Khuṣayb and his *kuttāb*; 100,000 *dinars* from Ibrāhīm bin Rayyāḥ and his *kuttāb*; 60,000 dinars from Najāḥ and 140,000 *dinars* from Abū al-Wazīr as a *ṣulḥ*: 'and that was other than what he took from the tax collectors because of their proxies.'[432]

The number of confiscations increased at the time of al-Mutawakkil and these became an important resource. The best example of the motives of al-Mutawakkil for these confiscations is mentioned by al-Ṭabarī:

> When al-Mutawakkil resolved to build [the palace city of] al-Ja'farīyah, Najāḥ, who was one of his confidants (*nudamā'*), told him, 'O Commander of the Faithful, I will name for you [certain] people. Hand them over to me so that I can extract from them money for you to build your city such that your majesty will be glorified and your remembrance magnified.' He replied to him, 'Name them.' So he put before him a piece of paper on which he mentioned Mūsā bin 'Abd al-Malik (in charge of the *diwān* of the *kharāj*), al-Ḥasan bin Makhlad (in charge of the *diwān* of *ḍiyā'* – estates)...and Ja'far al-Ma'lūf, the official (*mustakhrij*) in the *diwān* of the *kharāj* and other names of about twenty other men...and this matter pleased al-Mutawakkil very much. (In naming these senior functionaries and the *kuttāb* of the *diwān*, Najāḥ was recommending that the caliph confiscate from their wealth.)

None of these men escaped these machinations, except the vizier, 'Ubayd Allah bin Yaḥyā, who uncovered the plot of Najāḥ and exposed him to two of those on his list: Mūsā bin 'Abd al-Malik and al-Ḥasan bin Makhlad. 'Ubayd Allah bin Yaḥyā 'said to them, "He [Najāḥ] has gone to the Commander of the Faithful to hand you both over to him to kill you and to take what you own. However, first write a document to the Commander of the Faithful saying in it that you will guarantee the payment two million *dinars*."' They followed this advice, and subsequently tortured Najāḥ until he died in 245AH.[433]

In 233AH, al-Mutawakkil took 70,000 *dinars* from Ibrāhīm bin al-Junayd al-Naṣrānī and confiscated from his *kātib* Abū al-Wazīr '60,000 *dinars* and charged, in turn, whatever could be carried off in *dirhams* and jewellery. He took for him sixty-two *safaṭ*,[434] thirty-two servants (*ghulām* – lit. boys) and many furnishings from the goods of Egypt.' One of the *kuttāb* – Sa'ūn bin 'Alī – made a *ṣulḥ* agreement for '400,000 *dinars*' and two others made a *ṣulḥ* settlement 'approximately three-thousand *dinars* and he took their estates *(ḍiyāʿ)* in that'.[435] In 237AH, al-Mutawakkil was angered at Aḥmad bin Abī Dāwūd, so he took 120,000 *dinars* from his son and jewels worth a value of 20,000 *dinars* 'and he made a *ṣulḥ* settlement after that for 16 million *dirhams* and everyone (his brothers also) witnessed the sale of each estate *(ḍiyāʿ)* belonging to them'.[436] Also, in 233AH, 'Umar bin Faraj made a *ṣulḥ* settlement for 10,000. These examples illustrate the importance of confiscation – *muṣādarah* – at the end of the first ʿAbbāsid age as a resource for the treasury as well as the increasing recourse to it as a device, even to the extent that it resembled a [standard] tax on the senior *kuttāb*.

Taxes in the later ʿAbbāsid periods

I have researched the system of taxation in the later ʿAbbāsid period up to the mid-fifth century AH in some detail in my book *Tārīkh al-ʿIrāq al-Iqtiṣādī* (*The Economic History of Iraq*).[437] Similarly, I have explained the influence of the development which took place in taxation, its levying on the general situation and the emergence of social movements in another book *Dirasāt fī al-ʿUṣūr al-ʿAbbasīyah al-Muta'akhkhirah* (*Studies on the Late ʿAbbāsid Age*), so this will not be repeated here.[438] It is sufficient here to conclude by mentioning some useful points.

The later periods are characterised by the disruption of the ʿAbbāsid state and its takeover by foreign Turkish or Persian elements. This is in addition to the diminishing of its prestige without any corresponding diminution of its administrative machine, together with the increase in standards of living. If we add to this the lack of supervision over the governors, we can understand the reprehensible conduct and the effort to innovate new taxes termed *mukūs* (sg. *maks*), as well as the increases in the old taxes. For the *kharāj* tax,[439] we notice a sizeable increase in the usual tax such that the *kharāj* exceeded half the crop sometimes; the spread of the *ḍamān* tax farming system, along with its inherent abuses; the tyranny of the *iqṭāʿ* landowners and the collection of the *kharāj* before the ripening of the crops. For the *'ushr* tax, we notice an increase in its amount, the collection on the basis of the cadastral survey (*misāḥah*) and not the crop,[440] as well as constant grievances over the *'ushr* region of Baghdad.[441] Along with these increases, we notice a decrease in revenue which indicates a decline in agriculture, despite some of the attempts at reform.[442]

Aside from what relates to the Islamic-legal taxes, the levying of the *mukūs* was difficult because it was not defined or delimited by any system.

There was also much scope in it for brutality and injustice. It was imposed on individuals among the subjects without any distinction with regard to religion. It included the tax on inheritance (*ḍarībat al-irth*), which was introduced, it seems, during the caliphate of al-Muʿtamid (r. 256–279AH) and which was levied, at times, on all inheritance without regard for the heirs, and it was heavy. It continued throughout this period despite the attempt of some caliphs or their viziers to abolish it.[443]

There were duties on goods passing through sea or lands in specified places. They were fostered by political division and internal chaos. This was in addition to taxes at the borders and duties imposed on the waterways, which were known as *maʾāṣir* in these cases.[444] There were also the *mustaghallāt*, which were the taxes imposed on shops and markets (as well as market grounds). Furthermore, there were also taxes imposed on mills such that the trend in some cases was for these to become monopolies of the state, as was the case with the Ḥamānids in Mosul. Taxes imposed on buildings (*dūr*) were termed *ʿarṣah* (courtyard) taxes and were perhaps imposed on buildings constructed on government land and sometimes imposed generally.[445]

Taxes were imposed on all foodstuffs sold in the markets, such as flour, vegetables and fruit. They were imposed on sheep, beasts of burden, cows and horses which were sold, and likewise on the selling of wines (*khumūr*). Special taxes were imposed on silk and cotton products sometimes and proved a hindrance to production and a source of trouble and unrest. The situation came to the point where the *ʿushr* was imposed on sustenance (*rizq*) and salaries (*rawātib*) in the late fourth century AH.[446] Pastures were subject to new taxes and these clearly contradicted normative practice, in addition to the fact that they were ruinous. A new tax appeared which was taken by the *jahbadhs* (money changers, *jahābidhah*)[447] who used to be given the collection of some regions in return for a loan (*silfah*), which they offered to the state. They would take something from the people over and above the usual tax, and perhaps this took the place of delayed interest (*al-fāʾiḍ al-muʾajjal*) and the effort exerted. The tax was onerous for the people and termed the monies/commission of the *jahbadhs* (*māl al-jahbadhah*).[448]

As for the methods of tax collection, there were repeated grievances about these. If we are precise, we find that the abuses tended to preponderate when the central supervision was weak and when the control of the men of the army was strong. Therefore, there is repeated reference to attempts at reform and to ʿAlī bin ʿĪsā, the splendid vizier of al-Muqtadir, who made efforts worthy of mention in attempting reform.

Notes

1. *sūrat al-tawbah*, Q 9:29.
2. *sūrat al-mu'minūn*, Q 23:72.
3. Abū 'Ubayd al-Qāsim al-Harawī Ibn Salām, *al-Amwāl*, edited with commentary by Muḥammad Ḥāmid al-Fiqī, 4 vols. in 1 (Cairo: Maṭba'at Ḥijāzī, 1353/1934), pp. 65 and 120.
4. The term *ibn al-sabīl*, which literally means 'son of the way/path', is variously interpreted by the *mufassirūn* (exegetes) as connoting a 'traveller' or 'wayfarer', as well as someone who is 'cut off' either from his family or stranded in strange territory. It also is interpreted as connoting someone who is engaged in *jihād* – whether in the military sense or in the sense of an individual seeking to acquire knowledge (and religious knowledge in particular). This category constitutes a category of persons upon whom *zakāt* or *ṣadaqah* (alms) can be spent. [Editor's note.]
5. *sūrat al-anfāl*, Q 8:41; Ya'qūb bin Ibrāhīm Abū Yūsuf, *Kitāb al-Kharāj* (Cairo: al-Maṭba'ah al-Salafīyah, 1352/1933), p. 18.
6. In this context, there is difference of interpretation with regard to the intended designation of the term *ahlih* – either *its* or *his* people, where the Shī'ah understand this to refer to the *ahl al-bayt* – the 'people of the house' of the Prophet. [Editor's note.]
7. Ibn Salām, ibid., p. 21.
8. See ibid., p. 21; Abū Muḥammad 'Abd al-Malik Ibn Hishām, *al-Sīrah al-Nabawīyah*, edited and indexed by Muṣṭafā al-Saqqā, Ibrāhīm al-Ibyārī, 'Abd al-Ḥafīẓ Shalabī, 4 vols. (Cairo: Muṣṭafā al-Bābī al-Ḥalabī, 1936), pp. 364–367.
9. Ibn Hishām, ibid., vol. 3, pp. 364–365.
10. Ibid., vol. 3, p. 352.
11. Ibn Salām, ibid., p. 56.
12. Ibn Hishām, ibid., vol. 3, pp. 340 and 352.
13. Abū al-'Abbās al-Balādhurī, *Futūḥ al-Buldān* (Cairo: Sharikat Ṭab' al-Kutub al-'Arabīyah, 1901), p. 39.
14. Ibn Salām, *al-Amwāl*, p. 69.
15. Abū Yūsuf, *Kitāb al-Kharāj*, p. 39.
16. Ibid., p. 33.
17. al-Balādhurī, *Futūḥ al-Buldān*, p. 82.
18. Ibid., p. 82. Here he means by bucket instead of what is watered with *al-sawāqī* – waterwheels (*dāwalīb*) and waterwheels turned by animals (*garrāfāt*).
19. Ibid., p. 40.
20. Ibid., p. 71.
21. Ibid.
22. Ibid., p. 72; Ibn Salām, *al-Amwāl*, p. 100.
23. al-Balādhurī, *Futūḥ al-Buldān*, p. 71.
24. Ibid., p. 72; Ibn Hishām, *al-Sīrah al-Nabawīyah*, vol. 4, p. 164; Ibn Salām, ibid., p. 100.
25. al-Balādhurī, ibid., p. 86.
26. Ibid., p. 76.
27. Muḥammad bin Yaḥyā Abū Bakr al-Ṣūlī, *Adab al-Kuttāb*, edited with commentary by Muḥammad Bahjah al-Atharī, (Cairo; Baghdad: al-Maktabah al-'Arabīyah, 1341/1922), p. 214.
28. Abū Yūsuf, *Kitāb al-Kharāj*, p. 15.
29. See Abū Zakariyā Yaḥyā bin Sulaymān Ibn Ādam al-Qurashī, *Kitāb al-Kharāj* (Cairo: al-Maṭba'ah al-Salafīyah, 1417AH/1996AD), no. 229.

30. Abū al-ʿAbbās Aḥmad bin ʿAlī al-Maqrīzī, *Imtāʿ al-Asmaʿ bi-mā li-l-Rasūl min al-Abnāʾ wa al-Amwāl wa al-Ḥifdah wa al-Matāʿ*, edited with commentary by Maḥmūd Muḥammad Shākir (Cairo: Lajnat al-Ta'līf wa al-Tarjamah wa al-Nashr, 1941), p. 321 [see: *sūrat al-ḥashr*, Q 59:6].

31. Ibn Hishām, *al-Sīrah al-Nabawīyah*, vol. 3, p. 354.

32. Ibn Salām, *al-Amwāl*, p. 295.

33. Ibid., pp. 295–297 and 300–301.

34. Julius Wellhausen, *Das Arabische Reich und Sein Sturz*, trans. Margaret Graham Weir as *The Arab Kingdom and its Fall* (Calcutta: University of Calcutta, 1927), p. 31.

35. The *jarīb* is equivalent to 2,400m^2. See Christensen, Arthur, *L'Iran sous les Sassanides* (Copenhagen: Levin and Munksgaard, 1936), p. 316, see n. 3. [Author's note.] Ibn Mufliḥ, Abū Isḥāq Burhān al-Dīn bin Muḥammad bin ʿAbdullah (al-Ḥanbalī) defines a *jarīb* in his book *al-Mubdiʿ fī Sharḥ al-Muqniʿ* as 'ten *qaṣbāt* in ten *qaṣbāt*, where one *qaṣbah* is: six arm-lengths of average arm length with the fist clenched and the thumb extended'. In this sense, it would be an area of land and the quantity of wheat which would be harvested on such. Ibn Mufliḥ, Abū Isḥāq Burhān al-Dīn (Beirut: al-Maktab al-Islāmī, 2000), p. 381. [Editor's note.]

36. al-Balādhurī, *Futūḥ al-Buldān*, p. 134.

37. Ibid., p. 298.

38. Muḥammad Ḥamīdullāh al-Ḥyderābādī, ed., *Majmūʿat al-Wathāʾiq al-Siyāsīyah fī al-ʿAhd al-Nabawī wa al-Khilāfah al-Rāshidah* (Cairo: Lajnat al-Ta'līf wa al-Tarjamah wa al-Nashr, 1941), p. 219.

39. See the text of the treaty in ibid., p. 219; al-Balādhurī, ibid., p. 299.

40. al-Balādhurī, ibid., p. 329; Ibn Salām, *al-Amwāl*, p. 64.

41. Abū Yūsuf, *Kitāb al-Kharāj*, p. 26.

42. al-Balādhurī, ibid., p. 251; Ibn Salām, ibid., p. 58.

43. al-Balādhurī, ibid., p. 251.

44. Abū Yūsuf, *Kitāb al-Kharāj*, p. 26.

45. Ibid., p. 25.

46. Aḥmad bin Abī Yaʿqūb al-Yaʿqūbī, *Tārīkh al-Yaʿqūbī*, 3 vols. (al-Najaf: al-Maktabah al-Murtaḍawīyah), 1358/1939, vol. 2, pp. 151–152.

47. Ibn Ādam al-Qurashī, *Kitāb al-Kharāj*, p. 42.

48. Ibn Salām, *al-Amwāl*, p. 65.

49. Abū Yūsuf, *Kitāb al-Kharāj*, p. 25.

50. Ibn Ādam al-Qurashī, *Kitāb al-Kharāj*, p. 44.

51. Ibn Salām, *al-Amwāl*, pp. 64–65.

52. Ibid., p. 62; al-Balādhurī, *Futūḥ al-Buldān*, p. 329.

53. ʿIzz al-Dīn Abū al-Ḥasan ʿAlī bin Muḥammad Ibn al-Athīr, *Tārīkh al-Kāmil*, 12 vols. (Cairo: Muṣṭafā al-Bābī al-Ḥalabī, 1303AH/1885), vol. 2, p. 307.

54. *sūrat al-ḥashr*, Q 59:7.

55. *sūrat al-ḥashr*, Q 59:8–10; Ibn Ādam al-Qurashī, *Kitāb al-Kharāj*, p. 43; Ibn Salām, ibid., p. 66; Abū Yūsuf, *Kitāb al-Kharāj*, p. 26.

56. Abū ʿAbdullah Muḥammad bin ʿAbdūs al-Jahshiyārī, *al-Wuzarāʾ wa al-Kuttāb*, edited and indexed by Muṣṭafā al-Saqqā, Ibrāhīm al-Ibyārī, ʿAbd al-Ḥafīẓ Shalabī (Cairo: Maṭbaʿat Muṣṭafā al-Bābī al-Ḥalabī), 1938, p. 5; Abū Jaʿfar Muḥammad bin Jarīr al-Ṭabarī, *Tārīkh al-Rusul wa al-Mulūk*, 12 vols. (Cairo: al-Maṭbaʿah al-Ḥusaynīyah, 1336/1917), vol. 2, p. 122; Abū ʿAlī Aḥmad bin Muḥammad Ibn Miskawayh, *Tajārib al-Umam*, with selections from various histories relating to the matters mentioned therein, ed. H. F. Amedroz, 7 vols. (Cairo: [n.pb.], 1920–1921), vol. 1, p. 185; Abū Ḥanīfah al-Dīnawarī, *al-Akhbār al-Ṭiwāl*, eds. V. Guirgass and I. Kratchkovskii (Leiden: Brill, 1888–1912), p. 72.

57. Arthur Christensen, *L'Iran sous les Sassanides* (Copenhagen: Levin and Munksgaard, 1936), p. 316, also see n. 3.

58. al-Ṭabarī, *Tārīkh al-Rusul wa al-Mulūk*, vol. 2, p. 122; Ibn Miskawayh, *Tajarīb al-Umam*, vol. 1, p. 186.

59. al-Dīnawarī, *al-Akhbār al-Ṭiwāl*, p. 73; al-Ṭabarī, ibid., vol. 2, p. 123.

60. al-Ṭabarī, ibid., vol. 2, p. 122; Ibn Miskawayh, ibid., vol. 1, p. 186.

61. al-Dīnawarī, ibid., p. 73; al-Ṭabarī, ibid., vol. 2, p. 123.

62. Fateh contends that both the terms *jizyah* and *kharāj* were Arabicised versions of Persian terms: respectively 'Gesith' and 'Kharagh', where the first connoted a head-tax (of non-Persian Greeks and Jews in the Sassanian empire) and the second a land tax. A counter-argument could be made to the effect that, at least as far as the Arabic-language histories of the early 'Abbāsid period, which cover Persia and Byzantium that the then contemporary terminology in use might have been projected backwards and used to describe previous Persian practices – *ex post facto* – using the lexicon then current. See Mostafa Khan Fateh, 'Taxation in Persia: "A Synopsis from the Early Times to the Conquest of the Mongols"', *Bulletin of the School of Oriental Studies*, University of London, vol. 4, no. 4 (London: Cambridge University Press, 1928), pp. 723–743. [Editor's note.]

63. A note is, perhaps, instructive here about ancient measures and the lexicon for such. Terms of measure and weight had various equivalents as well as commonly accepted local definitions, where there might be a regional variation in the understanding of the quantity, weight or amount denoted by a single term; for example, in Iraq or in Syria. It should also be noted that there was not always a hard and fast distinction between types of measure so that a single measure might connote area, mass/volume or weight all at the same time – depending on the context. For example, a *jarīb* (pl. *jirbān)* was generally a measure of area – defined as six arm-lengths (of an average arm) with the fist clenched and the thumb extended – to denote a length but also an area *squared.* Likewise, as *Lisān al-'Arab* specifies, the term was not only a measure of 'land' (*arḍ*) but also 'food' (*ṭa'ām*), so when a *jarīb* of wheat was specified, it implied the *yield* of such an area ('that which can be cultivated on it'), and would, thus, connote a weight and a volume of wheat in this sense. According to *Lisān al-'Arab*, the Prophet used to perform his minor ritual ablutions – for a state of minor impurity (*wuḍū'*) – with one *mudd* [of water], and would wash his entire body in major ritual ablution – for a state of major impurity [i.e. a state of *janābah* such as obtains after intercourse or preparing a dead body for burial, etc.] (*ghusl*) – with one *ṣā'*. In Medina, four *amdād* (sg. *mudd*) were equivalent to one *ṣā'*. (In the *modern* context, a *mudd* is a unit of dry measure, where in Palestine it is equivalent to 18 litres and in Tangier it is equivalent to 46.6 litres. [See Hans Wehr, ed. Cowan, J. M. *Arabic English Dictionary, Fourth Edition* (Ithica: Spoken Language Services, 1994), p. 1053.].) Also according to *Lisān al-'Arab*, a *qafīz* is defined as being equivalent to eight *makākīk* (sg. *makūk*) and equivalent to one *ṣā'* and a half (i.e. that which would be equivalent to six Medinan *amdād*), and a *jarīb* is equivalent to four *aqfizah* (sg. *qafīz*), according to the same source. [Editor's note.]

64. al-Ṭabarī, ibid., vol. 2, pp. 122–123; Ibn Miskawayh, ibid., vol. 1, p. 187.

65. Abū Yūsuf, *Kitāb al-Kharāj*, pp. 7–8.

66. See ibid., pp. 21–22; al-Ya'qūbī, *Tārīkh al-Ya'qūbī*, vol. 2, p. 39; Christensen, *L'Iran sous les Sassanides*, p. 108.

67. Christensen, ibid., p. 119.

68. al-Jahshiyārī, *al-Wuzarā' wa al-Kuttāb*, p. 24.

69. See Charles Diehl, *Byzance, grandeur et decadence* (Paris, E. Flammarion, 1919); Norman H. Baynes, *The Byzantine Empire* (New York, London: H. Holt and

Company, 1939; Home University Library of Modern Knowledge, no. 114), p. 99 ff; H. M. Gwatkin and J. P. Whitney, (eds.), *The Cambridge Medieval History*, Vol. II, *The Rise of the Saracens and the Foundation of the Western Empire* (Cambridge: Cambridge University Press, 1913).

70. Jalāl al-Dīn ʿAbd al-Raḥmān bin Abī Bakr al-Suyūṭī, *Ḥusn al-Muḥāḍarah fī Akhbār Miṣr wa al-Qāhirah*, 2 vols. in 1 (Cairo: Fahmī al-Katbī, 1327/1909), vol. 1, p. 65.

71. Abū al-ʿAbbās Aḥmad bin ʿAlī al-Maqrīzī, *al-Khiṭaṭ al-Maqrīzīyah al-Musammāt bi-l-Mawāʿiẓ wa al-Iʿtibār bi-Dhikr al-Khiṭaṭ wa al-Āthār, yakhtaṣṣ dhalika bi-akhbār iqlīm Miṣr wa al-Nīl wa dhikr al-Qāhirah wa mā yataʿallaq bihā wa bi-iqlīmihā*, 5 vols. (Cairo: Maktabat al-Malījī, 1324–1326/1906–1908), vol. 1, p. 224.

72. See details in ibid., vol. 1, p. 224.

73. al-Balādhurī, *Futūḥ al-Buldān*, p. 328. Abū ʿUbayd reports that: ʿJarīr bin ʿAbdullah was the first person ʿUmar sent to Kūfah. He [ʿUmar] asked, "Will you go to Kūfah if I reward you with one-third after [i.e. as well as] the fifth?" He replied, "Yes" so ʿUmar sent him.' See Ibn Salām, *al-Amwāl*, pp. 67–68.

74. al-Balādhurī, ibid., p. 328; Ibn Ādam al-Qurashī, *Kitāb al-Kharāj*, pp. 29–30.

75. al-Yaʿqūbī, *Tārīkh al-Yaʿqūbī*, vol. 2, p. 135.

76. Abū Yūsuf, *Kitāb al-Kharāj*, p. 37.

77. See the texts of the treaties in Muḥammad Ḥamīdullāh al-Ḥyderābādī, *Majmūʿat al-Wathāʾiq al-Siyāsīyah fī al-ʿAhd al-Nabawī wa al-Khilāfah al-Rāshidah*, pp. 252–346. The following expressions appear here: 'It is incumbent on every adult male (*ḥālim*) in his wealth and the same according to his capacity (*bi-qadri ṭāqatihi*)', 'according to their capacity (*bi-qadri ṭāqatihim*)', 'the capacity of each male adult (*ṭāqat kulli ḥālim*) per year', 'from the hand of each male adult according to his capacity', 'according to their capacity (*ʿalā qadri ṭāqatihim*)', and so on.

78. al-Maqrīzī, *al-Khiṭaṭ al-Maqrīzīyah*, vol. 1, p. 225.

79. al-Maqrīzī, ibid., vol. 1, p. 229; al-Suyūṭī, *Ḥusn al-Muḥāḍarah fī Akhbār Miṣr wa al-Qāhirah*, vol. 1, p. 65; al-Balādhurī, *Futūḥ al-Buldān*, p. 253.

80. al-Maqrīzī, ibid., vol. 1, p. 224; al-Suyūṭī, ibid., vol. 1, p. 65.

81. Abū Yūsuf, *Kitāb al-Kharāj*, p. 125.

82. Abū al-Qāsim ʿAlī bin al-Ḥasan Ibn ʿAsākir, *al-Tārīkh al-Kabīr*, ed. ʿAbd al-Qādir Badrān, 5 vols. in 3 (Damascus: Maṭbaʿat Rawḍat al-Shām, 1329–1332/1911–1913), vol. 1, p. 174.

83. al-Ṭabarī, *Tārīkh al-Rusul wa al-Mulūk*, vol. 4, p. 346.

84. Abū Jaʿfar Muḥammad bin Jarīr al-Ṭabarī, *Ikhtilāf al-Fuqahāʾ*, ed. Joseph Schacht (Leiden: Brill, 1933), p. 225.

85. Abū Yūsuf, *Kitāb al-Kharāj*, p. 29; Ibn Salām, *al-Amwāl*, p. 83.

86. Ibn Salām, ibid., p. 85.

87. Wellhausen, *The Arab Kingdom and its Fall*, p. 276.

88. See Ibn Salām, ibid., pp. 73 and 252; Ibn Ādam al-Qurashī, *Kitāb al-Kharāj*, pp. 37–39 and 43–44.

89. See G. Van Vloten, *Recherches sur la Domination Arabe, le Chiitisme, les Croyances Messianiques sous la Khilafat des Omayades*, translated with commentary by Ḥasan Ibrāhīm Ḥasan and Muḥammad Zakī Ibrāhīm as *al-Siyādah al-ʿArabīyah wa al-Shīʿah wa al-Isrāʾīlīyāt fī ʿAhd Banī Umayyah* (Cairo: Maṭbaʿat al-Saʿādah, 1934), p. 50; al-Ṭabarī, *Tārīkh al-Rusul wa al-Mulūk*, vol. 8, p. 196; Muḥammad Ḥamīdullāh al-Ḥyderābādī, *Majmūʿat al-Wathāʾiq al-Siyāsīyah fī al-ʿAhd al-Nabawī wa al-Khilāfah al-Rashīdah*, pp. 205–215.

90. Abū Yūsuf, *Kitāb al-Kharāj*, p. 58; al-Balādhurī, *Futūḥ al-Buldān*, p. 181.

91. Ibn ʿAsākir, *al-Tārīkh al-Kabīr*, vol. 1, p. 183.
92. al-Balādhurī, ibid., p. 375.
93. al-Ṭabarī, *Tārīkh al-Rusul wa al-Mulūk*, vol. 5, p. 27.
94. V. V. Bartol'd, *Kul'tura musul'manstva*, trans. Ḥamzah Ṭāhir as *Tārīkh al-Ḥaḍārah al-Islāmīyah*; introduction by ʿAbd al-Wahāb ʿAzzām (Cairo: Dār al Maʿārif, 1942), vol. 1, p. 171.
95. al-Ṭabarī, ibid., vol. 3 , p. 589.
96. Abū Yūsuf, *Kitāb al-Kharāj*, p. 42.
97. al-Balādhurī, *Futūḥ al-Buldān*, p. 359; Ibn Salām, *al-Amwāl*, p. 54.
98. Abū Yūsuf, ibid., p. 9.
99. al-Balādhurī, ibid., p. 181.
100. al-Suyūṭī, *Ḥusn al-Muḥāḍarah fī Akhbār Miṣr wa al-Qāhirah*, vol. 1, p. 66.
101. Van Vloten, *al-Siyādah al-ʿArabīyah wa al-Shīʿah wa al-Isrāʾīlīyāt fī ʿAhd Banī Umayyah*, p. 19.
102. Ibn Ādam al-Qurashī, *Kitāb al-Kharāj*, p. 64.
103. Ibn Salām, *al-Amwāl*, p. 83.
104. Ibn Ādam al-Qurashī, *Kitāb al-Kharāj*, p. 38.
105. al-Suyūṭī, *Ḥusn al-Muḥāḍarah fī Akhbār Miṣr wa al-Qāhirah*, vol. 1, p. 67.
106. al-Balādhurī, *Futūḥ al-Buldān*, p. 359; Ibn Salām, ibid., p. 277.
107. Ibn Ādam al-Qurashī, ibid., pp. 1–8.
108. In his narrations, al-Balādhurī says there are ten categories but forgot to mention three of them. See al-Balādhurī, ibid., p. 334; Ibn Ādam al-Qurashī agrees on this number but there are four forgotten categories in his narration.
109. According to al-Masʿūdī, the *buyūt nīrān* were pre-Zoroastrian Persian fire temples wherein fire was worshipped, which were subsequently adopted by Zoroaster (Zarādasht – to whom al-Masʿūdī refers to as 'the prophet of the Majūs'). It is not clear whether these may have been left to function in their capacity or whether they may have been used simply as storehouses for tinder/firewood. A dimension of the question revolves around the status of the Zoroastrians and whether they are identical with the Majūs – as mentioned in the Qur'ān – and, hence, their legal status in Islamic *sharīʿah*. In his *tafsīr*, al-Qurṭubī reports a *ḥadīth* attributed to ʿAlī bin Abī Ṭālib to the effect that they have a 'book' and are, therefore, among the *ahl al-kitāb* – 'the people of the Book'. See Abū al-Ḥasan ʿAlī bin al-Ḥusayn al-Masʿūdī, *Murūj al-Dhahab wa Maʿādin al-Jawhar*, vol. 3, 7 vols. (Beirut: al-Jāmiʿah al-Lubnānīyah, 1965), p. 268. [Editor's note.]
110. See al-Balādhurī, ibid., pp. 272–273; al-Ṭabarī, *Tārīkh al-Rusul wa al-Mulūk*, vol. 3, p. 146; Ibn Ādam al-Qurashī, ibid., no. 199; Ibn al-Athīr, *Tārīkh al-Kāmil*, p. 407.
111. al-Balādhurī, ibid., pp. 334–335.
112. Ibn Ādam al-Qurashī, ibid., p. 64.
113. Ibid.
114. Ibn ʿAsākir, *al-Tārīkh al-Kabīr*, vol. 1, pp. 182–183.
115. See ibid., vol. 1, p. 186; Abū Bakr al-Ṣūlī, *Adab al-Kuttāb*, p. 212; Abū Yūsuf, *Kitāb al-Kharāj*, p. 32; al-Balādhurī, *Futūḥ al-Buldān*, p. 281.
116. See Adam Metz, *Der Renaissance des Islam*, trans. Muḥammad ʿAbd al-Hādī Abū Raydah as *al-Ḥaḍārah al-Islāmīyah fī al-Qarn al-Rābiʿ al-Hijrī*, 2 vols. (Cairo: Lajnat al-Ta'līf wa al-Tarjamah wa al-Nashr, 1940–1941), vol. 1, p. 187, as reported in Qudāmah bin Jaʿfar, Abū al-Faraj, *al-Kharāj*, ed. M. J. de Goeje; Bibliotheca Geographorum Arabicorum 6 (Leiden: Brill, 1889).
117. Ibn ʿAsākir, *al-Tārīkh al-Kabīr*, vol. 1, p. 182.

118. Abū Isḥāq Ibrāhīm bin Muḥammad al-Iṣṭakhrī, *Kitāb al-Masālik wa al-Mamālik, wa huwa Mu'awwal 'alā Kitāb Ṣuwar al-Aqālīm li-Abī Zayd bin Sahl al-Balkhī*, ed. M. J. de Goeje; Bibliotheca Geographorum Arabicorum 1 (Leiden: Brill, 1870), p. 158.

119. See Ibn Ādam al-Qurashī, *Kitāb al-Kharāj*, p. 9.

120. See Ibn Salām, *al-Amwāl,* p. 81; al-Balādhurī, *Futūḥ al-Buldān*, pp. 243–245.

121. al-Balādhurī, ibid., p. 298; al-Ḥyderābādī, *Majmū'at al-Wathā'iq al-Siyāsīyah fī al-'Ahd al-Nabawī wa al-Khilāfah al-Rāshidah*, p. 219.

122. Abū Yūsuf, *Kitāb al-Kharāj*, p. 27.

123. al-Ya'qūbī, *Tārīkh al-Ya'qūbī*, vol. 2, p. 152.

124. Abū Yūsuf, ibid., p. 38.

125. Ibn Salām, *al-Amwāl,* p. 45.

126. Abū al-Ḥasan 'Alī bin al-Ḥusayn al-Mas'ūdī, *al-Tanbīh wa al-Ishrāf*, ed. 'Abdullah Ismā'īl al-Ṣāwī (Cairo: al-Sharq al-Islāmīyah, 1938), p. 35.

127. Ibn Salām, ibid., p. 78; Ibn Ādam al-Qurashī, *Kitāb al-Kharāj*, no. 23; Muḥammad bin al-Ḥusayn Abū Ya'lā al-Farrā', *al-Aḥkām al-Sulṭānīyah*, edited with commentary by Muḥammad Ḥāmid al-Fiqī (Cairo: Maṭba'at Muṣṭafā al-Bābī al-Ḥalabī, 1938), p. 150.

128. Abū Yūsuf, *Kitāb al-Kharāj*, p. 38.

129. See Abū al-Ḥasan 'Alī bin Muḥammad al-Māwardī, *al-Aḥkām al-Sulṭānīyah wa al-Wilāyat al-Dīnīyah* (Cairo: Maṭba'at al-Sa'ādah, 1909), p. 143.

130. al-Ya'qūbī, *Tārīkh al-Ya'qūbī*, vol. 2, p. 130. There is an obscure narration (*riwāyah shādhah*) in al-Balādhurī, *Futūḥ al-Buldān*, p. 230.

131. al-Māwardī, *al-Aḥkām al-Sulṭānīyah*, p. 143.

132. al-Balādhurī, ibid., p. 231.

133. See ibid., p. 278; see ibid., p. 278; Abū al-Qāsim Muḥammad Ibn Ḥawqal, *al-Masālik wa al-Mamālik*, ed. J. H. Kramers, 2 vols.; Bibliotheca Geographorum Arabicorum 2 (Leiden: Brill, 1822), vol. 1, p. 234.

134. al-Balādhurī, ibid., p. 231.

135. Abū Yūsuf, *Kitāb al-Kharāj*, p. 36: 'He exempted the date palms to help them.' It seems that Abū Bakr al-Ṣūlī transmitted this sentence. See Abū Bakr al-Ṣūlī, *Adab al-Kuttāb*, p. 218.

136. Ibn Ḥawqal, *al-Masālik wa al-Mamālik*, vol. 1, p. 234; Abū Ya'lā al-Farrā', *al-Aḥkām al-Sulṭānīyah*, p. 150; Ibn Salām, *al-Amwāl*, p. 75; Abū Yūsuf, ibid., p. 36; al-Māwardī, *al-Aḥkām al-Sulṭānīyah*, p. 143. al-Balādhurī states: 'It was ten *dirhams*'. See al-Balādhurī, ibid., p. 333. Al-Ṣūlī reports: 'It was five *dirhams*.' See al-Ṣūlī, ibid., p. 218.

137. al-Balādhurī, ibid., p. 331; Abū Ya'lā al-Farrā', ibid., p. 150.

138. Abū Yūsuf, ibid., p. 21.

139. al-Balādhurī, *Futūḥ al-Buldān*, p. 332.

140. Abū Yūsuf, ibid., p. 38; al-Ṣūlī, *Adab al-Kuttāb*, p. 218.

141. Abū Yūsuf, ibid., p. 37; al-Ṣūlī, ibid.; al-Balādhurī, ibid., p. 331.

142. al-Balādhurī, ibid., p. 270; Abū Yūsuf, ibid., p. 37; al-Māwardī, *al-Aḥkām al-Sulṭānīyah*, p. 143; al-Ṣūlī, ibid., p. 218; Ibn Ḥawqal, *al-Masālik wa al-Mamālik*, vol. 1, p. 234.

143. Abū Yūsuf, ibid., p. 38; al-Ṣūlī, ibid., p. 218.

144. Ibn Salām, *al-Amwāl*, p. 75.

145. Ibid., p. 75.

146. Ibid.

147. Abū Yūsuf, *Kitāb al-Kharāj*, p. 38.

148. al-Ya'qūbī, *Tārīkh al-Ya'qūbī*, vol. 2, p. 152.
149. al-Balādhurī, *Futūḥ al-Buldān*, p. 333.
150. Abū Yūsuf, ibid., p. 38.
151. That is, their necks were marked – either tattooed or branded. See note 303 of this chapter.
152. al-Balādhurī, ibid., p. 332.
153. Ibn Ḥawqal, *al-Masālik wa al-Mamālik*, vol. 1, p. 234.
154. Ibn Salām, *al-Amwāl*, p. 74; Abū Yūsuf, *Kitāb al-Kharāj*, p. 36.
155. al-Ḥyderābādī, *Majmū'at al-Wathā'iq al-Siyāsīyah fī al-'Ahd al-Nabawī wa al-Khilāfah al-Rāshidah*, p. 219.
156. Abū Yūsuf, ibid., p. 38.
157. Ibid.; Ibn Salām, *al-Amwāl*, p. 159; al-Balādhurī, *Futūḥ al-Buldān*, p. 125.
158. Ibn Salām, ibid., p. 159.
159. Ibid., p. 160.
160. Ibid., no. 396.
161. al-Balādhurī, ibid., p. 205.
162. Ibid., p. 206.
163. Ibid., pp. 207–208.
164. Ibid., pp. 185–186.
165. Abū Yūsuf, *Kitāb al-Kharāj*, p. 41.
166. al-Balādhurī, ibid., p. 211.
167. Ibid., p. 209.
168. See A. S. Tritton, *The Caliphs and their Non-Muslim Subjects* (Oxford: Oxford University Press, 1930), p. 205.
169. Ibn 'Asākir, *al-Tārīkh al-Kabīr*, vol. 1, p. 155; al-Balādhurī, ibid., p.130.
170. al-Ṭabarī, *Tārīkh al-Rusul wa al-Mulūk*, vol. 3, p. 600; Ibn 'Asākir, ibid., vol. 1, p. 150. Here he confuses the city of Damascus (Dimashq) with the region of Dimashq.
171. al-Balādhurī, ibid., pp. 138 and 238. Here a narration reports that Abū 'Ubaydah made peace with the people of Hims for 170,000 *dinars* per year.
172. al-Ṭabarī, ibid., vol. 3, p. 600.
173. Ibid.; Ibn 'Asākir, *al-Tārīkh al-Kabīr*, vol. 1, p. 159.
174. al-Balādhurī, *Futūḥ al-Buldān*, pp.119 and 132.
175. Ibid., p. 174.
176. Ibid., p. 177.
177. Ibid., p. 164; al-Ṭabarī, ibid., vol. 3, pp. 609–610.
178. Ibn al-Athīr, *Tārīkh al-Kāmil*, vol. 2, p. 383.
179. al-Balādhurī, *Futūḥ al-Buldān*, p. 265.
180. Ibn 'Asākir, *al-Tārīkh al-Kabīr*, vol. 1, p. 150;
181. Ibn Salām, *al-Amwāl*, p. 149.
182. Ibn 'Asākir, ibid., vol. 1, p. 179.
183. There is a weak narration regarding the taxes in Greater Syria (*al-shām*); therefore, we have omitted it. See ibid., vol. 1, p. 179; al-Balādhurī, ibid., p. 139.
184. See Alfred J. Butler, *The Arab Conquest of Egypt and the last thirty years of the Roman dominion*, trans. Farīd Abū Ḥadīd as *Fatḥ al-'Arab li-Miṣr* (Cairo: Dār al-Kutub al-Miṣrīyah, 1933), pp. 240–241.
185. Ibid., p. 241.
186. al-Maqrīzī, *al-Khiṭaṭ al-Maqrīzīyah*, vol. 1, p. 807.
187. Butler, ibid., p. 275.
188. Ibid., p. 241.

189. al-Maqrīzī, ibid., vol. 1, p. 223.
190. al-Suyūṭī, *Ḥusn al-Muḥāḍarah fī Akhbār Miṣr wa al-Qāhirah*, vol. 1, p. 56.
191. al-Balādhurī, *Futūḥ al-Buldān*, p. 252.
192. Ibid., p. 252.
193. al-Maqrīzī, *al-Khiṭaṭ al-Maqrīzīyah*, vol. 1, p. 223.
194. Ibid., vol. 1, p. 223.
195. Ibid., vol. 1, p. 224.
196. al-Suyūṭī, *Ḥusn al-Muḥāḍarah fī Akhbār Miṣr wa al-Qāhirah*, vol. 1, p. 54.
197. Ibid., vol. 1, p. 63; al-Maqrīzī, ibid., vol. 1, p. 224.
198. Coptic names for the leaders and chiefs of the villages.
199. al-Suyūṭī, ibid.; al-Maqrīzī, ibid., vol. 1, p. 224 ff.
200. al-Balādhurī, *Futūḥ al-Buldān*, p. 252.
201. al-Maqrīzī, ibid., vol. 1, p. 224; al-Suyūṭī, ibid.
202. See Butler, *Fatḥ al-ʿArab li-Miṣr*, pp. 393–394.
203. al-Suyūṭī, ibid., vol. 2, p. 64.
204. Ibid., vol. 2, p. 65; al-Maqrīzī, *al-Khiṭaṭ al-Maqrīzīyah*, vol. 1, pp. 227–229.
205. al-Suyūṭī, ibid., vol. 1, p. 65; al-Maqrīzī, ibid., vol. 1, p. 223 ff; Ibn Ḥawqal, *al-Masālik wa al-Mamālik*, p. 78. al-Yaʿqūbī reports that ʿUmar collected 12 million in the first year, then 10 million in the second year.
206. Ibn Ḥawqal, ibid., p. 87.
207. al-Maqrīzī, ibid., vol. 1, p. 284.
208. [lit. 'the abode of war' – *dār al-ḥarb*: the territories bordering *dār al-Islām* (abode of Islam) without non-aggression or peace treaty with the Muslims]. Ibn Ādam al-Qurashī, *Kitāb al-Kharāj*, p. 173. This narration has its value, although we doubt there was a commercial relationship with the lands which had not submitted to the Muslims in these circumstances.
209. Ibn Salām, *al-Amwāl*, no. 532.
210. Ibid., no. 530; Ibn Ādam al-Qurashī, ibid., pp. 135–136 and 173.
211. Ibn Salām, ibid., p. 531.
212. Ibn Ādam al-Qurashī, ibid., p. 172.
213. Abū ʿUbayd attempts to make the lowest limit ten *dinars* or 100 *dirhams*, whereas Yaḥyā bin Ādam (523) puts it at 200 *dirhams*. See Ibn Salām, ibid., p. 534.
214. Ibid., p. 533; Ibn Ādam al-Qurashī, ibid., p. 173.
215. See Butler, *Fatḥ al-ʿArab li-Miṣr*, pp. 393–394.
216. See Van Vloten, *al-Siyādah al-ʿArabīyah wa al-Shīʿah wa al-Isrāʾīlīyāt fī ʿAhd Banī Umayyah*, pp. 2–4.
217. Julius Newman, *The Agricultural Life of the Jews in Babylonia between the Years 200 C.E. and 500 C.E.* (London: Oxford University Press, Humphrey Milford, 1932), p. 161 ff.
218. Muḥammad Ḥamīdullāh al-Ḥyderābādī, *Majmūʿat al-Wathāʾiq al-Siyāsīyah fī al-ʿAhd al-Nabawī wa al-Khilāfah al-Rāshidah*, p. 227.
219. Jurjī Zaydān, *Tārīkh al-Tamaddun al-Islāmī*, 5 vols. (Cairo: Dār al-Hilāl, 1918–1922), vol. 2, p. 19.
220. al-Ṭabarī, *Tārīkh al-Rusul wa al-Mulūk*, vol. 6, p. 44; Ibn al-Athīr, *Tārīkh al-Kāmil*, vol. 4, p. 90.
221. Abū Muḥammad ʿAbdullah Ibn ʿAbd al-Ḥakam, *Futūḥ Miṣr wa Akhbāruhā*, ed. Henri Massé (Cairo: Institut Français [d'Archeologie Orientale], 1914), p. 81.
222. The terms here appear to be used in contradistinction; that is, the term slave – *raqīq* – in the literal sense, and the term *ʿabd* in the common Classical parlance, which

denotes a human being along the lines of the term *insān* as is commonly used today. [Editor's note.]

223. al-Ṭabarī, *Ikhtilāf al-Fuqahā'*, p. 225.

224. Ibn 'Abd al-Ḥākim, ibid., p. 78; al-Balādhurī, *Futūḥ al-Buldān*, p. 225.

225. al-Maqrīzī, *al-Khiṭaṭ al-Maqrīzīyah*, vol. 3, p. 767.

226. al-Ṭabarī, *Tārīkh al-Rusul wa al-Mulūk*, vol. 7, p. 269.

227. See Zaydān, *Tārīkh al-Tamaddun al-Islāmī*, vol. 2, p. 23; Van Vloten, *al-Siyādah al-'Arabīyah wa al-Shī'ah wa al-Isrā'īlīyāt fī 'Ahd Banī Umayyah*, p. 33.

228. See al-Muṭahhar bin Ṭāhir al-Maqdisī, *al-Bid' wa al-Tārīkh (al-mansūb) li-Abī Zayd Aḥmad bin Sahl al-Balkhī* (*Le Livre de la Création et de l'Histoire de Motahhar ben Tahir el-Maqdisi, attribué à Abou-Zéïd Ahmed ben Sahl el-Balkhi*), 6 vols., ed. and trans. Clément Huart (Paris, Ernest Leroux, 1899–1919), vol. 6, p. 4; Ibn al-Athīr, *Tārīkh al-Kāmil*, vol. 5, p. 17; al-Jahshiyārī, *al-Wuzarā' wa al-Kuttāb*, p. 29; al-Ya'qūbī, *Tārīkh al-Ya'qūbī*, vol. 2, p. 211; Idem, ibid., vol. 3, p. 44; al-Ṭabarī, *Tārīkh al-Rusul wa al-Mulūk*, vol. 8, p. 187.

229. al-Ṭabarī, ibid., vol. 8, p. 139.

230. al-Ya'qūbī, ibid., vol. 3, p. 45.

231. See al-Maqrīzī, *al-Khiṭaṭ al-Maqrīzīyah*, vol. 4, p. 395.

232. Ibid., vol. 8, p. 264.

233. al-Ya'qūbī, ibid., vol. 2, p. 209.

234. Ibn al-Athīr, *Tārīkh al-Kāmil*, vol. 4, p. 59.

235. Muḥammad Kurd 'Alī (ed.), *Rasā'il al-Bulaghā'* (Cairo: Lajnat al-Ta'līf wa al-Tarjamah wa al-Nashr, 1913), p. 275.

236. Abū Yūsuf, *Kitāb al-Kharāj*, pp. 23–24.

237. al-Jahshiyārī, *al-Wuzarā' wa al-Kuttāb*, p. 24; al-Ya'qūbī, *Tārīkh al-Ya'qūbī*, vol. 2, p. 194.

238. Here there is a difference in some of the ancient narrations where it is variously reported that the wages of the minters – literally those who 'strike [coins]' (*ujūr al-ḍarrābīn*) – are specified or, alternatively, the wages of money changers – *ujūr al-ṣarrāfīn*. This could be a scribal error in transcription or even in recording a text being dictated. Al-Dūrī has assumed that the reference is to minters of coins, wherein the charge is apparently not directly linked to the *kharāj* or those paying it, but rather to an independent need of the state, which may have been to mitigate against the pilfering of coins from the mint by paying those striking them through payment of good salaries. Ghaida Katbi admits this possibility, but tends towards the hypothesis that the intended referent is to money changers who would have been involved directly in the *kharāj* and in dealing with the exchange of different coinage, as well as inspecting coinage for purity. See Ghaida Khazna Katbi, *Islamic Land Tax – al-Kharaj* (London: I.B.Tauris, 2010). [Editors note.]

239. al-Ṭabarī, *Tārīkh al-Rusul wa al-Mulūk*, vol. 8, p. 139.

240. See 'Abd al-'Azīz al-Dūrī, *Tārīkh al-'Irāq al-Iqtiṣādī fī al-Qarn al-Rābi' al-Hijrī* (Baghdad: Maṭba'at al-Ma'ārif, 1948), pp. 233–234.

241. Ibn Salām, *al-Amwāl*, p. 47.

242. See al-Dūrī, pp. 210–211.

243. al-Ya'qūbī, *Tārīkh al-Ya'qūbī*, vol. 3, p. 55.

244. Bandalī Jawzī, *Min Tārīkh al-Ḥarakāt al-Fikrīyah fī al-Islām* (Jerusalem: Maṭba'at Bayt al-Maqdis, 1928), p. 42.

245. al-Ṭabarī, *Tārīkh al-Rusul wa al-Mulūk*, vol. 8, p. 129.

246. Ibid., vol. 8, p. 129.

247. al-Ya'qūbī, ibid., vol. 2, p. 232.

248. Abū al-'Abbās Aḥmad bin Yaḥyā al-Balādhurī, *Anṣāb al-Ashrāf*, 5 vols. (Jerusalem: Maṭba'at al-Jāmi'ah al-'Arabīyah, 1936–1940), vol. 4, pt. 2, p. 45.

249. al-Ya'qūbī, ibid., vol. 2, p. 233.

250. al-Balādhurī, *Anṣāb al-Ashrāf*, vol. 4, pt. 2, pp. 245–246.

251. al-Balādhurī, *Futūḥ al-Buldān*, p. 302.

252. al-Māwardī, *al-Aḥkām al-Sulṭānīyah*, p. 183.

253. See Ibn 'Asākir, *al-Tārīkh al-Kabīr*, vol. 1, p. 184 ff.

254. Ibn Ādam al-Qurashī, *Kitāb al-Kharāj*, p. 62.

255. al-Ṭabarī, *Tārīkh al-Rusul wa al-Mulūk*, vol. 6, p. 381.

256. See ibid.; Wellhausen, *The Arab Kingdom and its Fall*, pp. 279–280.

257. al-Māwardī, *al-Aḥkām al-Sulṭānīyah*, p. 134.

258. Ibn Ādam al-Qurashī, *Kitāb al-Kharāj*, p. 42.

259. See ibid., no. 50 and p. 193; Wellhausen, ibid., p. 251.

260. Ibn Ādam al-Qurashī, ibid., no. 148.

261. al-Ya'qūbī, *Tārīkh al-Ya'qūbī*, vol. 2, p. 306.

262. Ibid., vol. 2, p. 312.

263. al-Ṭabarī, *Tārīkh al-Rusul wa al-Mulūk*, vol. 7, p. 269.

264. Qudāmah bin Ja'far, *al-Kharāj*, p. 170.

265. al-Jahshiyārī, *al-Wuzarā' wa al-Kuttāb*, p.118.

266. 'Abd al-'Azīz al-Dūrī, *Tārīkh al-'Irāq al-Iqtiṣādī fī al-Qarn al-Rābi' al-Hijrī*, pp. 34–35.

267. al-Balādhurī, *Futūḥ al-Buldān*, pp. 355–356; Qudāmah bin Ja'far, ibid., p. 240.

268. al-Balādhurī, ibid., p. 360; Qudāmah bin Ja'far, ibid., p. 240 ff.

269. al-Ya'qūbī, *Tārikh al-Ya'qūbī*, vol. 2, p. 303.

270. See al-Ṭabarī, *Tārīkh al-Rusul wa al-Mulūk*, vol. 3, p. 597; al-Balādhurī, ibid., p. 365.

271. Van Vloten, *al-Siyādah al-'Arabīyah wa al-Shī'ah wa al-Isrā'īlīyāt fī 'Ahd Banī Umayyah*, pp. 48–50.

272. M. Kurd 'Alī, *Rasā'il al-Bulaghā'*, p. 270.

273. Gholam Hossien Sadighi, *Les Mouvements Religieux Iraniens au IIe et au IIIe siècle de l'Hégire* (Paris: Les Press moderns, 1938), p. 8.

274. al-Ṭabarī, *Tārīkh al-Rusul wa al-Mulūk*, vol. 8, p. 252; Ibn al-Athīr, *Tārīkh al-Kāmil*, vol. 3, p. 12.

275. al-Balādhurī, *Futūḥ al-Buldān*, p. 365.

276. al-Ṭabarī, ibid., p. 54.

277. See Van Vloten, *al-Siyādah al-'Arabīyah wa al-Shī'ah wa al-Isrā'īlīyāt fī 'Ahd Banī Umayyah*, p. 50.

278. Bartol'd, *Tārīkh al-Ḥaḍārah al-Islāmīyah*, p. 65.

279. al-Ṭabarī, *Tārīkh al-Rusul wa al-Mulūk*, vol. 6, p. 605.

280. Ibid., vol. 6, p. 19.

281. al-Maqdisī, *al-Bidī' wa al-Tārīkh*, vol. 6, p. 1.

282. al-Ṭabarī, ibid., vol. 7, p. 56.

283. al-Ya'qūbī, *Tārīkh al-Ya'qūbī*, vol. 3, p. 44; Ibn al-Athīr, *Tārīkh al-Kāmil*, vol. 5, pp. 7 and 40; al-Jahshiyārī, *al-Wuzarā' wa al-Kuttāb*, p. 23.

284. See details in Van Vloten, *al-Siyādah al-'Arabīyah wa al-Shī'ah wa al-Isrā'īlīyāt fī 'Ahd Banī Umayyah*, pp. 48–50.

285. al-Ṭabarī, *Tārīkh al-Rusul wa al-Mulūk*, vol. 6, pp. 559 and 569; al-Ya'qūbī, ibid., vol. 3, p. 45.

286. Van Vloten, *al-Siyādah al-'Arabīyah wa al-Shī'ah wa al-Isrā'īlīyāt fī 'Ahd Banī Umayyah*, p. 51.

287. al-Ṭabarī, ibid., vol. 7, p. 55; Ibn al-Athīr, *Tārīkh al-Kāmil*, vol. 5, p. 54; W. Barthold [V. V. Bartol'd], *Turkestan Vèpokhu Mongol'skago Nashestviia*, translated from the original Russian and revised by the author with the assistance of H. A. R. Gibb, 2nd edn (London: Luzac and Co., 1928; E. J. W. Gibb memorial series. New series 5), pp. 189–190.

288. Sadighi, *Les Mouvements Religieux Iraniens au IIe et au IIIe siècle de l'Hégire*, p. 18.

289. al-Ṭabarī, ibid., vol. 7, pp. 173–174; Wellhausen, *The Arab Kingdom and its Fall*, pp. 478–488.

290. al-Balādhurī, *Futūḥ al-Buldān*, p. 225; Ibn 'Abd al-Ḥakam, *Futūḥ Miṣr wa Akhbāruhā*, p. 78.

291. See al-Maqrīzī, *al-Khiṭaṭ al-Maqrīzīyah*, vol. 3, p. 766; Sāwīrūs [Severus] bin al-Muqaffa', *Siyar al-Ābā' al-Baṭārikah* (n.p.: n.pb., n.d.).

292. Zaydān, *Tārīkh al-Tamaddun al-Islāmī*, vol. 2, p. 20.

293. Sāwīrūs bin al-Muqaffa', ibid., vol. 2, p. 55.

294. al-Maqrīzī, *al-Khiṭaṭ al-Maqrīzīyah*, vol. 3, p. 767.

295. Ibid., vol. 1, p. 226.

296. al-Jahshiyārī, *al-Wuzarā' wa al-Kuttāb*, pp. 51–52.

297. al-Maqrīzī, *al-Khiṭaṭ al-Maqrīzīyah*, vol. 3, p. 767.

298. Ibid., vol. 1, p. 226.

299. Sayyidah Ismā'īl Kāshif, *Miṣr fī Fajr al-Islām: min al-Fatḥ al-'Arabi ilā Qiyām al-Dawlah al-Ṭulūnīyyah* (Cairo: Dār al-Fikr al-'Arabī, 1947), pp. 56–57.

300. Sāwīrūs bin al-Muqaffa', *Siyar al-Ābā' al-Baṭārikah*, vol. 2, p. 72.

301. Ibid., vol. 2, p. 73.

302. al-Maqrīzī, *al-Khiṭaṭ al-Maqrīzīyah*, vol. 1, p. 227.

303. It is mentioned that Yazīd bin Abī Muslim, governor of Ifrīqiyah for Yazīd II, in 102AH wanted to follow the policy of al-Ḥajjāj with the *māwalī*, who had recently adopted Islam and left their villages to go to the garrison cities: 'He returned them to their rural areas and imposed the *jizyah* on their necks in the same way it was taken from them when they were unbelievers.' However, he did not succeed because the population revolted against him and killed him.

304. The text of al-Maqrīzī specifies: *wasama aydī al-ruhbān bi-ḥalaqat ḥadīd*, where the term *wasama* denotes: branding, marking or tattooing; and the phrase *bi-ḥalaqat ḥadīd* denotes: *with* or *by* a ring or disc (*ḥalaqah*) of metal/iron/lead. This has been interpreted variously by historians as: a branding of the hand with hot iron; an iron bracelet which was secured about the wrist; or a tattoo using lead. The logical argument in favour of a lead tattoo would be that it would be efficient to mark a large number of individuals, which if used in conjunction with a register would appear to be an effective means of record keeping. (That is, tattooing could be rapidly implemented, and if checked against a written record – especially one which included a date – could obviate against individuals tattooing themselves to avoid taxes.) Also, there is a report in al-Ṭabarī of a tattoo (*wisām*) of an *image* of a lion being used during the reign of Hishām bin 'Abd al-Malik, which would lend support to the contention that the reference in al-Maqrīzī is to a *tattoo* applied with lead. (See the following paragraph in the text on page 123 and note 306 below.) The contention that al-Maqrīzī's text refers to an *iron* bracelet which was affixed to the wrist is possible, but the idea that *iron* – either as a unique bracelet or a custom-made brand – suggests a costly, inefficient and labour-intensive process (even if such would militate against deception). Lastly, it might be possible that this was a bracelet of *lead* attached about the wrist – which would be softer to impress and more efficient than iron – assuming that it was used in conjunction with a written

register. For this reason, the text has been rendered as 'marked the hands of the monks with a ring of metal', even if the concept of a tattoo seems most likely in light of the above considerations. [Editor's note.]

305. al-Jahshiyārī, *al-Wuzarā' wa al-Kuttāb*, p. 57; Ibn Khallikān, Shams al-Dīn Abū al-'Abbās Aḥmad bin Muḥammad, *Wafayāt al-A'yān wa Anbā' Abnā' al-Zamān*, following on *Fawāt al-Wafayāt* by al-Ṣalāḥ al-Katbī, in the notes of *al-Shaqā'iq al-Nu'mānīyah fī 'Ulamā' al-Dawlah al-'Uthmānīyah* following on al-'Iqd al-Manẓūm fī Dhikr Afāḍil al-Rūm, 2 vols. (Cairo: Maṭba'at Muṣṭafā al-Bābī al-Ḥalabī, 1310/1892), vol. 2, p. 277.

306. al-Ṭabarī, *Tārīkh al-Rusul wa al-Mulūk*, vol. 8, p. 167.

307. See Kāshif, *Miṣr fī Fajr al-Islām*, pp. 55–58.

308. al-Maqrīzī, *al-Khiṭaṭ al-Maqrīzīyah*, vol. 2, p. 122.

309. A sufficient collection of papyri was not available to me, so I must refer the reader to: the category 'Miṣr [Egypt]', in *Dā'irat-al-Ma'ārif al Islāmīyah*; Tritton, 'The Caliphs and their Non-Muslim Subjects', pp. 211–220.

310. It is clear to me from a comparison of the Arabic sources that the *sawād* extended between Ḥarbī and al-'Alath northwards, to the Persian Gulf southwards, and from Ḥilwān eastwards to Qādisīyah westwards. See al-Dūrī, *Tārīkh al-'Irāq al-Iqtiṣādī fī al-Qarn al-Rabi' al-Hijrī*, pp. 5–7.

311. For details of the rivers in this region, see Suhrāb, *'Ajā'ib al-Aqālīm al-Sab'ah ilā Nihāyat al-'Imārah wa Kayf Hay'at al-Mudun wa Iḥāṭat al-Biḥār bihā wa Tashaqquq Anhārihā wa Ma'rifat Jibālihā wa Jamī' ma warā' Khaṭ al-Istiwā' wa al-Ṭūl wa al-'Ard bi-l-Misṭarah wa al-Ḥisāb wa al-'Adad wa al-Baḥth 'alā Jamī' mā Dhukir* (*Das Kitab 'Aga'ib al-Akalim as-Sab'a des Suhrab*), ed. Hans von Mžik (Vienna: Adolf Holtzhausen, 1929), pp. 129–135; *Journal of the Royal Asiatic Society* (JRAS) 1895, pp. 20–28.

312. al-Balādhurī, *Futūḥ al-Buldān*, pp. 293–294.

313. Qudāmah bin Ja'far, *al-Kharāj*, pp. 241–242.

314. al-Balādhurī, ibid., p. 273.

315. Ibid., p. 297; al-Jahshiyārī, *al-Wuzarā' wa al-Kuttāb*, p. 177.

316. al-Balādhurī, ibid., p. 291.

317. Abū Yūsuf, *Kitāb al-Kharāj*, p. 131.

318. Ibid., p. 133.

319. See Ibn Ḥawqal, *al-Masālik wa al-Mamālik*, vol. 1, p. 243; al-Iṣṭakhrī, *Kitāb al-Masālik wa al-Mamālik*, p. 84.

320. al-Jahshiyārī, *al-Wuzarā' wa al-Kuttāb*, p. 186.

321. He calls this type of *kharāj*: '*kharāj al-waẓīfah*'.

322. See al-Balādhurī, *Futūḥ al-Buldān*, pp. 280–281; Muḥammad bin 'Alī Ibn al-Ṭaqṭaqī, *al-Fakhrī fī al-Ādāb al-Sulṭānīyah wa al-Duwal al-Islāmīyah* (Cairo: Sharikat Tab' al-Kutub al-'Arabīyah, 1317/1899), p. 134; al-Māwardī, *al-Aḥkām al-Sulṭānīyah*, p. 170; Abū Ya'lā al-Farrā', *al-Aḥkām al-Sulṭānīyah*, p. 169.

323. Qudāmah bin Ja'far, *al-Kharāj*, p. 170.

324. al-Māwardī, ibid., p. 168.

325. al-Jahshiyārī, *al-Wuzarā' wa al-Kuttāb*, p. 151.

326. Ibn al-Ṭaqṭaqī, *al-Fakhrī fī al-Ādāb al-Sulṭānīyah wa al-Duwal al-Islāmīyah*, p. 162.

327. Abū al-Ḥasan 'Alī bin al-Ḥusayn al-Mas'ūdī, *Murūj al-Dhahab wa Ma'ādin al-Jawhar*, edited with commentary by Muḥammad Muḥyī al-Dīn 'Abd al-Ḥamīd, 4 vols. (Cairo: Dār al-Rajā', 1938), vol. 4, p. 169.

328. Abū Yūsuf, *Kitāb al-Kharāj*, p. 85.

329. Ibid., p. 109.

330. Ibid., p. 110.
331. Ibid.
332. al-Jahshiyārī, *al-Wuzarā' wa al-Kuttāb*, pp. 91–92.
333. Abū Yūsuf, ibid., p. 86.
334. Abū 'Alī al-Muḥsin bin 'Alī al-Tanūkhī, *al-Faraj Ba'da al-Shiddah*, 2 vols. in 1 (Cairo: Maḥmūd Riyāḍ, 1904), vol. 1, p. 79.
335. al-Ṭabarī, *Tārīkh al-Rusul wa al-Mulūk*, vol. 8, p. 259.
336. Abū Yūsuf, *Kitāb al-Kharāj*, p. 3.
337. Ibid., pp. 84–85.
338. Ibid., p. 85.
339. Ibid., p. 110.
340. He says that he wronged the people, oppressing them in a draconian fashion, and that he 'harrassed their nobles, took their wealth and belittled their men'. See al-Ṭabarī, ibid., vol. 8, pp. 315 and 324.
341. al-Jahshiyārī, *al-Wuzarā' wa al-Kuttāb*, p. 217.
342. al-Ṭabarī, ibid., vol. 8, p. 236.
343. Ibn al-Ṭaqṭaqī, *al-Fakhrī fī al-Ādāb al-Sulṭānīyah wa al-Duwal al-Islāmīyah*, p. 126.
344. al-Jahshiyārī, *al-Wuzarā' wa al-Kuttāb*, p. 279.
345. al-Ya'qūbī, Tārīkh al-Ya'qūbī, vol. 3, p. 460.
346. *Muḥaḍarāt al-Majma' al-'Ilmī al-'Arabī, Dimashq* [Arab Academy in Damascus] 1925–1954, 3 vols. (Damascus: al-Majma', 1954), vol. 1, pp. 49–50.
347. Abū Yūsuf, *Kitāb al-Kharāj*, pp. 108–109.
348. Ibid., p. 107.
349. Ibid., p. 108.
350. al-Maqrīzī, *al-Khiṭaṭ al-Maqrīzīyah*, vol. 2, pp. 761–762.
351. See ibid., vol. 2, pp. 762–763; Abū al-Rayḥān Muḥammad bin Aḥmad al-Bīrūnī, *al-Āthār al-Bāqiyah 'an al-Qurūn al-Khāliyah = Chronologie orientalischer Völker*, ed. Eduard Sachau (Leipzig: [n.pb.], 1878).
352. al-Maqrīzī, ibid., vol. 1, pp. 762–763.
353. al-Jahshiyārī, *al-Wuzarā' wa al-Kuttāb*, pp. 142–143.
354. Abū Yūsuf, *Kitāb al-Kharāj*, p. 109.
355. al-Maqrīzī, *al-Khiṭaṭ al-Maqrīzīyah*, vol. 1, p. 235.
356. al-Ya'qūbī, *Tārīkh al-Ya'qūbī*, vol. 2, p. 415.
357. Cited in Metz, *al-Ḥaḍārah al-Islāmīyah fī al-Qarn al-Rābi' al-Hijrī*, vol. 1, p. 1222.
358. al-Jahshiyārī, *al-Wuzarā' wa al-Kuttāb*, p. 197.
359. Al-Suyūṭī discusses a *ḥadīth* reported in most of the major Sunni compendia, where the Prophet is reported to have said: '*Al-kharāj bi-l-ḍamān*'. Abū 'Ubayd explains that the context of this utterance had to do with a man who purchased a slave from another and used him for a time before discovering a [physical] defect (*'ayb*), whereupon he returned him to the original owner. The original owner demanded compensation from the buyer for lost time and labour (when the slave was in the other's possession), and the matter was taken before the Prophet who made his pronouncement. The *fuqahā'* discussed the import of the *ḥadīth*, but the general consensus seems to have been that the beneficiary is entitled to benefit when bearing risk (or the risk of loss). That is, the buyer who purchased the slave with the defect bore the risk, was entitled to benefit, and therefore nothing was due in the way of compensation to the original owner. It should be noted that the context of this *ḥadīth* is *not* the *kharāj* land tax, although, given the usage of like terms, it may very well be the case that something similar was intended and

that there might have been an attempt to insure against crop loss in the extracting of the *kharāj*. It would seem – given the suggestion here in the narration of *hardship* – that a burden of guarantee against loss may have been imposed on the peasant farmers. It also seems logical that a guarantee against loss – *ḍamān* – might be the basis of the 'surplus' which the tax collector extracts over and above the *kharāj*. See al-Suyūṭī, 'Abd al-Raḥmān bin Abī Bakr, *al-Ashbāh wa al-Naẓā'ir* (Beirut: Dār al-Kutb al-'Ilmīyah, 1983. [Editor's note.]

360. Abū Yūsuf, *Kitāb al-Kharāj*, p. 105.

361. al-Maqrīzī, *al-Khiṭaṭ al-Maqrīzīyah*, vol. 1, p. 235.

362. In this context, keeping in mind the variability and fluidity of the definitions of terms over time, the *qibālah* here appears to be essentially the same thing as the *ḍamān*, in the sense that it referred to 'lands set aside against a pre-determined tax payment'. In other words, introduced into the *kharāj* system was a system of *ḍamān* or *qibālah*, which amounted to a setting aside of lands [or crops] apparently to ensure the *kharāj* was paid in full – ostensibly as against liability for poor yield or crop failure, etc. [Editor's note.]

363. Ibid., vol. 1, p. 239.

364. See Abū al-Ḥusayn Hilāl bin al-Muḥsin al-Ṣābī, *Tuḥfat al-Umarā' fī Tārīkh al-Wuzarā' = The Historical Remains of Hilal al-Sabi: first part of his Kitāb al-Wuzarā' and fragment of his History*, 389–393AH, edited with notes and glossary by H. F. Amedroz (Beirut: Catholic Press [Maṭba'at al-Ābā' al-Kathūlīkiyīn], 1904), pp. 10–11.

365. Abū Yūsuf, *Kitāb al-Kharāj*, p. 106.

366. Abū al-Faraj 'Abd al-Raḥmān bin 'Alī Ibn al-Jawzī, *al-Muntaẓam fī Tārīkh al-Mulūk wa al-Umam*, 10 vols. (Hyderabad-Deccan: Dā'irat al-Ma'ārif al-'Uthmānīyah, 1357–1358/1938–1939), vol. 5, p. 53; Abū 'Abdullah Muḥammad bin Aḥmad al-Khawārizmī, *Kitāb Mafātīḥ al-'Ulūm*, ed. G. Van Vloten (Leiden: Brill, 1895), p. 60. [Author's note.] One of the major challenges of working with the sparse accounts left by chroniclers of taxation and the details of its procedures, who assumed that their readers would be familiar to a degree with such, is that there are cases of terms which may or may not have been cognate, or where their precise designation is unclear. Thus, if the term *ḍamān* is understood to be cognate with *īghār* (a practice and mode which persisted into the late Ottoman period), then it is also possible it may be, in certain historical epochs, also related to or cognate with *iljā'*. As Elad has demonstrated, the meaning of the term *īghār* is not certain as even the Medieval lexicographers – in their sparse treatment of it – presented sometimes contradictory definitions of it and what it connoted. Modern scholars have not reached a consensus about the term, but there are general views that it was a protective arrangement within the *kharāj* system, whereby through payment of a fixed and lesser tax directly to the treasury – *bayt al-māl* – the taxpayer could be relived of part or possibly all of the *kharāj* tax. Apparently, this also meant that the landowner was not obliged to deal with the tax collectors. There are also particular types of special *īghār*, some of which continue into the later Ottoman period. See Amikam Elad, 'Two Identical Inscriptions from Jund Filasṭīn from the Reign of the Abbasid Caliph, Al-Muqtadir', *Journal of the Economic and Social History of the Orient*, vol. 35, no. 4 (Leiden: Brill, 1992), pp. 301–360. [Editor's note.]

367. al-Maqrīzī, *al-Khiṭaṭ al-Maqrīzīyah*, vol. 1, p. 854.

368. Ibid.

369. Ibid., vol. 1, p. 855.

370. Ibid., vol. 1, p. 857.

371. Ibid., vol. 1, p. 859.

372. al-Ya'qūbī, *Tārīkh al-Ya'qūbī*, vol. 2, p. 466.

373. Abū ʻAbdullah Muḥammad bin Aḥmad al-Muqaddasī, *Kitāb Aḥsan al-Taqāsīm fī Maʻrifat al-Aqālīm*, ed. M. J. de Goeje; Bibliotheca Geographorum Arabicorum 3 (Leiden: Brill, 1877), p. 448.
374. Ibid., p. 451.
375. Ibid., p. 421.
376. al-Iṣṭakhrī, *Kitāb al-Masālik wa al-Mamālik*, pp. 157–159; Metz, *al-Ḥaḍārah*, vol. 1, p. 206.
377. This involved registering the land (by those who lacked high status) in the name of a proxy who was typically an influential personage who would tender a fee to the treasury – *bayt al-māl* – directly, and thus avoid having to pay or deal with the tax collectors of the *kharāj*. It involved using the name of influential personage – to avoid paying the *kharāj* – but sometimes resulted in the lands ultimately being transferred to the individual. [Editor's note.]
378. al-Jahshiyārī, *al-Wuzarāʼ wa al-Kuttāb*, p. 7; *Muḥāḍarāt al-Majmaʻ al-ʻIlmī al-ʻArabī*, Dimashq 1925–1954, vol. 2, p. 56.
379. al-Jahshiyārī, ibid., p.118.
380. al-Iṣṭakhrī, *Kitāb al-Masālik wa al-Mamālik*, p. 158.
381. Bartol'd, *Tārīkh al-Ḥaḍārah al-Islāmīyah*, pp. 65–66.
382. al-Balādhurī, *Futūḥ al-Buldān*, p. 365.
383. Qudāmah bin Jaʻfar, *al-Kharāj*, p. 170.
384. al-Jahshiyārī, *al-Wuzarāʼ wa al-Kuttāb*, p. 90; al-Tanūkhī, *al-Faraj Baʻda al-Shiddah*, vol. 1, p. 52.
385. al-Ṭabarī, *Tārīkh al-Rusul wa al-Mulūk*, vol. 9, p. 172.
386. Ibn al-Jawzī, *al-Muntaẓam fī Tārīkh al-Mulūk wa al-Umam*, vol. 6, p. 25.
387. al-Iṣṭakhrī, *Kitāb al-Masālik wa al-Mamālik*, p. 158.
388. Qudāmah bin Jaʻfar, *al-Kharāj*, p. 170; al-Balādhurī, *Futūḥ al-Buldān*, p. 368.
389. al-Balādhurī, ibid., p. 371.
390. Ibid.
391. Qudāmah bin Jaʻfar, ibid., p. 170; al-Balādhurī, ibid., p. 368. The purchase of the lands of al-Sabyīn was before the caliphate of al-Maʼmūn. See al-Jahshiyārī, *al-Wuzarāʼ wa al-Kuttāb*, p. 306.
392. Qudāmah bin Jaʻfar, ibid.
393. al-Ṭabarī, *Tārīkh al-Rusul wa al-Mulūk*, vol. 9, p. 323.
394. al-Iṣṭakhrī, *Kitāb al-Masālik wa al-Mamālik*, p. 82; Ibn Ḥawqal, *al-Masālik wa al-Mamālik*, p. 213.
395. Abū al-Qāsim ʻUbayd Allah bin ʻAbdullah Ibn Khordadhbeh, *Kitāb al-Masālik wa al-Mamālik*, ed. M. J. de Goeje; Bibliotheca Geographorum Arabicorum 6 (Leiden: E. J. Brill, 1306/1889), p. 12.
396. See al-Balādhurī, *Futūḥ al-Buldān*, p. 272.
397. The *ṣawāfī* in the *sawād* were originally the lands of Khusrau and the Sassanian ruling family, the postal stations, bequests for the fire temples (*buyūt nīrān*) [see note 108, in this chapter], marshes, lands of those who died in the war at the Islamic conquest, wetlands, the swamps of the '*al-baṭīḥah*' and the lands of those inhabitants who had fled during the Islamic conquest. See ibid., pp. 272–273; Ibn Ādam al-Qurashī, *Kitāb al-Kharāj*, p. 199; Ibn al-Athīr, *Tārīkh al-Kāmil*, vol. 2, p. 407; Abū Yūsuf, *Kitāb al-Kharāj*, p. 57.
398. Abū Yūsuf, ibid., p. 58.
399. Ibid., p. 57. Here it says 7 million.
400. Qudāmah bin Jaʻfar, *al-Kharāj*, p. 251.
401. al-Balādhurī, *Futūḥ al-Buldān*, p. 318.

402. al-Ṭabarī, *Tārīkh al-Rusul wa al-Mulūk*, vol. 9, p. 203.
403. Dionysius, cited in Metz, *al-Ḥaḍārah*, vol. 1, p. 72.
404. Ibrāhīm bin Hilāl al-Ṣābī, *Rasā'il al-Ṣābī*, edited with commentary by Shakīb Arslān (B'abdā, Lebanon: al-Maṭba'ah al-'Uthmānīyah, 1898), vol. 1, p. 112.
405. Ibid., pp. 139–141.
406. Abū Yūsuf, ibid., p. 123.
407. Ibid., p. 125.
408. Cited in Metz, *al-Ḥaḍārah*, vol. 1, p. 72.
409. Ibid., vol. 1, p. 76.
410. al-Ṭabarī, *Tārīkh al-Rusul wa al-Mulūk*, vol. 9, p. 172.
411. Abū Yūsuf, *Kitāb al-Kharāj*, p. 124.
412. Qudāmah bin Ja'far, *al-Kharāj*, p. 184.
413. al-Maqrīzī, *al-Khiṭaṭ al-Maqrīzīyah*, vol. 1, p. 766.
414. There is insufficient space to mention this here. See Abū Bakr al-Ṣūlī, *Adab al-Kuttāb*, pp. 199–200; al-Ṣābī, *Rasā'il al-Ṣābī*, vol. 1, pp. 111 and 139–140; al-Māwardī, *al-Aḥkām al-Sulṭānīyah*, pp. 109, 112–116 and 146; Ibn Ādam al-Qurashī, Abū Zakariyā Yaḥyā bin Sulaymān, *Kitāb al-Kharāj*, ed. A. W. T. Juynboll (Leiden: Brill, 1896), pp. 81, 84 and 126; Ibn Salām, *al-Amwāl*, pp. 423–533; Abū Yūsuf, *Kitāb al-Kharāj*, p. 76 ff; al-Dūrī, 'Abd al-'Azīz, *Studies on the Economic Life of Mesopotamia in the 10th century* (PhD Thesis, University of London, School of Oriental and African Studies, 1942), pp. 203–205; Nicolas Prodromou Aghnides, *Mohammedan Theories of Finance* (New York: Colombia University Press, 1911), p. 244 ff.
415. Aḥmad Zakī Ṣafwat, ed., *Jamharat Rasā'il al-'Arab fī 'Uṣūr al-'Arabīyah al-Zāhirah*, 4 vols. (Cairo: Muṣṭafā al-Bābī al-Ḥalabī, 1937–1938), vol. 3, p. 152.
416. Abū Yūsuf, *Kitāb al-Kharāj*, p. 107.
417. al-Ṭabarī, *Tārīkh al-Rusul wa al-Mulūk*, vol. 9, pp. 203–206.
418. Metz, *al-Ḥaḍārah*, vol. 1, p. 89. Transmitted in the manuscript of Qudāmah.
419. Abū Yūsuf, *Kitāb al-Kharāj*, p. 188.
420. Abū al-Faraj 'Abd al-Raḥmān bin 'Alī Ibn al-Jawzī, *Manāqib Baghdād*, ed. Muḥammad Bahjah al-Atharī (Baghdad: Maṭba'at Dār al-Salām, 1342/1923), pp. 13–14.
421. Zaydān, *Tārīkh al-Tamaddun al-Islāmī*, vol. 2, p. 84; al-Iṣṭakhrī, *Kitāb al-Masālik wa al-Mamālik*, p. 158.
422. Aḥmad bin Abī Ya'qūb al-Ya'qūbī, *al-Buldān* (al-Najaf: al-Maṭba'ah al-Ḥaydarīyah, 1939), p. 22.
423. Ibid., p. 30.
424. al-Iṣṭakhrī, ibid., p. 158.
425. Metz, *al-Ḥaḍārah*, vol. 1, p. 206.
426. al-Khawārizmī, *Kitāb Mafātīh al-'Ulūm*, vol. 3, p. 208.
427. al-Ya'qūbī, *Tārīkh al-Ya'qūbī*, vol. 2, p. 483.
428. al-Ṭabarī, *Tārīkh al-Rusul wa al-Mulūk*, vol. 9, p. 483.
429. al-Ya'qūbī, ibid., vol. 2.
430. Reinhart Dozy, *Supplement aux Dictionnaires Arabes*.
431. al-Jahshiyārī, *al-Wuzarā' wa al-Kuttāb*, p. 149.
432. al-Ṭabarī, *Tārīkh al-Rusul wa al-Mulūk*, vol. 9, p. 125.
433. Ibid., vol. 9, p. 126.
434. The term can refer to a basket or also a container such as a money pouch. Here the reference would seem to be the former, where such were used to contain women's valuables such as perfumes and jewellery. [Editor's note.]
435. Ibid., vol. 9, p. 189; al-Mas'ūdī, *Murūj al-Dhahab wa Ma'ādin al-Jawhar*, vol. 5, p. 15.

436. al-Ṭabarī, ibid., vol. 9, p. 161; al-Ya'qūbī, *Tārīkh al-Ya'qūbī*, vol. 2, p. 485; Ibn al-Athīr, *Tārīkh al-Kāmil*, vol. 7, pp. 26–27.

437. al-Dūrī, *Tārīkh al-'Irāq al-Iqtiṣādī fī al-Qarn al-Rābi' al-Hijrī*, pp. 203–229.

438. 'Abd al-'Azīz al-Dūrī, *Dirāsāt fī al-'Uṣūr al-'Abbāsīyah al-Muta'akhirah* (Baghdad: Sharikat al-Rābiṭah li al-Ṭab' wa al-Nashr, 1946), pp. 17 ff and 191 ff.

439. al-Dūrī, *Tārīkh al-'Irāq al-Iqtiṣādī fī al-Qarn al-Rabi' al-Hijrī*, pp. 188–190.

440. In the event that explicit mention of the possible implication of these two practices is warranted: the collection of the *kharāj* before the ripening of crops and on the basis of the cadastral survery (*misāḥah*), and *not* the actual crop yield, imply that the farmers and taxpayers would be obliged to pay in *cash* rather than in kind, as it would not be possible to harvest a crop early, and as there would definitely appear to be greater liability for the taxpayer if assessments were made on the basis of estimates of the surveys for what the land *might* yield as opposed to actual crop yield. [Editor's note.]

441. Ibid., pp. 191–193.

442. See ibid., pp. 22 and 192–195.

443. Ibid., pp. 198–200.

444. Ibid., pp. 200–202.

445. Ibid., pp. 202–204.

446. Ibid., pp. 204–206.

447. The *jahbadhs* were money changers, financial clerks, financiers and essentially bankers – often Jewish – who came into prominence in the Baghdad of the caliph al-Muqtadir. See Walter Fischel, 'The Origin of Banking in Mediaeval Islam: A Contribution to the Economic History of the Jews of Baghdad in the Tenth Century', in *Journal of the Royal Asiatic Society of Great Britain and Ireland*, no. 3 (July 1933), pp. 569–603. [Editor's note.]

448. Ibid., pp. 206–207. The reader may notice modification in the terms of the book indicated, and this is at my discretion.

Chapter 3

Administrative Systems

The Diwāns

The beginning – the diwān *of 'Umar*

Like the rest of the Islamic institutions, the *diwāns* (*dāwāwīn*),[1] or government bureaus, originated as a result of the Arabs' need for financial, administrative and military systemisation. They began in a simple and limited way, and then developed, multiplied and branched out according to the developing needs and circumstances. In studying their formation, there is a need to distinguish between the central *diwāns* and the local *diwāns* in the provinces (*wilāyāt*) and garrison cities (*amṣār*). The former were instituted by the Arabs themselves and utilised the Arabic language, whereas the local *diwāns* were a continuation of the local Sassanian and Byzantine *diwāns*, and the Arabs initially retained these in their original state, in accordance with their general practice. Therefore, they continued to use the local languages, such as Pahlavi (Middle Persian) in Iraq and Iran, Greek in Greater Syria and Coptic in Egypt, until their Arabicisation was undertaken in the middle of the Umayyad state, at the time of 'Abd al-Malik bin Marwān and al-Walīd bin 'Abd al-Malik. Similarly, the foundations of these *diwāns* and their functions gradually converged, and were integrated until they took a single form for each type of *diwān* in the various provinces, characterised by a unified standard like other institutions.

Our study will focus on the central *diwāns*, since the local departments became miniature versions of these with the passage of time and this was after the stage of Arabicisation. The historians' account of the formation of the *diwāns* points to the *diwān* (or *diwāns*) of the centre (i.e., in the capital). The local *diwāns* are only referred to in the historical accounts of the beginnings of the process of Arabicisation during the caliphate of ʿAbd al-Malik bin Marwān. The sources agree unanimously on the fact that the first *diwān* in Islam was set up through the actions of the caliph ʿUmar bin al-Khaṭṭāb: 'ʿUmar was the first to set up the *diwān* (register) of the Arabs in Islam.'[2] Some of the sources indicate that the direct catalyst for establishing the first *diwān* was the vast wealth coming in from the conquered lands. The caliph's desire was to systematise their distribution. Al-Jahshiyārī and al-Balādhurī mention that Abū Hurayrah came from Bahrain with 500,000 *dirhams*, which the caliph regarded to be a huge amount. Then, he ascended the *minbar* (pulpit) and said to the people: '"Great wealth has come to us. If you so will, we will count it out, or if you wish, we will weigh it for you." A man said, "O Commander of the Faithful, I have seen those people [the Persians] keeping a register – *diwān* – (*yudawwinūn diwānan*) according to which they give to the people."' Thus, ʿUmar initiated the *diwān*.[3] It is narrated that Abū Sufyān asked ʿUmar: '"Is it a *diwān* like the *diwān* of the Banī Aṣfar (the Byzantines)? If you allocate money to the people they will come to rely on the *diwān* and abandon trade." ʿUmar replied, "This is unavoidable as the *fay'* (common booty) of the Muslims has become abundant."'[4]

We may mention that ʿUmar intended to make the Arabs into a militant *ummah* (nation) and to orient it towards struggle (*jihād*) in the interest of Islam. Therefore, he wanted to assign salaries (*rawātib*) and stipends (*ʿaṭīyāt*) to the fighters from the treasury – *bayt al-māl* – to suffice for them as recompense (*maʿūnah*) for their labour. He wanted to keep a register (*sijil*) of the names of the fighters and their families. Al-Yaʿqūbī reports: 'He [ʿUmar] imposed the *ʿaṭā'*..., saying that the wealth had become abundant so it was suggested to him to institute a *diwān* and he did so.'[5] In this, he gave priority to the allocation of the *ʿaṭā'* – a stipend for the fighters – which led to the creation of the *diwān*. Al-Jahshiyārī and al-Maqrīzī mention that the caliph sent a [military] expedition, and al-Firuzan or al-Hurmuzan (satrap of Fars) was present and he said to them, '"[As for] this delegation you have given money to its people [i.e., those entitled to it]. However, if one among them were to stay behind and leave his place, how would you know?" He advised him to establish a register for them.'[6] Al-Balādhurī narrates that al-Walīd bin Hishām bin al-Mughīrah said to ʿUmar: '"I went to Syria and I saw its kings had instituted a *diwān* and enlisted soldiers. So set up a *diwān* and enlist an army." And ʿUmar accepted his suggestion.'[7] Thus, we find confirmation of the direct connection between organising the soldiers, and systematising the stipends (*'aṭīyāt*) and the instituting of the *diwān*.

It appears that 'Umar, in his predilection for centralisation of policy and preparation of a stable resource for the state, came to prefer the system of the *diwān*. Abū Yusūf says:

> When Allah granted conquest to him ['Umar] and he conquered Persia and Byzantium, he assembled some of the companions of the Prophet and inquired, 'What is your opinion, I see fit to establish a stipend *'aṭā'* – for the people every year, and to collect money, as it will be the greatest blessing.'[8]

Despite the existence of narrations indicating that the second caliph did not approve of hoarding wealth, his actions show clearly his sentiments about the importance of having money at the disposal of the caliph, and that he paid heed to financial systemisation and stability which led to the existence of the *diwān* for the state. Historians differ over the origin of the concept for the establishment of the *diwān*. Some narrations[9] ascribe it to the influence of the Persians, while others[10] attribute it to Byzantine influence. Nevertheless, all the narrations refer to perceptions about the necessity for systemisation and consider this to have been the catalyst for initiating the *diwān*. This *diwān* was the register of soldiers in its first form, and at that time it was simply called '*al-diwān*' (*the diwān*) as it was the only one in Medina.

From analysis of information on this original '*diwān*', the type of elements which were recorded in it are clear to us and they pertained to the fighters. Abū 'Ubayd explains this in some detail:

> As for the large-scale distribution of the *'aṭā'* to the fighters and the provisioning of rations (*arzāq*) for the families, there has not come to us anything from the Messenger of Allah or from anyone of the *imāms* after him that he did that, except in regard to the settled people/urban dwellers (*ahl al-ḥāḍirah*) in Islam who are not in need of such.[11]

Then he reports on the authority of Ibn 'Umar that the second caliph 'did not used to give the *'aṭā'* to the people of Mecca or impose [recruitment for] military expeditions/campaigns on them'. He comments on this by saying: 'Do you not see, he did *not* stipulate a perpetual stipend – *'aṭā'* – for them since they were not made to carry out military expeditions.' He elucidates the policy of the caliph on this on the basis of Ibn 'Umar's assertion that:

> His opinion about the *fay'* is well-known, that no one had a right to it. This indicates to you that by the rights of settled people/urban dwellers in that from

> which the Muslims benefit, he had in mind the stipend – *aʿṭiyah* – and rations – *arzāq* – and by the rights of others he intended to mean what was for exigencies [i.e., only in the case of need].[12]

Al-Maqrīzī supports this approach since he narrates that the caliph said: 'I am the one who enlists the Muslims [for military service] on the basis of the *aʿṭiyah*, and the one who records them in the *diwān* and the one who strives for the truth.'[13] In clarifying this approach and its cause, al-Ṭabarī adds that ʿUmar:

> allocated it to the people entitled to the *fay'* which had been granted to them by Allah, and they were the people of al-Madā'in...They moved to Kūfah, Basra, Damascus, Homs, al-Urdunn (Jordan), Palestine and Egypt. He said, 'The *fay'* belongs to the people of these garrison cities (*amṣār*) and to those who joined them, helped them and stayed with them.' It was not allocated to anyone other than them. It was due to this that the cities and the villages were inhabited; *ṣulḥ* (peace) agreements applied to them, and compensation (*jazā'*) was paid, and the breaches frontiers were defended by them and the enemy was repelled.[14]

Thus, it is clear the *'aṭā'* in the *diwān* was for the first fighters who carried out the conquests, and for the inhabitants of the Peninsula who emigrated to them [and the lands] and assisted them in the conquest, or in maintaining the existence of the Islamic entity, because they constituted the pride of Islam and the mainstays of its power. Abū ʿUbayd demonstrates ʿUmar's attitude towards the rest of the Arabs by mentioning his famous commendation and bequest: 'The caliph after me is advised (thus...) and I advise him to treat the Bedouin Arabs (*al-aʿrāb*) well as they are progenitors of the Arabs and the core of Islam, and to take from their surplus wealth and return it to their poor.' He also mentions that he said: 'Verily, I will return it – meaning the alms (*ṣadaqah*) – to them until each one of them owns a hundred camels.'[15] Therefore, we see that the second caliph did not assign the *'aṭā'* in the register to all the Arabs. He recorded the inhabitants of Medina who were the heart of the Islamic *ummah*, then the fighting tribes that had participated in the conquests and those who joined these, among tribes, in order to reinforce the military power of the Muslims. He did not include the inhabitants of Mecca in the *diwān* because he did not send them on raids (*ghazawāt*). Nor did he include the Bedouin Arabs (*al-aʿrāb*) who remained in the Peninsula. Rather, he used to distribute from the funds of the *ṣadaqah* to the needy among them.

'Umar did not follow Abū Bakr's line in the *'aṭā'*, wherein the first caliph had not taken 'precedence (*sawābiq*), seniority/priority (*qidam*) and excellence (*faḍl*)' into consideration in the assessment of the *'aṭā'* . He said: 'That is something which is rewarded by Allah, glorified be His praise. This is for subsistence (*ma'āsh*), so equality [among people] in it is better than preference.'[16] 'Umar proceeded along new lines, saying: 'Abū Bakr had an opinion on this wealth, yet I have another view on it. I will not make [the share of] those who fought against the Messenger of Allah the same as those who fought with him.'[17] 'Umar explained the principle which he followed:

> There is no one entitled to it [the *fay'*] even a slave (*'abd mamlūk*). I am like any one of you in regard to it. Each of us is according to that which was sent down in the Book of Allah [or: each of us according to the status described in the Book of Allah] and our share as apportioned by the Messenger of Allah, hence [these categories are]: the man and his immediate family (*tilād*) in Islam; the man and his precedence in Islam; the man and his wealth in Islam [i.e. the one who is wealthy not in need of such]; and the man and his need in Islam.[18]

'Umar, thus, categorised the Muslims into ranks according to their previous service for Islam; precedence in converting to Islam (*sabq/qidam*); devotion to Islam; and then – lastly – according to need. When some of the Companions suggested to him that he begin the register – *al-sijil* – with his name, he refused, saying: 'The Messenger of Allah is our *imām*, so we will begin with his closest relatives, then with the next closest and the next.'[19] Another narration reports that he said: 'I put myself in whatever station Allah has placed me. Begin with the family of the Messenger of Allah.'[20] Al-Balādhurī says: 'He began with the Banū Hāshim in the call to Islam, then the people who were closest to the Messenger of Allah. If they were equal in their kinship (*qarābah*), he prioritised those who had precedence;' and that he 'favoured those with precedence and the witnesses – *mushāhid* [i.e. those who had witnessed the expeditions and the conquests] in the allocations.'[21]

In order to institute this plan, he appointed a special group to undertake the registration of the people according to their tribes and clans. It was composed of 'Aqīl bin Abī Ṭālib, Makhramah bin Nawfal and Jubayr bin Muṭ'im, who were the scribes of the Quraysh, and he said to them: 'Write [them down] according to their ranks/statuses (*manāzilihim*).'[22] The narrations differ with regard to the number of ranks and their *'aṭā'*. Having analysed the narrations of al-Ṭabarī, al-Balādhurī (two different narrations), al-Ya'qūbī, Abū Yūsuf and al-Maqrīzī, I have inferred the following: (figures are in *dirhams*)

1 12,000 for al-'Abbās and 'Ā'ishah.[23]
2 10,000 in total for all the 'mothers of the believers' (*ummahāt al-mu'minīn*).[24]
3 5,000 annually for those *muhājirūn* (emigrants) and *anṣār* (helpers [from Medina]) who witnessed the battle of Badr,[25] and for four people who joined them and were not from the people of Badr, who were al-Ḥasan, al-Ḥusayn, Abū Dhar and Sulaymān al-Fārisī.[26]
4 3,000 for those [who became Muslim] after Badr until al-Ḥudaybīyah,[27] and the Abyssinian emigration and Usāmah bin Zayd.[28]
5 3,000 for those [who became Muslim] after al-Ḥudaybīyah until Abū Bakr had finished with the 'people of apostasy' (*ahl al-riddah,* i.e. those whom he defeated in the so-called *riddah* wars),[29] as well as 'Abd Allah bin 'Umar[30] and those who emigrated before the conquest.[31]
6 2,000 for the people of [the battles of] Qādisīyah and those of Yarmūk.[32]
7 1,000 for those [who became Muslim] after Qādisīyah and Yarmūk.[33]

The *'aṭā'* was not assigned in these ranks for men only. 'Umar designated *aṭā'* for women, which amounted to one-tenth of the *'aṭā'* for the men of the same rank.[34] While al-Ṭabarī mentions that the second caliph treated as equals those people who were ranked below the people of Qādisīyah and Yarmūk.[35] We find al-Balādhurī specifying payments going down to 500 and 300 *dirhams*,[36] whereas al-Ya'qūbī goes down to 200 *dirhams* for the Rabī'ah tribe[37] and al-Maqrīzī also mentions this figure for some groups.[38]

There is some other curious information, to the effect that the caliph allocated 100 *dirhams* to each new-born child at birth, 200 *dinars* when he entered youth (lit. begins moving/walking), and above this amount if he attained to the age of maturity. More interesting than this is that he apportioned 100 *dirhams* for abandoned children:

> He allocated to him [the foundling] a ration for his sustenance, which his guardian took every month in the amount appropriate to him, and then he renewed it from year to year. He used to advise that the foundlings should be treated well and [what was necessary for] their contentment and their expenses was to be [taken] from the treasury – *bayt al-māl*.

He specified their assistance as being in kind for all, and apportioned 'two *mudd* of wheat, two *qisṭ* of oil and two *qisṭ* of vinegar for each Muslim soul every year'.[39]

He assigned to the commanders of the armies and the villages the *'aṭā'* in the requisite amount for them for food and their affairs, according to the narration of Abū Yūsuf.[40] 'Umar made the *mawālī* (non-Arab clients) and the Arabs equal in the ranks for the *'aṭā'*, as he did for the *muhājirūn* and their *mawālī*, and the *anṣār* and their *mawālī*, according to the narration of Abū 'Ubayd.[41] He also placed those who fought at the battle of Badr (*al-badrīyīn*) and their *mawālī* on an equal footing.[42] He wrote to the commanders of the armies: 'Those set free among the non-Arabs (*ḥumrā'* – lit. the 'red' people or Romans/Byzantines) who then become Muslim, are to be of the same status as the *mawālī*, they have the same [rights] as they have and the same [duties] as are germane to them.'[43] It is narrated that a group of people came to the governor of 'Umar bin al-Khaṭṭāb. He gave to the Arabs but not the *mawālī*. 'Umar wrote to him: 'A man is deemed evil if he despises his Muslim brother.'[44]

'Umar assigned the *'aṭā'* to 'tribal nobility (*ashrāf*) and non-Arabs (*a'ājim*)'. Abū 'Ubayd mentions that he gave 2,000 *dirhams* to Hurmuzan [a Persian advisor to him]. Al-Balādhurī counts two *dihqān*, who were both given 1,000 *dirhams* by 'Umar; and al-Ya'qūbī refers to two *dihqāns*, each given 2,000 *dirhams* by the caliph.[45]

Some of the narrations state that the initiation of the *diwān* took place in 15AH.[46] However, more trustworthy narrations among those from Ibn Sa'd (as well as al-Wāqidī and from al-Zahrī in al-Balādhurī and al-Ya'qūbī) put the timing of this at the beginning of 20AH.[47] It should be noted that '*diwān*' during the rule of 'Umar used to connote the record or register – *sijil* – which contained the names of the fighters and their family members, and the amount of their *'aṭā'* and provisions. When the *diwāns* multiplied, the term came to connote the register – *sijil* – in a general sense. Eventually, the meaning came to be applied to the place in which the register was kept. Hence, al-Qalqashandī specified it as being 'the name of the place (*mawḍi'*) in which the *kuttāb* (secretaries) sit'.[48]

Next to the *diwān* of soldiers (*diwān al-jund*), there was the treasury (*bayt al-māl*) where the funds accruing from the booty (*ghanā'im*) were stored, as well as those from the *jizyah*, *kharāj* and *ṣadaqah* taxes. There were a number of *kuttāb* employed by the caliph to write his correspondence, but there was no special *diwān* for correspondence during this period.[49] This was in Medina. In the provinces, there were *diwāns* for the *kharāj* and for expenditure (*nafaqāt*), which were a legacy from the previous era. There were also *diwāns* for the army, similar to that of Medina.[50]

The Umayyad diwāns

When the Umayyads came to power, they adopted Damascus as their capital. Their activities were gradually expanded and their needs multiplied in tandem with the unfolding circumstances. This led to the *diwāns* being developed and becoming numerous as commensurate with the needs of the state. New *diwāns* emerged, but it is often difficult for us to specify when this transpired. However, we may notice during which caliph's reign the name of the *diwāns* appears for the first time and will regard this as the time of its appearance.

Although the *diwāns* only assumed their final form during the 'Abbāsid age and were constantly in a state of development, we can say that their general foundations were laid down in the Umayyad age. The main Umayyad *diwāns* were the following:

- ***diwān al-kharāj*** was the most important bureau among the *diwāns*. It was in charge of the *kharāj* land tax, its collection and evaluation of its problems, and it constituted the fiscal mainstay. This was the Byzantine *diwān* for land tax and its language had been Byzantine Greek: 'Sarjūn bin Manṣūr al-Rūmi [i.e. the Byzantine] used to serve as a scribe (lit. to write) for the *diwān al-kharāj*.'[51] Its primary importance is clear from the fact that it came simply to be called '*the diwān*'.[52]
- ***diwān al-jund*** for the army (*jund*) was established on the same foundation by 'Umar bin al-Khaṭṭāb. The register contained the names of the soldiers, their descriptions, their genealogies and their stipends – '*aṭā*'.
- ***diwān al-khātam*** – the bureau of signet/registry – was first established by Mu'āwiyah (r. 4–60AH/66–80AD), following the forgery of a letter to Ziyād [bin Abīhi] ordering him to pay the courier the amount of 'one-hundred thousand', which the courier had changed to 'two-hundred thousand'. The *diwān* kept a copy of the caliph's correspondence and his directives after the original copy had been closed and impressed with a seal (*khātam*) in wax.[53]
- ***diwān al-rasā'il*** handled the caliph's correspondence and directives internally and his formal diplomatic documents (*mukātabāt*) for the outside. Al-Qalqashandī says: 'The matters of the sultan of the *mukātabāt* and the provinces originate from it and emanate from it.'[54] Then he explains that this was 'the first *diwān* established in Islam and that the Prophet would correspond with his commanders,

Companions and leaders of military...and he wrote to those kings of the neighbouring lands to invite them to Islam'.[55] There are references to *kuttāb* specialising in letters from the beginning of the Umayyad state. However, al-Jahshiyārī does not name this *diwān* explicitly, except in his account about 'Abd al-Malik bin al-Marwān (r. 65–86AH/685–705AD).[56] *Kuttāb* from among the Arabs and *mawālī* used to work for it. For example, Abū al-Zu'ayzi'ah, the *mawlā* of 'Abd al-Malik, and Rawḥ bin Zinbā' al-Judhāmī were among its *kuttāb*. 'Abd al-Malik described Rawḥ bin Zinbā' al-Judhāmī as being 'Persian of writing (*fārisī al-kitābah*)'.[57]

- ***diwān al-barīd*** or the postal bureau had the main and primary task of transmitting information and correspondence between the capital and the provinces, or between provinces. It appears that it also used to transport certain essentials and materials of state. For example, al-Walīd I used it to transport mosaics from Constantina to Damascus.[58] Its establishment is attributed to Mu'āwiyah, and he made use of the expertise of the Persians and Byzantines in this.[59]
- ***diwān al-nafaqāt*** monitored all expenditure (*nafaqāt*): 'everything which was spent on and for the army and other.'[60] That is to say, it dealt with all expenditures. It seems that its function was connected closely to the treasury. Al-Jahshiyārī mentions it for the first time in the caliphate of Sulaymān (r. 96–99AH/715–717AD) and he says: 'Al-Raqīq bin 'Abdullah bin 'Amr al-Ḥārith used to serve as *kātib* (lit. to write) for the [*diwāns*] of expenditure and the treasuries.'[61]
- ***diwān al-ṣadaqah*** dealt with the alms of *zakāt* and *ṣadaqāt* and their distribution among those entitled to them, in accordance with the Qur'ān and the Prophetic *sunnah*. Al-Jahshiyārī refers to it for the first time during the caliphate of Hishām bin 'Abd al-Malik (r. 105–125AH/724–743AD).[62]
- ***diwān al-mustaghallāt*** perhaps used to deal with the administration of the immovable/non-portable revenues of the state accrued from buildings, shops and real estate [such as taxes on market grounds].[63]
- ***diwān al-ṭarāz*** had the task of overseeing the factories which wove the official clothing, banners and emblems, and these were the factories for embroidery (*ṭarz*). Al-Jahshiyārī mentions it for the first time in his account about Hishām bin 'Abd al-Malik.[64] This *diwān* may have been set up at the time of 'Abd al-Malik or after him, or when he initiated the Arabicisation of the institutions of the dominion.

The most significant undertaking of the Umayyads was the Arabicisation of the *diwāns* or, to be more precise, the Arabicisation of the *diwāns* of the *kharāj*. Al-Jahshiyārī says:

> In Kūfah and Basra there were still two *diwāns*: one of them in Arabic for the census of the people and their stipends – *a'ṭīyāt* – and this was the one laid down by 'Umar; and another one for documenting types of revenues which was administered in Persian. In Syria it was similar to that [with two *diwāns*], one of them in Greek and the other in Arabic. It was like this until the time of 'Abd al-Malik bin Marwān.[65]

Thus, the language used in the *diwāns* of the *kharāj* continued to be the local language, just as was the case before the Islamic conquest, Pahlavi in Iraq, Byzantine Greek in Syria, and Coptic and Greek in Egypt. This is to be expected given the lack of Arab expertise in these matters and because the art of the scribe constituted a specialised field. However, the Arabs' expanding expertise, the development of the state, and its trajectory towards centralisation and unified standards, all necessitated modification and change. We cannot accept the trivial reasons offered by historians for this change, such as the annoyance of a particular *kātib* or a quarrel between two of the *kuttāb*.[66] The Arab policy followed by the Umayyads, the stability of the state and the affirmation of its edifice, as well as the supremacy of the Arabic language, demanded this Arabicisation.

The process of Arabicisation was long and essential. The Arabicisation of the *diwāns* of Iraq and Greater Syria was completed during the caliphate of 'Abd al-Malik bin Marwān,[67] and the *diwāns* of Egypt were Arabicised during the caliphate of al-Walīd bin 'Abd al-Malik (r. 86–96AH/705–715AD). The process was completed when the *diwāns* of Khurasān were Arabicised under the governorship of Naṣr bin Sayyār during the late Umayyad rule around the year 124AH. Arabicisation was the first vast and systematic process of translation, and it led to the transmission of much Persian and Greek terminology into Arabic. Moreover, it factored in circulating and spreading the Arabic language among the *mawālī*, and in the fact that Arabic became the *lingua franca* of administration and culture in addition to the language of politics and religion.

The 'Abbāsid diwāns

The 'Abbāsids inherited this legacy and they developed it in accordance with their circumstances. They increased centralisation, especially after creating the position of the vizier – *wazīr* (pl. *wuzarā'*), or state minister.

They created new departments and extended the authority of the vizier to include supervision over all the *diwāns*. Here it is sufficient for us to indicate some of the ʿAbbāsid developments. The ʿAbbāsids perhaps made some use of Persian administrative traditions, even if the *mawālī* were inclined towards exaggerating the influence of the Persians. This is clear from the *Kitāb al-Tāj fī Akhlāq al-Mulūk* (*Book of the Crown in the Conduct of Kings*), attributed to al-Jāhiẓ, where he says: 'Let us begin with the kings of the Persians...from them we took the laws (*qawānīn*) of the king and the dominion, the ordering of the elite and common people, the policy for the subjects and compelling each class to fulfil its duties on the basis of their traditions.'[68] The ʿAbbāsids were also influenced by Persian social traditions relating to fashion and clothing, and some customs of the court. As for their own influence on the administrative systemisation, I am inclined to regard it as insignificant, if it existed, because the ʿAbbāsid administrative systems differed from those of the Sassanians[69] and for the reason that they were essentially the same systems of the Umayyads. Therefore, it was natural that they should grow in conformity with the norm of development according to needs and evolving circumstances.[70]

During the caliphate of Abū al-ʿAbbās (r. 132–136AH/749–753AD), a systemisation of the registers (*sijilāt*) took place in that they were put into codices (*dafātīr*) instead of being recorded on separate sheets (*ṣuḥuf*), and this was done to prevent their loss. This was undertaken by Khālid al-Barmakī. Al-Jahshiyārī says: 'The means for recording in the *diwāns* was to write on the sheets. Then, Khālid was the first to put it into codices.'[71]

When Abū al-ʿAbbās confiscated the possessions and estates (*ḍiyāʿ*) of the Umayyads, he set up a special *diwān* to manage them: 'Abū al-ʿAbbās entrusted to ʿAmārah bin Ḥamzah the estates of Marwān and the family of Marwān.'[72] After his account of the building of Baghdad, al-Yaʿqūbī refers to the *diwāns* which al-Manṣūr (r. 136–158AH/754–775AD) transferred there.[73] After indicating the treasury and the arsenal (*khizānat al-silāḥ*), he mentions the *diwāns* for correspondence (*diwān al-rasāʾil*), the *diwān* of the *kharāj*, the seal (*diwān al-khātim*), the army (*diwān al-jund*) and expenditure (*diwān al-nafaqāt*), as well as the *diwān* of those in the service of the royal court (*diwān al-aḥshām*)[74] and the *diwān* of the court (*diwān al-ḥawāʾij*). It appears that the head of this last had the function of collecting notes and pleas, and presenting them to the caliph[75] so that he could look into them and see that justice was being served to the complainants in them. Al-Yaʿqūbī mentions, in another place, the *diwān al-ṣadaqāt*, and it was dedicated to matters of *zakāt* on livestock in particular.[76]

Al-Manṣūr created a temporary *diwān* where the names of those whose possessions had been confiscated were recorded, along with the amount which had been seized from them. This was the *diwān al-muṣādarah* (confiscation) and, perhaps, was abolished at the time of al-Mahdī.[77]

Al-Mahdī's rule (r. 158–169AH/775–785AD) was a period of relative calm in which the organisation of the *diwāns* was consolidated and the supervision of their workers was intensified. The *diwāns* of audits/comptrollers – *dawāwīn al-azimmah* – were created in 162AH[78] to oversee the work of the major *diwāns* and to supervise the financial side of them in particular. Al-Ṭabarī narrates:

> The first to set up the *diwān al-zimām* [lit. the *diwān* of the 'reigns', i.e. that for control] was 'Umar bin Buzaygh during the caliphate of al-Mahdī. That was when he subsumed for him all the *diwāns*. He thought he could not control these except with reins – *zimām* – which he would have over each *diwān*. So he saw fit to create the *dawāwīn al-azimmah* and appoint a man for each *diwān*.[79]

This systemisation points to the expansion of the work of the original *diwāns* and their increasing complexity. Al-Mahdī took another step in 168AH towards centralisation, and that was by creating a *diwān* to oversee the *diwāns* of audit and to systematise their work. This was the supreme audit/comptroller's office – the *diwān zimām al-azimmah*.[80] It appears that the creation of the *dawāwīn al-azimmah* spread into the provinces.[81] Subsequently, al-Mahdī set up a new *diwān* to take up his subjects' complaints about the governors and to protect them from their transgressions, especially in tax collection. This was the department for the assessment of grievances (lit. those wronged) – *diwān li-l-naẓar fi al-maẓālim*. He used to hear the cases himself personally, and the judges used to participate with him in this.[82] Al-Mahdī also systematised the working hours for the *kuttāb* in the *diwāns* and their days off. He ordered that 'the day of Thursday shall be appointed for the *kuttāb* [as a day] on which to take rest and deal with their own affairs, when they did not have to be present at the *diwāns* and the day of Friday shall be for prayer and worship'. This protocol was followed until al-Mu'taṣim annulled the Thursday as a day of respite.[83]

During the caliphate of Hārūn al-Rashīd (r. 170–193AH/786–809AD), we find reference to a special *diwān* called the *diwān al-ṣawāfī* for state lands. Its function, so it seems, was to deal with matters relating to the lands belonging to the caliph in his capacity as leader of the Muslims.[84] There was also a *diwān* of estates (*diwān ḍiyā'*), which supervised the management of the caliph's private estates and those of his family. These were extensive and spread across the various far reaches of the empire.[85]

At the time of al-Ma'mūn (r. 198–218AH/813–833AD), we find mention of the *diwān al-jahbadhah*; that is, the *diwān* for money changers (*jahbādh*, pl. *jahābidhah*). It appears that this was a branch of the treasury – *bayt al-māl* – and its function was to scrutinise the accounts of the treasury and the nature of its resources. Al-Tanūkhī relates a story about an individual who became al-Ma'mūn's '*jahbadh* (money changer) and the chief of his treasury' and he describes the premises of the *jahbadhah*. The narrator says:

> I went into the building...in it there were many chambers with many opulent furnishings and in the centre there was a young man. Before him were the *kuttāb* and the money changers – *jahābidhah* – and the accounts with which they were dealing. There were *jahābidhah* in the porticos and the chambers of the buildings with money, wooden benches and balances before them, collecting and receiving.[86]

Al-Ya'qūbī, in his account about the Ja'farīyah – the palace city of al-Mutawakkil (r. 232–247AH/847–861AD) – indicates its *diwāns* and mentions 'the *diwān* of the *mawālī* and slave soldiers (*diwān al-mawālī wa al-ghilmān*)'. It seems that this *diwān* looked into the concerns of the servants and *mawālī* connected to the palace court. Al-Ya'qūbī calls the *diwān* for the army (*diwān al-jund*) the '*diwān al-jund wa al-shākirīyah*', in reference to the Turkish troops known as the *shākirīyah*, and he also mentions the auditing/comptroller *diwān* over the *diwān* of expenditure (*diwān zimām al-nafaqāt*).[87] This is a glimpse into the innovations in the *diwāns* until the end of the first 'Abbāsid age (which ends with the death of the caliph al-Wāthiq).

The *kuttāb*, or state secretaries, used to carry out the directives of the *diwāns*. These men represented the elite among the intelligentsia. We are able to grasp this from the advice to the *kuttāb* attributed to 'Abd al-Ḥamīd bin Yaḥyā (d. 132AH/750AD). From this, it was clear that the *kātib* should:

> have studied every category of knowledge (*'ilm*) and mastered it; and if he cannot master it, he should draw from it an amount which is sufficient for him...Therefore, you, O company of *kuttāb*, compete with each other in the categories of knowledge and literature (*adab*) and become versed in *fiqh* and the matters of religion. Begin with the knowledge of the Book of Allah (Qur'ān) and the religious duties (*farā'iḍ*), then the Arabic language as it is the edification of your tongues (speech). Excel in calligraphy (*khaṭṭ*) as it is the ornament of your letters. Recite poetry and be acquainted with their unusual words (*gharīb*) and their meanings, recite the histories (*ayyām*) of the Arabs

> and non-Arabs (*'ajam*), their traditions and biographies. That will assist you in that for which you strive in your endeavours. And, do not neglect or falter in your study of accounting/mathematics (*ḥisāb*) as it is the backbone of the *kuttāb* of the *kharāj* among you.[88]

In order words, the *kātib* should have the most comprehensive education in all branches of knowledge of the Islamic age.

It seems that the increasing complexity of administration and the expansion of the sciences both led to a kind of specialisation among the *kuttāb*, such that we find one elderly *kātib* at the time of al-Ma'mūn distinguishing between five types of specialisations in the *diwāns*:

- The ***kātib kharāj*** for the land tax must be knowledgeable about conditions, taxes,[89] accounting, cadastral surveys (*misāḥah*), the arts (*funūn*) and parchments (*ruqūq*).
- The ***kātib aḥkām*** for the judiciary must know what is lawful (*ḥalāl*), prohibited (*ḥarām*), legal argumentation (*iḥtijāj*), consensus (*ijmā'*) and the branches of jurisprudence (*furū'*).
- The ***kātib ma'ūnah*** for the constabulary must be knowledgeable in the rules of retaliation (*qiṣāṣ*), the fixed punishments of Islamic law (*ḥudūd*), injuries (*jirāḥāt*), handling of claims in the presence of witnesses (*muwathabāt*) and discretionary punishment (*siyāsah*) because he was dealing with criminal matters.
- The ***kātib jaysh*** for the army must have familiarity with the equipment and armour of the men, the shoeing and maintaining of riding animals, etiquette and edification of the irregular soldiers (*awliyā'*), and some knowledge of genealogy (*nasab*) and accounting.
- The ***kātib rasā'il*** for correspondence must know about salutations (*ṣudūr*) and closings (*fuṣūl*) [i.e. beginning and ending correspondence], lengthening (*iṭālah*) and conciseness (*ījāz*), eloquence in rhetoric (*ḥusn al-balāghah*), and calligraphy.[90]

The letter of appointment from the caliph al-Ṭā'i' (r. 363–381AH/974–991AD) to the chief judge – *qāḍī al-quḍāt* – Abū Muḥammad 'Abdullah bin Aḥmad bin Ma'rūf clarifies the qualifications for the *kātib* of the *qāḍī*:

> I command him to take as a companion a *kātib* practised in note-taking and record-keeping, skilled in legal matters, state matters, knowledgeable in conditions and punishments, familiar with what is permitted and what is not, and able to cope with the high-ranking judges and acceptable witnesses – in his righteousness, his purity, his preserving of himself from the evils of eating and

> drinking and yielding to doubt and suspicion. The *kātib* constitutes the reigns (*zimām*) of the authority (*ḥākim*) for whom he is his recourse and helper and through him, he guards against disastrous intrigues and hidden evils.[91]

The central *diwāns* initially had small similar, representative *diwāns* in the provinces. For example, at the time of al-Rashīd there was, in addition to the central *diwān* of the *kharāj*, a *diwān* of the *kharāj* for Basra and its districts, a *diwān* of the *kharāj* for Kūfah and its districts, a *diwān* of the *kharāj* for Egypt, and a *diwān* of the *kharāj* in Khurasān.[92] However, we notice that after the confused circumstances in the kingdom, which ensued after the taking of control by the Turks, each province came to have a special *diwān* in Baghdad to examine its affairs.[93] Then during the caliphate of al-Mu'taḍid (r. 189–279AH/892–902AD), these *diwāns* were combined into a singled *diwān* called the *diwān* of the palace (*diwān al-dār*) or the grand *diwān* (*diwān al-kabīr*), and Aḥmad bin al-Furāt was put in charge of it.[94] After a brief period, the affairs of the eastern provinces were separated out and he created the *diwān al-mashriq* for it, just as the affairs of the western provinces were separated, and he instituted the *diwān al-maghrib* for them. The affairs of the Sawād (Iraq) were left to the *diwān al-sawād*. However, it appears the *diwān al-dār* remained central to these important *diwāns*.[95] At the beginning of the fourth century AH, 'Alī bin 'Īsā instituted the charities *diwān – diwān al-birr wa al-ṣadaqāt*. Its task was the administration of the endowments (*awqāf*) which the caliph had established in Iraq. Its revenue was 93,000 *dinars* for the two sanctuaries of Mecca and Medina (*al-ḥaramayn al-sharīfayn*), and for defending the borders.[96]

The unsettled affairs of the caliphate had an effect on these developments as a large share of the lands came to be given out for tax farming (*ḍamān*). The tax farmer (*ḍāmin*) was required to pay an amount of money in order to have a free hand with the tax collection.[97] In my opinion, the diminishing influence of the caliphate was a reason for the decrease in the works of the *diwān* of expenditure (*nafaqāt*) for which the needs of the *diwān* of the caliphate became its greatest task at the end of the third century AH and the beginning of the fourth century AH.[98] Perhaps the control of the Turks in the second third of the third century AH, and their financial misconduct, led to the distinction between the private treasury of the caliph (*bayt māl al-khāṣṣah*) and the state treasury (*bayt al-māl*). It also led to making the vizier, or those in whose power was the general administration, supervisors of the state treasury, while the caliphs controlled the private treasury and spent from it on whatever matters were associated with them.

Perhaps we may explain that the third century AH witnessed a reversal in administrative institutions and a decline in their activities due to the domination of the Turks. Despite the fact that some of their glory and prestige returned to the administrative institutions during the caliphates of al-Muʿtaḍid, al-Muktafī (r. 289–296AH/902–908AD) and al-Muqtadir (r. 295–320AH/908–932AD), nevertheless these were dealt a crushing blow during the period of the *imārat al-umarāʾ* (see Chapter 1) and they declined considerably in the Buwayhid era.[99] Metz authored an interesting study on the *diwāns* of the fourth century AH.[100] However, he depended considerably on what he cited from Qudāmah bin Jaʿfar (d. 337AH/948AD). This makes his study more idealistic rather than one based on reality because it appears to me that Qudāmah was researching the regulations of the *diwāns* and what they *ought* to be, rather than what they were in fact. As I was unable to obtain all the sources which I wanted (at the time of writing this book), including the manuscript of Qudāmah on which Metz relied, I will draw Qudāmah's information from what has been cited from him by Metz. For this reason, I am only able to sketch an outline of the important *diwāns* and their activities after they had acquired the characteristic of systemisation of them in the ʿAbbāsid age preceding the Buwayhid conquest.

Let us begin with the treasury:

> This *diwān* was known as the sublime *diwān* – *diwān al-sāmī*. It was the original source *diwān* and the authoritative reference to which the *diwāns* referred. Its function was that all the sources of the royal assets were confirmed in its registers, according to their categories of assets/commodities in kind (*ʿayn*), crops, *fayʾ*, booty (*ghanāʾim*), tithes (*ʿushr*) and fifths (*khums*). It also verified what was obtained from these and taken by the treasuries for the categories of revenue, and it assigned *diwāns* and administrators for them. Money and cloth had the *diwān al-khizānah* (treasury), the crops had the *diwān al-ahrāʾ* (granaries) and weapons and materials had the *diwān khizānat al-silāḥ* (of the arsenal).[101]

The head of the treasury (*ṣāḥib bayt al-māl*) was required to:

> supervise the revenue which is returned to the treasury and incoming and outgoing expenditure and payments. The documents which concerned the revenue had to pass through it [the treasury] to be verified there before they arrived at the respective [provincial] *diwāns*, and likewise the remainder of the documents sent to the head of the treasury and all the *diwāns* that exact revenue. The head of this *diwān* must be knowledgeable in documents,

> contracts (*ṣikāk*) and payments (*iṭlāqāt*), which the vizier and his caliphs should examine, supervise and demand.[102]

The *diwān* of the *jahbadhah* (money changer) was a derivative branch of the treasury, where the *kuttāb* specialising in financial matters and the *jahābidhah* (money changers) worked. Its activities, as I have noted, consisted of monitoring and assessing income revenues and spending. Among the duties of the head of this *diwān* was to present an account at the end of each month in a synopsis known as a *khatmah* and another final and comprehensive one at the end of each year – *khatmah jāmi'ah* – about revenue and expenditure, which he submitted to the treasury.[103]

The *diwān* of the *kharāj* was described as comprehensively subsuming the handling of *kharāj* taxes of the *ḍiyā'* (estates), the *jawālī* tax and the *zakāt* tax. Among the requisite requirements to work for this *diwān* were knowledge of arithmetic, multiplication and division, as well as trustworthiness and fairness in order to take what was due and not cause ruin or waste.[104]

As for the *diwān* of expenditure – *nafaqāt*, the affairs of the *diwāns* and their requirements were referred to its head. Their accounts were submitted to him so that he could pay them in full, and demand funds and whatever was earmarked for requirements. The head of this *diwān* had to excel in arithmetic, multiplication, division, measures, weights, prices and taxes, in addition to knowing all categories of clothing, food, equipment, animals and their value, and knowing the corresponding crown charges.[105] The head of this *diwān* also had to be in direct contact with the treasury in order to retain certificates (*tawāqī'*) to verify that monies were spent correctly in expenditure.[106]

According to [the lexicographer] al-Khalīl bin Aḥmad, the term *barīd* (post) was Arabic, while others were of the opinion that it was an Arabicised form of a Persian word.[107] The *diwān al-barīd* used to make use of mules, horses and camels, and its fast camels (*jammāzāt*, 'quick-paced') were desired for the desert areas.[108] Al-Ḥasan bin 'Abdullah remarked: 'The Persians use excellent horses for that and the Arabs use the high-bred camels, and they are faster than the horses and have greater endurance for travelling.'[109] They used to make use of messengers who were fast at running and this had become a widespread practice, particularly in the Buwayhid era. Al-Ḥasan bin 'Abdullah said: 'The people of Iraq are known to be the swiftest. They are men – light and fit – who are accustomed to running and enduring travel so as to pass three days' journey in a single day.'[110]

The postmaster (*ṣāḥib al-barīd*) oversaw and received 'the documents sent from all reaches of the domain...so that he is the one who collects all of them and distributes each to its designated location. He is in charge of presenting to the caliph the post and the news from all the regions of the caliphal domain or summarising this.'[111] The postmaster had subordinates in various towns, called the deputies of the postal service, and their effectiveness appears manifestly during the caliphate of al-Manṣūr, as al-Ṭabarī narrates:

> The deputies of the postal service in all the remote regions used to write to al-Manṣūr at the time of his caliphate about all the food prices, the decisions made by judges in their districts and the actions of the governor, what revenue was returned to the treasury and every event. After they prayed the evening prayer, they would write to him all night about whatever there was.[112]

The nature of this position is elucidated by what is transmitted of the duties entrusted to the head of the postal service in 315AH when the postmaster was required:

> ...to know the state of the officials of the [*diwāns* of] the *kharāj* and the estates and to follow this satisfactorily in detail, with transparency and handling it correctly and honestly; to know the state of the cultivation of the lands and what is perfect and defective of it; the affairs of the subjects in how they are treated as regards justice and equity, injustice, compassion and tyranny and to write an official report on it; to know the rulings and conduct of the judges and the rest of their views and ways; to know the state of the money mint and what gold coins (*'ayn*) and silver coins (*waraq*) are struck there, and what those coming there are charged and to write what is correct and honest thereby what is necessary for the suppliers of expenses and wages (for the minters), and to write what is correct and honest thereby; to assign persons to supervise the pensions *majlis* for the army irregulars and their stipends – *'aṭā'* – those who be thoroughly informed about what transpires in it; and to write information about what the situation is at the time [it occurs] so that whatever he reports is accurate and verifiable; to devote a document to each of the categories of information about important personages: a document to information on the judges, the police officials and events/crimes; as well as to author documents on the *kharāj*, on the estates, on sustenance/pensions and the like so that each document is channelled to its proper place.[113]

It was not sufficient for the postmaster to simply transmit official reports. Rather, he was obliged to engage in scrutiny and espionage. Thus, the agents of the postal service were 'in the station of being the seeing eyes and hearing ears' of the ruler.[114] For this reason:

> they were obliged to know news (*aṣḥāb al-akhbār*) and to attend the gatherings of the people, their banquets, preaching sessions and the marketplaces as it is in these places that noteworthy information is to be found. Likewise, they discover the conditions of the common people, their seditious talk and rumours and what words and actions are known of them at all times.[115]

This necessitated that the agent of the *barīd* would know 'the schemes of women, boys, guards, bathhouses, tradesmen and craftsmen';[116] in other words, he should have spies in all of the various professions and social classes. Hence, the importance of the work of the postmaster is obvious, and this required a person who was trustworthy and cautious in his work.

The official highways (*ṭuruq*) were under the supervision of the postmaster and it was expected of him to know them adequately so as not to require any observations other than his own:

> If the caliph were to inquire of him at the time of his need to travel or to dispatch an army or other than these which demanded someone who knew the roads, he would find – in the person of the postmaster – someone before him who was knowledgeable and dependable and not in need of delegating others or making further inquiries.[117]

He was responsible for maintaining and preserving the roads, and securing them from highway robbers, spies, enemies and the infiltration of spies by land and sea.[118] The roads were divided into waystations – *maḥaṭāt* – with spare riding animals and riders, and there were two *farsangs*[119] or four *farsakhs* (sg. *farsakh*, pl. *farāsikh*; approximately 5km) between every two stations.[120]

The postal service was in the service of the 'Abbāsid caliphs[121] and used to transport goods in addition to correspondence. For example, watermelons from Khawārizm [Khiva in Uzbekistan] were brought by the post for al-Ma'mūn,[122] and dates were sent to al-Ma'mūn, to the frontiers of Byzantium, by the postal camels.[123] The post was used in exceptional circumstances to transport travellers. When al-Hādī (r. 169–170AH/785–786AD) heard the news of the death of al-Mahdī – he was in Jurjān – he rushed to Baghdad on riding animals of the postal service.[124] Al-Rashīd was informed about an exceptionally talented *'oud* (lute) virtuoso in Persia: 'He sent...for the Persian, and the musician was brought by the post.'[125] In addition to the requirements of the usual post, a special post service was sometimes organised, as al-Mahdī did when he sent his son to attack the lands of Byzantium.[126] When al-Mu'taṣim (r. 218–227AH/833–842AD) sent his commander al-Afshīn to war against Bābak al-Kharmī, he organised the post so that the messages went from the stations of al-Afshīn in Azerbaijan to Sāmarrā' in four days or less.[127]

Carrier pigeons came to constitute the fastest service for the post, and al-Qalqashandī indicates that al-Mahdī used them.[128] Similarly, there is reference to it at the time of al-Mu'taṣim when he was informed about the capture of Bābak. There are other details which Metz reports narrating from Qudāmah with regard to the branches of the *diwāns* of the army and expenditure. However, it is not necessary to mention these here since I do not attach great importance to these details, as they were either theoretical (i.e. not actually in practice) or were of temporary significance.

The inception and development of the *wizārah*

Introduction

Arab writers consider the term *wazīr* – vizier – to be Arabic, and to have been applied to the advisor or aide to the king. Al-Mas'ūdī explains that the Umayyads used to presume that [the term] '*wazīr* derives from *mu'āzarah* (assistance or support)', and he holds that the 'Abbāsids took the word from the Qur'ānic verse: '[O Allāh] Appoint a *wazīr* (a supporter/helper) from my family: Hārūn (Aaron) – my brother. Who will support me [lit. who will "straighten/support my back" – *wizrī*] and let him share my task'.[129] Al-Māwardī and Abū Sālim assert that there are three approaches to the derivation of the word *wazīr*. One is

> that it is taken from *wizr* meaning 'burden' because he [the *wazīr*] relieves the king of his burdens. The second is that it is taken from *wazr* meaning 'refuge'. Thus, he is called by this because the king takes refuge in his opinion and assistance. The third is that it is taken from *izr* meaning 'back (or strength)' because the king is strengthened through his *wazīr* like the body is strengthened by the back.[130]

Ibn al-Ṭaqṭaqī supports the first two derivations, mentioning: 'How the inversion of the phonation/articulation of the word *wazīr* was indicatory of refuge and burden.'[131]

Ibn Khaldūn refers to the Arabs' knowledge of the *wizārah*, or ministerial office, among other nations since the beginnings of Islam. He says the

Messenger [i.e. the Prophet Muḥammad] used to solicit the advice of his Companions: 'and in that, he singled out Abū Bakr for other particular matters/private affairs, to the extent that the Arabs who were familiar with the dynasties and circumstances of Khusrau, Caeser and the Negus used to refer to Abū Bakr as his *wazīr*.'[132] The *Tafsīr al-Jalālayn* (of al-Suyūṭī) explains the meaning of the word *wazīr* as being 'helper (*al-muʿīn*)', just as it appears in the Qur'ān.[133] Al-Zamakhsharī says: 'The *wazīr* of the king is the one who bears the burdens of the king. That is, he bears it [a burden] with him [the king], and it is not from the word *mu'āzarah* meaning to help someone.'[134] Al-Fīrūzābādī confirms the Arabic origin of the word and says: 'The *wazīr* is a companion for the king (*ḥaba'* – i.e. *jalīs* or someone who 'sits with him') who bears his burden and helps him with his opinion.'[135]

From the discussion above, it is clear that the word is Arabic, even if the office of *wazīr* to which it refers is not Arab in origin. Babinger's opinion on its meaning was that the origin of the word is Iranian. In Avestan (old Persian) the word *vicira* connoted 'arbiter' or 'judge', and in Pahlavi (middle Persian) the word *v(i)cir* had the same meaning, and he believes that the Arabs adopted the word during the Sassanian era.[136] However, the similarity in the terms does not serve as a proof that it was borrowed or adapted, especially as the concept of the *wizārah* differs from that of the *judiciary* and Pahlavi includes a term for minister/*wazīr* other than the word mentioned by Babinger. This is in addition to the fact that the Arab linguists were concerned with distinguishing loanwords and attempted to trace them back to their origins. In light of this, they concurred unanimously that the word *wazīr* was Arabic as it had been mentioned in the Qur'ān and the Muslims had utilised it since the dawn of Islam.

The origin of the wizārah

The *wizārah* did not appear within the practical sphere in Islam until the 'Abbāsid era. Before that time the office did not exist, despite the Arabs' knowledge of its existence among the Sassanians.[137] The Arab historians have stated this decisively. Al-Masʿūdī refers to the non-existence of the *wizārah* among the Umayyads.[138] Ibn Khalkān says about the first 'Abbāsid *wazīr*: 'No one before him was known by this description, not in the state of the Banī Umayyah (Umayyads), nor in others.'[139] Ibn al-Ṭaqṭaqī says:

> The foundations of the *wizārah* were not laid down and its rules were not specified except during the state of the Banī al-'Abbās ('Abbāsids). Before that,

> the bases were indeterminate and the regulations not standardised. Rather, each one of the kings had his followers and entourage. When something transpired, he would seek the advice of those possessing perspicacity, discretion and probity, and each of them would proceed along the lines of a *wazīr*.[140]

However, the emergence of the office of *wazīr*, coterminous with the rise of the ʿAbbāsids, does attract attention. Al-Jahshiyārī mentions that:

> When Ibn Hubayrah was defeated and was heading for Wāsiṭ, Humayd and al-Ḥasan, the sons of Qaḥṭabah, entered Kūfah on 11 Muḥarram 132AH. They recognised Abū Salamah (al-Khallāl) and handed over the leadership to him, naming him the *wazīr* of the people of the Prophet Muḥammad's house. He took over affairs and proclaimed the Hashemite *imamate*.[141]

The significance of this is that the appointment of the first *wazīr* and his being named by this term were both effected through the view of the Khurasānī supporters of the ʿAbbāsids. This may point to the concept being from Iran and that the office symbolises the involvement of the Persians in the new authority. However, it is not sufficient a reference to explain the appearance of the *wizārah*. Undoubtedly, the general circumstances were favourable for the creation of such an office and in ensuring its growth and stability, as actually transpired.

The Umayyad administration had been gradually heading towards centralisation, to the effect that the Umayyad caliph began to select a *kātib* from those around him and favour him with his trust. Such was the position of ʿAbd al-Ḥamīd, the *kātib* for the last Umayyad caliph Marwān II. The effect of the trend towards centralisation dictated that there be a person to supervise and to assist the caliph, and in this we can comprehend the emergence of the *wizārah*. If we examine the jurisdiction of the early viziers, we find that it is not very far removed from that of the position of ʿAbd al-Ḥamīd. It is apparent that the Arab historians realised this, as al-Masʿūdī says: 'Banū al-ʿAbbās chose to name the *kātib* as *wazīr*.'[142] Ibn al-Ṭaqṭaqī writes: 'When the Banū al-ʿAbbās took power, the naming of the *wizārah* was decided and the vizier came to be termed *wazīr*. Before that he had been called a *kātib* or advisor/counsel (*mushīr*).'[143]

The ʿAbbāsid system of the *wizārah* had grown gradually in accordance with the position of the caliphs and their power, as well as the development of administrative orientations. As for the theoretical foundations laid by the *fuqahāʾ*, they were relative and influenced by reality.

It is useful for us to consider the foundations of the scribal profession and the *wizārah* in the Sassanian era in order to find a means for comparison of what transpired in the ʿAbbāsid age. The vizier had been the chief of central administration and had been called the *hazārbadh* (grand vizier) since the Achaemenid age. The *hazārbadh*, who was originally the supreme commander of the army/praetorian guard, became the first official in the empire and the emperor ruled the state with his assistance. This name remained in currency during the Parthian and the Sassanian eras. In the Sassanian era, the official title of the *wazīr* was *vuzurg framadhar*, as Mihr Narsī, the grand vizier for Yazdegerd II, referred to himself in a letter to the Armenians.[144] We understand from al-Ṭabarī, al-Masʿūdī and al-Yaʿqūbī that the name *vuzurg framadhar* was given to the vizier until the end of the Sassanian period.[145] Al-Ṭabarī explains the title of *wazīr*: 'His rank in Persian is *buzurgfarmadhār* which in Arabic means chief minister (*wazīr al-wuzarāʾ*) or supreme chief (*raʾīs al-ruʾasā*).'[146]

Christensen acknowledges that our primary information about the powers of the Sassanian viziers is scant; however, he believes that they were not limited to directing the affairs of the state with the supervision of the king. In his opinion, the *wazīr* served as the king's representative and vicegerent while he was absent travelling or at war; he also used to undertake political negotiations and might lead the army. In general, Christensen thinks that the *wazīr* was the main advisor to the king, overseeing and being involved in all matters of the state.[147] Al-Masʿūdī narrates:

> The Persians used to call the minister of the king 'the bearer of burden' (*ḥāmil al-thiql*), the underpinning of support (*wisād al-ʿaḍd*), the chief of the competent [experts] and the grand administrator and disposer of affairs since the proper arrangement of affairs, the splendour of the dominion and the majesty of the sultan inhered in him. The *wazīrs* are the elocutors of the kings, the treasurers of their wealth and their trustees over their subjects and lands.[148]

The perfect *wazīr* is described as being educated, noble, with praiseworthy qualities, and superior to his contemporaries in everything. He combines the highest morals, patient deliberateness, theoretical wisdom and practical experience.[149] Al-Ṭabarī says: 'When Yazdegerd took power, he appointed as *wazīr* the wisest of his age. Narsī was perfect in his conduct, virtuous in all his beliefs, ahead of the people of his time.'[150] He also says of him: 'He was revered by all the kings of Persia by virtue of his conduct, the excellence of his opinions and the reassurance of the people with him.'[151] Those whom the king might appoint as his *wazīr* would not be among the very powerful, and those who would be so were of his own making (from his servile dependants). This is clarified in the advice of Khusrau Parviz (Chosroes Abruizus) to his son Shīrawayh (Shiruyah): 'and let whoever you choose for your ministry be a person who was [of] humble [origin], whose stature was lowly, whom you then raised up and made him [into something].'[152]

The conduct of the Sassanian *wazīr* delegated that he was to hide secrets, and to be a truthful and sincere advisor. Abriyz said, addressing his *wazīr*, 'Conceal secrets, speak truthfully, strive to arrive at the correct conclusions in your advice and be cautious and on your guard.'[153] The Persian King Sābūr Dhū al-Aktāf (Shapur II) had two viziers. He would consult each of them separately and individually: 'Doing so keeps secrets, engenders decisive and correct opinions and leads to peace and well-being.'[154]

Christensen believes that the system of the *wizārah* in the caliphate derived directly from the Sassanian state, and that what the Arabic sources mention about the powers of the *wazīr* (on the theoretical side) is found in the clarification of the powers of the Sassanian vizier.[155] However, I am unable to support this because the endeavour of the *fuqahā'* in elaborating their theories was to refine experiences and to direct them a long time after their occurrence. This is contrary to the impression which they give, that reality proceeded according to and in light of the theory that they propounded. What strengthens this opinion is that the system of the *wizārah* began obscurely, then developed, and was defined gradually. If we consider the concept of the *wizārah* and its priorities with regard to the influence of the Persian systems, we can affirm that the 'Abbāsid *wizārah* had a life of its own and corresponding development; there is no evidence to support the contention that it was completely derived (or borrowed). Rather, the evidence does not suggest more than inspiration for the primary elements.

The Sassanian vizier used to appoint *kuttāb* (scribes). He would insist that the *kātib* be: 'noble in his morals; of sound opinion; profound in his thought; knowledgeable of the classes and ranks of his age; logical; erudite and capable in correspondence; conversant with laws, politics and poetry and possessing excellent style. He also approved of his having excellent handwriting.'[156] Vishtaspa [Kishtāsib] used to say to the *kuttāb*: 'You must be virtuous and render loyalty in everything delegated to you and discipline your instincts and your minds to upright etiquette and manners.'[157] The *kuttāb* constituted a single class with a special chief called the *Eran dibherbedh*. They used to have to undergo examinations before they were employed for duties. The king ordered his senior chief *kuttāb* to examine the young (incoming) *kuttāb*:

> and to test their intellects. As for any of those with whom they were satisfied, his name was presented to him [i.e. the *eran dibherbedh*] and he was retained

> and ordered to remain ready for service. Subsequently, the king would command them to join the officials and to be given a free hand in their work.[158]

Al-Khawārizmī (d. 387AH) enumerated the secretarial positions and scribal categories – *kitābah* – of the Persian *kuttāb* (according to function), and these were:

> the *kitābah* (secretary) of legal rulings (*aḥkām*); the *kitābah* of land for the land tax – *kharāj*; the *kitābah* of accounting for the royal exchequer – *ḥisāb dār al-malik*; the *kitābah* for the treasuries; the *kitābah* for the stables; the *kitābah* for accounting firewood/tinder – *ḥusbānāt al-nīrān*; and the *kitābah* for endowments (*awqāf*).[159]

The *kuttāb* had exceptional status, says al-Jahshiyārī:

> The kings used to promote the *kuttāb* and to acknowledge the virtue of the craft of *kitābah*, and its practitioners enjoyed a high social station as they combined in their persons virtuous opinion and deftness in the craft. [They used] to say, 'They are the disposers of affairs, the perfection of the dominion and the splendour of the ruler. They are the elocutors of the kings, the treasurers of their wealth and their trustees over their subjects and lands.'[160]

Among their distinctions was that they used to ride horses (*barādhīn*): 'and no one rode these except the kings, *kuttāb* and judges.'[161] The foundation principles of this *kitābah* became a model in the 'Abbāsid era in particular.[162]

In order to fathom the development of the *wizārah* system, we must make note of the prominent issues among the viziers of the 'Abbāsid age. We have mentioned the appointment of Abū Salamah al-Khallāl; however, we must not infer that the plan for the *wizārah* in its commonly understood administrative connotation was drawn from this because the 'Abbāsids embarked on the system of the *wizārah* in a simple form – somewhat influenced by the views of their Persian aides on the one hand, and inclining towards the vestiges of the Umayyad systemisations on the other. Therefore, we find al-Mas'ūdī putting the 'Abbāsid *wazīr* in the (category and) place of the Umayyad *kātib*, as he considers the change to be – in the first instance – one of preference in terminology.[163]

Al-Khallāl was only an influential advisor by virtue of his circumstances, and not all the *diwāns* were under his control. Rather, the two important *diwāns* – the *diwān* of the army and the *kharāj* – were controlled by Khālid bin Barmak.[164] Among that which points to the ambiguity of the new post was that 'everyone appointed as *wazīr* after Abū Salamah used to attempt to avoid being called *wazīr* seeing it as a bad omen in light of what happened to Abū Salamah'.[165] Khālid al-Barmakī 'took the place of the *wazīr*' after the misfortune of al-Khallāl, and 'he was...doing the work of the viziers yet not called a *wazīr*'.[166] It appears that al-Khallāl was among the group of *kuttāb* given that he was 'eloquent, knowledgeable and informed, adept in poetry, biographies, debate and [Qur'ānic] exegesis, and prepared for argumentation'.[167] The main cause of al-Khallāl's demise was that he attempted to transfer the caliphate to the 'Ālids,[168] and Ibn Qutaybah adds that al-Khallāl's powerful reach and influence bordered on the dangerous.[169] This misfortune was a manifestation precipitated by the ambiguity of the station of the *wizārah*, and the clash between the caliph's authority and the power of the *wazīr*.

If we scrutinise the history of the first 'Abbāsid era meticulously, we find it was a theatre for the constant clash between the caliphs and their viziers due to the lack of clarity about the powers and definition of the post of the *wazīr*. The *wazīr* wanted to control everything, while the caliph desired to render him strictly as an advisor and assistant. Therefore, the problems multiplied and so too did the misfortunes of the *wazīrs*. The first 'Abbāsid age ended with the affirmation of the authority of the caliph and the circumscribing of the general lines for the powers of the *wazīr*. For this reason, it is correct to consider the first 'Abbāsid era as a trial period for the *wizārah* system. It is to be noted about al-Khallāl, and Khālid al-Barmakī after him, that – in addition to their extensive education and culture – they were both among the most prominent propagandists of the 'Abbāsid claim and of those who had service worthy of mention in establishing the 'Abbāsid state.

The caliphate of Abū al-'Abbās ended with a position for viziers which was somewhere between that of a *wazīr* and a *kātib*. Al-Manṣūr came to power and was involved, looking into all major and minor matters. Therefore, it was natural that there should be a relatively perfunctory and insignificant *wazīr* with him so that his function – in the first instance – would be limited to carrying out orders, and secondly, to providing counsel when such was asked of him. Al-Manṣūr did not have a permanent *wazīr*, but a *wazīr* at some times and a *kātib* at others. Al-Manṣūr 'used to always seek advice on matters'. Yet, 'during his reign, the *wizārah* did not have any power due to his [al-Manṣūr's] despotism and his tendency to rely on his own opinion and abilities and to do without those of his viziers...His prestige used to diminish that of the viziers and they remained in fear and dread of him.'[170] One of the viziers tells us about the *wazīr* closest to al-Manṣūr, Abū Ayyūb al-Muryānī: 'We were sitting with Abū Ayyūb in his chamber. Then the messenger of Abū Ja'far came to him and he turned pale and his aspect changed.'[171]

Al-Manṣūr did not take a *wazīr* at the beginning of his rule, but selected a *kātib*, 'Abd al-Malik bin Ḥamīd 'and he appointed him in charge of the offices of his *kuttāb* and *diwāns*'. 'Abd al-Malik sought the services al-Muryānī as his *kātib*, deputising for him during his illness, and finally al-Manṣūr appointed him as his *wazīr*. It seems that al-Muryānī's position had been good with him, so he appointed him simultaneously over 'the *diwāns* with the *wizārah*' and granted him authority to investigate all matters. Then he removed him and the direct cause for this was that he had entrusted him with 300,000 *dirhams* to invest for his son – prince Ṣāliḥ – in an estate, but he did not do this despite pretending to do so.[172] Al-Mas'ūdī says: 'When he appointed him as *wazīr*, he was accused of things, including pilfering money and bad intent, so it was his downfall.'[173] After that, he sought the services of Abān bin Ṣadaqah as his *kātib*, until he died.[174] Finally, he appointed al-Rabī' bin Yūnis as *wazīr*, and this latter remained *wazīr* for al-Manṣūr until the death of the caliph.[175]

It is to be noted and worthy of mention that 'Abd al-Malik was 'an exceptional *kātib*' and that he was a *mawlā*.[176] Al-Muryānī was from Khuzistān: 'Al-Manṣūr bought him before [attaining to] the caliphate and educated him.' In addition to his intelligence, virtue and generosity, he was extensively educated: 'He had become familiar with everything and used to say, "There is nothing which I have not looked into, except *fiqh* (jurisprudence). I have never delved into it. I have studied chemistry, medicine, astrology (*al-nujūm*) and magic (*al-siḥr*)."'[177] Similarly, al-Rabī' bin Yūnis was a *mawālī* who had come from slavery and distinguished himself through his nobility, eloquence, acumen and decisiveness, as well as his experience in accounting and his skill in the affairs of the king, just as he loved good deeds.[178]

We noticed in the foregoing that al-Manṣūr did not always appoint himself a *wazīr*. He had a *kātib* at one time and a *wazīr* at another time, and the position of that official in both cases did not extend beyond that of rendering advice and carrying out the orders of the caliph. This indicates that the foundations of the *wizārah* were not firmly established at the time of al-Manṣūr. Rather, there was a kind of hesitation or a tendency towards not taking a *wazīr*, out of a caution that his powers might become too great. We notice subsequently that the viziers of al-Manṣūr were *mawālī* whom he appointed for their proficiency in writing and their administrative ability, and not due to their great effect or influence. Perhaps the 'Abbāsids' experience with Abū Salamah had an effect on that. Thus, we find the caliph dismissing or removing his *wazīr* or *kātib* without any hesitation or danger arising from this, as he was merely a functionary dependent on the power and satisfaction of the caliph for his existence.

The time of al-Mahdī was also a period of political and administrative stability. During his reign 'the splendour of the *wizārah* emerged due to the competence of his viziers'.[179] Initially, al-Mahdī appointed Abū 'Ubayd Allah Mu'āwiyah bin Yasār (r. 159–163AH) as *wazīr*, who was his *kātib* and a commander, and he 'delegated to him the administration of the dominion and handed the *diwāns* over to him',[180] thereby making his powers extremely powerful and comprehensive. It appears that Ibn Yasār was one of the extraordinary *kuttāb* who had exceptional administrative ability. Ibn al-Ṭaqṭaqī praises him, saying: 'He was the *kātib* of the world and most unique in his skill, knowledge and experience.' He also mentions that he 'organised the *diwāns* and specified the rules'.[181] Even the worst of his enemies acknowledged his unwavering integrity, decency, intellect and competence, and that he was the most brilliant of the people.[182] The credit for systemising the *muqāsamah* tax on crops for the *kharāj* in the *sawād* goes to him, just as 'he composed a book on the *kharāj* in which he detailed its legal rulings, intricacies and foundations, and he was the first to compile a book on the *kharāj*'.[183] This indicates his extensive knowledge and understanding of matters, and it is regrettable that no part of this book has come down to us.

His successor in the *wizārah* was Ya'qūb bin Dāwūd (163–166AH). Ya'qūb 'was a Shī'ite' and one of the supporters of the family of al-Ḥasan of the Zaydīyah. His appointment had a political basis which was al-Mahdī's attempt to please the family of al-Ḥasan on the one hand, and to find out about their affairs on the other, and subsequently his mutual understanding with al-Rabī' bin Yūnis and their cooperation in the plot against Ibn Yasār.[184] Ya'qūb was among the superior *kutāb* and he was 'highly literate, understanding and versatile in all categories of knowledge'.[185] Al-Mahdī appointed Ya'qūb as *wazīr* and called him 'a brother in faith [*akhan fī-lāh*]. Confirming this is that the edicts (*tawqī'āt*) in the *diwāns* were produced under this [appellation].' This appellation is indicative of his absolute trust and total reliance. Thus, al-Mahdī handed over to him the *diwāns* and his extensive authority is clear from the statement by al-Jahshiyārī to the effect: 'He [al-Mahdī] blindly relinquished all his power and his *wizārah*;' and: 'Ya'qūb was unique in managing all affairs.'[186] Then, upon hearing the words of [the poet] Bashshār:

Banū Umayyah, wake up, your slumber has been so long
that the caliph is Ya'qūb bin Dāwūd!

Al-Mahdī appointed al-Fayḍ bin Ṣāliḥ as *wazīr* after him, a *mawlā* from the people of Nishapur and from the class of *kuttāb*: 'He was raised...in the 'Abbāsid state and was highly literate and masterfully skilled.'[187] He became renowned for his generosity and his draconian omnipotence, remaining as *wazīr* until the death of al-Mahdī.

Ibn Yasār was dismissed because of intrigues that revolved around al-Rabī' bin Yūnis and for personal reasons.[188] As for Ya'qūb bin Dāwūd, he distressed and maltreated the family and relatives of Ibn Yasār, and dismissed his associates in the east and west for political reasons. There are two views about this. The first has been narrated by multiple narrators and is that he inclined towards the Ṭālibīyūn (the 'Ālids).[189] The second view, which is unique to al-Mas'ūdī, is that he 'used to hold that the *imamate* rightfully belonged to the eldest descendant of al-'Abbās and that one of the uncles of al-Mahdī was more entitled to it'.[190]

From the foregoing we notice that the foundations of the *wizārah* had become firmly established and its authority had widened until it was spread throughout all the *diwāns*. In spite of the existence of this vast power and authority, the caliph was able to withdraw it whenever he wanted without hesitation or warning. The viziers were outstanding *kuttāb* because of their education and qualifications, and we notice that plots and intrigues played an important role in the removal of some and the appointment of others.

The system of the *wizārah* began to become deeply rooted during the age of al-Rashīd, and this was due to his trust in the Barmakids and to their activities. Al-Rashīd appointed Yaḥyā al-Barmakī as *wazīr* and delegated extensive powers to him. He assigned to him the supervision of all the *diwāns* except the *diwān al-khātam* (the *diwān* of the signet),[191] but subsequently this *diwān* was added as well in 171AH. The significance of this is readily apparent from al-Ṭabarī's words: 'The two *wizārah* were combined for him.'[192] Al-Rashīd conferred distinctions on him, including the fact that he was 'the first among viziers to be made an emir'; and he entrusted him with the signature of the documents issued from the *diwān* of *kharāj*, which formerly had been issued by the caliph himself.[193]

With the agreement of al-Rashīd, Yaḥyā was assisted by his two sons al-Faḍl and Ja'far, and they constituted a powerful triumvirate whose influence extended to all matters of state.

Al-Rashīd favoured Ja'far for his companionship and service,[194] and they were inseparable until 180AH/796–797AD, when he sent him to pacify the tribal strife in Syria.[195] He used to call him 'my brother' and did not give preference to anyone over him.[196] He enjoyed his company extremely, and the historians exaggerated this relationship to the extent of insinuating that it reached the degree of a homosexual relationship.[197] Al-Rashīd honoured him with distinctions of great moral and material significance, and he had him join with him in deliberating cases of grievances (*maẓālim*), which no one had done previously. He entrusted him with the postal service for the outlying regions and general supervision over the *ṭarz* (embroidery factories) and the money mints.[198] Al-Rashīd was the first caliph to delegate the overseeing of the money mint's standard – *'iyār* (i.e. to verify the weight and quality of the coinage) – and with this he authorised Ja'far the minting of the *dirhams* and *dinars*: 'This is what distinguished the name of Ja'far bin al-Barmakī since it was something with which no one had been honoured before.'[199] Despite this, it was problematic to give him a sensitive role in politics or administration like his father and his brother al-Faḍl.[200]

It seems that Ja'far's role derived from his familiarity with al-Rashīd, as is clear from his story with 'Abd al-Malik Ṣāliḥ al-'Abbāsī[201] even to the extent that his father was anxious about the consequences of that familiarity.[202] Furthermore, al-Rashīd entrusted him with the edification of al-Ma'mūn and he had an influence on the covenant of succession for him.[203] Al-Faḍl was the foster brother of al-Rashīd through a milk-relationship (i.e. they shared the same wet nurse) and was serious in his nature.[204] It seems that his father had depended on him often and he would serve as his deputy, and his role was more powerful than that of Ja'far.[205] He had been charged with crucial and dangerous matters, such as subduing the revolt of Yaḥyā bin 'Abdullah the 'Ālid. He was also put in charge of some of the vital provinces, such as Khurasān.[206] He was entrusted with the education of al-Amīn[207] and is also attributed a role in the covenant of succession to him, although this is doubtful.[208] Above all, his significance was in official works, and he did not participate in the gatherings of the palace court.[209]

The Barmakids were distinguished by their ability in the arts of the secretary. Despite our misgivings about many of the exaggerations attributed to them, their culture and outstanding skill in the craft of *kitābah* and their magnanimity is famous. Thus, Yaḥyā became well-known for his sagacity and the eloquence of his writing,[210] and Ja'far excelled in his germane, eloquent edicts, which were a model followed by the *kuttāb*.[211] The Barmakids played an indispensable role in the caliphate of al-Rashīd. However, he was not oblivious of their conduct. Rather, he used to monitor them meticulously, and began to gradually clip their wings after the death of his mother who was their ally.[212] Eventually, he removed them after seventeen years (187AH/803AD). There were several reasons for this dismissal, including their influence and danger, as well as their political inclinations which were incompatible with the interests of the ʿAbbāsids, their squandering of state funds, their monopolisation of positions, their closeness to the Persians and resistance towards the Arabs.[213] Then al-Rashīd appointed al-Faḍl bin al-Rabīʿ as *wazīr* and did not delegate to him the supervision of the *diwāns*: 'rather he conferred on him the handling of his expenses and the administration of his affairs.'[214] He remained *wazīr* until the death of al-Rashīd in Ṭūs (d. 193AH/809AD).

Al-Faḍl bin al-Rabīʿ was made the *wazīr* for al-Amīn (r. 193–198AH/809–813AD) after al-Rashīd. It appears that al-Amīn had relied on him before he came into the caliphate, as is clear from al-Amīn's letter to his brother Ṣāliḥ about the camp of al-Rashīd shortly before his death: 'Take care not to implement an idea or settle any affair without the opinion of your sheikh – the entrusted of your fathers, al-Faḍl bin al-Rabīʿ.'[215] Al-Faḍl's role was not one of distinction during the dispute between al-Amīn and al-Ma'mūn. He had justified his return to the army of Khurasān to al-Amīn, saying: 'I will not abandon a king who is present for another whose future I do not know.'[216] Al-Ṭabarī attributes to him the urging of al-Amīn to depose al-Ma'mūn[217] and al-Jahshiyārī explains this by the fact that al-Faḍl 'was fearful that he [al-Ma'mūn] might attain to rule'. However, al-Faḍl renounced his caliph (al-Amīn) in his hour of need and al-Jahshiyārī says: 'When al-Faḍl bin al-Rabīʿ saw the power of al-Ma'mūn's situation and the weakness attaching to Muḥammad (al-Amīn), and the breaking away of the people from him as well as the loss of the wealth which had been in his hands, he went into hiding in Rajab of 196AH.'[218]

Perhaps the *wizārah* reached its climax at the apex of the power of the caliphate, at the time of al-Ma'mūn. He accorded his *wazīr*, al-Faḍl bin Sahl, unlimited authority over matters: 'and he named him Dhū al-Riyāsatayn (possessor of the two leaderships), meaning the leadership of the army [lit. 'war' – *ḥarb*] and the leadership of the administration (*tadbīr*).'[219] There had not been any such combination for any previous *wazīr*. Al-Ma'mūn delegated al-Faḍl his mandate 'in all his authority, power and dominion from the east and west of the land'.[220] Similarly, we find the *wizārah* delegating to al-Faḍl a special signed edict (*tawqīʿ*). This was the first honour of its kind and perhaps the contents of the edict explain its significance. It read: 'I have made for you...the rank of those who say and hear everything, and the rank of any other shall not exceed so long as you do what I have commanded you of deeds for Allah and for the Prophet to engage in the welfare of the state in what you are entrusted to do.'[221]

Al-Faḍl followed the precedent of the Sassanian viziers, even in appearance, due to his nationalistic tendencies. Al-Jahshiyārī narrates:

> Dhū al-Riyāsatayn used to sit on a winged throne and he was carried on it, when he wanted to call on al-Ma'mūn; and he would be continued to be carried until al-Ma'mūn's eyes fell on him. Then the throne would be put down and he would descend. He would then walk and the throne would be carried and put in front of al-Ma'mūn. Then Dhū al-Riyāsatayn would greet him and return to sitting on it... Dhū al-Riyāsatayn followed the ideas of the Khusraus (Persian kings) in this since one of their viziers used to be carried on such a throne and sit on it before them.[222]

Al-Faḍl was a recent convert to Islam because his father, a Majūsī, had become a Muslim at the time of al-Rashīd. He was an expert in astrology, and was known for his eloquence, sagacity and magnanimity in which he tried to emulate the Barmakids. However, al-Faḍl was autocratic in matters.[223] He hid information from the caliph and was not hesitant in falsifying it for his own aims, to the extent that he concealed the news of the oath of allegiance (*bay'ah*) to Ibrāhīm bin al-Mahdī and told the caliph that the people of Baghdad 'have [only] made Ibrāhīm bin al-Mahdī an emir who governs their affairs'.[224] His political principles contradicted the interests of the 'Abbāsids because they were Persian in form and reality such that Na'īm bin Khāzim accused him, in the presence of al-Ma'mūn: 'You want to remove power from the Banū al-'Abbās and transfer it to the descendants of 'Alī, then deceive them so you become the king like Khusrau.'[225] The era of al-Faḍl ended with al-Ma'mūn's return from Merv.

When al-Ma'mūn returned to Baghdad, he appointed al-Ḥasan bin Sahl as *wazīr* for a brief period, which points to the influence of the Sahl family [Ḥasan was Faḍl's brother]. Al-Ma'mūn also married his daughter Būrān in order to please him. However, he used to supervise matters himself, and he severed the last link to the Sahl family when he dismissed al-Ḥasan from the *wizārah*. Some have posited al-Ḥasan's illness as the reason for his dismissal,[226] but the conversations between al-Ma'mūn and his new *wazīr* Aḥmad bin Abī Khālid al-Aḥwal reveal that al-Ma'mūn removed his *wazīr* in order to be rid of him.[227] The successors to the position of al-Ḥasan bin Sahl were skilled *kuttāb*, but they had no influence or significance.[228]

The *wizārah* had passed through a period of harsh experiences during the first 'Abbāsid era, but had made progress gradually in favourable circumstances as well as in others, which were more critical. Al-Ma'mūn is attributed with advising his successor not to appoint anyone as *wazīr*. However, the institution was fixed and had become one of the cornerstones of the systemisations of the 'Abbāsids. After the first 'Abbāsid era, the *wizārah* was to be found alongside the caliphate at most times. There was struggle between it and the ascendant military power until it almost ceased to exist in the period of the Nine Years (247–256AH) from the killing of al-Mutawakkil to the accession of al-Mu'tamid (r. 256–279AH/870–892AD). Similarly, it became nominal and *pro-forma* during the period of the *imārat al-umarā'*. The *wizārah* of the 'Abbāsids was abolished during the Buwayhid period and the *wizārah* of the Buwayhid emirs themselves took its place. In spite of that, the *wizārah* and its ceremonies continued to develop and crystallise. Our attention is drawn to some of the periods of this age when: the *wazīr* had priority over the generals and they deferred to him; the chamber of the *wizārah* (*dār al-wizārah*) was designated; a semi-hereditary *wizārah* emerged for some families such as the family of al-Furāt, and the *wazīrs* were given honorific titles which resounded into the late fourth century AH.[229]

The theory of the *wizārah*

The *wizārah* originated from simple exigencies and developed gradually. Therefore, the theory of the *wizārah* and its constitution were laid down later on, making use of previous experiences, along with adding some refinement admixed with considerable theoretical opinion. Therefore, in studying the theory of the *wizārah*, we perceive the presence of a discrepancy between it and the reality, as well as difficulty in delimiting the practical *wizārah* in light of theoretical bases. Despite this, defining the theory of the *wizārah* is crucial for understanding political and administrative thought in Islamic society. The time of al-Māwardī (d. 450AH/1058AD) was the end of the period, so he is our guide here, with reference to others as well.

Al-Mas'ūdī says:

> The caliphs and the kings only appointed as *wazīr* the perfect among the *kuttāb*, the decent and loyal from their retinue, the honest advisors of their men, and those who were trusted with their secrets and wealth, reliable in their discretion, virtuous of opinion and sound of management of their affairs.[230]

It is related that al-Ma'mūn wrote on the selection of a *wazīr*:

> I have sought out for my affairs a man who combines all the superior qualities. He is of decent disposition, uncommonly righteous, refined by the arts and fortified by experience. I entrust him my secrets which he keeps and if he is given authority for important matters, he is adept at them. He keeps silence in discretion, made to speak by knowledge and a glance or subtle hint is sufficient for him. He has the fearlessness of the commanders [in battle] and the patience of the wise, the modesty of the scholars and the perspicacity of the *fuqahā'*. If he is favoured he is grateful, and if he is wronged he is patient. He does not sell today's share for tomorrow's deprivation, and he softens the hearts of men with the charm of his speech and the beauty of his eloquence.[231]

This is the best example of the ideal in the extreme. Ibn al-Ṭaqṭaqī says:

> The *wazīr* is the mediator/intermediary (*wasīṭ*) between the king and his subjects. Therefore, there must be in his nature one half which is suited to the qualities of the kings and one half which is appropriate to the qualities of the common people so that he can treat both of the two parties with the acceptance and affection which is requisite for him. Loyalty and honesty are his capital. It is said, 'If the mediator is treacherous, planning is worthless', as it is said 'The liar has no say'. Competence and magnanimity are his most important [qualities] and discretion, vigilance, astuteness and resolve are among his necessary [qualities]. He cannot do without entertaining guests often to win over [people] with this so that they will show gratitude to him with every word. There is no doubt he must have kindness, patience and conviction in matters, prudence, sobriety, ability and influential of speech.[232]

Al-Māwardī, Abū Ya'lā and Abū Sālim Muḥammad bin Ṭalḥah the *wazīr* give a precise definition of the qualifications and powers of the *wazīr*. They put the *wizārah* into two categories: the *wizārah* of delegation (*wizārat al-tafwīḍ*), and the *wizārah* of execution (*wizārat al-tanfīdh*). What is intended by the *wizārah* of delegation is 'that the *imām* (ruler) appoints someone to whom he delegates the management of affairs according to his opinion and to execute this according to his *ijtihād* [i.e. independent discretion/judgment]...Everything which is accepted from the *imām* is accepted from this *wazīr*.'[233] The *wazīr* benefits from this trusteeship (*wilāyah*) from the free hand which it affords him, enforcing judgments in the affairs of the dominion and acting independently in the affairs of the state, according to what is demanded by his insight and *ijtihād* as regards to making appointments, dismissals, releases, spending, usage and cutting off stipends – *'aṭā'*.[234] This *wazīr* is allowed to rule by himself, to appoint judges, to address grievances and to appoint a deputy for handling them, to lead *jihād* by himself: 'and it is permitted from him to proclaim the execution of orders which he has devised, and to appoint a deputy for their execution because the preconditions for (independent) judgement (*ra'y*) and management (*tadbīr*) inhere in him.'[235]

The authority of the *wizārat al-tafwīḍ* is limited by the powers of the *imām*, since the *wazīr* must 'inform the *imām* of the measures which he has carried out and appointments and authorisations which he has made so as not to come to have autocratic powers like the *imām*'. The *imām* must 'scrutinise the actions of the *wazīr* and his management of affairs in order for him to affirm which of them agrees with what is correct and to rectify what is contrary to this because the management of the *ummah* (nation/community) is entrusted to him and referred back to his judgement (*ijtihād*)'.[236]

As for the executive *wizārah* (*wizārat al-tanfīdh*):

> The handling of it is constrained to the decision of the *imām* and his administration. This *wazīr* is the intermediary between him, the subjects and the provincial governors. He carries out [an order] when he is ordered, he implements what is said to him, he executes whatever is decided, he announces the appointment of the governors and the recruitment of the armies. He presents him (the *imām*) with important news so that he may be informed and act accordingly. He is an aide in implementing orders and is not in charge of them, nor charged with them.[237]

Al-Māwardī sets forth the characteristics of the *wizārat al-tafwīḍ*:

> In the commissioning of this *wizārah*, the same conditions as those for the *imamate* (leadership by the *imām*) are considered, except for lineage itself, because he [the *wazīr*] executes decisions and exercises independent discretionary judgment (*ijtihād*). Therefore, it is required for him to have the qualities of the *mujtāhidūn*. In these an additional condition is required to [those for] the *imamate*, and this is that he be competent (lit. from the people of competence) in what is entrusted to him in the two matters of war and the *kharāj* tax, and experienced in both of them and familiar with their details.[238]

As regards the *wizārat al-tanfīdh*, the executive *wazīr* should possess seven characteristics:

1 Loyalty, so that he is not disloyal in what has been entrusted to him or is disingenuous in what advice has been sought from him.

2 Honest (straightforward) language, so that what he says can be trusted and carried out.
3 Lack of greed and avarice, so that he is not susceptible to bribes in regard to that of which he has been placed in charge, and so that he is not submissive or apt to be deceived.
4 That he should be impervious to any enmity and hatred in what is between him and the people, as enmity diverts [him] from just treatment and prevents sympathy.
5 That he should be mindful and recollect whatever he takes to or from the caliph because he is witness to it.
6 Intelligence and acumen.
7 That he should not be among those who follow their whims [and base desires] (*ahl al-ahwāʾ*), so that his passions should divert him from the truth to what is false.

Then he adds an eighth characteristic:

8 Sophistication and being worldly-wise (*ḥinkah*), and experience (*tajribah*) if he is called to participate in decision-making.[239]

It is obvious that this theory reflects the influence of expertise, and that experience reflects the influence of expertise and surpasses it in many points.

Notes

1. As is the case with many if not most of the technical terms found in this study, there was variability across both geographical regions as well as historical periods. The term *diwān* originally connoted a written record (*sijil*) or roster for the Arab Muslim fighters in the period of the second caliph ʿUmar bin al-Khaṭṭāb, which was used for recording stipends, and the provisioning of them and their families. Later, and naturally, the term came to be associated with the actual bureau of scribes – *kuttāb* – who were tasked with recording and maintaining the records; often the physical premises of the building were situated next to the treasury – *bayt al-māl*. [Editor's note.]

2. Abū ʿAbdullah Muḥammad bin ʿAbdūs al-Jahshiyārī, *al-Wuzarāʾ wa al-Kuttāb*, edited and indexed by Muṣṭafā al-Saqqā, Ibrāhīm al-Ibyārī, ʿAbd al-Ḥafīẓ Shalabī (Cairo: Maṭbaʿat Muṣṭafā al-Bābī al-Ḥalabī, 1938), p. 16.

3. Ibid., pp. 16–17; Abū al-ʿAbbās Aḥmad bin Yaḥyā al-Balādhurī, *Futūḥ al-Buldān* (Cairo: Sharikat Tabʿ al-Kutub al-ʿArabīyah, 1901), p. 458.

4. al-Balādhurī, ibid., p. 463.

5. Aḥmad bin Abī Yaʿqūb al-Yaʿqūbī, *Tārīkh al-Yaʿqūbī*, 3 vols. (al-Najaf: al-Maktabah al-Murtaḍawīyah, 1358/1939), vol. 2, p. 153.

6. al-Jahshiyārī, *al-Wuzarā' wa al-Kuttāb*, p. 17; Abū al-'Abbās Aḥmad bin 'Alī al-Maqrīzī, *al-Khiṭaṭ al-Maqrīzīyah al-Musammāt bi-l-Mawā'iẓ wa al-I'tibār bi-Dhikr al-Khiṭaṭ wa al-Āthār, yakhtaṣṣ dhalika bi-akhbār iqlīm Miṣr wa al-Nīl wa dhikr al-Qāhirah wa mā yata'allaq bihā wa bi-iqlīmihā*, 5 vols. (Cairo: Maktabat al-Malījī, 1324–1326/1906–1908), vol. 1, p. 265.

7. al-Balādhurī, *Futūḥ al-Buldān*, p. 454. Al-Maqrīzī attributes this suggestion to Khālid bin al-Walīd. See al-Maqrīzī, ibid., vol. 1, p. 265.

8. Ya'qūb bin Ibrāhīm Abū Yūsuf, *Kitāb al-Kharāj* (Cairo: al-Maṭba'ah al-Salafīyah, 1352/1933), p. 44.

9. As in al-Maqrīzī and al-Jahshiyārī, and perhaps in al-Balādhurī.

10. As in al-Balādhurī and al-Maqrīzī.

11. Ibn Salām, Abū 'Ubayd al-Qāsim al-Harawī, *al-Amwāl*, edited with commentary by Muḥammad Ḥāmid al-Fiqī, 4 vols. in 1 (Cairo: Maṭba'at Ḥijāzī, 1353/1934), no. 562.

12. Ibid., p. 231.

13. al-Maqrīzī, *al-Khiṭaṭ al-Maqrīzīyah*, vol. 1, p. 267.

14. Abū Ja'far Muḥammad bin Jarīr al-Ṭabarī, *Tārīkh al-Rusul wa al-Mulūk*, 12 vols. (Cairo: al-Maṭba'ah al-Ḥusaynīyah, 1336/1917), vol. 3, p. 615.

15. *al-Amwāl*, Ibn Salām, nos. 567–568.

16. Abū Yūsuf, *Kitāb al-Kharāj*, p. 42.

17. Ibid.

18. Ibid., p. 46.

19. Ibn Salām, ibid., p.243. In al-Ṭabarī: 'No, rather I will begin with the uncle of the Messenger of Allah, then the next closest and the next.' See al-Ṭabarī, *Tārīkh al-Rusul wa al-Mulūk*, vol. 3, p. 614.

20. al-Balādhurī, *Futūḥ al-Buldān*, pp. 453–454.

21. Ibid., pp. 454–455; al-Maqrīzī, *al-Khiṭaṭ al-Maqrīzīyah*, vol. 1, p. 148.

22. al-Ya'qūbī, *Tārīkh al-Ya'qūbī*, vol. 2, p. 44; al-Maqrīzī, ibid., vol. 1, p. 148.

23. al-Ṭabarī, *Tārīkh al-Rusul wa al-Mulūk*, vol. 2, p. 614; Abū Yūsuf, *Kitāb al-Kharāj*, p. 26; Ibn Salām, *al-Amwāl*, p. 226; al-Balādhurī, ibid., pp. 455–457, 460 and 466. He renders it to 'the wives of the Prophet' and in other narrations 'the wives of the Prophet with whom he engaged in conjugal relations'. See al-Ya'qūbī, ibid., vol. 2, p. 44. He adds Umm Ḥabīb and Ḥafṣah.

24. al-Ṭabarī, ibid., vol. 3; al-Balādhurī, ibid., p. 460; Abū Yūsuf, *Kitāb al-Kharāj*, p. 44; Ibn Salām, ibid., p. 226. Al-Balādhurī makes the *'aṭā'* for Ṣafīyah and Juwayrīyah 6,000 because they were among the *fay'* granted by Allah to His Messenger, whereas al-Ya'qūbī gives that amount (10,000) to the 'mothers of the believers' (i.e. the wives of the Prophet) and gives 6,000 to Ṣafīyah and Juwayrīyah.

25. al-Ṭabarī, ibid., vol. 2, p. 44; Abū Yūsuf, ibid., p. 25; al-Balādhurī, ibid., pp. 455 and 458, where al-Balādhurī makes this for the first *muhājirūn*. Abū 'Ubayd says the *muhājirūn* were those who witnessed the battle of Badr. See Ibn Salām, ibid., p. 255. Al-Ya'qūbī makes it for the people of Mecca, the senior Quraysh. See al-Ya'qūbī, ibid., vol. 2, p. d131.

26. Abū 'Ubayd makes the *'aṭā'* of Salmān four thousand. See Ibn Salām, ibid., no. 476.

27. al-Ṭabarī, ibid., vol. 2, p. 614; al-Maqrīzī, *al-Khiṭaṭ al-Maqrīzīyah*, p. 267; al-Balādhurī, ibid., p. 458; Abū Yūsuf, ibid., p. 25. In al-Ya'qūbī and Abū 'Ubayd bin Salām, there is a narration about al-Balādhurī which makes it for those *anṣār* who witnessed the battle of Badr.

28. al-Ya'qūbī, *Tārīkh al-Ya'qūbī*; al-Balādhurī, ibid.

29. al-Ṭabarī, ibid., vol. 2, p. 614; al-Maqrīzī, ibid., vol. 1, p. 267.

30. al-Balādhurī, ibid.; Abū Yūsuf, *Kitāb al-Kharāj*.
31. al-Balādhurī, ibid.
32. al-Maqrīzī, al-Balādhurī and Abū Yūsuf describe the sons of the *muhājirūn* and the *anṣār*. See ibid.; al-Maqrīzī, ibid.; Abū Yūsuf, ibid.
33. al-Ṭabarī, *Tārīkh al-Rusul wa al-Mulūk*, vol. 3, p. 614.
34. Ibid.; al-Maqrīzī, ibid., vol. 1, p. 268.
35. al-Ṭabarī, ibid., vol. 3, p. 615.
36. al-Balādhurī, *Futūḥ al-Buldān*, pp. 456–457.
37. al-Ya'qūbī, *Tārīkh al-Ya'qūbī*, vol. 2, p. 153.
38. al-Maqrīzī, ibid., vol. 1, p. 268.
39. al-Balādhurī, *Futūḥ al-Buldān*, pp. 456–457.
40. Abū Yūsuf, *Kitāb al-Kharāj*, p. 46.
41. Ibn Salām, *al-Amwāl*, nos. 569–570.
42. For those who witnessed the battle of Badr, their confederates and the *mawālī* on an equal basis, see al-Balādhurī, *Futūḥ al-Buldān*, p. 455. Abū Yūsuf wrote that those who witnessed Badr were among the *mawālī* or Arabs. See Abū Yūsuf, ibid., p. 26.
43. Ibn Salām, ibid., p. 235, no. 570.
44. Ibid., p. 236.
45. See al-Ya'qūbī, *Tārīkh al-Ya'qūbī*, vol. 2, p. 153; Ibn Salām, ibid., no. 577; al-Balādhurī, ibid., p. 464.
46. al-Ṭabarī, *Tārīkh al-Rusul wa al-Mulūk*, vol. 3, p. 613; al-Maqrīzī, *al-Khiṭaṭ al-Maqrīzīyah*, vol. 1, p. 266.
47. al-Maqrīzī, ibid., vol. 1, p. 266; al-Ya'qūbī, ibid., vol. 2, p. 44; al-Balādhurī, ibid., p. 462.
48. Abū al-'Abbās Aḥmad bin 'Alī al-Qalqashandī, *Ṣubḥ al-A'shā fī Kitābat al-Inshā*, 14 vols. (Cairo: Dār al-Kutub al-Miṣrīyah, 1913–1919), vol. 1, p. 123.
49. See al-Jahshiyārī, *al-Wuzarā' wa al-Kuttāb*, p. 16 ff.
50. Ibid., vol. 3, p. 38.
51. Ibid., p. 24.
52. Ibid., p. 32.
53. Ibid., pp. 22–25; Kurd 'Alī, Muḥammad, *al-Idārah al-Islāmīyah fī 'Izz al-'Arab* (Cairo: Maṭba'at Miṣr, 1934), p. 18.
54. al-Qalqashandī, *Ṣubḥ al-A'shā fī Kitābat al-Inshā*, vol. 1, p. 124.
55. Ibid., vol. 1, p. 91.
56. al-Jahshiyārī, *al-Wuzarā' wa al-Kuttāb*, p. 35.
57. Ibid.
58. al-Qalqashandī, ibid., vol. 14, p. 413.
59. Ibid., vol. 14, p. 368.
60. al-Jahshiyārī, ibid., p. 3.
61. Ibid., p. 49.
62. Ibid., p. 60.
63. Ibid., p. 47.
64. Ibid., p. 60.
65. Ibid., p. 38.
66. Ibid., pp. 39–40.
67. Ibid., p. 67.
68. (Pseudo) Abū 'Uthmān 'Amr bin Baḥr al-Jāḥiẓ, *al-Tāj fī Akhlāq al-Mulūk* (Cairo: Aḥmad Zakī Pāshā, 1914), p. 23.
69. See Arthur Christensen, *L'Iran sous les Sassanides* (Copenhagen: Levin and Munksgaard, 1936).

70. See the article 'Banī Umayyah' in *Dā'irat al-Ma'ārif al-Islāmīyah*.
71. al-Jahshiyārī, *al-Wuzarā' wa al-Kuttāb*, p. 98.
72. Ibid., p. 90.
73. Aḥmad bin Abī Ya'qūb al-Ya'qūbī, *al-Buldān* (al-Najaf: al-Maṭba'ah al-Ḥaydarīyah, 1939), p. 9.
74. Idem, *al-Buldān*, trans. Gaston Wiet as *Les Pays*; Publications de l'Institut Français d'Archéologie Orientale; Textes et traductions d'auteurs orientaux, tome 1 (Cairo: Institut Français d'Archéologie Orientale, 1937), p. 15.
75. Abū Faḍl Aḥmad Ibn Ṭayfūr, *Kitāb Baghdād*.
76. al-Ya'qūbī, *al-Buldān*, p. 11.
77. See al-Ya'qūbī, *Tārīkh al-Ya'qūbī*, vol. 2, p. 226; Muḥammad bin 'Alī Ibn al-Ṭaqṭaqī, *al-Fakhrī fī al-Ādāb al-Sulṭānīyah wa al-Duwal al-Islāmīyah* (Cairo: Sharikat Tab' al-Kutub al-'Arabīyah, 1317/1899), p. 115.
78. al-Jahshiyārī, *al-Wuzarā' wa al-Kuttāb*, p. 146.
79. al-Ṭabarī, *Tārīkh al-Rusul wa al-Mulūk*, vol. 8, p. 142.
80. al-Jahshiyārī, ibid., p. 168.
81. Ibid., p. 168.
82. Ibn al-Ṭaqṭaqī, *al-Fakhrī fī al-Ādāb al-Sulṭānīyah wa al-Duwal al-Islāmīyah*, p. 131; Abū Ṭālib 'Alī bin Anjab Ibn al-Sā'ī, *Mukhtaṣar Akhbār al-Khulafā' al-'Abbāsīyīn* (Bulāq: al-Maṭba'ah al-Amīrīyah, 1309/1891), p. 20; Jamīl Nakhlah al-Mudawwar, *Ḥaḍārat al-Islām fī Dār al-Salām* (Cairo: Maṭba'at al-Mu'ayyid, 2nd edn, 1905), pp. 65–66.
83. al-Jahshiyārī, ibid., p. 166.
84. See ibid., p. 166.
85. Ibid., p. 277; 'Abd al-'Azīz al-Dūrī, *Tārīkh al-'Irāq al-Iqtiṣādī fī al-Qarn al-Rābi' al-Hijrī* (Baghdad: Maṭba'at al-Ma'ārif, 1948), pp. 25–27.
86. Abū 'Alī al-Muḥsin bin 'Alī al-Tanūkhī, *al-Faraj Ba'd al-Shiddah*, 2 vols. in 1 (Cairo: Maḥmūd Riyāḍ, 1904), vol. 1, pp. 39–40.
87. See al-Ya'qūbī, *al-Buldān*, p. 23; Idem, *al-Buldān*, *Les Pays*, p. 61.
88. al-Jahshiyārī, *al-Wuzarā' wa al-Kuttāb*, pp. 74–75. This advice applies more to the first 'Abbāsid age more than to the Umayyad age. The composition of the advice and its attribution to powerful personalities is well known so that their content would acquire literary force.
89. *ṭasūt* (sic.) Perhaps the word intended here is *ṭasūq*, the plural of *ṭasq* (from the Persian word *tashak*), that is, the *kharāj* (tax).
90. al-Tanūkhī, *al-Faraj Ba'd al-Shiddah*, vol. 2, p. 36.
91. Ibrāhīm bin Hilāl al-Ṣābī, *Rasā'il al-Ṣābī*, edited with commentary by Shakīb Arslān (B'abdah, Lebanon: al-Maṭba'ah al-'Uthmānīyah, 1898), pp. 121–122.
92. See al-Jahshiyārī, *al-Wuzarā' wa al-Kuttāb*, pp. 124, 141 and 167.
93. Adam Metz, *Der Renaissance des Islam*, trans. Muḥammad 'Abd al-Hādī Abū Raydah as *al-Ḥaḍārah al-Islāmīyah fī al-Qarn al-Rābi' al-Hijrī*, 2 vols. (Cairo: Lajnat al-Ta'līf wa al-Tarjamah wa al-Nashr, 1940–1941), pp. 121–122.
94. Abū al-Ḥusayn Hilāl bin al-Muḥsin al-Ṣābī, *Tuḥfat al-Umarā' fī Tārīkh al-Wuzarā' = The Historical Remains of Hilāl al-Ṣābī: first part of his Kitāb al-Wuzarā' and fragment of his History, 389–393AH*, edited with notes and glossary by H. F. Amedroz (Beirut: Catholic Press [Maṭba'at al-Ābā' al-Kathūlīkiyīn], 1904), p. 131; Harold Bowen, *The Life and Times of "Alī Ibn 'Īsā', 'the Good Vizier'* (Cambridge: Cambridge University Press, 1928), p. 32.
95. al-Ṣābī, ibid., p. 132; Metz, ibid., vol. 1, p. 124; Bowen, ibid., p. 32.
96. See al-Dūrī, *Tārīkh al-'Irāq al-Iqtiṣādī fī al-Qarn al-Rābi' al-Hijrī*, pp. 37–38.

97. See al-Ṣābī, ibid., pp. 10–11.

98. Metz, *al-Ḥaḍārah al-Islāmīyah fī al-Qarn al-Rābiʿ al-Hijrī*, vol. 1, p. 125 [translation of Adam Metz, *The Islamic Civilization in the Fourth Century of the Hejirah*].

99. See chapter 'al-Buwayhīyūn' in *Dirāsāt fī al-ʿUṣūr al-ʿAbbāsīyah al-Mutaʾakhirah* (Baghdad: Sharikat al-Rābiṭah li-l-Ṭabʿ wa al-Nashr, 1946).

100. Metz, ibid., vol. 1, p. 124 ff.

101. al-Ḥasan bin ʿAbdullah al-ʿAbbāsī, *Āthār al-Uwal fī Tartīb al-Duwal* (Cairo: Bulāq, 1295/1878), p. 72.

102. Jaʿfar bin Qudāmah cited in Metz, ibid., vol. 1, pp. 126–127.

103. Abū ʿAbdullah Muḥammad bin Aḥmad al-Khawārizmī, *Kitāb Mafātīḥ al-ʿUlūm*, ed. G. Van Vloten (Leiden: Brill, 1895), pp. 154–156; al-Ḥasan bin Muḥammad bin Ḥasan al-Qummī, *Tārīkh Qumm* ([n.p.: n.pb., n.d.]), pp. 149–151; al-Dūrī, *Tārīkh al-ʿIrāq al-Iqtiṣādī fī al-Qarn al-Rābiʿ al-Hijrī*, pp. 206–207.

104. al-ʿAbbāsī, *Āthār al-Uwal fī Tartīb al-Duwal*, p. 71.

105. Ibid., p. 74.

106. Ibid., p. 72.

107. al-Qalqashandī, *Ṣubḥ al-Aʿshā fī Kitābat al-Inshā*, vol. 14, p. 366; al-Khawārizmī, *Kitāb Mafātīh al-ʿUlūm*.

108. Abū al-Faraj Qudāmah bin Jaʿfar, *al-Kharāj*, ed. M. J. de Goeje; Bibliotheca Geographorum Arabicorum 6 (Leiden: Brill, 1889), p. 184; al-Tanūkhī, *al-Faraj Baʿd al-Shiddah*, vol. 8, p. 343; al-Qalqashandī, ibid., vol. 14, p. 369.

109. al-ʿAbbāsī, *Āthār al-Uwal fī Tartīb al-Duwal*, p. 88.

110. Ibid., p. 88.

111. Qudāmah bin Jaʿfar, *al-Kharāj*, p. 184.

112. al-Ṭabarī, *Tārīkh al-Rusul wa al-Mulūk*, vol. 8, p. 96.

113. Qudāmah cited in Metz, *al-Ḥaḍārah al-Islāmīyah fī al-Qarn al-Rābiʿ al-Hijrī*, vol. 1, p. 129.

114. al-ʿAbbāsī, *Āthār al-Uwal fī Tartīb al-Duwal*, p. 87.

115. Ibid.

116. Ibid., pp. 89–90.

117. Qudāmah bin Jaʿfar, *al-Kharāj*, p. 87.

118. al-ʿAbbāsī, pp. 58–86.

119. Abū ʿAbdullah Muḥammad bin Aḥmad al-Muqaddasī, *Kitāb Aḥsan al-Taqāsīm fī Maʿrifat al-Aqālīm*, ed. M. J. de Goeje; Bibliotheca Geographorum Arabicorum 3 (Leiden: Brill, 1877), p. 66; al-Khawārizmī, *Kitāb Mafātīh al-ʿUlūm*, p. 63.

120. al-Qalqashandī, *Ṣubḥ al-Aʿshā fī Kitābat al-Inshā*, vol. 14, p. 214.

121. Abū al-Ḥasan ʿAlī bin al-Ḥusayn al-Masʿūdī, *Murūj al-Dhahab wa Maʿādin al-Jawhar*, edited with commentary by Muḥammad Muḥyī al-Dīn ʿAbd al-Ḥamīd, 4 vols. (Cairo: Dār al-Rajāʿ, 1938), vol. 1, p. 263.

122. Abū Manṣūr ʿAbd al-Malik bin Muḥammad al-Thaʿālibī, *Laṭāʾif al-Maʿārif*, ed. Pieter de Jong (Leiden: Brill, 1867), p. 129.

123. al-Qalqashandī, *Ṣubḥ al-Aʿshā fī Kitābat al-Inshā*, vol. 14, p. 414.

124. al-Jahshiyārī, *al-Wuzarāʾ wa al-Kuttāb*, p. 167.

125. (Pseudo) al-Jāḥiẓ, *al-Tāj fī Akhlāq al-Mulūk*, p. 40.

126. al-Qalqashandī, *Ṣubḥ al-Aʿshā fī Kitābat al-Inshā*, vol. 14, p. 414.

127. al-Ṭabarī, *Tārīkh al-Rusul wa al-Mulūk*, vol. 9, p. 52.

128. al-Qalqashandī, ibid., vol. 14, p. 435.

129. *sūrat ṭāhā*, Q 20:29–32; Abū al-Ḥasan ʿAlī bin al-Ḥusayn al-Masʿūdī, *al-Tanbīh wa al-Ishrāf*, ed. ʿAbdullah Ismāʿīl al-Ṣāwī (Cairo: al-Sharq al-Islāmīyah, 1938), p. 294.

130. Abū al-Ḥasan 'Alī bin Muḥammad al-Māwardī, *al-Aḥkām al-Sulṭānīyah wa al-Wilāyāt al-Dīnīyah* (Cairo: [Maṭba'at al-Sa'ādah], 1909), p. 23; Abū Sālim Muḥammad bin Ṭalḥah [al-Qurashī] al-'Adawī, *al-'Iqd al-Farīd li-l-Malik al-Sa'īd* (Cairo: Maṭba'at al-Waṭan, 1283/1866), p. 142.

131. Ibn al-Ṭaqṭaqī, *al-Fakhrī fī al-Ādāb al-Sulṭānīyah wa al-Duwal al-Islāmīyah*, p. 153.

132. Abū Zayd 'Abd al-Raḥmān bin Muḥammad Ibn Khaldūn, *al-Muqaddimah* ([n.p.: n.pb., n.d.]), p. 198.

133. Muḥammad bin Aḥmad Jalāl al-Dīn al-Maḥallī and 'Abd al-Raḥmān bin Abī Bakr Jalāl al-Dīn al-Suyūṭī, *Tafsīr al-Jalālayn* (n.p.: n.pb., n.d.), p. 414.

134. See 'kalimat wazīr' in Abū al-Qāsim Maḥmūd bin 'Umar al-Zamakhsharī, *Asās al-Balāghah*, 2 vols. (Cairo: Dār al-Kutub al-Miṣrīyah, 1922–1923), vol. 2, p. 503.

135. See 'wizr' in al-Fīrūzābādī, Abū al-Ṭāhir Muḥammad bin Ya'qūb, *al-Qāmūs al-Muḥīṭ* (n.p.: n.pb., n.d.).

136. *Encyclopedia of Islam*[1], vol. 4, p. 1135.

137. See ibid., vol. 4, p. 135; al-Mas'ūdī, *al-Tanbīh wa al-Ishrāf*, p. 310.

138. al-Mas'ūdī, ibid., p. 310.

139. Ibn Khallikān, Shams al-Dīn Abū al-'Abbās Aḥmad bin Muḥammad, *Wafayāt al-A'yān wa Anbā' Abnā' al-Zamān*, following on *Fawāt al-Wafayāt* by al-Ṣalāh al-Katbī, see the notes of Shaqā'iq al-Nu'mānīyah fī 'Ulamā' al-Dawlah al-'Uthmānīyah, following on *al-'Iqd al-Manẓūm fī Dhikr Afāḍil al-Rūm*, 2 vols. (Cairo: Maṭba'at Muṣṭafā al-Bābī al-Ḥalabī, 1310/1892), vol. 1, pp. 110–111.

140. Ibn al-Ṭaqṭaqī, *al-Fakhrī fī al-Ādāb al-Sulṭānīyah wa al-Duwal al-Islāmīyah*, p. 153.

141. al-Jahshiyārī, *al-Wuzarā' wa al-Kuttāb*, p. 85.

142. al-Mas'ūdī, *al-Tanbīh wa al-Ishrāf*, p. 310. He also says: 'The kings of the Banū Umayyah disapprove of addressing a *kātib* as *wazīr* and they say *wazīr* is derived from the word help (*mu'āzarah*) while the caliph is more glorified than to be in need of assistance.'

143. Ibn al-Ṭaqṭaqī, *al-Fakhrī fī al-Ādāb al-Sulṭānīyah wa al-Duwal al-Islāmīyah*, p. 153.

144. Christensen, *L'Iran sous les Sassanides*, p. 108.

145. Ibid., p. 513.

146. Abū Ja'far Muḥammad bin Jarīr al-Ṭabarī, *Tārīkh al-Rusul wa al-Mulūk*, ed. M. J. de Goeje (Leiden: Brill, 1879–1901), vol. 1, p. 80.

147. Christensen, ibid., p. 109.

148. al-Mas'ūdī, *al-Tanbīh wa al-Ishrāf*, p. 310.

149. al-Ṭabarī, *Tārīkh al-Rusul wa al-Mulūk* (Leiden ed.) vol. 1, p. 64; Christensen, ibid., p. 109.

150. al-Ṭabarī, ibid., vol. 1, p. 64.

151. Ibid., vol.1, p. 79.

152. al-Jahshiyārī, *al-Wuzarā' wa al-Kuttāb*, p. 10.

153. Ibid., p. 8.

154. Ibid., p. 11.

155. Christensen, *L'Iran sous les Sassanides*, pp. 111–112.

156. Ibid., pp. 127–129.

157. al-Jahshiyārī, ibid., p. 8.

158. Ibid., pp. 3–4.

159. al-Khawārizmī, *Kitāb Mafātīh al-'Ulūm*, pp. 117–118.

160. al-Jahshiyārī, ibid., p. 8.

161. Ibid., p. 9.

162. Christensen, *L'Iran sous les Sassanides*, p. 128.
163. al-Mas'ūdī, *al-Tanbīh wa al-Ishrāf*, p. 310.
164. al-Jahshiyārī, *al-Wuzarā' wa al-Kuttāb*, p. 88.
165. Ibn al-Ṭaqṭaqī, *al-Fakhrī fī al-Ādāb al-Sulṭānīyah wa al-Duwal al-Islāmīyah*, p. 156.
166. Ibid., p. 156; al-Jahshiyārī, ibid., p. 290.
167. Ibn al-Ṭaqṭaqī, ibid., p. 155.
168. Ibid.; al-Ṭabarī, *Tārīkh al-Rusul wa al-Mulūk*, vol. 7, p. 429; (Pseudo) Ibn Qutaybah, Abū Muḥammad 'Abdullah bin Muslim, *al-Imāmah wa al-Siyāsah* (Cairo: Maṭba'at al-Nīl, 1904), p. 113; al-Mas'ūdī, Abū al-Ḥasan 'Alī bin al-Ḥusayn, *Murūj al-Dhahab wa Ma'ādin al-Jawhar*, ed. and trans. C. Barbier de Meynard and Pavet de Courteille as *Les Prairies d'Or et les Mines de Pierres Precieuses*, 9 vols. [in Arabic and French] (Paris: Impr. Impériale, 1861–1877), vol. 6, pp. 134–136; al-Jahshiyārī, *al-Wuzarā' wa al-Kuttāb*, pp. 86–87.
169. (Pseudo) Ibn Qutaybah, ibid., pp. 113–114.
170. Ibn al-Ṭaqṭaqī, *al-Fakhrī fī al-Ādāb al-Sulṭānīyah wa al-Duwal al-Islāmīyah*, p. 174.
171. al-Jahshiyārī, *al-Wuzarā' wa al-Kuttāb*, p. 102.
172. Ibid., pp. 117–118; Ibn al-Ṭaqṭaqī, ibid., p. 172.
173. al-Mas'ūdī, *Murūj al-Dhahab wa Ma'ādin al-Jawhar*, vol. 3, p. 212.
174. Ibid., vol. 3, p. 213.
175. Ibn al-Ṭaqṭaqī, ibid., p. 178.
176. al-Jahshiyārī, *al-Wuzarā' wa al-Kuttāb*, p. 96.
177. Ibid., p. 97; Ibn al-Ṭaqṭaqī, ibid., p. 175.
178. al-Jahshiyārī, ibid., p. 125; Ibn al-Ṭaqṭaqī, ibid., p. 176.
179. See Ibn al-Ṭaqṭaqī, ibid., p. 181.
180. Ibid., p. 134; al-Jahshiyārī, ibid., p. 146.
181. Ibn al-Ṭaqṭaqī, ibid., p. 181.
182. Ibid., p. 183; al-Jahshiyārī, ibid., p. 153.
183. Ibn al-Ṭaqṭaqī, ibid., p. 182.
184. Ibid., p. 184; al-Jahshiyārī, ibid., p. 155.
185. al-Jahshiyārī, ibid., p. 155.
186. Ibid., p. 157.
187. Ibn al-Ṭaqṭaqī, ibid., p. 187.
188. For details, see ibid., pp. 182–183; al-Jahshiyārī, ibid., p. 153 ff.
189. Ibn al-Ṭaqṭaqī, ibid., p. 185; al-Jahshiyārī, ibid., pp. 160–161 ff; al-Ṭabarī, *Tārīkh al-Rusul wa al-Mulūk*, vol. 8, p. 155.
190. al-Mas'ūdī, *Murūj al-Dhahab wa Ma'ādin al-Jawhar*, vol. 3, p. 236.
191. I doubt the narration which says that al-Rashīd told Yaḥyā when he appointed him: 'I have charged you with the matter of care and supervision of the affairs of the subjects; and, I have removed this burden from my neck and placed it on yours. So, judge as you see fit, employ whom you will, and dismiss whomever you see to be in error. I will not partake in your decisions in any way.' See al-Ṭabarī, ibid., vol. 10, p. 50; al-Jahshiyārī, ibid., p. 177; Ibn Khallikān, *Wafayāt al-A'yān wa Anbā' Abnā' al-Zamān*, vol. 2, p. 443. That is because this delegation contradicted the principles of the 'Abbāsid caliphate from the religious viewpoint and because al-Rashīd used to always supervise the Barmakids.
192. al-Ṭabarī, ibid., vol. 8, p. 239.
193. al-Jahshiyārī, ibid., p. 178.
194. Ibn al-Ṭaqṭaqī, *al-Fakhrī fī al-Ādāb al-Sulṭānīyah wa al-Duwal al-Islāmīyah*, p. 205.

195. al-Jahshiyārī, *al-Wuzarā' wa al-Kuttāb*, pp. 208–210; al-Ṭabarī, *Tārīkh al-Rusul wa al-Mulūk*, vol. 8, p. 260.
196. al-Jahshiyārī, ibid., pp. 189 and 204.
197. Ibid., p. 204; 'Abd al-Malik bin 'Abdullah Ibn Badrūn, *Sharḥ Qaṣīdah Ibn 'Abdūn* (n.p.: n.pb., n.d.), pp. 222–223.
198. al-Jahshiyārī, ibid., p. 204; Appendix, see article: 'Ṭiraz', *Dā'irat al-Ma'ārif al-Islāmīyah*, eds. M. Th. Houtsma *et al.*, 13 vols. (Cairo: Dār al-Shāb, 1908–1938).
199. See, for example, al-Jahshiyārī, ibid., p. 190; 'Abd al-Raḥmān bin Abī Bakr Jalāl al-Dīn al-Suyūtī, *Ḥusn al-Muḥāḍarah fī Akhbār Miṣr wa al-Qāhirah*, 2 vols. in 1 (Cairo: Fahmī al-Katbī, 1327/1909), vol. 2, pp. 8–9; al-Ṭabarī, *Tārīkh al-Rusul wa al-Mulūk*, vol. 10, p. 86; 'Izz al-Dīn Abū al-Ḥasan 'Alī bin Muḥammad Ibn al-Athīr, *Tārīkh al-Kāmil*, 12 vols. (Cairo: Maṭba'at Muṣṭafā al-Bābī al-Ḥalabī, 1303/1885), vol. 6, p. 61.
200. Ibn Khallikān, *Wafayāt al-A'yān wa Anbā' Abnā' al-Zamān*, vol. 1, pp. 105–106; al-Jahshiyārī, ibid., pp. 213–214; Ibn al-Ṭaqṭaqī, *al-Fakhrī fī al-Ādāb al-Sulṭānīyah wa al-Duwal al-Islāmīyah*, pp. 198-204; Abū Muḥammad 'Abdullah bin As'ad al-Yāfi'ī, *Mir'āt al-Jinān wa 'Ibrat al-Yaqẓān fī Ma'rifat mā Yu'tabar min Ḥawādith al-Zamān*, 4 vols. (Hyderabad Deccan: Dā'irat al-Ma'ārif al-Niẓāmīyah, 1337–1339/1918–1920), vol. 1, pp. 405–406.
201. al-Jahshiyārī, ibid., pp. 213–214; Ibn al-Ṭaqṭaqī, ibid., pp. 206–206; Ibn Khallikān, ibid., vol. 1, pp. 105–106.
202. al-Ṭabarī, *Tārīkh al-Rusul wa al-Mulūk*, vol. 10, p. 84; al-Jahshiyārī, ibid., pp. 224–225.
203. al-Jahshiyārī, ibid., p. 211; al-Mas'ūdī, *Murūj al-Dhahab wa Ma'ādin al-Jawhar*, vol. 3, p. 272.
204. Ibn al-Ṭaqṭaqī, *al-Fakhrī fī al-Ādāb al-Sulṭānīyah wa al-Duwal al-Islāmīyah*, pp. 201–202.
205. al-Jahshiyārī, ibid., p. 189. Ibn Kathīr says: 'Al-Faḍl was higher-ranked than Ja'far in the esteem of al-Rashīd, but Ja'far was more favoured and preferred by al-Rashīd'. See Abū al-Fidā' Ismā'īl bin 'Umar Ibn Kathīr, *al-Bidāyah wa al-Nihāyah fī al-Tārīkh*, 14 vols. (Cairo: Maṭba'at al-Sa'ādah, 1929–1939), vol. 10, pp. 210–211.
206. See al-Ṭabarī, *Tārīkh al-Rusul wa al-Mulūk*, vol. 8, pp. 242 and 257.
207. al-Jahshiyārī, ibid., p. 193.
208. Ibid.; al-Ṭabarī, ibid., vol. 8, p. 240; al-Ya'qūbī, *Tārīkh al-Ya'qūbī*, vol. 3, p. 140.
209. See al-Jahshiyārī, ibid., p. 194; al-Ṭabarī, ibid., vol. 8, p. 293.
210. Ibn al-Ṭaqṭaqī, *al-Fakhrī fī al-Ādāb al-Sulṭānīyah wa al-Duwal al-Islāmīyah*, p. 198; al-Jahshiyārī, ibid., p. 203.
211. Ibn al-Ṭaqṭaqī, ibid., p. 205; al-Jahshiyārī, ibid., pp. 204 and 210 ff.
212. See 'Abd al-'Azīz al-Dūrī, *al-'Aṣr al-'Abbāsī al-Awwal: Dirāsah fī al-Tārīkh al-Siyāsī wa al-Idārī wa al-Mālī*; Manshūrāt Dār al-Mu'allimīn al-'Āliyah 1 (Baghdad: Maṭba'at al-Tafīḍ al-Ahlīyah, 1945), pp. 163–164.
213. Ibid., pp. 165–175.
214. See Ibn al-Ṭaqṭaqī, ibid., p. 211; al-Jahshiyārī, ibid., pp. 265 and 277.
215. al-Jahshiyārī, ibid., p. 276.
216. al-Ṭabarī, *Tārīkh al-Rusul wa al-Mulūk*, vol. 8, p. 370.
217. Ibid., vol. 8, p. 374.
218. al-Jahshiyārī, ibid., pp. 290 and 292; Ibn al-Ṭaqṭaqī, *al-Fakhrī fī al-Ādāb al-Sulṭānīyah wa al-Duwal al-Islāmīyah*, pp. 220–221; Ibn Khaldūn, *al-Muqaddimah*, vol. 3, p. 221.

219. al-Jahshiyārī, ibid., pp. 301–302.
220. Ibid., p. 305.
221. Aḥmad Zakī Ṣafwat, ed., *Jamharat Rasā'il al-'Arab fī 'Uṣūr al-'Arabīyah al-Zāhirah*, 4 vols. (Cairo: Maṭba'at Muṣṭafā al-Bābī al-Ḥalabī, 1937–1938), vol. 3, p. 417.
222. al-Jahshiyārī, ibid., p. 306.
223. Ibn al-Ṭaqṭaqī, *al-Fakhrī fī al-Ādāb al-Sulṭānīyah wa al-Duwal al-Islāmīyah*, p. 221.
224. Ibid., p. 218.
225. al-Jahshiyārī, ibid., p. 313.
226. Ibn al-Ṭaqṭaqī, ibid., p. 223; al-Mas'ūdī, *al-Tanbīh wa al-Ishrāf*, p. 304.
227. Ibn al-Ṭaqṭaqī, ibid., p. 224; al-Mas'ūdī, ibid., p. 320 ff.
228. Ibn al-Ṭaqṭaqī, ibid., pp. 225–227.
229. I do not know anything of the available sources which can be added to the existing studies and there is no reason to summarise them here. See Metz, *al-Ḥaḍārah al-Islāmīyah fī al-Qarn al-Rābi' al-Hijrī*, vol. 1, pp. 144–181; 'Abd al-'Azīz al-Dūrī, *Dirāsāt fī al-'Uṣūr al-'Abbāsīyah al-Muta'akhirah* (Baghdad: Sharikat al-Rābiṭah li-l-Ṭab' wa al-Nashr, 1946), pp. 29, 48–49, 190–191, 194–197, 199–207 and 219 ff; Idem, *Tārīkh al-'Irāq al-Iqtiṣādī fī al-Qarn al-Rābi' al-Hijrī*, especially chapters 'al-Zirā'ah', 'al-Jahbadhah wa al-Ṣayrafah' and 'Mustawā al-Ma'īshah'. See also Abū al-Ḥusayn Hilāl bin al-Muḥsin al-Ṣābī, *Tuḥfat al-Umarā' fī Tārīkh al-Wuzarā' = The Historical Remains of Hilāl al-Ṣābī: first part of his Kitāb al-Wuzarā' and fragment of his history, 389–393AH*, edited with notes and glossary by H. F. Amedroz (Beirut: Catholic Press [Maṭba'at al-Ābā' al-Kathūlīkiyīn], 1904); Abū 'Alī Aḥmad bin Muḥammad Ibn Miskawayh, *Tajārib al-Umam*, with selections from various histories relating to the matters mentioned therein, ed. H. F. Amedroz, 7 vols. (Cairo: [n.pb.], 1920–1921); Abū al-Faraj 'Abd al-Raḥmān bin 'Alī Ibn al-Jawzī, *al-Muntaẓam fī Tārīkh al-Mulūk wa al-Umam*, 10 vols. (Hyderabad-Deccan: Dā'irat al-Ma'ārif al-'Uthmānīyah, 1357–1358/1938–1939); Bowen, *The Life and Times of "Alī Ibn 'Īsā', 'the Good Vizier'*.
230. al-Mas'ūdī, *al-Tanbīh wa al-Ishrāf*, p. 310.
231. al-Māwardī, *al-Aḥkām al-Sulṭānīyah wa al-Wilāyāt al-Dīnīyah*, p. 21.
232. Ibn al-Ṭaqṭaqī, *al-Fakhrī fī al-Ādāb al-Sulṭānīyah wa al-Duwal al-Islāmīyah*, p. 152.
233. Muḥammad bin al-Ḥusayn Abū Ya'lā al-Farrā', *al-Aḥkām al-Sulṭānīyah*, edited with commentary by Muḥammad Ḥāmid al-Fiqī (Cairo: Maṭba'at Muṣṭafā al-Bābī al-Ḥalabī, 1938), pp. 29–30; [al-Qurashī] Abū Sālim al-'Adawī, *al-'Iqd al-Farīd li-l-Malik al-Sa'īd*, p. 143.
234. [al-Qurashī] al-'Adawī, ibid., pp. 143–144.
235. al-Māwardī, *al-Aḥkām al-Sulṭānīyah wa al-Wilāyāt al-Dīnīyah*, p. 24.
236. Ibid., p. 23; Abū Ya'lā al-Farrā', *al-Aḥkām al-Sulṭānīyah*, p. 30; [al-Qurashī] al-'Adawī, ibid., p. 144.
237. al-Māwardī, ibid., p. 25; Abū Ya'lā al-Farrā', ibid., p. 31; al-'Adawī, p. 144 ff.
238. al-Māwardī, ibid., p. 21.
239. Ibid., pp. 25–26.

Bibliography

Primary sources

al-ʿAbbāsī, al-Ḥasan bin ʿAbdullah, *Āthār al-Uwal fī Tartīb al-Duwal* (Cairo: Maṭbaʿat Bulāq, 1295/1878).

Abū Bakr al-Ṣūlī, Muḥammad bin Yaḥyā, *Akhbār al-Rāḍī bi-Lāh wa al-Muttaqī li-Lāh, aw Tārīkh al-Dawlah al-ʿAbbāsīyah min 322 ilā 333 hijrī min Kitāb al-Awrāq*, ed. J. Heyworth Dunne (Cairo: Maṭbaʿat al-Ṣāwī, 1935).

——— *Adab al-Kuttāb*, edited with commentary by Muḥammad Bahjah al-Atharī (Cairo, Baghdad: al-Maktabah al-ʿArabīyah, 1341/1922).

Abū Shujāʿ al-Iṣfahānī, Taqī al-Dīn Aḥmad bin al-Ḥusayn, *Matn al-Ghāyah ʿalā Madhhab al-Imām al-Shāfiʿī* [*Mukhtaṣar Abū Shujāʿ*] (n.p., n.pb., n.d.).

Abū Yaʿlā al-Farrāʾ, Muḥammad bin al-Ḥusayn, *al-Aḥkām al-Sulṭānīyah*, edited with commentary by Muḥammad Ḥāmid al-Fiqī (Cairo: Maṭbaʿat Muṣṭafā al-Bābī al-Ḥalabī, 1938).

Abū Yūsuf, Yaʿqūb bin Ibrāhīm, *Kitāb al-Kharāj* (Cairo: al-Maṭbaʿah al-Salafīyah, 1352/1933).

[al-Qurashī] al-ʿAdawī, Abū Sālim Muḥammad bin Ṭalḥah, *al-ʿIqd al-Farīd li-l-Malik al-Saʿīd* (Cairo: Maṭbaʿat al-Waṭan, 1283/1866).

al-Baghdādī, ʿAbd al-Qāhir, *Uṣūl al-Dīn* (Istanbul: Maṭbaʿat al-Dawlah, 1928).

——— *al-Farq bayna al-Firāq*, edited with commentary by Muḥammad Muḥyī al-Dīn ʿAbd al-Ḥamīd (Cairo: Maktabat al-Maʿārif, 1910).

al-Balādhurī, Abū al-ʿAbbās Aḥmad bin Yaḥyā, *Anṣāb al-Ashrāf*, 5 vols. (Jerusalem: Maṭbaʿat al-Jāmiʿah al-ʿArabīyah, 1936–1940).

——— *Futūḥ al-Buldān* (Cairo: Sharikat Ṭab' al-Kutub al-'Arabīyah, 1901).

Bar Hebraeus, Ibn al-'Ibrī Abū al-Faraj Yūḥannā Grīgūryūs (Gregorius), *Tārīkh Mukhtaṣar al-Duwal*, ed. Fr. Antoine Ṣālḥānī (Beirut: al-Maṭba'ah al-Kāthūlīkiyah, 1890).

al-Bīrūnī, Abū al-Rayḥān Muḥammad bin Aḥmad, *al-Āthār al-Bāqiyah 'an al-Qurūn al-Khāliyah* (*Chronologie orientalischer Völker*), ed. Eduard Sachau (Leipzig: [n.pb.], 1878).

——— *al-Jamāhir fī Ma'rifat al-Jawāhir*, ed. F. Krenkow (Hyderabad-Deccan: Jam'īyat Dā'irat al-Ma'ārif al-'Uthmānīyah, 1355/1936).

al-Dīnawarī, Abū Ḥanīfah, *al-Akhbār al-Ṭiwāl*, eds. V. Guirgass and I. Kratchkovskii (Leiden: Brill, 1888–1912).

al-Fīrūzābādī, Abū al-Ṭāhir Muḥammad bin Ya'qūb, *al-Qāmūs al-Muḥīṭ* (n.p., n.pb., n.d.).

[al-Ḥyderābādī] Ḥamīdullāh, Muḥammad, ed., *Majmū'at al-Wathā'iq al-Siyāsīyah fī al-'Ahd al-Nabawī wa al-Khilāfah al-Rāshidah* (Cairo: Lajnat al-Ta'līf wa al-Tarjamah wa al-Nashr, 1941).

Ibn 'Abd al-Ḥakam, Abū Muḥammad 'Abdullah, *Futūḥ Miṣr wa Akhbāruhā*, ed. Henri Massé (Cairo: Institut Français [d'Archeologie Orientale], 1914).

Ibn 'Abd Rabbih, Abū 'Umar Aḥmad bin Muḥammad, *al-'Iqd al-Farīd* (*The Unique Necklace*), ed. and commentary by one of the most distinguished personages of the age, 4 vols. (Cairo: Maḥmūd Shākir, 1913).

Ibn Abī al-Ḥadīd, Abū Ḥāmid 'Abd al-Ḥamīd bin Hibat Allah, *Sharḥ Nahj al-Balāghah*, 4 vols. (Cairo: Dār al-Kutub al-'Arabīyah al-Kubrā, [n.d.]).

Ibn Ādam al-Qurashī, Abū Zakariyā Yaḥyā bin Sulaymān, *Kitāb al-Kharāj* (Cairo: al-Maṭba'ah al-Salafīyah, 1417/1996).

——— *Kitāb al-Kharāj*, ed. A. W. T. Juynboll (Leiden: Brill, 1896).

Ibn 'Asākir, Abū al-Qāsim 'Alī bin al-Ḥasan, *al-Tārīkh al-Kabīr*, ed. 'Abd al-Qādir Badrān, 5 vols. in 3 (Damascus: Maṭba'at Rawḍat al-Shām, 1329–1332/1911–1913).

Ibn al-Athīr, 'Izz al-Dīn Abū al-Ḥasan 'Alī bin Muḥammad, *Tārīkh al-Kāmil*, 12 vols. (Cairo: Maṭba'at Muṣṭafā al-Bābī al-Ḥalabī, 1303/1885).

——— *al-Kāmil fī al-Tārīkh*, ed. Carolus Johannes Tornberg, 12 vols. (Leiden: Brill, 1851–1871).

Ibn Badrūn 'Abd al-Malik bin 'Abdullah, *Sharḥ Qaṣīdat Ibn 'Abdūn* (n.p., n.pb., n.d.).

Ibn Ḥassūl, Abū 'Alā' Muḥammad bin 'Alī, *Tafḍīl al-Atrāk 'alā Sā'ir al-Ajnād*, ed. 'Abbās al-'Azzāwī (Istanbul: [n.pb.], 1940).

Ibn Ḥawqal, Abū al-Qāsim Muḥammad, *al-Masālik wa al-Mamālik*, ed. J. H. Kramers, 2 vols., Bibliotheca Geographorum Arabicorum 2 (Leiden: Brill, 1822).

Ibn Hishām, Abū Muḥammad 'Abd al-Malik, *al-Sīrah al-Nabawīyah*, edited and indexed by Muṣṭafā al-Saqqā, Ibrāhīm al-Ibyārī, 'Abd al-Ḥafīẓ Shalabī, 4 vols. (Cairo: Muṣṭafā al-Bābī al-Ḥalabī, 1936).

Ibn al-Jawzī, Abū al-Faraj 'Abd al-Raḥmān bin 'Alī, *Talbīs Iblīs*, ed. Muḥammad Munīr al-Dimashqī (Cairo: Maktabat al-Nahḍah, 1928).

——— *Manāqib Baghdād*, ed. Muḥammad Bahjah al-Atharī (Baghdad: Maṭba'at Dār al-Salām, 1342/1923).

——— *al-Muntaẓam fī Tārīkh al-Mulūk wa al-Umam*, 10 vols. (Hyderabad-Deccan: Dā'irat al-Ma'ārif al-'Uthmānīyah, 1357–1358/ 1938–1939).

Ibn Kathīr, Abū al-Fidā' Ismā'īl bin 'Umar, *al-Bidāyah wa al-Nihāyah fī al-Tārīkh*, 14 vols. (Cairo: Maṭba'at al-Sa'ādah, 1929–1939).

Ibn Khaldūn, Abū Zayd 'Abd al-Raḥmān bin Muḥammad, *al-Muqaddimah* (n.p., n.pb., 1377).

Ibn Khallikān, Shams al-Dīn Abū al-'Abbās Aḥmad bin Muḥammad, *Wafayāt al-A'yān wa Anbā' Abnā' al-Zamān*, following on *Fawāt al-Wafayāt* by al-Ṣalāḥ al-Katbī, see the notes of Shaqā'iq al-Nu'mānīyah fī 'Ulamā' al-Dawlah al-'Uthmānīyah in margins, following on *al-'Iqd al-Manẓūm fī Dhikr Afāḍil al-Rūm*, 2 vols. (Cairo: Maṭba'at Muṣṭafā al-Bābī al-Ḥalabī, 1310/1892).

Ibn Khurradadhbih, Abū al-Qāsim 'Ubayd Allah bin 'Abdullah, *Kitāb al-Masālik wa al-Mamālik*, ed. M. J. de Goeje; Bibliotheca Geographorum Arabicorum 6 (Leiden: E. J. Brill, 1306/1889).

Ibn Miskawayh, Abū 'Alī Aḥmad bin Muḥammad, *Tajārib al-Umam*, with selections from various histories relating to the matters mentioned therein, ed. H. F. Amedroz, 7 vols. (Cairo: [n.pb.], 1920–1921).

(Pseudo) Ibn Qutaybah, Abū Muḥammad 'Abdullah bin Muslim, *al-Imāmah wa al-Siyāsah* (Cairo: Maṭba'at al-Nīl, 1904).

Ibn Sa'd, Abū 'Abdullah Muḥammad bin Manī', *al-Ṭabaqāt al-Kubrā*, eds. Eduard Sachau *et al.*, 8 vols. in 3 parts (Leiden: E. J. Brill, 1904–1918).

Ibn al-Sā'ī, Abū Ṭālib 'Alī bin Anjab, *al-Jāmi' al-Mukhtaṣar fī 'Unwān al-Tawārīkh wa-'Uyūn al-Siyar*, ed. Muṣṭafā Jawād, Fr. Anastase-Marie al-Karmali [Carmelite] (Baghdad: al-Maṭba'ah al-Suryānīyah al-Kāthūlīkīyah, 1934).

——— *Mukhtaṣar Akhbār al-Khulafā' al-'Abbāsīyīn* (Bulāq: al-Maṭba'ah al-Amīrīyah, 1309/1891).

Ibn Salām, Abū 'Ubayd al-Qāsim al-Harawī, *al-Amwāl*, edited with commentary by Muḥammad Ḥāmid al-Fiqī, 4 vols. in 1 (Cairo: Maṭba'at Ḥijāzī, 1353/1934).

Ibn al-Ṭaqṭaqī, Muḥammad bin 'Alī, *al-Fakhrī fī al-Ādāb al-Sulṭānīyah wa al-Duwal al-Islāmīyah* (Cairo: Sharikat Tab' al-Kutub al-'Arabīyah, 1317/1899).

Ibn Ṭayfūr, Abū Faḍl Aḥmad, *Kitāb Baghdād* (n.p., n.pb., n.d.).

al-Irbilī, 'Abd al-Raḥmān Sunbuṭ, *Khulāṣat al-Dhahab al-Masbūk, Mukhtaṣar min Siyar al-Mulūk* (Beirut: Maṭba'at al-Qiddīs Georgios, 1885).

al-Iṣṭakhrī, Abū Isḥāq Ibrāhīm bin Muḥammad, *Kitāb al-Masālik wa al-Mamālik, wa huwa mu'awwal 'alā Kitāb Ṣuwar al-Aqālīm li-Abī Zayd bin Sahl al-Balkhī*, ed. M. J. de Goeje; Bibliotheca Geographorum Arabicorum 1 (Leiden: Brill, 1870).

al-Jāḥiẓ, Abū 'Uthmān 'Amr bin Baḥr, *Rasā'il al-Jāhiẓ: al-Rasā'il al-Siyāsīyah* (n.p., n.pb., n.d.).

(Pseudo) al-Jāḥiẓ, Abū 'Uthmān 'Amr bin Baḥr, *al-Tāj fī Akhlāq al-Mulūk* (Cairo: Aḥmad Zakī Pāshā, 1914).

al-Jahshiyārī, Abū 'Abdullah Muḥammad bin 'Abdūs, *al-Wuzarā' wa al-Kuttāb*, edited and indexed by Muṣṭafā al-Saqqā, Ibrāhīm al-Ibyārī, 'Abd al-Ḥafīẓ Shalabī (Cairo: Maṭba'at Muṣṭafā al-Bābī al-Ḥalabī, 1938).

al-Khawārizmī, Abū 'Abdullah Muḥammad bin Aḥmad, *Kitāb Mafātīḥ al-'Ulūm*, ed. G. van Vloten (Leiden: Brill, 1895).

al-Kulaynī, Abū Ja'far Muḥammad bin Ya'qūb, *Uṣūl al-Kāfī* [includes the gloss (*sharḥ*) of al-Mullā Muḥammad Ṣāliḥ al-Māzandarānī in the notes] (Tehran: Ṭab' Ḥajar, [n.d.]).

Kurd 'Alī, M., ed., *Rasā'il al-Bulaghā'* (Cairo: Lajnat al-Ta'līf wa al-Tarjamah wa al-Nashr, 1913).

al-Maḥallī, Jalāl al-Dīn, Muḥammad bin Aḥmad and Jalāl al-Dīn 'Abd al-Raḥmān ibn Abī Bakr al-Suyūṭī, *Tafsīr al-Jalālayn* (n.p., n.pb., n.d.).

al-Maqdisī, al-Muṭahhar bin Ṭāhir, *al-Bid' wa al-Tārīkh (al-mansūb) li-Abī Zayd Aḥmad bin Sahl al-Balkh* (*Le Livre de la Création et de l'Histoire de Motahhar ben Tahir el-Maqdisi, attribué à Abou-Zéïd Ahmed ben Sahl el-Balkhi*), ed. and trans. Clément Huart, 6 vols. (Paris, Ernest Leroux, 1899–1919).

al-Maqrīzī, Abū al-'Abbās Aḥmad bin 'Alī, *Imtā' al-Asma' bi-mā li-l-Rasūl min al-Abnā' wa al-Amwāl wa al-Ḥifdah wa al-Matā'*, edited with commentary by Maḥmūd Muḥammad Shākir (Cairo: Lajnat al-Ta'līf wa al-Tarjamah wa al-Nashr, 1941).

——— *al-Khiṭaṭ al-Maqrīzīyah al-Musammāt bi-l-Mawā'iẓ wa al-I'tibār bi-Dhikr al-Khiṭaṭ wa al-Āthār, yakhtaṣṣ dhalika bi-akhbār iqlīm Miṣr wa al-Nīl wa dhikr al-Qāhirah wa mā yata'allaq bihā wa bi-iqlīmihā*, 5 vols. (Cairo: Maktabat al-Malījī, 1324–1326/1906–1908).

al-Mas'ūdī, Abū al-Ḥasan 'Alī bin al-Ḥusayn, *al-Tanbīh wa al-Ishrāf*, ed. 'Abdullah Ismā'īl al-Ṣāwī (Cairo: al-Sharq al-Islāmīyah, 1938).

——— *Murūj al-Dhahab wa Ma'ādin al-Jawhar*, ed. and trans. C. Barbier de Meynard and Pavet de Courteille as *Les Prairies d'Or et les Mines de Pierres Precieuses*, 9 vols. [in Arabic and French] (Paris: Impr. Impériale, 1861–1877).

——— *Murūj al-Dhahab wa Ma'ādin al-Jawhar*, edited with commentary by Muḥammad Muḥyī al-Dīn 'Abd al-Ḥamīd, 4 vols. (Cairo: Dār al-Rajā', 1938).

——— *Murūj al-Dhahab wa Ma'ādin al-Jawhar*, vol. 3, 7 vols. (Beirut: al-Jāmi'ah al-Lubnānīyah, 1965), p. 268.

al-Māwardī, Abū al-Ḥasan 'Alī bin Muḥammad, *al-Aḥkām al-Sulṭānīyah wa al-Wilāyāt al-Dīnīyah* (Cairo: [Maṭba'at al-Sa'ādah], 1909).

al-Mubarrad, Abū al-'Abbās Muḥammad bin Yazīd, *al-Kāmil*, ed. W. Wright from the manuscripts of Leiden, St. Petersburg, Cambridge and Berlin, 2 vols. (Leipzig: F.A. Brockhaus/Kreysing, 1874–1893).

al-Muqaddasī, Abū 'Abdullah Muḥammad bin Aḥmad, *Kitāb Aḥsan al-Taqāsīm fī Ma'rifat al-Aqālīm*, ed. M. J. de Goeje; Bibliotheca Geographorum Arabicorum 3 (Leiden: Brill, 1877).

al-Minqarī, Naṣr ibn Muzāḥim, Abū al-Faḍl, *Waq'at Ṣiffīn* (Cairo: al-Mu'assasah al-'Arabīyah al-Ḥadīthah, 1962).

al-Nawbakhtī, Abū Muḥammad al-Ḥasan bin Mūsā, *Firaq al-Shī'ah*, ed. H. Ritter (al-Najaf: al-Maṭba'ah al-Ḥaydarīyah, 1936).

al-Qalqashandī, Abū al-'Abbās Aḥmad bin 'Alī, *Ṣubḥ al-A'shā fī Kitābat al-Inshā*, 14 vols. (Cairo: Dār al-Kutub al-Miṣrīyah, 1913–1919).

Qudāmah bin Ja'far, Abū al-Faraj, *al-Kharāj*, ed. M. J. de Goeje; Bibliotheca Geographorum Arabicorum 6 (Leiden: Brill, 1889).

al-Qummī, al-Ḥasan bin Muḥammad bin Ḥasan, *Tārīkh Qumm* (n.p., n.pb., n.d.).

al-Qurṭubī, 'Arīb bin Sa'd, *Ṣilat Ta'rīkh al-Ṭabarī*, ed. M. J. de Goeje (Leiden: Brill, 1897).

al-Ṣābī, Ibrāhīm bin Hilāl, *Rasā'il al-Ṣābī*, edited with commentary by Shakīb Arslān (B'abdā, Lebanon: al-Maṭba'ah al-'Uthmānīyah, 1898).

al-Ṣābī, Abū al-Ḥusayn Hilāl bin al-Muḥsin, *Tuḥfat al-Umarā' fī Tārīkh al-Wuzarā'* (*The Historical Remains of Hilāl al-Ṣābī: first part of his Kitāb al-Wuzarā' and fragment of his History*, 389–393AH), edited with notes and glossary by H. F. Amedroz (Beirut: Catholic Press [Maṭba'at al-Ābā' al-Kathūlīkiyīn], 1904).

Ṣafwat, Aḥmad Zakī, ed., *Jamharat Rasā'il al-'Arab fī 'Uṣūr al-'Arabīyah al-Zāhirah*, 4 vols. (Cairo: Maṭba'at Muṣṭafā al-Babī al-Ḥalabī, 1937–1938).

Sāwīrūs [Severus] bin al-Muqaffa' (al-Anbā), *Siyar al-Ābā' al-Baṭārikah* (n.p., n.pb., n.d.).

al-Shahrastānī, Abū al-Fatḥ Muḥammad bin 'Abd al-Karīm, *al-Milal wa al-Niḥal* [repr. of William Cureton's ed., 1846], 2 vols. (Leipzig: Otto Harrassowitz, 1923).

al-Shaykh al-Mufīd, Muḥammad bin al-Nu'mān, *Awā'il al-Maqālāt fī al-Madhāhib wa al-Mukhtārāt*, ed. Mahdī Muḥaqqiq (Tehran: Institute of Islamic Studies, McGill University, 1323/1944).

Suhrāb, *'Ajā'ib al-Aqālīm al-Sab'ah ilā Nihāyat al-'Imārah wa Kayf Hay'at al-Mudun wa Iḥāṭat al-Biḥār bihā wa Tashaqquq Anhārihā wa Ma'rifat Jibālihā wa Jamī' ma warā' Khaṭ al-Istiwā' wa al-Ṭūl wa al-'Ard bi-l-Misṭarah wa al-Ḥisāb wa al-'Adad wa al-Baḥth 'alā Jamī' mā Dhukir* (*Das Kitab 'Aga'ib al-Akalim as-Sab'a des Suhrab*), ed. Hans von Mžik (Vienna: Adolf Holzhausen, 1929).

al-Suyūṭī, Jalāl al-Dīn 'Abd al-Raḥmān bin Abī Bakr, *Ḥusn al-Muḥāḍarah fī Akhbār Miṣr wa al-Qāhirah*, 2 vols. in 1 (Cairo: Fahmī al-Katbī, 1327/1909).

——— *al-Ashbāh wa al-Naẓā'ir* (Beirut: Dār al-Kutb al-'Ilmīyah, 1983).

al-Ṭabarī, Abū Ja'far Muḥammad bin Jarīr, *Ikhtilāf al-Fuqahā'*, ed. Joseph Schacht (Leiden: Brill, 1933).

——— *Tārīkh al-Rusul wa al-Mulūk*, ed. M. J. de Goeje (Leiden: Brill, 1879–1901).

——— *Tārīkh al-Rusul wa al-Mulūk*, 12 vols. (Cairo: al-Maṭba'ah al-Ḥusaynīyah, 1336/1917).

al-Tanūkhī, Abū 'Alī al-Muḥsin bin 'Alī, *al-Faraj Ba'da al-Shiddah*, 2 vols. in 1 (Cairo: Maḥmūd Riyāḍ, 1904).

al-Tha'ālibī, Abū Manṣūr 'Abd al-Malik bin Muḥammad, *Laṭā'if al-Ma'ārif*, ed. Pieter de Jong (Leiden: Brill, 1867).

al-Yāfi'ī, Abū Muḥammad 'Abdullah bin As'ad, *Mir'āt al-Jinān wa 'Ibrat al-Yaqẓān fī Ma'rifat mā Yu'tabar min Ḥawādith al-Zamān*, 4 vols. (Hyderabad Deccan: Dā'irat al-Ma'ārif al-Niẓāmīyah, 1337–1339/1918–1920).

al-Ya'qūbī, Aḥmad bin Abī Ya'qūb, *al-Buldān* (al-Najaf: al-Maṭba'ah al-Ḥaydarīyah, 1939).

——— trans. Gaston Wiet as *Les pays*; Publications de l'Institut Français d'Archéologie Orientale; textes et traductions d'auteurs orientaux, tome 1 (Cairo: Institut Français d'Archéologie Orientale, 1937).

——— *Tārīkh al-Ya'qūbī*, 3 vols. (al-Najaf: al-Maktabah al-Murtaḍawīyah, 1358/1939).

al-Zamakhsharī, Abū al-Qāsim Maḥmūd bin 'Umar, *Asās al-Balāghah*, 2 vols. (Cairo: Dār al-Kutub al-Miṣrīyah, 1922–1923).

Secondary sources

Abbott, Nabia, 'An Arabic Papyri of the Reign of Ga'far al-Mutawakkil 'alā allāh (232–247AH/847–861AD)', *Zeitschrift der Deutschen Morgen-ländischen Gesellschaft* (ZDMG), vol. 92, nos. 1–3 (1938), pp. 88–135.

'Abd al-Nūr, Jabbūr, *Naẓrāt fī Falsafat al-'Arab* (Beirut: Dār al-Makshūf, 1945).

Aghnides, Nicolas Prodromou, *Mohammedan Theories of Finance* (New York: Colombia University Press, 1911).

Akhtar, Aḥmad Mian, *Studies: Islamic and Oriental*, with a foreword by Muhammad Shafi (Lahore: Sh. M. Ashraf, 1945).

Amīn, Aḥmad, *Ḍuḥā al-Islām* (Cairo: Maktabat al-Nahḍah al-Miṣrīyah, 1936).

——— *Fajr al-Islām* (Cairo: Maktabat al-Nahḍah al-Miṣrīyah, 1945).

Andrae, Tor, *Mohammed: sein Leben und sein Glaube*, trans. Theophil Menzel as *Mohammed: The Man and His Faith* (London: George Allen & Unwin, 1936).

Arnold, Thomas W., *The Caliphate* (Oxford: Clarendon Press, 1924).

Barthold, W. [Bartol'd, V. V.], *Kul'tura musul'manstva*, trans. Ḥamzah Ṭāhir as *Tārīkh al-Ḥaḍārah al-Islāmīyah*; introduction by 'Abd al-Wahāb 'Azzām (Cairo: Dār al Ma'ārif, 1942).

——— *Turkestan Vèpokhu Mongol'skago Nashestviia (Turkestan Down to Mongol Invasion)*, translated from the original Russian and revised by the author with the assistance of H. A. R. Gibb, 2nd edn; E. J. W. Gibb memorial series. New series 5 (London: Luzac and Co., 1928).

Baynes, Norman H., *The Byzantine Empire* (New York, London: H. Holt and Company, 1939; Home University Library of Modern Knowledge, no. 114).

Bowen, Harold, *The Life and Times of 'Alī Ibn 'Īsā, 'the Good Vizier'* (Cambridge: Cambridge University Press, 1928).

Browne, Edward G., *A Literary History of Persia*, 4 vols. (Cambridge: Cambridge University Press, repr. 1928–1929).

Butler, Alfred J., *The Arab Conquest of Egypt and the Last Thirty Years of the Roman Dominion*, trans. Farīd Abū Ḥadīd as *Fatḥ al-ʿArab li-Miṣr* (Cairo: Dār al-Kutub al-Miṣrīyah, 1933).

Cevdet, Muallim, *al-Ākhīyah wa al-Fityān* (Istanbul: [n.pb.], 1916).

Christensen, Arthur, *L'Iran sous les Sassanides* (Copenhagen: Levin and Munksgaard, 1936).

Diehl, Charles, *Byzance, Grandeur et Decadence* (Paris, E. Flammarion, 1919).

Dozy, Reinhart, *Histoire des Musulmans d'Espagne: jusqu'à la Conquête de l'Andalousie par les Almoravides*, 711–1110, 3 vols., New edn, rev. E. Lévi-Provençal (Leiden: E. J. Brill, 1932).

——— *Supplement aux Dictionnaires Arabes* (n.p., n.pb., n.d.).

al-Dūrī, ʿAbd al-ʿAzīz, *Tārīkh al-ʿIrāq al-Iqtiṣādī fī al-Qarn al-Rābiʿ al-Hijrī* (Baghdad: Maṭbaʿat al-Maʿārif, 1948).

——— *Dirāsāt fī al-ʿUṣūr al-ʿAbbāsīyah al-Mutaʾakhirah* (Baghdad: Sharikat al-Rābiṭah li-l-Ṭabʿ wa al-Nashr, 1946); repr. *al-Aʿmāl al-Kāmilah li-l-Duktūr ʿAbd al-ʿAzīz al-Dūrī* – 4 (Beirut: Centre for Arab Unity Studies, 2007).

——— *al-ʿAṣr al-ʿAbbāsī al-Awwal: Dirāsah fī al-Tārīkh al-Siyāsī wa al-Idārī wa al-Mālī*; Manshūrat Dār al-Muʿallimīn al-ʿĀliyah – 1 (Baghdad: Maṭbaʿat al-Tafīḍ al-Ahlīyah, 1945); repr. *al-Aʿmāl al-kāmilah li-l-Duktūr ʿAbd al-ʿAzīz al-Dūrī* – 3 (Beirut: Centre for Arab Unity Studies, 2006).

——— *Studies on the Economic Life of Mesopotamia in the 10th century* (PhD Thesis, University of London, School of Oriental and African Studies, 1942).

Elad, Amikam, 'Two Identical Inscriptions from Jund Filasṭīn from the Reign of the Abbasid Caliph, Al-Muqtadir', *Journal of the Economic and Social History of the Orient*, vol. 35, no. 4 (Leiden: Brill, 1992).

Faris, Bisr, *L'Honneur chez les Arabes avant l'Islam* (Paris: Adrien-Maisonneuve, 1932).

Fateh, Mostafa Khan, 'Taxation in Persia: "A Synopsis from the Early Times to the Conquest of the Mongols"', *Bulletin of the School of Oriental Studies*, University of London, vol. 4, no. 4 (London: Cambridge University Press, 1928).

Fischel, Walter, 'The Origin of Banking in Mediaeval Islam: A Contribution to the Economic History of the Jews of Baghdad in the Tenth Century', in *Journal of the Royal Asiatic Society of Great Britain and Ireland*, no. 3 (July 1933).

Gibb, H. A. R., 'Al-Mawardi's theory of the Khilafa', *Islamic Culture*, 11 (1937), pp. 291–302.

Goldziher, Ignác [Ignaz], *Vorlesungen uber den Islam*, trans. Felix Arin as *Le Dogme et la Loi de l'Islam: histoire du développement dogmatique et juridique de la religion musulmane* (Paris: Librairie Orientaliste Paul Geuthner, 1926).

Guidi, Ignazio, *L'Arabie Antéislamique: Quatre Conférences Données à l'Université Egyptienne du Caire en 1909* (Paris: Librairie Paul Geuthner, 1921).

Gwatkin, H. M. and J. P. Whitney, eds., *The Cambridge Medieval History*, vol. II, *The Rise of the Saracens and the Foundation of the Western Empire* (Cambridge: Cambridge University Press, 1913).

——— *The Cambridge Medieval History*, vol. IV, *The Eastern Roman Empire (717–1453)* (Cambridge: Cambridge University Press, 1923).

Gwatkin, H. M. and J. P. Whitney *et al.*, *The Cambridge Medieval History*, 8 vols. (Cambridge: Cambridge University Press, 1911–1936).

Ḥamīdullāh, Muḥammad, 'The City State of Mecca', *Islamic Culture*, vol. 12, 1938.

——— *Documents sur la Diplomatie Musulmane à l'Epoque du Prophète et des Khalifes Orthodoxes*. Préface de Monsieur M. Gaudefroy-Demombynes (Paris: G.-P. Maisonneuve, 1935).

al-Ḥanafī [al-Nahrawālī], Quṭb al-Dīn, *al-I'lām bi-A'lām Bayt Allāh al-Ḥarām* (n.p., n.pb., n.d.).

Ḥasan, Ḥasan Ibrāhīm and Ḥasan, 'Alī Ibrāhīm, *al-Nuẓum al-Islāmīyah* (Cairo: Maktabat al-Nahḍah al-Miṣrīyah, 1939).

Hitti, Philip K., *History of the Arabs*, 2nd edn (London: Macmillan and Co. Ltd, 1940).

Ibn Mufliḥ, Abū Isḥāq Burhān al-Dīn, *al-Mubdi' fī Sharḥ al-Muqni'* (Beirut: al-Maktab al-Islāmī, 2000).

M. Th. Houtsma *et al.* (eds.), article 'Ṭiraz', *Dā'irat al-Ma'ārif al-Islāmīyah*, 13 vols. (Cairo: Dār al-Shāb, 1908–1938).

——— *The Encyclopædia of Islam: A Dictionary of the Geography, Ethnography and Biography of the Muhammadan Peoples*, 4 vols. and Suppl. (Leiden: E. J. Brill and London: Luzac, 1913–1938).

——— Levi della Vida, G., *Kharidjite*, vol. 2, pt. 2, pp. 904–908.

——— Pedersen, Johannes, *Masdjid*, vol. 3, pt. 1, pp. 314–389.

——— Lévi-Provençal, E., *Mu'taḍid*, vol. 3, pt. 2, pp. 777–778.

——— Taeschner, F., *al-Nāṣir li-Dīn Allāh*, vol. 3, pt. 2, pp. 860–862.

——— Levi della Vida, G., *Umaiyads*, vol. 4, pt. 2, pp. 998–1012.

Jawzī, Bandalī, *Min Tārīkh al-Ḥarakāt al-Fikrīyah fī al-Islām* (Jerusalem: Maṭba'at Bayt al-Maqdis, 1928).

Journal of the Royal Asiatic Society (JRAS), 1895.

Kāshif, Sayyidah Ismāʿīl, *Miṣr fī Fajr al-Islām: min al-Fatḥ al-ʿArabi ilā Qiyām al-Dawlah al-Ṭulūnīyyah* (Cairo: Dār al-Fikr al-ʿArabī, 1947).

Katbi Ghaida Khazna, *Islamic Land Tax – al-Kharaj* (London: I.B.Tauris, 2010).

Khuda Bukhsh, Salahuddin, *Contributions to the History of Islamic Civilization*, 2 vols. (Calcutta: University of Calcutta, 1924).

Köprülü, M. F. [Mehmet Fuat/Mehmed Fuad], *Les Origines de l'Empire Ottoman* (Paris: Publiés aux Editions E. de Boccard par L'Institut Français d'Archéologie de Stamboul, 1935).

Kurd ʿAlī, Muḥammad, *al-Idārah al-Islāmīyah fī ʿIzz al-ʿArab* (Cairo: Maṭbaʿat Miṣr, 1934).

Lammens, Henri, *L'Islam: Croyances et Institutions*, trans. by E. Denison Ross as *Islam: Beliefs and Institutions* (London: Methuen and Co. Ltd, 1929).

——— *La Mecque à la Veille de l'Hégire*, vol. 9 (Beirut: Imprimerie Catholique, 1924).

Lane-Poole, Stanley, *Catalogue of Oriental Coins in the British Museum*, 10 vols. (London: Trustees of the British Museum, 1875–1890).

——— *The Mohammedan Dynasties: Chronological and Genealogical Tables with Historical Introductions* (London: A. Constable and Company, 1894).

Lavoix, Henri, *Catalogue des Monnaies Musulmanes de la Bibliothèque Nationale*, 3 vols. (Paris: Imprimerie nationale, 1887–1896).

Lewis, Bernard, 'The Islamic Guilds', *Economic History Review*, vol. 8, no. 1, 1937–1938, pp. 20–37.

Metz, Adam, *Der Renaissance des Islam*, trans. Muḥammad ʿAbd al-Hādī Abū Raydah as *al-Ḥaḍārah al-Islāmīyah fī al-Qarn al-Rābiʿ al-Hijrī*, 2 vols. (Cairo: Lajnat al-Ta'līf wa al-Tarjamah wa al-Nashr, 1940–1941).

Minorsky, Vladimir, '*La domination des Dailamites*' (Paris: Publications de la Societé des Etudes Iraniennes, 1932).

al-Mudawwar, Jamīl Nakhlah, *Ḥadārat al-Islām fī Dār al-Salām* (Cairo: Maṭbaʿat al-Mu'ayyid, 2nd edn, 1905).

Muḥāḍarāt al-Majmaʿ al-ʿIlmī al-ʿArabī, Dimashq [Arab Academy in Damascus] 1925–1954, 3 vols. (Damascus: al-Majmaʿ, 1954), vol. 1.

Newman, Julius, *The Agricultural Life of the Jews in Babylonia between the Years 200 C.E. and 500 C.E.* (London: Oxford University Press, Humphrey Milford, 1932).

Nicholson, Reynold A., *A Literary History of the Arabs*, 2nd edn (Cambridge: Cambridge University Press, 1930).

al-Qalmāwī, Suhayr, *Adab al-Khawārij fī al-ʿAṣr al-Umawī* (Cairo: Lajnat al-Taʾlīf wa al-Tarjamah wa al-Nashr, 1945).

Sadighi, Gholam Hossien, *Les Mouvements Religieux Iraniens au IIe et au IIIe siècle de l'Hégire* (Paris: Les Press moderns, 1938).

Sanhoury, ʿAbd al-Razzāq Aḥmad, *Le Califat: son Evolution vers une Société des Nations Orientale*, préface d'Edouard Lambert; Travaux du Séminaire Oriental d'Etudes Juridiques et Sociale, tome 4 (Paris: Librairie Orientaliste Paul Geuthner, 1926).

Sherwani, Haroon Khan, *Studies in Muslim Political Thought and Administration* (Lahore: Sh. Muḥammad Ashraf, 1945).

Ṣiddīqī, Amīr Ḥasan, 'Caliphate and Kingship in Medieval Persia', *Islamic Culture*, vol. 9 (1935), pp. 560–579.

Smith, W. Robertson, *Kinship and Marriage in Early Arabia* (Cambridge: Cambridge University Press, 1885).

Tritton, A. S., *The Caliphs And Their Non-Muslim Subjects* (Oxford: Oxford University Press, 1930).

Van Vloten, G., *Recherches sur la Domination Arabe, le Chiitisme, les Croyances Messianiques sous la Khilafat des Omayades*, translated with commentary by Ḥasan Ibrāhīm Ḥasan and Muḥammad Zakī Ibrāhīm as *al-Siyādah al-ʿArabīyah wa al-Shīʿah wa al-Isrāʾīlīyāt fī ʿAhd Banī Umayyah* (Cairo: Maṭbaʿat al-Saʿādah, 1934).

Wehr, Hans and Cowan, J. M., eds., *Arabic English Dictionary*, Fourth Edition (Ithica: Spoken Language Services, 1994).

Wellhausen, Julius, *Das Arabische Reich und Sein Sturz*, trans. Margaret Graham Weir as *The Arab Kingdom and its Fall* (Calcutta: University of Calcutta, 1927).

Wittek, Paul, *The Rise of the Ottoman Empire: Studies in the History of Turkey, 13th–15th Centuries*; Royal Asiatic Society monographs, vol. xxiii (London: Royal Asiatic Society, 1938).

Zaydān, Jurjī, *Tārīkh al-Tamaddun al-Islāmī*, 5 vols. (Cairo: Dār al-Hilāl, 1918–1922).

Index